LANGUAGE CONTACT, CREOLIZATION, AND GENETIC LINGUISTICS

Language Contact, Creolization, and Genetic Linguistics

Sarah Grey Thomason
and
Terrence Kaufman

UNIVERSITY OF CALIFORNIA PRESS
Berkeley   Los Angeles   London

University of California Press
Berkeley and Los Angeles, California

University of California Press, Ltd.
London, England

Copyright © 1988 by The Regents of the University of California

Library of Congress Cataloging in Publication Data

Thomason, Sarah Grey.
    Language contact, creolization, and genetic
linguistics.

    Bibliography: p.
    Includes indexes.
    1. Languages in contact.   2. Interference
(Linguistics)   3. Linguistic change.   4. Languages,
Mixed.   5. Comparative linguistics.   I. Kaufman,
Terrence, 1937–   .   II. Title.
P130.5.T46   1988   417'.2   87–19441
ISBN 0–520–05789–9 (alk. paper)

Printed in the United States of America

1 2 3 4 5 6 7 8 9

This book is dedicated

to three men who helped us become historical linguists:
to Kaufman's teacher Eric Hamp

and

to the memories of Thomason's teachers
Bernard Bloch and Warren Cowgill

Contents

Preface

This book grew out of a paper entitled 'Toward an Adequate Definition of Creolization', which we presented at the 1975 International Conference on Pidgins and Creoles in Honolulu. The main text of that paper—forty-one pages in all—functioned, in effect, as an outline for the book. The remainder of the paper consisted of several case studies; two of these, extensively revised, appear here in chapter 9 (9.2 and 9.8).

Each of us wrote about half of the original paper: the introductory section, laying out the basic theoretical framework, was a joint effort; Kaufman wrote the sections on borrowing and retrospection; and Thomason wrote the sections on language shift and pidgins. Since 1975 Kaufman's research on other topics has kept him fully occupied, so Thomason is responsible for the present form of chapters 1–8 of this book (though we have, of course, discussed the theoretical issues together). The only part of the main body of the book that was not prefigured in the 1975 paper is chapter 2. The discussions in chapters 4 (Language Maintenance) and 8 (Retrospection) still reflect Kaufman's original formulation, and chapter 8 still contains parts that he wrote. We each wrote parts of chapter 9. Kaufman wrote the most substantial section, on French and Norse interference in English (9.8), and Thomason wrote the other case studies. Finally, we have revised each other's sections as needed.

We are very grateful to several people who gave us helpful comments on part or all of previous drafts: Warren Cowgill, Jeffrey Heath, John Holm, Dell Hymes, Paul Kroskrity, and Ilse Lehiste.

December, 1985   Sarah G. Thomason

1
Introduction

"Es gibt keine Mischsprache"
  —Max Müller (1871.1:86)
"Es gibt keine völlig ungemischte Sprache"
  —Hugo Schuchardt (1884:5)

For well over a hundred years, mainstream historical linguists have concentrated heavily on system-internal motivations and mechanisms in studying language change. The methodological principles embodied in the powerful Comparative Method include an assumption that virtually all language change arises through intrasystemic causes. Most historical linguists, therefore, would probably still agree with Welmers' view that, in phonology and morphosyntax, external influences "are insignificant when compared with internal change . . . the established principles of comparative and historical linguistics, and **all we know about language history and language change,** demand that . . . we seek explanations first on the basis of recognized processes of internal change" (1970:4–5; emphasis ours). Max Müller's claim that mixed languages do not exist reflects this prejudice, both because a mixed language could not arise without extensive foreign

influence and because the existence of mixed languages would constitute a potential threat to the integrity of the family tree model of
genetic relationship (and hence to the Comparative Method itself).

It is surely no accident that it was the first great creolist, Hugo
Schuchardt, who provided an extreme counterclaim to Müller's extreme claim about mixed languages. Pidgins and creoles were obviously the prime candidates for mixed-language status. But Schuchardt's interests were by no means confined to pidgins and creoles,
and his research on contact-induced language changes of all sorts
confirmed his belief in the universality of language mixture. Since
1884, most reactions to Schuchardt's challenge have fallen into three
main categories. First, some historical linguists have simply ignored
the position Schuchardt represents, along with the massive amount
of data that he and many others have adduced in support of the claim
that contact-induced language change at all levels of linguistic structure is a pervasive phenomenon. Oksaar, for instance, observes that
there are "no clear cases that would permit the generalization of
statements that grammatical paradigms, bound morphemes, word
order etc. can be subject to interference" (1972:492).

Other linguists have accepted the challenge but rejected
Schuchardt's conclusion. Arguments along this line are of two types.
One is that some linguistic subsystem—in practice, either the basic
vocabulary or the inflectional morphology—is relatively impervious
to foreign influence and is therefore a safe diagnostic tool for classifying a language genetically. That is, that subsystem is taken to be a
reliable indicator of the oldest, and thus inherited, linguistic material
in the language. The other is the claim that no language is so mixed
that it cannot be fit unambiguously into a family tree: it will always
be possible to show that the bulk of a language's lexicon and grammatical structures come from the same source.

The third major reaction to the proposal that all languages are
mixed is an acceptance of the proposition, with all its apparent consequences for genetic linguistics. Arguments for this approach make
explicit reference to pidgins and creoles, but they often go beyond
the languages traditionally called pidgins and creoles to claim that all
languages are in effect creoles, since probably all have undergone
considerable foreign interference in the course of their development.
In this view, "the traditional Stammbaum theory of linguistic relationships cannot be upheld" (Mühlhäusler 1980:34), because (among

other things) probably "every system or node on a family tree should have at least two parents" (Bailey 1973:20).

We disagree with all three of these positions on the interrelations among genetic linguistic theory, contact-induced language change in general, and language mixture in particular. We believe, with Schuchardt, Bailey, and Mühlhäusler, that foreign interference in grammar as well as in lexicon is likely to have occurred in the histories of most languages. So, although we have no quarrel with the Comparative Method's **methodological** requirement that the possibility of interference be ignored in its application, we do not accept the common assumption that this requirement is also a **theoretical** principle. On the other side, however, we do not find cogent either the extreme arguments for or the extreme arguments against hypotheses of language mixture. The former reflect an underdifferentiation of the linguistic results of contact; the latter suffer from a confusion about the nature of genetic relationship as a historical hypothesis.

In fact, the entire literature on this subject lacks a unified framework for the discussion, a framework that is based on the substantive claims underlying the metaphors of genetic linguistics and on a systematic historical investigation of pidgins, creoles, and all kinds and degrees of contact-induced language change. It is our goal in this book to propose such a framework and to provide arguments and evidence to support it. Since generalizations in this domain depend crucially on the quantity as well as on the quality of the evidence, the main arguments are followed by a set of case studies (chap. 9) that show in some detail how our approach works.

Our major conclusions are these: there are indeed mixed languages, and they include pidgins and creoles but are not confined to them; **mixed languages** do not fit within the genetic model and therefore **cannot be classified genetically at all; but most languages are not mixed,** and the traditional family tree model of diversification and genetic relationship remains the main reference point of comparative-historical linguistics owing to the fact that it is usually possible (except in relatively rare borderline cases) to distinguish mixed languages, whose origins are nongenetic, from languages whose development has followed the much more common genetic line. There are, finally, two very different kinds of contact situations that can lead to the emergence of mixed languages. These two kinds of situations, which are usually (but not consistently) distinguished as cases of "borrowing" and "substratum" interference, differ sharply in their linguistic results, especially in less extreme cases.

In the rest of this chapter and in chapters 2 and 3 we will lay some theoretical groundwork to provide a starting point for the detailed discussion to follow. The first step is to formulate the notion of genetic relationship in such a way as to make it possible to interpret the linguistic results of language contact in a genetic context (1.1, 1.2). Chapter 2 reviews some theoretical and empirical claims that have been made about the results of language contact. Chapter 3 outlines the main points of our own approach, and chapters 4 to 9 fill in this outline.

The key to our approach—and the single point on which we stand opposed to most structuralists (including generativists) who have studied these issues—is our conviction that the history of a language is a function of the history of its speakers, and not an independent phenomenon that can be thoroughly studied without reference to the social context in which it is embedded. We certainly do not deny the importance of purely linguistic factors such as pattern pressure and markedness considerations for a theory of language change, but the evidence from language contact shows that they are easily overridden when social factors push in another direction. The opposing position has been stated perhaps most dogmatically by the creolist Derek Bickerton (1980:125): "At the level of *parole,* social forces do have an effect on language; at the level of *langue,* they hardly ever do so." From a broader viewpoint, therefore, our book is meant as a contribution to the efforts of such scholars as Uriel Weinreich, William Labov, and Dell Hymes to remind the linguistic profession that languages are a product of, and a vehicle for, communication among people.

We should emphasize, however, that our study is not primarily a sociolinguistic one. We have examined cases in which contact-induced language change has occurred, and have correlated the linguistic results with what is known (and sometimes it is very little) of the sociohistorical circumstances of the various contact situations. Our purpose is to provide as complete a picture as possible of the scope and distribution of such changes; and we hope that the evidence presented here about what has happened in the past will help in the interpretation of ongoing linguistic change in directly observable current contact situations.

Throughout the book, our discussion of other authors' ideas and examples is selective and representative rather than exhaustive. We have not tried to emulate the dissertation-style comprehensiveness of bibliographical reference in Weinreich (1953) or Vildomec (1971), and we refer readers to these two sources for further examples (especially Weinreich) and for details on various theoretical positions (especially Vildomec, and especially for European views). In general, we have tried to be as thorough as possible in mentioning authors who have anticipated our ideas, but we have concentrated only on the most influential scholars in discussing views that we reject.

1.1. BOAS VS. SAPIR ON FOREIGN INFLUENCE VS. GENETIC INHERITANCE

To most American linguists, the famous Boas-Sapir controversy is by far the best known discussion of the possibility (or not) of distinguishing, for purposes of genetic classification, inherited similarities in two languages from similarities that result from language contact. This controversy and its background have been described recently by Darnell & Sherzer, who characterize Boas' position as a belief that "at a certain time depth it [is] impossible to distinguish results of borrowing from those of common origin," and Sapir's position as a belief that there will always be "a recognizable structural distinction between the two kinds of similarity" (Darnell & Sherzer 1971:25). Sapir, of course, followed through on his belief by proposing very broad genetic groupings based on structural similarities, usually without adducing the traditionally required evidence of regular sound/meaning correspondences (although, according to Darnell & Sherzer [1971:26], he "clearly believed that his hypothesized relationships would be confirmed through discovery of regular sound correspondences"). Sapir distinguished between superficial elements of grammar that might be diffused from language to language and a "deeper" kernel of grammar that must be inherited (Darnell & Sherzer 1971:26).

In practice, Sapir's "deeper kernel" was morphological, as can be seen from (among others) his Na-Déné grouping. This practice in turn reflected the widespread belief that the morphology, in particular the inflectional morphology, is especially stable, because it is so highly structured that it resists both internally- and externally-motivated changes. Other influential scholars besides Sapir have also held this view, among them Meillet, Hoijer, Swadesh, and Hymes, though only Hymes has explored carefully the possibility of using morphology alone as a sole criterion for establishing genetic relationship (Hymes 1955, 1956; see Thomason 1980b for a criticism of the superstable morphology hypothesis). The continuing popularity of this position can be established by reference to more recent literature. To give just two examples, Hancock appeals to the "retention [sic] of grammatical items as a criterion for establishing the core of direct retention, and thereby the genetic affiliation of the language" (1980: 86n); and Dolgopol'skij classifies Ma'a (Mbugu) as a Bantu language because of its Bantu morphology (1973, cited by Zaborski 1976:83; see 9.2 and Thomason 1983b for discussion of the Ma'a case).

But the morphology is not the only subsystem that has been proposed as a single definitive criterion for establishing genetic relationship. The other popular view is that the vocabulary, specifically the basic vocabulary, is **the** criterion. Weinreich, for instance, believed that genetic relationship is established by "the existence of cognates in the basic morpheme stock, with parallelism in allomorphic alternations as a powerful supplement" (1958:376), and he advocated using this criterion to group creoles with their vocabulary-base languages. Greenberg's widely used and largely successful technique of mass lexical comparison in setting up genetic groupings is of course based on this criterion, and Greenberg has stated explicitly his belief that there is no danger of having the results disconfirmed by the effects of massive foreign interference (e.g., 1953:275–276). For linguists who hold the view that neither lexical nor grammatical interference will affect the validity of their lexically determined genetic groupings, Tok Pisin (Neomelanesian) must be related to English in spite of its strikingly un-English grammar, and Ma'a (Mbugu), with its Cushitic basic vocabulary, is related to Cushitic, in spite of its fully elaborated Bantu morphology and its near-total lack of productive Cushitic grammatical features.

Unfortunately, neither the inflectional morphology nor the basic vocabulary is sufficiently stable internally and sufficiently impervious to restructuring or replacement through foreign interference to justify giving it status as the sole criterion for genetic relationship. A simple thought experiment shows what the difficulty is. If a group of English speakers replaced all their English lexical morphemes with Russian ones, but continued to use English phonology and morphosyntax, then surely they no longer speak English; and the language they speak, though identical to English grammatically, is not related to English in the usual sense of being a changed (later) form of English. And it isn't Russian, either, in spite of its 100 percent Russian vocabulary. It is, in fact, a mixed language.

There are several possible responses to this hypothetical example. The most obvious, perhaps, is to insist that no real-life cases of this sort exist—that it will always be possible to show that even the (apparently) most mixed languages, e.g., creoles, share most of their nonlexical structures with their vocabulary-base languages. Meillet (1921*b*) and Hall (1958), among others, offer this argument. But their hope is vain, because real cases of this exact type do exist. Ma'a is one: it consists of mainly Cushitic lexicon, especially basic vocabulary, and almost entirely Bantu grammar. Tok Pisin and other English-based Pacific pidgins and creoles, e.g., Bislama, are others: nonlexical English structures are few, or altogether lacking. AngloRomani is a form of speech with a Romani lexicon and a completely English grammar; in this case, the lexicon is that of the English Gypsies' ethnic heritage, while the entire grammar has been borrowed (in effect) from English (see chap. 4 for discussion).

Meillet, Weinreich, Hall, and others, in focusing their attention on the Caribbean creoles, may have been misled by a crucial feature of the history of most of these languages subsequent to their period of origin: with some notable exceptions, these creoles are spoken in a social context in which their various vocabulary-base languages have official national-language status. As a result, the best-known creoles have been converging toward the vocabulary-base languages for two hundred years or more. They therefore presumably share more grammatical structures with the vocabulary-base languages now, when linguists are studying them, than they originally shared, at a period from which there are few or no attestations.

Our claim that the cases mentioned above are mixed languages in the strongest sense of the phrase brings us back to Boas' side of the controversy with Sapir. Boas also believed in the existence of mixed languages, and, from his work on cultural diffusion in the Pacific

Northwest, he concluded that "we have to recognize that many of the languages (of America) have multiple roots" (1929:7; cited by Darnell & Sherzer 1971:25, 26). Darnell's and Sherzer's reaction to Boas' position is interesting, because it is representative of the strong tradition exemplified by the Müller and Welmers quotes given above, and it suggests a reason why so many historical linguists have tried so hard to deny the possibility of truly mixed languages:

> Such a position, of course, made the comparative method as under-stood in linguistics untenable. If mixed languages could occur, then no language could be proven to be the descendant of an earlier stage of a single other language. (Darnell & Sherzer 1971:26)

But this view of the consequences of Boas' position is unnecessarily pessimistic, and Boas himself pointed the way toward the solution to the methodological dilemma:

> On the basis of Indo-European experience, we should be very much inclined to seek for a common origin for all those languages that have a far-reaching morphological similarity; but it must be acknowledged, that, when the results of classifications based on different linguistic phenomena conflict, we must recognize the possibility of the occurrence of morphological assimilation. . . . We ought to inquire . . . into the possibility of mutual influences, which will be revealed, in part at least, by lack of correspondence between lexicographic, phonetic, and detailed morphological classifications. Boas 1917:4

In other words, given the possibility of diffused linguistic features of all sorts (and, by implication, to all degrees), no single subsystem is criterial for establishing genetic relationship. In fact, genetic relationship in the traditional sense of one parent per language can only be posited when systematic correspondences can be found in **all** linguistic subsystems—vocabulary, phonology, morphology, and (we would add) syntax as well.[1] If only languages that meet this criterion are considered candidates for genetic classification, then those languages that do not meet the criterion will pose no threat to the Comparative Method. The latter group includes not only mixed languages, which have followed a nongenetic path of development, but also, we will argue (chap. 8), languages whose genetic links date from a time too remote to permit establishment of the necessary systematic correspondences.

1.2. WHAT "GENETIC RELATIONSHIP" MEANS

In accepting Boas' basic position, however, we must still ask **why** it should be the case that genetic relationship entails systematic correspondences in all parts of the language. That is: why, exactly, is it inappropriate to claim that the basic vocabulary or the inflectional morphology is "the language" for purposes of genetic classification? To answer this question, we need to look at the fundamental theoretical assumptions that underlie the concept of genetic relationship. These assumptions provide the context for our consideration of the implications of our analysis for the historical interpretation of the products of contact-induced language change.

First, **all languages change through time.** The main stimuli for change are **drift**, i.e., tendencies within the language to change in certain ways as a result of structural imbalances; **dialect interference**, both between stable, strongly differentiated dialects and between weakly differentiated dialects through the differential spread (in 'waves') of particular changes; and **foreign interference.** Just as it is often difficult to tell whether two speech forms are dialects of one language or separate languages, so the borderline between dialect interference and foreign interference is often fuzzy. Nevertheless, many clear cases attest to the basic difference between these two types of interference. A language's geographical area may become fragmented, through physical and/or social factors, from the point of view of regular intercommunication. In such cases, change over time can result in dialect diversity and even language splits. Metaphorically, then, **a language can have multiple offspring.**

The second assumption is that **change can occur at any and all levels of the linguistic system.** Insofar as phonological units are used, singly or in combinations, only to represent morphemes and have no one-to-one associated ("symbolic") meanings, that is, most of the time, internally motivated **sound change is regular.**[2] Grammatical change, involving changes in elements and patterns that are meaningful, is neither regular nor thoroughgoing in the sense that sound change is; but internally motivated grammatical change can be accounted for, under a variety of rubrics, as the result of a dynamic interchange among various parts of the linguistic system.

Third, **a language is passed on** from parent generation to child generation and/or via peer group from immediately older to immediately younger, **with relatively small degrees of change over the short run**, given a reasonably stable sociolinguistic context. There has been a good deal of speculation about what kinds of rapid and drastic linguistic change might occur under highly unstable sociolinguistic situations, involving stresses among different cultural, political, economic, and religious systems, but our position is that most responses to such situations can be classed under **normal historical development** (i.e., according to assumptions 1–3) or **language shift**. That is, in general, either a language responds normally—changes gradually, is transmitted through generations and peers, and exhibits regular internally motivated sound change—or else it is given up.

In addition to these rather standard assumptions, we would like to propose two more principles which will help to define, by exclusion, genetic relationship or **normal transmission**.

Our fourth assumption is that **the label "genetic relationship" does not properly apply when transmission is imperfect.** If a whole population acquires a new language within possibly as little as a single lifetime, therefore necessarily other than by parental or peer-group enculturation, the linguistic system which results may have massive interference from the structure(s) of the language(s) originally spoken by the group. If this population is not integrated into the group that provided it with a new language, this deviant form of speech may crystallize into a new language. Or, to take another extreme possibility, a population may come under such heavy cultural (including sociopolitical and economic) pressure from another group that the entire pressured population becomes bilingual in the dominant group's language. The bilingual population may then actually shift completely to the second language, while retaining the lexicon of the original language for use, with the other language's grammar, as an ethnic-group code or jargon. Children born to members of that group might then begin to learn, not the whole original ethnic-group language, but only its vocabulary, in addition to the entire language of the dominant group. Cases of these two types are not known to be frequent, but they do exist, and they arise through imperfect transmission. Some of the languages traditionally called creoles constitute a special case of the first type (see chap. 6 for discussion); pidgins probably belong here too (chap. 7). We would claim that languages arising outside of normal transmission are **not** related (in the genetic sense) to **any** antecedent systems.[3]

Although many historical linguists might be willing to accept this assumption, some will surely be dubious about the possibility of detecting in a language a prior history of interrupted transmission. Weinreich, for instance, considered and rejected this possibility before settling on basic vocabulary as the safest guide to genetic affiliation: "to use relative continuity or discontinuity of transmission as a **criterion** [for genetic relationship] . . . would probably be unwise, since past circumstances of transmission cannot easily be reconstructed" (1958:375). It is likely, as Thomason (1980*a*) has pointed out, that the very understandable caution expressed in this remark accounts in large part for the fact that most linguists interested in the question have preferred to rely on the asocial (and ahistorical) criterion of synchronic linguistic features in determining genetic relationship. But the passage quoted above from Boas (1917:4) provides our methodological guideline: if transmission has been interrupted, then there should be, as he predicted, a **lack** of correspondence among the various subsystems of the language, most probably between the lexicon as a whole and the grammar as a whole. In other words, in such a language it will not be possible to show that both grammar and lexicon derive from the same source. In cases like Ma'a and Anglo-Romani, lexicon comes from one source and grammar from another; in most pidgins and creoles, lexicon comes from one source and grammar comes neither from that language nor from any other single language.

To answer the question posed at the beginning of this section, then, a claim of genetic relationship entails systematic correspondences in all parts of the language because that is what results from normal transmission: what is transmitted is an entire language—that is, a complex set of interrelated lexical, phonological, morphosyntactic, and semantic structures. This is the meaning of one of the first principles students learn when they study historical linguistics—namely, that a daughter language in a family tree is a changed later form of its single parent language.

Our fifth and final assumption is a corollary to the fourth: **a language can not have multiple ancestors in the course of normal transmission.** To be sure, mixed languages in a nontrivial sense exist, but by definition they are unrelated genetically to the source(s) of any of their multiple components. We disagree strongly, therefore, with Mühlhäusler's assertion that one would get wrong results by using the "traditional static comparative method" to determine the relationship between Tok Pisin and the Melanesian language Tolai (1980:38). If properly applied, the Comparative Method will yield no results at all for Tok Pisin, because it will not be possible to find systematic correspondences in all its linguistic subsystems with any other single language. This is because Tok Pisin did not arise through normal transmission.

Our approach to the study of genetic relationship is thus based theoretically on the social fact of normal transmission rather than merely on the linguistic facts themselves. But, like everyone else, we must rely on the attested linguistic evidence to fill in the many gaps in the linguistic history of a speech community. We will show, in chapters 3–8, that Boas' prediction about a lack of sufficient systematic correspondences in mixed languages is borne out by the evidence available from well-documented cases. We will also show that—as Boas apparently also suspected, and as one should expect in any set of phenomena where one kind of thing can change gradually into another—there are languages whose history hovers on the borderline between genetic and nongenetic (see especially the case study on Ma'a, 9.2).

Moreover, genetic classification is not the only aspect of our investigation that turns out on close inspection to rest on a social foundation. After showing in chapter 2 that no linguistic constraints that have been proposed provide a reliable guideline to the actual results of interference, we will give a socially oriented reason in chapter 3 for the failure of all such constraints.

2
The Failure of Linguistic Constraints on Interference

In a 1973 article on areal linguistics, Werner Winter remarked of contact-induced language change that "the inspection of a wide array of observations . . . leads to the conclusion that in this field nearly everything can be shown to be possible, but . . . not much progress has been made toward determining what is probable" (1973:135). Winter's article appeared in the *Current Trends in Linguistics* volume entitled *Diachronic, areal, and typological linguistics,* and the content of that 604-page book provides indirect support for Winter's comment: aside from his own twelve-page article, contact-induced language change receives no systematic attention in the book. Today, Weinreich's 1953 book *Languages in contact* still stands as the best known and most authoritative study of the subject; but even that impressive work provides no means of predicting, however roughly, what types of contact-induced changes will occur when.

The reason for this discouraging state of affairs, we believe, is that most linguists have been approaching the problem from the wrong direction. From Meillet, Sapir, and the Prague linguists to Weinreich to the most modern generativists, the heirs of Saussure have proposed linguistic constraints on linguistic interference. These constraints are all based ultimately on the premise that the structure of a language determines what can happen to it as a result of outside influence. And they all fail. As far as the strictly linguistic possibilities go, any linguistic feature can be transferred from any language to any other language; and implicational universals that depend solely on linguistic properties are similarly invalid. This assertion flatly contradicts most older views on the subject and some newer ones as well, but solid evidence has been available and in print for many years. Before examining the major source of misunderstanding in this area (in chap. 3), we will survey some of the linguistic constraints that have been proposed.

2.1. TYPOLOGICAL CONSTRAINTS[1]

Meillet believed that **grammatical** loans are possible only between very similar systems, especially dialects of a single language (1921b:87). Many linguists have shared this view, often with the corollary assumption that, since similar systems will share (most of) the same categories, grammatical categories cannot be transferred from one language to another. This widespread view arose (we suspect) not from the examination of actual language contact data, but from the standard structuralist belief that the most highly structured subsystems are the most stable.

This belief seems to be as popular now as it was in the early decades of this century. Haugen, in a review of Weinreich (1953), comments approvingly that "following hints advanced by other linguists, the author offers material in support of the thesis that the likelihood of morphemic transfer . . . is in inverse proportion to its structural integration. . . . On those relatively rare occasions when bound morphemes are actually transferred from one language to another, they are such as fit readily into a preexistent category in the recipient language" (1954:385–386). Vildomec observes that "if the structuralists are right, we can really say, with L. Tesnière (1939:85), that a language will the better resist foreign influence the better developed and organized systems it contains" (1971:100). Winter asserts that "the ease of adoption of outside features depends on the degree of variation admitted in the respective component of a language," so that the lexicon will be most susceptible and the paradigmatic morphology least susceptible (1973:144). Givón believes that "it is relatively unlikely for languages to 'borrow grammar'," because borrowing grammar would be disruptive "for the interlocking, highly nonarbitrary part of the system" (1979:26). And, as a final example, Bickerton says that "languages . . . are systems, systems have structure, and things incompatible with that structure cannot be borrowed" (1981:50). Statements of this sort can be found throughout the literature, some more dogmatic than others but all confident about the soundness of the reasoning.[2]

But the structuralist reasoning is not consistent with the available data, for two reasons. First, the claim that a language has "a complex resistance to interference" (Weinreich 1953:44) is only relevant to borrowing situations, not to cases of substratum interference; and second, though it is true that some kinds of features are more easily transferred than others (and we will outline the empirical evidence below), social factors can and very often do overcome structural resistance to interference at all levels. These points will be elaborated on in chapter 3, but we will mention a few examples here to show that the more dogmatic versions of the above argument from linguistic structure are false.

In his historical analysis of Chinookan tense-aspect and pronominal categories, Silverstein argues convincingly that "Proto-Chinookan must have been under heavy categorial influence from the languages surrounding on the coast, before the speakers started moving upriver" (1977:154; see also 1974:S65). He cites this external influence as the cause of, among other things, the "adventitious rise of gender categories" in Chinookan (1977:154). Similarly, Boas believed that the obviative (fourth person) category had been diffused into western Sahaptian languages from neighboring Kutenai in the Pacific Northwest (1929:4). On the other side of the world, some Indic languages have acquired very un-IndoEuropean morphological categories and syntactic construction types from Dravidian. One is the characteristic Dravidian exclusive/inclusive 'we' distinction that has been acquired by some Indic languages, e.g., Sindhi and Gujarati (Emeneau 1980 [1962]:59; Southworth MS). Another is the development of negative verbs in languages such as Bengali and Marathi under Dravidian influence (Klaiman 1977:311; Southworth 1971:264). A third case is discussed by Andronov (1964:124), who describes the Bengali plural suffixes -rā (human) and -gulō, -guli (non-human) both as direct morpheme borrowings (the suffixes themselves are of Dravidian origin) and as categorial borrowing, since

the noun classification categories came from Dravidian with the suffixes. Some interference in India goes in the other direction, from
Indic to Dravidian, often as a result of Sanskrit influence on literary
Dravidian languages. Sridhar cites such examples as old Malayalam
inscriptions that show un-Dravidian concord between modifiers and
head nouns (1978:212 n. 7, citing Sekhar 1959:161), and the development in Kannaḍa of subordinate clauses with finite verbs beside
typical Dravidian participial constructions (1978:204, citing Nadkarni
1970). There are now numerous well-documented examples in the
literature of categorial diffusion between languages that are (as far as
linguists can tell) unrelated and that do not, or did not originally,
have similar grammars.

Most linguists would probably accept the suggestion that
generativists' grammatical rules—phonological as well as morphosyntactic ones—fall under Meillet's ban on grammatical interference between very different systems, on the premise that rule systems are
highly integrated and thus likely to be especially stable. Certainly the
constraint proposed by Bybee Hooper for phonological interference
is in harmony with Meillet's constraint. Working within the
framework of natural generative phonology, Bybee Hooper claims
that genuine phonological rules (as opposed to morphophonemic
rules) cannot be borrowed, though "minor via-rules can develop
through borrowing, and on a very restricted scale, it is possible for
morphophonemic rules to enter a language with borrowed forms"
(1973:186, 191; cited by Campbell 1976:186). But phonological rules
of all sorts do diffuse from language to language. Campbell (1976)
presents counterexamples to Bybee Hooper's prediction; for instance,
Mayan languages show changes in which quite regular automatic
morphophonemic rules like /m,n/ → [ŋ]/__ # and allophonic rules
like palatalization have been transferred from languages of one Mayan
subgroup to neighboring languages of another. Several languages
have been shown to have stress rules acquired under foreign influence.
These include the word-initial stress pattern in Czech (Winter
1973:144), the stress of a group of Serbocroatian dialects, which was
fixed under Hungarian influence (Ivić 1964; see 3.3 below for details),
and the fixed stress of Sri Lanka Portuguese Creole, changed from a
phonemic stress system under the influence of Sri Lanka Tamil and
Sinhala (Smith 1977).[3] So, again, the purely linguistic constraint on
contact-induced change will not work: phonological rules—in fact,

grammatical rules of all sorts—are among the linguistic features that can be transferred from one language to another.[4]

A less absolute linguistic constraint than Meillet's is the one proposed by Jakobson in 1938: "a language accepts foreign structural elements only when they correspond to its own tendencies of development" (1962 [1938]:241). This echoes a constraint proposed specifically for phonological interference by Sapir, who believed that foreign sounds might enter a language as nondistinctive variants "provided always that these new variations . . . are in the direction of the native drift" (1921:200). Like Meillet's constraint, this one has been, and continues to be, widely accepted. Jakobson's view is a faithful manifestation of the Prague Circle's emphasis on the structuredness of language, so it is not surprising that his Prague colleagues shared it. Havránek, for instance, argued as early as 1931 that the structure of a language would determine its acceptance or rejection of foreign features (Vachek 1962:434), and Vachek says that his examples from English have "confirmed that the influence of external factors upon the development of the structure of a language could only assert itself because its assertion was in harmony with the needs and wants of the structure exposed to that influence" (1962:447). (Vachek adds, however, that exceptions do occur, and that consequently one must formulate the hypothesis with caution.) Beyond Prague, many other linguists have cited Jakobson's constraint with apparent approval, for example Weinreich (1953:25), Vogt (1954:372), and Jeffers and Lehiste (1979:143), or (re)formulated a similar constraint of their own. Mühlhäusler belongs in the latter group when he asserts that a pidgin's grammar "determines what can be borrowed and what cannot" (1980:41) and that, in fact, borrowing will occur only if the results agree with natural tendencies (1980:36).[5]

Jakobson's claim is particularly hard to disprove, because it has at least the potential of being circular: if a language has accepted foreign structural elements, then, on Jakobson's hypothesis, it must already have had a tendency to develop in that direction. Case studies like Silverstein's analysis of Chinookan tense-aspect developments, with different dialects undergoing interference from different sources and thus developing in quite different ways, provide a check of sorts on Jakobson's claim: if the tendencies were all already present in the language, why didn't the dialects develop in more similar ways? Other examples of this type are easy to find. A particularly convincing one is Leslau's description (1945, 1952) of changes in Ethiopic Semitic languages under Cushitic influence. Most of these changes, which include such developments as glottalized emphatic consonants, plural formation via reduplication, a distinct future tense, and SOV (Subject-Object-Verb) word order, are unique in Semitic (except for the SOV word order, which is also dominant in Akkadian, thanks to Sumerian influence [S. Kaufman 1974:132]).

Vogt's argument that foreign elements must correspond to "innovation possibilities offered by the receiving system" (1954:372) hints at a solution to the problem of dialect divergence under foreign influence, because the different interference features in different dialects could be ascribed to different "innovation possibilities" already present in the language. But the circularity problem remains. Moreover, there are more extreme cases than the Chinookan and Ethiopic Semitic ones, and these offer compelling evidence against Jakobson's hypothesis, even with Vogt's refinement. One such example is the massive introduction of Turkish features into all aspects of the grammar of Asia Minor Greek, as described by Dawkins (1916). These interference features include word order patterns, relative clause formation, phonetics, phonemic inventory, phonological rules (including vowel harmony), agglutination, and borrowed morphemes of every category. These features can hardly be explained as following tendencies already existing in Greek, because, with one exception,[6] no other dialects of Greek have undergone any of the changes (see 9.1 for a discussion of this case). An even more spectacular example than Asia Minor Greek is found in the dialect of Aleut that is spoken on Mednyj Island. On Menovščikov's account (1969), the highly agglutinative Aleut verb inflectional system has become flexional under very strong Russian influence. It has also lost its dual number category, and in the past tense the inherited person distinctions have vanished. These and other drastic changes were brought about by the replacement of native Aleut inflectional suffixes by borrowed Russian ones, and the resulting verb system is strikingly different from those of other Aleut dialects (see 9.4).

Weinreich proposes a constraint on grammatical interference that is more cautious than Meillet's or Jakobson's (because it is hedged): "in the interference of two grammatical patterns it is ordinarily the one which uses relatively free and invariant morphemes in its paradigms . . . which serves as the model for imitation" (1953:41).

As examples he cites the replacement of suffixed pronominal possessors on nouns by analytic constructions in Estonian (under Germanic
influence), Amharic (under Cushitic influence), and colloquial Israeli
Hebrew (under Yiddish and other European influence) (41–42). In a
similar vein, Mühlhäusler states that "inflectional and derivational
morphology are . . . the first victims of language contact" (1980:38).
But there are counterexamples here, too. Asia Minor Greek, for
instance, sometimes adds third person possessive suffixes to nouns
on the Turkish model (Dawkins 1916:201); and Mednyj Aleut also
runs counter to Weinreich's and Mühlhäusler's prediction, since
agglutinative morphology is more readily segmentable than flexional
morphology.

In fact, counterexamples are sufficiently common that Weinreich's proposal cannot be used to predict the results of contact unless
some principled way can be found of separating cases that follow it
from cases that do not. As we will see, the only way to do this is to
rely on social predictors: it is the social context, not the structure of
the languages involved, that determines the direction and the degree
of interference. Turkish influenced Greek in Asia Minor because it
was the Greeks who were under cultural pressure and (therefore) the
Greeks who became bilingual. Greek could not have influenced Turkish structurally (though lexical borrowing from Greek did occur in
Turkish), no matter how much Greek structures might have favored
such interference, when few Turks learned Greek and Greeks who
shifted to Turkish were too few to introduce their learners' errors
into Turkish as a whole. And, in that particular context, Turkish
influence was powerful enough to introduce morphological features
as well as the more readily borrowed features of phonology and
syntax into local Greek dialects.

Another of Weinreich's suggested constraints is one against the
adoption of a full set of inflectional morphemes: "the transfer of a full
grammatical paradigm, with its formant morphemes, from one language to another has apparently never been recorded" (1953:43–44).
This fits well with Sapir's view that "nowhere do we find any but
superficial morphological interinfluencings . . . [we have] no really
convincing examples of morphological influence by diffusion"
(1921:203, 206). It may also be considered a special case of Meillet's
more sweeping constraint on possible grammatical interference.
Winter agrees that the chances for such extensive interference are

around zero (1973:145), and the idea is so bizarre that probably most linguists would accept Weinreich's observation as a minimal constraint on contact-induced language change.

Nevertheless, though we do not claim that such changes are common, they do occur. One example is Ma'a in Tanzania, which consists of mostly Cushitic basic vocabulary, a few Cushitic grammatical patterns, and a rather full Bantu grammar that includes much inflectional morphology and even some allomorphy (9.2; see Thomason 1983*b* for a fuller discussion). Other examples are Dawkins's Asia Minor Greek case, where Turkish personal suffixes are used with native Greek verbs in some villages (9.1),[7] and Menovščikov's Mednyj Aleut case, where the vocabulary and the bulk of the grammar are clearly Aleut, but the entire finite verb morphology is Russian (9.4).

2.2. IMPLICATIONAL UNIVERSAL CONSTRAINTS

Most recent claims about linguistic constraints on interference fall into two general (and overlapping) categories: implicational universals and constraints based on naturalness. In the former category, some of the claims would be valid if confined to **borrowing**, as opposed to **substratum interference**; but it is clear in context that most authors use the term 'borrowing' in the broadest sense, to refer to all kinds of linguistic interference. That is, the following definition is the one most linguists operate with, usually implicitly, in discussing contact-induced language change: "the term 'borrowing' will be understood to refer to a process whereby a language acquires some structural property from another language" (Moravcsik 1978:99).

This is the meaning of the term that underlies the most commonly expressed implicational universal about contact-induced change: no structural borrowing without lexical borrowing. Moravcsik gives this as a firm constraint: "no non-lexical . . . property can be borrowed unless the borrowing language already includes borrowed lexical items from the same source language" (1978:110). Many other linguists have proposed the same constraint (though often with more caution), e.g., Frachtenberg (1918:177), Hoijer (1948), and Comrie (1981*a*:202–203). This prediction is valid for borrowing proper, but substratum interference need **not** be accompanied by extensive lexical transfer, as one can see from, for instance, the small number of Indic (and Dravidian) words in the variety of English known as Indian English.

Nor is this a recent discovery. In his seminal paper on phonological Sprachbund phenomena, Jakobson pointed out that 'borrowings of vocabulary . . . do not suffice to produce phonological contagion; **nor are they a necessary condition for it** (1962 [1938]:240–241; translation and emphasis ours). Vildomec (1971:116) cites Deeters' claim (1939:53) that "substrata influence vocabulary only very slightly but exercise great influence on sound-changes, simplifications in morphology, and on the changes of the *innere Form* (i.e., mainly syntax)." (Deeters was wrong only in his claim that substratum influence will always simplify the morphology.) Vildomec himself remarks on the strikingly low number of loanwords in some cases of substratum interference (1971:97).

It might be objected that most of these sources refer to "few loanwords" rather than "no loanwords," so that Moravcsik's (and others') constraint could be upheld as long as at least one or two loanwords can be found. But such an objection would trivialize the constraint. The interesting point is that in borrowing proper many words will be borrowed before any structural interference at all occurs; but in substratum interference, as we will argue below, structural interference comes first. So the constraint is not universal in the usual very general formulation. In fact, the distinction between borrowing and substratum interference is so important that, in spite of a reluctance (which we share with many of our colleagues) to proliferate technical vocabulary, we will hereafter use the term **"borrowing"** to refer only to **the incorporation of foreign elements into the speakers' native language**, not to interference in general.

Other implicational universals that have been proposed by Moravcsik (1978), Comrie (1981a), and others are also valid in principle only for borrowing situations. The most popular ones are constraints against the transfer of affix morphemes and function words without lexical morphemes; in particular, it is often claimed that affixes are transferred only as adjuncts on lexical morphemes. Although pure cases are hard to find, since even substratum interference usually involves at least a few lexical items, counterexamples can be found in substratum situations.

2.3. CONSTRAINTS BASED ON NATURALNESS

Constraints based on considerations of naturalness are currently enjoying a prominent position in theoretical discussions of both internally and externally induced language change. Many of the proposed constraints discussed above can be subsumed under the general category of naturalness constraints, but in this section we will look at claims based explicitly on naturalness. Before doing so, however, we need to comment on the theoretical foundations of this approach to the study of language change.

One of the few dissenting views in the current literature on naturalness is Hymes' discussion (1980:399–403), which begins with this statement: "At the risk of offending even more colleagues, I should like to propose that we abandon talk of 'natural' change" (399). He goes on to argue that, since all change is natural in some sense, the identification of certain types of changes as natural carries the unfortunate, and false, implication that changes in the opposite direction are somehow unnatural. Although we share Hymes' reservation to some extent, we feel that the notion of naturalness, at least in the context of universal markedness theory, has an important role to play in theories of language change: natural changes are produced from general principles, while other changes arise in circumstances where they would not be expected. However, we also believe that most of the claims that have been made to date using markedness theory as a general predictor of change are so simplistic that they have little hope of success. (This objection applies only to general claims; many explanations based on markedness that have been proposed for specific changes strike us as entirely reasonable.) Since naturalness claims for internal and external motivations are closely linked, we will give reasons for our general skepticism before turning to claims about externally motivated change in particular.

The commonest form of markedness constraint is some version of the claim that, at least in internally motivated change, more marked structures ($\overset{>}{m}$) will become less marked ($\overset{\smallfrown}{m}$). This view may be most familiar to historical linguists from the writings of Charles-James N. Bailey and his colleagues, especially Mühlhäusler and Mayerthaler (see, for instance, Bailey 1977:8), but it is widespread elsewhere in the literature as well. (Much of Paul Kiparsky's work on phonological

and analogic change, for instance, fits into the same general picture.)
We agree with Bailey that many linguistic changes are best seen as
simplifications, i.e., as changes from more marked to less marked in
systematic terms. However, in principle any predictions based on
such observations must always be hedged with an "all other things
being equal" reservation.[8] The reason is that a language is not just
one system, but a system of systems. All its systems interact, and,
as we were taught when we were beginning students of historical
linguistics, a change that simplifies one subsystem is likely to complicate another.

Most of the textbook illustrations of this truism have to do with
the interplay between sound change and analogy—specifically, with
interactions between phonology and morphology. To take a typical
example, the Serbocroatian sound change that merged the inherited
phonemes /i/ and /ï/ into /i/—a clear simplification, and a clear
change m̂ > m̌ in the phonemic inventory—complicated the morphophonemics of nominal and verbal inflection by making the previously
automatic morphophonemic rule $k\,g\,x \rightarrow c\,z\,s$ / ___ i nonautomatic
(or opaque, in Kiparsky's terms). In some dialects the rule remained
in this form; in others it was extended to apply before the new
suffix-vowel $+i$ ($<ï$) in noun declension. This change moved the
nonautomatic rule toward an automatic one and was thus a simplification, resulting in a less marked rule system as far as the noun
morphology was concerned. But since no such extension occurred in
the verb morphology, a gap was introduced between noun and verb
morphophonemics—a complication.

Nor can this sort of difficulty be avoided by restricting the domain of markedness constraints to changes within one subsystem,
e.g., the phonology or the morphology. A natural, phonetically
based sound change may result in a more marked phonemic inventory
or phonological rule system; a simplification of a rule may produce
a more marked phonetic system; an analogic change that extends a
pattern and can thus be viewed as a change from more to less marked
may nevertheless result in a more complicated morphology. Here are
a few examples. The rather common sound change VN > Ṽ / ___ C,
e.g., in French and in Proto-Slavic, may simplify the syllable structure (in Slavic this change was part of a diachronic conspiracy called
the Law of Open Syllables, a group of changes that led in various

ways to a pattern in which all syllables ended in a vowel). But it produces at least a surface contrast between oral and nasal vowels and often a new morphophonemic rule too, and this is a complication.

Another common change is palatalization, e.g., k or $t > č$ / ___ i, which is a phonetically motivated change from marked to less marked. Subsequent generalization of this change to new environments is likely to simplify the phonological rule of palatalization, but the new environments may not be phonetically well motivated. A rule like the Papago one that changes /t/ to [č] before any high vowel /i ɨ u/ is less marked in terms of generality but certainly more marked phonetically than $t \rightarrow č$ / ___ i. In most Salishan languages all instances of /k/ changed to /č/, leaving (in those languages that did not develop a new /k/ from another source) an inventory with /q/ but no /k/— even though the presence of /q/ is generally believed to imply the presence of /k/. Campbell (1980:21) argues that this does not represent a violation of the implicational universal because the change is externally motivated. But, though this palatalization is indeed a widespread areal feature in the Pacific Northwest, it must have started somewhere, and the original change presumably moved from a phonetically well motivated one to a phonetically unmotivated one that generalized the rule but made the inventory more marked.

Another Pacific Northwest areal feature is the change of nasal phonemes to voiced oral stops in contiguous languages of three different families (Salishan, Chimakuan, and Wakashan). It is not clear that this change is $\overset{>}{m} > \tilde{m}$ in any sense. The languages had no voiced/voiceless contrast before the change $m, n > b, d$, so there was no reduction in the number of phonemes, and an inventory that lacks nasal phonemes is generally believed to be highly unnatural. So, wherever this change started, it looks like a move toward greater markedness, and in addition it often complicated the morphophonemics to a considerable degree. (Haas 1969 and Campbell 1980 discuss this change in more detail.)

As for analogic change, cases of morphological expansion such as the spread of the animacy category in Slavic noun declension provide examples of complicating changes. In Czech, for instance, changes that extended the pattern distinguishing animate masculines from other declensional types destroyed partially (but not totally) the pattern uniting one group of animate masculines with feminine nouns in one declension (see Thomason 1976 for discussion). The result is a declensional system which in this aspect is more complicated than the antecedent system.

We conclude from these and similar examples that, while many internally motivated linguistic changes do move unambiguously in the direction $\overset{>}{m} > \overset{<}{m}$, others move from $\overset{<}{m} > \overset{>}{m}$, and still others have both systemic effects (depending on which subsystem one examines) or neither. It is possible that successful, i.e., regular, internally motivated sound changes always **begin** with a phonetic motivation that can be identified as $\overset{>}{m} > \overset{<}{m}$ in character; we find the recent work by Ohala, Hombert, and others on phonetic explanation cogent and valuable (see, e.g., Hombert and Ohala 1982). But they make no claim for exclusivity, and in general they state their conclusions with commendable caution. (Certainly other internally motivated changes have an initial analogic motivation, but perhaps they never sweep through the entire lexicon. See Malkiel [1976] for a highly suggestive discussion of two such changes.) In any case, subsequent phonetic **extension** of initially natural changes and their **effects** on other subsystems are by no means predictably $\overset{>}{m} > \overset{<}{m}$.

Once we move away from the area of sound change, in which theory is more highly developed, the picture becomes even murkier. Analogic morphological change is often simplificatory, at least in languages whose morphology is shrinking, but not always. Efforts to predict its direction have been notoriously unsuccessful. Syntactic analyses like the ones presented by Bever and Langendoen (1972) and Naro (1981) represent promising lines of investigation into the possibilities of using naturalness to explain some syntactic changes, but it is not yet clear how or if these approaches can be extended more generally. Other efforts by syntacticians, including most of the research based on Greenberg's implicational word order universals, have been less fruitful, mainly because of circularity in the argumentation (see, for instance, Mithun and Campbell's [1982] and Lightfoot's [1979:154 ff.] discussions of methodological problems in this area). In morphology and syntax, there is little agreement on which specific structures and rules are marked and which are unmarked. This is not to say, of course, that consensus is totally lacking. Many linguists believe (not always correctly) that morphological coding of a given function can be assumed to be more marked than a corresponding syntactic construction. Another point on which there is quite general agreement is that a language that has, for example, prefixes and prepositions combined with SOV word order is more highly marked as far as word order is concerned than an SOV language with suffixes and postpositions.

In sum, we see two continuing difficulties with applications of markedness theory to the study of language change. One is a pervasive tendency to underestimate the complexity of change processes and their systemic results. The other is widespread disagreement about what constitutes a marked feature or combination of features. Nevertheless, a start has been made in attacking both problems, so our skepticism about the results of such historical investigations so far inspires us rather to caution than to rejection of the whole line of research.

We believe (in agreement, probably, with most linguists) that markedness is a genuine linguistic phenomenon; that it rests on a basis, however ill defined, of relative productive and perceptual ease; and that it can be expected, therefore, to play a role in all kinds of language learning and language use. We also find cogent Bever and Langendoen's argument (1972) that language change involves competition between ease of learning and ease of perception. Conflicts should thus be expected to arise between these different aspects of markedness, and such conflicts will account for some of the complexities presented by the data on language change. Consider, for instance, the case of the nasalless languages of the Pacific Northwest. The normal ("unmarked") position of the velum for breathing is lowered (i.e., set for nasality), but some research shows that it is at least partly raised when a person begins to speak (see, e.g., Ohala 1975:291), so that the raised position may be "unmarked" during speech. Perhaps, then, the near-universal presence of one or more nasal phonemes is unmarked for perceptual reasons: *p* may be easier to distinguish from *m* than *p* from *b*. But it may be easier to learn to produce *b* than *m*, in that no articulatory movement needs to be programmed, ever, to lower the velum after it has been raised for speech.

In the discussion that follows in this and later sections, we will adopt the usual practice of making proposals about markedness based on evidence primarily from typology (more widespread = less marked), and secondarily from first-language acquisition (first learned = less marked). It should be noted, however, that our awareness of some of the gaps in the research on markedness will not make us more knowledgeable than other scholars—only, we hope, more cautious than some.

Turning now to proposed markedness constraints on contact-induced change, we find an interesting split between people who claim that foreign interference complicates the grammar (increases its markedness) and people who claim that interference simplifies the grammar (decreases its markedness). Distinguishing substratum interference from borrowing resolves part, but by no means all, of the conflict.

Bailey (1973) and Traugott (1973) argue that, in Sherzer's words (1977:185), "internal language change typically involves simplification, i.e., loss of marked features, while creolization, language change through external contact, involves linguistic complication, the development of marked features." (It should be noted that Bailey, unlike Traugott, applies the term 'creolization' to all externally-motivated change.) Campbell argues more cautiously that externally-induced changes, specifically sound changes, **may** be unnatural: in general, "it can be said that sound changes induced by internal factors are natural and regular, and that unnatural changes and exceptions to natural changes typically have external motivation" (1980:24). The dichotomy expressed in these proposals is important. The reasoning, usually implicit, seems to be roughly this: if all internal change is $\overset{>}{m} > \overset{<}{m}$, then why do all languages have lots of marked elements and structures instead of a maximally unmarked system? The need to maintain enough distinctions, enough structure, to provide for communicative adequacy will set a lower limit on possible reduction, but no human language is anywhere near any imagined limit of that type. Therefore, external influence is proposed as the major or only source of complications in the system. Since Bailey, at least, believes that such influence is universal in language history, the dichotomy would account both for natural tendencies and for the universal presence of marked features. Mühlhäusler makes a similar claim for external change but (following Givón; see below) contrasts pidgins with other languages: generally, he says, "language mixing with pidgins results in added natural rules whilst mixing between two full-fledged languages can result in unnaturalness" (1980:21).

As we observed above, we do not agree with the first half of Bailey's (and others') dichotomy. Our data on contact-induced changes do not support the second half, either. Both borrowing and substratum interference do frequently complicate the grammar, but both simplify it just as often, at least in cases involving moderate to heavy interference. Here are a few examples of simplifying changes. Asia Minor Greek lost /θ,ð/ (through merger with /t,d/) and grammatical gender through borrowing from Turkish, and Ma'a lost such marked Cushitic features as ejectives, labialized dorsal phonemes, and the singulative number category through borrowing from Bantu. Adstratum interference caused the loss of dual number and plural markers on nouns in Ethiopic Semitic (Leslau 1952).

On the other side of the fence, the most prominent claim about contact as a simplifying force is probably the one made by Givón, who argues, in his section on "Why languages do not borrow grammar" (1979:25–28), that disrupting the morphosyntactic patterns would cause the grammar to "gain in markedness" (26): " . . . if conflicts of grammar did arise, then rather than increase the markedness of his specific grammar by borrowing, the speaker is more likely to revert to the universal competence shared by all humans—Universal Grammar" (Givón 1979:26–27).

This argument simply is not justified by the available data on language contact. We do not claim that overall morphosyntactic leveling in the direction $\overset{>}{m} > \overset{<}{m}$ never occurs as a result of contact. But one case that is often cited in support of this claim, Kupwar in India (Gumperz and Wilson 1971), in fact shows few clearly simplificatory changes, together with a larger number of apparently neutral ones and one complicating change (see 4.3 for a fuller discussion). Moreover, the long-term contact between Ma'a and Bantu led to the wholesale adoption by Ma'a of highly marked Bantu inflectional structures. Givón would perhaps explain away the Ma'a case in a manner analogous to his explanation of the apparent counterexample of interference in Amharic from a Cushitic substratum: there was "no communicative stress" because the shift by Cushitic speakers to Amharic "proceeded gradually, without need to resort to the extreme compromise of Universal Grammar" (1979:27–28). If this is his response to the Ma'a borrowing situation, then he cannot use his theory to explain the simplificatory Kupwar results, because that contact situation is at least as old as the Ma'a/Bantu one.

Since, as we have mentioned, moderate to heavy interference is likely to complicate the grammar of the borrowing language or the target language in a shift situation about as often as it simplifies it, Givón's prediction will not hold. A number of relevant examples have already been given; others will be given in following sections. To mention just four here, Kupwar Urdu developed an inclusive/exclusive 'we' distinction under the influence of Kupwar Marathi and Kupwar Kannaḍa; Ethiopic Semitic acquired a future tense distinction from its Cushitic substratum; Russian owes its partitive ("second genitive") case to a Uralic substratum (see 9.5 for discussion); and Ma'a borrowed many noun classes, and their prefixal concord systems, from Bantu.

Givón may wish to restrict his claims about borrowing to pidgins and creoles, where the need to arrive at a common medium of communication is often, though not always, urgent. (This is a risky restriction, since in the **creation** of a grammar 'borrowing' is not really an appropriate label for the development of grammatical features. See chapters 6 and 7 for discussion of this point.) But a comparison of, for example, Chinook Jargon with a Bantu-based pidgin like Kituba shows little grammatical similarity and no demonstrable reversion to Universal Grammar. Chinook Jargon grammar can be entirely, or almost entirely, explained by reference to typological characteristics shared by Pacific Northwest Amerindian languages (*pace* Silverstein 1972; see Thomason 1983*a*). Similarly, Bantu-based pidgins owe their morphosyntax primarily to the Bantu languages spoken by their originators.

Mühlhäusler (1980), who cites Givón's notion of speakers reverting to Universal Grammar, asserts that morphology is one of the first victims of language contact (38) and that "second-language pidgins will generally not borrow grammar or lexicon that will make their syntax or morphology less natural" (43). His belief that fully crystallized pidgins react differently under foreign-language influence than non-pidgins do strikes us as unmotivated. His first specific claim here, in any case, is false. Morphology is by no means always reduced in contact situations, as we have already shown. And pidgins, as far as we can tell, are just as likely to acquire marked features through contact as is any other language. We have very little actual evidence on this point, however. Too few long-lived pidgins are well enough attested from their earliest stages to permit safe generalizations. The grammar of Chinook Jargon, for instance, has changed very little during its recorded history, but one small morphosyntactic complication is the sporadic addition, for both Indian and white speakers especially during the twentieth century, of the English plural suffix -*s* to a few nouns, including some derived from Indian languages. Morever, if Mühlhäusler (1981) is right about the early grammatical simplicity of Tok Pisin, the developments of dual and trial pronouns and (if it was not there to begin with) of an exclusive/inclusive 'we' distinction, through continuing contact with Austronesian languages, are counterexamples to his claim.

Another of Mühlhäusler's proposed principles in this general line is that "mixing of linguistic subsystems tends to lead to leveling or a kind of common-core grammar" (1980:28). In his article he does not provide criteria for distinguishing between "linguistic subsystems" and his contrasting notion of "separate systems," but presumably dialects of a single language would fall into the former category and thus be subject to his leveling constraint.

Now, dialect leveling is one of the oldest traditional notions in historical linguistics. But in its traditional sense "leveling" merely refers to change toward greater similarity of dialects and not, as Mühlhäusler's use of the term suggests, to change toward a less marked overall system. All the evidence we have indicates that the traditional notion is correct and Mühlhäusler's more constrained prediction is not.

Dialect interference, like cross-language interference, very often leads to replacement of a structure in one dialect by a partially or entirely corresponding structure from another. This replacement may of course constitute an overall change $\overset{>}{m} > \overset{<}{m}$, but it is just as likely to result in a change $\overset{<}{m} > \overset{>}{m}$ or one that is equivalent in markedness. Most changes that are not simple replacements are partial reinterpretations, with the same variation in their effects on the markedness of the system. Many of the clearest (recent, well documented) examples involve pressure from a standard on a nonstandard dialect. Here is a typical instance. Most dialects of Serbocroatian have six cases in the plural inflection of nouns: nominative, accusative, genitive, instrumental, dative, and locative; of these, the last four are generally known as the **oblique** cases. In Standard Serbocroatian, masculine and neuter nouns of the major declensional type have a single suffix -*ima* for three oblique plural cases (instrumental, dative, and locative) and -*ā* for the fourth oblique plural case, the genitive. Most Serbo-croatian dialects of the čakavian dialect group, by contrast, either distinguish all four oblique cases in the plural or have genitive-locative or instrumental-locative syncretism. But those čakavian dialects on which standard-dialect pressure is strongest have undergone (or are undergoing) changes that upset the old regularities and replace them with the standard ones. One example is the dialect of the Adriatic island Hvar: in 1935, older people in some villages were still using a genitive-locative plural suffix -*īh* that was opposed to the suffixes in the other oblique cases, but younger speakers were using -*īh* only in the genitive, and the suffix -*ima,* borrowed from the standard dialect, for the other three oblique plural cases (Hraste 1935:17–25). These changes run counter to the historical structural tendencies of the čakavian dialects themselves, and they do not result in a demonstrable loss or gain in markedness.

Givón's is not the only prominent claim in the literature about clashes of different systems producing universal structures rather than more marked ones. Bickerton's is similar in effect: "there are likely to be partial reemergences of bioprogram features in a number of linguistic situations, prominent among these being . . . contacts between typologically different languages . . . which set in motion extreme change processes in one party or the other" (Bickerton 1981:293). Now, Bickerton's bioprogram features cannot be equated with universally unmarked features in the more usual sense, since the bioprogram is claimed to be (and is pictured as) an innate system gradually evolved on a neo-Darwinian model. In particular, some or all of the bioprogram features may not be easier to perceive, produce, or learn in any sense independent of the innate program, with the result that some universally unmarked features will not be identified by Bickerton as bioprogram features. Moreover, there is no particular reason, according to Bickerton, to expect bioprogram features to be common in the languages of the world. Nevertheless, Bickerton's suggestion that bioprogram features will resurface in contact situations is close enough to Givón's that most of the counterevidence for the one will also apply to the other. The application here is particularly clear when this point of Bickerton's is taken together with another statement he makes on the subject of interference: "we can be reasonably certain that [constraints on a language's development] exist," so that if a marked structure is acquired through foreign-language interference, "it can only be because the language, at that particular stage of its development, has to have some such rule" (1981:50).[9] Bickerton thus allows for the acquisition of marked features from other languages, but only under specific constraints (which we showed above, in 2.1, to be invalid). Otherwise, conflicts between typologically diverse systems should cause leveling toward the innate grammar. This position, like Givón's and for the same reason, is untenable.

Various other claims about the effects of contact-induced change can be grouped loosely with the ones in this section. Heath (1978), for instance, cites Vogt (1948) and Coteanu (1957) as examples of authors who believe that language contact leads to morphosyntactic simplification. Heath himself observes that his data from Arnhem Land in Australia do not show significant simplification, at least in what he calls "indirect" diffusion, i.e., diffusion of patterns without the morphemes that express them (1978:125). Jeffers and Lehiste (1979:157) and Whinnom (1980:206) argue that substratum interference, specifically, generally leads to morphosyntactic simplification. Examples of complicating changes in the morphosyntax, including substratum changes, have already been given, and more will be given later. But in the morphology, at least, as we will see, significant complications are likely to occur only in cases of moderate to heavy substratum interference. Cases of light to moderate interference usually do result in simplification.

In a line of research that is largely independent of the work discussed above, a number of phonologists have made predictions about the phonological results of language contact. Hyman (1970) and Lovins (1973, 1974) in particular believe that "among the data that must be considered in trying to construct a tenable phonological theory are those of phonic interference" (Lovins 1974:240).[10] In discussing the point, Lovins argues that her evidence from the phonological adaptation of English loanwords in Japanese "supports the . . . claim that innate processes determine phonic interference" (1974:246). But even if this is true in some sense, no phonological analysis or innateness claims can be used as predictors of the results of phonological interference in the absence of precise information about the social situation in which the interference takes place. The need for such information is illustrated by the two sets of loanwords in table 1, from Russian into Asiatic Eskimo. The earlier set is from the pre-Soviet period, when there was little bilingualism among Eskimos; the later borrowings date from the Soviet period, during which Eskimos have lived among Russians and have been taught in Russian schools, so that Russian has become established as a second language for them.[11]

TABLE 1

RUSSIAN LOANWORDS IN ASIATIC ESKMO

Russian	Earlier borrowings	Later borrowings	gloss
bljudce [bl'útcə]	pljusa	bljutca	saucer
čaj	saja	čaj	tea
tabak	tavaka	tabak	tobacco
pačka	paska-q	pačka	bundle

In the earlier period, the Eskimos simply replaced the foreign sounds in the Russian words, e.g., *b*, *c* [ts], and *č*, by the closest sounds in their own language: *p* for *b* initially and *v* for *b* intervocalically, *s* for *c* and *č*, and so forth. They also simplified un-Eskimo consonant sequences like *tc* and made other changes that produced a syllable structure closer to that of native words. In the later period, after Russian had become better known among the Eskimos, they kept most of the Russian sounds and syllable structures in loanwords. In order to predict the extent to which non-Eskimo Russian sounds will be altered in loanwords, therefore, we would need to know (at the very least) the level of bilingualism among the Eskimos. Knowledge of native (pre-borrowing) Eskimo phonology alone is clearly not enough. This point is not merely academic as far as Lovins's Japanese research is concerned. Our student Sono Takano (1985) has recently conducted research on Japanese phonology that shows clear evidence of English interference comparable to the interference in later Russian borrowings into Asiatic Eskimo.

Paul Kiparsky (1973) makes a similar distinction between what he calls "casual contact" and "extensive bilingualism." He predicts results comparable to those of Hyman and Lovins for casual contact situations, but when there is extensive bilingualism, he believes, speakers of the borrowing language will tend to preserve "the distinctness between lexical items of the lending language by means of the phonetic repertoire of the borrowing language" (1973:112). Certainly this subtle—even invisible—type of phonological interference exists, as Kiparsky's examples (among others) demonstrate. But Kiparsky's two categories are still not enough, because they do not allow for the actual phonemic borrowing that has occurred in Asiatic Eskimo and in Japanese. We will present a more detailed borrowing scale in chapter 4.

2.4. CONCLUSION

The review of proposed linguistic constraints on contact-induced change that we have presented in this chapter, though not exhaustive, is representative of the literature on the general topic of interference. We believe that all these proposals ultimately arise from a conviction that—as some authors explicitly say—a language's structure determines its subsequent development. The reasons for this conviction are partly historical, having to do with the development of linguistics as a science, and partly methodological. We in no way reject, and in fact support, the very widespread view that it is acceptable, appropriate, and even necessary to study the structure of a language abstracted from the circumstances of its use. But however useful this approach might be for some analytic purposes, it has no value for the development of a predictive theory of linguistic interference. The next chapter describes an approach which offers more hope for the eventual prediction of at least some kinds of interference.

3
Contact-Induced Language Change: An Analytic Framework

The starting point for our theory of linguistic interference is this: it is the sociolinguistic history of the speakers, and not the structure of their language, that is the primary determinant of the linguistic outcome of language contact. Purely linguistic considerations are relevant but strictly secondary overall. Ultimately, all the proposed structural constraints discussed in chapter 2 fail because linguistic interference is conditioned in the first instance by social factors, not linguistic ones. Both the direction of interference and the extent of interference are socially determined; so, to a considerable degree, are the kinds of features transferred from one language to another.

Like most of the individual ideas in this book, this one did not originate with us. Our contribution lies mainly in the particular arrangement and development of ideas that have appeared elsewhere over the past hundred years or so. We have found two emphatic statements about the general importance of social factors in linguistic interference. The first was made by Valentin Kiparsky (1938:176) in a comment to Vočadlo's 1938 paper "Some observations on mixed languages," specifically with reference to lexical borrowing:

> Die Fähigkeit der sogenannten "homogenen" Sprachen, Entleh-
> nungen (mots communs de l'Europe) aufzunehmen, hängt *nicht*
> von der linguistischen Struktur der Sprache, sondern von der polit-
> isch-sozialen Einstellung der Sprecher ab.[1]

The second comment appears in Coteanu's 1957 paper "A propos des langues mixtes (sur l'istro-roumain)" (cited by Heath 1978:71):

> Selon nous, cette question ne dépend pas du caractère de la structure grammaticale des langues en contact, mais d'une série de facteurs de nature sociale. Coteanu 1957:147[2]

A thorough search of the literature would no doubt turn up other comments of this sort. In addition to these generalizations, it is easy to find comments on the significance of specific social factors. To give just one example, in discussing the different degrees of hospitality of Amerindian languages to Spanish loanwords, Bright (1976:149) suggests that "the Californian situation might also be explained in sociocultural terms, rather than in terms of linguistic structure alone." What Bright has in mind is the relevance of attitudinal factors resulting from differential Spanish policies toward the treatment of various Indian tribes.

Although a number of scholars have recognized the deciding role played by social factors in this domain, their views have not convinced the majority of linguists—as the continuing popularity of the constraints we saw in chapter 2, both old and new, indicates. We have already shown that these constraints do not make valid predictions. We will now outline a way of making some valid predictions and of explaining the failure of the proposed linguistic constraints.

The first step in developing a viable theory is to draw a sharp distinction between two fundamentally different types of linguistic interference. Then, under conditions of roughly similar intensity of contact within each type, we can begin to make general predictions about the kinds of expected interference, based on linguistic criteria like markedness and the typological distance between the source language and the language undergoing the interference.

Before beginning this discussion, we should remind the reader that our perspective is that of the historical linguist, not of the sociolinguist. To anthropologists and sociolinguists, the sociolinguistic/sociocultural aspect of our analysis will seem very shallow. As we have said, our main goal is to describe and analyze linguistic results of language contact situations, and to correlate these results with certain fairly general kinds of social factors. So, although we argue that social factors are the primary determinants of the linguistic outcome of contact situations, our focus is on systematizing the linguistic facts rather than on the various kinds of social influences.

3.1. BORROWING VS. INTERFERENCE THROUGH SHIFT

We have already mentioned the two basic types of interference in discussing some of the examples in chapter 2. Traditionally, they are known as **borrowing** and **substratum interference** (but, as we will show, the label "substratum" is inappropriate because it is too narrow).

Borrowing is the incorporation of foreign features into a group's native language by speakers of that language: the native language is maintained but is changed by the addition of the incorporated features. Invariably, in a borrowing situation the first foreign elements to enter the borrowing language are words. Typically, though not always, the borrowed words are treated as stems in the borrowing language—that is, they take the usual affixes for the appropriate stem-class. As Heath (personal communication 1985) points out, "these stems may really be words, including affixes, in the source language." If there is strong long-term cultural pressure from source-language speakers on the borrowing-language speaker group, then structural features may be borrowed as well—phonological, phonetic, and syntactic elements, and even (though more rarely) features of the inflectional morphology. Although lexical borrowing frequently takes place without widespread bilingualism, extensive structural borrowing, as has often been pointed out, apparently requires extensive (though **not** universal)[3] bilingualism among borrowing-language speakers over a considerable period of time.

Deshpande, for instance, points out that Southeast Asian languages have undergone no structural interference from Indic in spite of the fact that their speakers have adopted hundreds of Indic loanwords along with Hindu and Buddhist religious systems and a living tradition of Pāli texts. Even the characteristic retroflex Indic consonants in the loanwords are simply replaced by (and merged with) non-retroflex apicals, e.g., Indic t, $ṭ$ → t and Indix n, $ṇ$ → n in Old Cambodian and Old Siamese (Deshpande 1979:258). Since the speakers of Old Cambodian and Old Siamese were apparently not bilingual in the relevant Indic languages, this lack of phonological interference is predictable. Similarly, monolingual English-speaking British citizens living in India during the days of British rule adopted many Indian words for local items, but they apparently did not pronounce the words with retroflex or other non-English sounds. By contrast, once they had learned Russian the Soviet Asiatic Eskimos did borrow

Russian sounds along with Russian words; and younger Japanese speakers, all of whom have studied English throughout their schooling, have to some extent phonemicized former allophonic variants such as [č] and [ǰ] under the influence of English (Takano 1985).

Incorporation of phonological features that enter the borrowing language with loanwords may seem the first and most obvious kind of structural borrowing to be expected in such cases as the Japanese and Eskimo ones. But all the evidence we have gathered indicates that structural (as opposed to merely lexical) interference is not so compartmentalized, at least in cases of **moderate** to **heavy** borrowing (discussed below, chap. 4.1). In such cases, where there is phonological interference, there will be a comparable degree of syntactic interference too. Morphological interference lags behind these somewhat, but not as much as many authors have assumed. (See, for instance, the case studies of Ma'a and Asia Minor Greek in chap. 9.)

Even in cases of minor phonological interference, it may well be that minor syntactic interference is to be expected: if a person knows a second language well enough to incorporate some of its phonemes, s/he probably knows it well enough to incorporate some of its syntax as well. A possible example is Wallace's argument (1977) that the Japanese "passive" construction in *-(r)are* has lost its original adversative sense and taken on expanded syntactic functions under the influence of English. However, this example is complicated by two factors. First, Japanese has been in contact with other European languages besides English over the past four hundred years, and some of them, notably Portuguese, Dutch, and German, could have exerted the same influence as English on passives. Second, syntactic interference of this sort can arise through knowledge of another language in its written form alone, so it does not presuppose extensive verbal contact. It may therefore be independent of phonological interference. A clearer example of minor interference in both phonology and syntax is found in India. Certain literary (but not colloquial) Dravidian languages have acquired Indic syntactic features such as relative constructions with relative pronoun + finite verb and noun-modifier concord markers, along with phonological features like phonemic aspiration of stops, from Sanskrit, the sacred language of their Hindu religion (Sridhar 1978).

Substratum interference is a subtype of interference that results from imperfect group learning during a process of language shift.

That is, in this kind of interference a group of speakers shifting to a target language fails to learn the target language (TL) perfectly. The errors made by members of the shifting group in speaking the TL then spread to the TL as a whole when they are imitated by original speakers of that language. Of course, we do not mean to imply that imperfect learning has anything to do with lack of ability to learn; attitudinal factors may often be the crucial determinant for the shifting speakers' version of the TL, and in other cases the main factor is availability of the TL. So "errors" are identified solely from the viewpoint of preexisting TL structure.

As we observed in chapter 2, unlike borrowing, interference through imperfect learning does **not** begin with vocabulary: it begins instead with sounds and syntax, and sometimes includes morphology as well before words from the shifting group's original language appear in the TL. Often, in fact, the TL adopts few words from the shifting speakers' language. This makes sense if one thinks about it a bit. If the speakers' goal is to give up their native language and speak some other language instead, vocabulary is the first part of the TL they will need, so it is the first part they will learn. (Hoenigswald [1971:479] makes this same point.) They will probably keep their own native-language words only for things the TL has no words for: foods and other cultural items, and (if the TL speakers are invaders from elsewhere) names for local animals, plants, and so forth. Attitudinal factors may interfere with this prediction, but for substrata, at least in **light** to **moderate** interference (see chap 5.2), we expect the prediction to hold.

For instance, to take India as an example again, Emeneau's hypothesis about the origin of retroflexion and other Dravidian features in Sanskrit and later Indic languages clearly involves substratum interference. This is evident in his remark that "absorption, not displacement, is the chief mechanism in radical language changes of the kind we are considering" (1964:644). If we interpret his proposal in the present context, the two basic assumptions are that Dravidian speakers, shifting in considerable numbers to the language of the Indo-Aryan invaders, imposed their own habits of (among other things) retroflex-vs.-dental articulation on Indic as they learned it; and that they were numerous enough to influence Indic as a whole, through the eventual imitation of their flawed Indic by original Indic speakers. This interference in Indic from Dravidian is striking in view of the fact that, as has frequently been observed, there are few old Dravidian loanwords in Indic. In sharp contrast, Sanskrit influence on some literary Dravidian languages has come about through borrowing—native speakers of Dravidian languages are the initiators of the structural changes—and accordingly we expect, and indeed find, large numbers of Sanskrit loanwords in Dravidian.

A very neat picture of this overall difference between borrowing and interference through shift can be seen in Rayfield's description (1970:85) of mutual interference between the Yiddish and the English spoken by a group of bilinguals in the United States (table 2). As the table shows, the Yiddish spoken by these bilinguals—that is, their native language, into which English features have been borrowed—has much more lexical than structural interference. As is usual in borrowing situations, words are borrowed first and structural features later, if at all. But in their English—their second language, in which interference features will be, in effect, adstratum features—there is more structural than lexical interference.[4]

TABLE 2

DEGREES OF INTERFERENCE IN BILINGUALS' LANGUAGES

	English → Yiddish (borrowing)	Yiddish → English (adstratum)
lexicon	very strong	moderate
phonology	weak	strong
morphosyntax	moderate	strong

A similar example, probably, is the case of a Cree-French-English-speaking Métis community in Lac le Biche, Alberta, Canada. As described by Douaud (1980:396), all three languages in the community underwent interference: "French and English borrowings into Cree were largely lexical, whereas the Cree contribution is mainly phonological and morphosyntactic." Douaud observes that none of the three languages is prestigious. And, though he does not say so explicitly, it is likely that (as in other Métis communities) native speakers of Cree are more likely to learn French and/or English than vice versa.

This is the expected pattern in all cases of borrowing and shift; and, since predictions about the types of expected interference features and the order in which they will appear depend crucially on which of these two situations applies, it follows that we must investigate the social setting before we can predict, or interpret historically, the areal diffusion of linguistic features.

Another important difference between borrowing and interference through shift has to do with the time required for far-reaching structural modification. All the cases of borrowing that we have found that involve extensive structural changes in the borrowing language have a history of several hundred years of intimate contact (e.g., Asia Minor Greek, Ma'a, and Cypriot Arabic; see chap. 4). Two possible exceptions to this generalization are Mednyj Aleut and Michif (chaps. 4 and 9); but the Mednyj Aleut case, at least, may have included interference through shift as well as borrowing, and both cases involved contact over a period of a hundred years or more.

By contrast, a process of language shift may take as little as a generation. In such a case the interference features will enter the TL as spoken by the shifting speakers quite rapidly, though the adoption of these features by original TL speakers may take more time. In fact, substratum features are more likely to enter a TL rapidly than slowly: if the shift takes place over long centuries, then the shifting population is likely to be truly bilingual in the TL. In such a case there is no imperfect learning, and consequently no interference in the TL. However, shifting speakers' attitudes may well affect the linguistic outcome even with a long-term process of shift. In the case of Ile de Groix French, for instance, Breton interference has apparently been considerable; see chapter 5.2 for discussion. In cases of rapid shift, by contrast, it is much more likely that the shifting speakers will fail to learn some of the TL patterns. So the greatest amount of interference through shift will occur in the **absence** of full (perfect) bilingualism, though of course the shifting group will normally be partially bilingual during the shifting period. (Early-creolized creoles may provide an exception to this general rule; see chap. 6 for discussion.) TL speakers may be completely monolingual or at least some of them may know the native language of the shifting group. In either case their language may be considerably changed through the influence of the shifting group.

We should emphasize that the distinction we are drawing here is not a new one. The notions of borrowing and substratum interference have been standard in linguistics for a long time, and the refinements of superstratum and adstratum in the second category are also rather old. Nevertheless, few linguists have recognized the implications of these two categories for types of expected interference features. Both Winter (1973) and Vildomec, for instance, make the distinction, and Vildomec even points out that in borrowing situations the major foreign influence is loanwords, while in shift situations the major influences will be in phonetics and perhaps also syntax (1971:97). But Vildomec is still puzzled by what he sees as a discrepancy:

> Whereas some adherents of substratum theories maintain that pronunciation, particularly intonation, melody and rhythm of speech, are among the features most persistently dictated by the L^m . . . it has often been observed that, after a relatively short stay, immigrants to America speak their L^m with an English "accent." (Vildomec 1971:91)

The problem here is that prosodic and other phonological features are being viewed as having an existence of their own, independent of the context in which they occur. It is true that prosodic features of the original native language are very frequently maintained in a shifting group's version of a TL; intonation is one of the most striking features of both Irish English and Indian English, for instance. But the immigrants Vildomec refers to are **borrowing** English phonology into their native language. This is a quite different process, one that is dictated by different social factors and often connected with language death, at least as far as the phonology of particular individuals is concerned. Shifting speakers maintain their original language's prosodic patterns if they haven't learned those of the TL. But immigrants who have succeeded in learning the prosodic patterns of a language their group is shifting to may use those patterns so often in speaking the TL, and their own so seldom (and/or with a feeling that low prestige adheres to the native language), that they replace the native patterns with the ones borrowed from the TL.

Perhaps the most common error made by historical linguists in weighing the evidence of language contact is to assume that (as we observed in chap. 2) a lack of numerous loanwords critically weakens the case for any structural interference. One such argument is the frequently-made claim that, since there are few early Dravidian loanwords in Indic, there is little likelihood of early contact between Dravidian and Indic. This conclusion is not justified, however. The lack of numerous loanwords means only that if there was sufficient early contact for Dravidian features to be diffused into Indic, that contact must have involved shift of Dravidian speakers to Indic, not borrowing by Indic from Dravidian.[5] Similarly, it has often been argued that the lack of old Uralic loanwords in Slavic means that there cannot have been any other early interference from Uralic in Slavic either; but in fact that lack only means, again, that if there was any such early interference, it must have come about through shift as Slavic speakers spread into Uralic territory and absorbed speakers of Uralic languages. (Timing is, however, a problem for this claim; for a discussion of this case, see 9.5.)

One important aspect of the distinction is that some of the linguistic constraints that have been suggested are relevant only for borrowing situations. Most notably, Weinreich's belief that a language will have "a complex resistance to interference" (1953:44), and Jakobson's proposal about a language accepting only those foreign structural elements that correspond to its own internal tendencies, can only apply to cases of borrowing (and only then when the cultural pressure is not strong). In changes resulting from imperfect learning of a second language, the TL is not so much accepting the changes as giving in to them, since it is the shifting speakers, not the original TL speakers, who initiate the changes. Of course attitudinal factors can influence the degree to which original TL speakers will imitate the altered TL as spoken by shifting speakers, but such attitudes do not seem to protect a TL from interference if the shifting group is numerically strong. So, for instance, Irish-influenced English is spoken in Ireland by descendants of English-speaking settlers from England as well as by descendants of Gaelic speakers; in this case, the English settlers presumably had no positive motive for imitating Irish-influenced English, but the more numerous shifting Gaelic speakers' speech habits prevailed anyway.

A social factor that is frequently invoked in discussions of language contact is prestige. Moravcsik (1978:109) puts forward the hypothesis that "nothing can be borrowed [i.e., "borrowed" in the broadest sense, not in our narrow usage] from a language which is not regarded [as] prestigious by speakers of the borrowing language." She concedes that there is a convincing counterexample in the literature (in Nadkarni 1975, on interference from Kannaḍa in Konkani), but believes that the constraint is "otherwise plausible." Similarly, Pinnow argues that shared animal names in Na-Déné languages cannot be due to borrowing because no one language (group) in Sapir's proposed Na-Déné stock is dominant, and borrowing generally occurs only from a dominant to a nondominant language (1969:98). To some extent this widespread view is supported by common sense: why would you replace some of your native lexicon and grammatical features with those of another language unless you wanted to emulate the speakers of that language because of admiration or respect for them? But common sense is an unreliable guide in historical linguistics, and the fallacy in this view has been recognized for decades—at least since the following statement by Jakobson in his influential 1938 paper on phonological Sprachbund phenomena:

> Contrairement à l'opinion courante l'action qu'une langue exerce sur la structure phonologique d'une autre langue ne suppose pas nécessairement la prépondérance politique, sociale ou culturelle de la nation parlant la première langue. Jakobson 1962 [1938]:241[6]

This assertion is as true for other parts of the grammar as it is for phonology. The most obvious flaw in the prestige claim is that it can hardly be true for cases of interference through shift when the shifting group is a true substratum (rather than an adstratum or superstratum). In such cases the dominance relationship is clear, and the interference features are sure to be nonprestigious, if not definitely stigmatized. Moreover, prestige often seems to be irrelevant in cases of borrowing as well. Certainly this is true of dialect interference; here is a small but suggestive personal example. One of the authors grew up (either from birth or from early schooling) with a fully internalized rule of *who/whom* usage that matched the literary standard rule: *who* as subject only, *whom* as object or oblique case, regardless of its position in the sentence. She applied this rule without hesitation even in tricky sentences like *Who did you say was coming?*. But by the time she reached the age of thirty, the spreading colloquial usage of sentence-initial *who* regardless of case, as in *Who did you see?* and *Who did he give it to?*, began to interfere with her original rule, and she would occasionally catch herself in a hypercorrection: *Whom did you say was coming?* At that point (finding hypercorrection offensive) she dropped sentence-initial *whom* altogether in speaking and now conforms consistently to the colloquial usage except in formal prose.

Now, this was the opposite of a prestige borrowing. The colloquial usage initially sounded wrong and uneducated to her, and she tried for some years to avoid adopting it. Nevertheless, it interfered with the original rule against the speaker's **conscious** effort not to change her grammar. If this can happen in the speech of a self-conscious speaker, why should one expect speakers in general to adopt only features from languages or dialects that strike them as prestigious? We do not mean to deny the existence of prestige borrowing—certainly it is a common phenomenon—but there is no sociolinguistic or psycholinguistic reason to expect prestige borrowing to exhaust the possibilities even in borrowing proper, let alone in linguistic interference in general.

Now that we have carefully distinguished the two basic mechanisms of contact-induced language change, we must emphasize that there is unfortunately no reason to expect these two types of interference to take place in mutually exclusive contexts. Sometimes, to be sure, we find one without the other. Indic speakers did not, apparently, borrow much from Dravidian while shifting Dravidian speakers were changing their version of the Indic target language. Similarly, in many cases of borrowing we find no interference through shift to the borrowing language. In Asia Minor Greek, for instance, Dawkins (1916) reports widespread continuing shift from Greek to Turkish, but none from Turkish to Greek, so that all the Turkish interference in Greek can be assumed to be due to borrowing. In some cases, however, a language undergoes both types of interference at once. Target-language speakers may be borrowing words and possibly even structural features from a language whose speakers are in the process of shifting to the target language and incorporating their learners' errors into it. To judge by the very large number of loanwords, this was probably what happened when Cushitic speakers shifted to Ethiopic Semitic (see chap. 5 for a fuller discussion).

3.2. PREDICTING EXTENT AND KINDS OF INTERFERENCE

So far we have mentioned only very broad sociolinguistic differences among contact situations and their significance for predicting the linguistic results of contact. We have been able to distinguish between, and generalize about, the overall effects of borrowing vs. interference through shift, and we have argued that social factors such as prestige and long-term bilingualism cannot be used to develop **overall** predictive constraints for contact-induced change. In this section we will consider, in addition to purely linguistic factors, just one social factor: intensity of contact. Beyond this, we will have little to say about the general predictive value of more specific social factors, especially attitudes, because these are as varied as the contact situations in which they are embedded. For instance, we can say with confidence that the Ma'a language owes its spectacularly mixed structure to its speakers' refusal to acculturate completely to their Bantu-speaking milieu (Thomason 1983*b* and 9.2); but we could not have predicted in advance that some Ma'a clans would show this extreme cultural resistance while others simply shifted to Bantu.

In subsequent chapters we will refer frequently to specific social circumstances, but we do not believe that the information now available permits broad generalizations to be made about their effects on the linguistic outcomes of contact situations. We do not feel quite as pessimistic as Emeneau about the chances for making useful generalizations in this domain in the future; but his comment on the subject will serve as a salutary warning about the complexity of the phenomenon:

> Students of the historical aspects of bilingualism have usually discussed the historical situations that they studied in terms of an analysis of factors which had general application. It was almost as if they hoped to be able, once all factors were identified, to produce a calculus which, allowing for all factors and the various weightings to be given them, would on the one hand explain the past and on the other predict the future. It is a vain hope. Historical events, being unique, do not yet admit of such a calculus, and in all probability never will. (Emeneau 1980 [1962]:43)

In particular, we agree with Emeneau that simplistic socially based predictions will inevitably fail, just as the simplistic linguistic predictions that we discussed in chapter 2 fail. (Indeed, it is our hope that the arguments and evidence presented in this book will introduce some subtlety into discussions of contact-induced language change, as an antidote to the reductionism that is prevalent in many writings on the topic—especially, perhaps, in the pidgin/creole literature.)

Intensity of contact is not the same for shift and maintenance situations. In cases of language shift, where the shifting group is very small relative to the TL speaker group, there will be little or no interference in a TL as a whole (as opposed to an isolated subgroup like Indian English or Irish English speakers). In such cases the shifting speakers, in the absence of attitudinal barriers, will most likely have ready access to the TL as spoken by its native speakers; and even if the learners produce errors, the occurrence of the errors will not be so pervasive that original TL speakers acquire them. Exceptions might be expected (and have been claimed) in cases of superstratum interference, but we have found no convincing examples of extensive structural interference in such cases (see chap. 5 for further discussion).

There will also be little or no interference, probably, if the shift occurs after the shifting group has become fully bilingual and well integrated into the TL speech community, because then the learning of the TL is likely to be perfect, not imperfect. However, possible situations of this type are difficult to interpret historically, because (as mentioned above) long-term shift situations, especially those with mutual bilingualism, are likely also to involve at least lexical borrowing by TL speakers from the shifting group's language—not just interference initiated by the shifting speakers. But if shift occurs rapidly, and if the shifting group is so large numerically that the TL model is not fully available to all its members, then imperfect learning is a probability, and the learners' errors are more likely to spread throughout the TL speech community.

Intensity of contact in a borrowing situation crucially involves factors of time and of level of bilingualism. If few speakers of the borrowing language are bilingual in the potential source language, then normally only words will be borrowed (but see chap. 4 for a group of exceptions). However, if there is extensive bilingualism on the part of borrowing-language speakers, and if this bilingualism persists over a long period of time, then substantial structural borrowing is a probability. Extensive bilingualism does **not**, however, imply that virtually every borrowing-language speaker is bilingual. In many cases of borrowing, e.g., some Asia Minor Greek dialects and some of the Arnhem Land cases, only one subgroup of borrowing-language speakers is bilingual in the source language—all the men, perhaps, or all the men whose mothers belong to a particular clan (see chap. 3. n. 3). In other cases, notably Ma'a, all the borrowing-language speakers are bilingual in the source language.

As we will argue in chapters 4 and 6, both maintenance and shift situations have as their most extreme outcome the emergence of a language whose lexicon is not from the same source as the bulk of its grammar. Such languages are, by our definition, not genetically related to any of their source languages; their origin is nongenetic. In language shift situations, these extreme cases are ones in which the availability of the TL is so limited that the shifting speakers have successfully acquired only the vocabulary of the TL, but little or none of its grammar. Examples include, and are, for social reasons, probably confined to, those creole languages that did not develop directly from fully crystallized pidgins. Some creolists do not believe that such languages exist; but certainly, as we will argue, there are a number of creoles for which a definite pidgin stage is not attested, and whose structure can be accounted for under a hypothesis of extreme unsuccessful acquisition of a TL. Mauritian Creole, Seychelles Creole, and some of the Caribbean creoles probably fall into this category. We call this process "abrupt creolization," and its products correspond to what Bickerton has termed "early-creolized creoles" (e.g., Bickerton 1979). In these languages the features of the new language do not spread to the TL as a whole but (for social reasons) remain—as in much less extreme cases like Indian English—confined to a socially and/or geographically isolated subgroup.

In a comparably intense borrowing situation, whole subsystems or even the entire grammar may be borrowed along with large numbers of words; or, alternatively, the phenomenon known as language death may occur. In the most extreme cases, only portions of the vocabulary, including much of the basic vocabulary, are successfully maintained. The cases of this type that we have studied involve a stubborn and persistent resistance to total cultural assimilation in the face of overwhelming long-term cultural pressure from source-language speakers. A case like AngloRomani apparently represents actual language shift with maintenance of Romani vocabulary for use as a secret code; in a case like Ma'a, no shift has occurred, but almost all of the original Cushitic grammar and at least half (according to Christopher Ehret, personal communication, 1982) of the Cushitic vocabulary have been replaced by Bantu grammar and lexicon.

In between the least and most extreme cases, there are of course many intermediate ones. In table 3 we give a rough scale of interference levels in each of the two major categories. The double line separates those linguistic outcomes which, we will argue, can be interpreted retrospectively within the standard model of genetic relationship from those which cannot. That is, above and to the left of the double line, the linguistic products of contact represent cases of normal transmission; below the line, the resulting languages reflect a break in normal transmission.

Pidgins are placed off to the side in the table because we believe that, as new linguistic creations, they do not represent any kind of transmission, broken or unbroken—neither the tradition of a shifted-to TL nor the tradition of a maintained language. A well-established pidgin may become creolized (nativized) in the course of time; Tok Pisin is an example. If this occurs, the problems of interpreting the new creole retrospectively will be similar or identical to those that arise with early-creolized creoles. But the processes by which these two types of creole arise strike us as different enough to warrant putting them into separate developmental categories: pidgins themselves do not arise through a process of language shift. As we will see, historical interpretation in cases of (near-)total grammatical replacement presents different problems. In these cases, only two languages are involved, while all or almost all creoles of both types arise out of contact among more than two languages.

In chapters 4 through 7 we will discuss and provide examples for each section of table 3. However, before turning to questions specific to contact situations resulting in language maintenance, language shift, or pidgin genesis, we will outline our general views on the role played by the linguistic factors of markedness and typological distance in linguistic interference.

Universally marked linguistic features are those that are hardest to learn, both for perceptual and for productive reasons. In a phonet-

TABLE 3

Linguistic Results of Language Contact

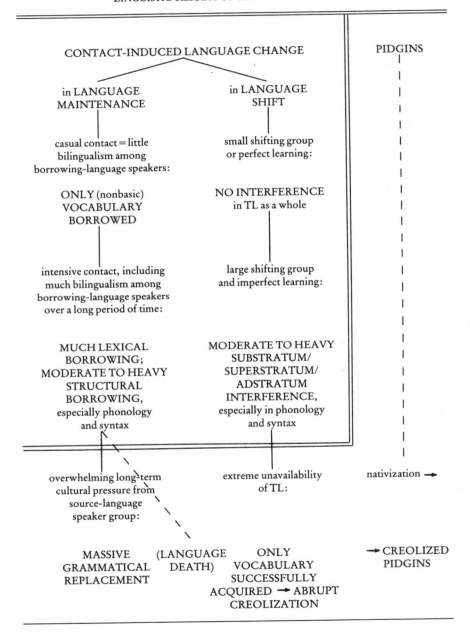

ically complex language such as the Salishan language Flathead, for instance, an English-speaking learner has trouble hearing the difference between /ɫ/ and /š/, or between /kʷ/ and /qʷ/; so, unless corrected repeatedly, s/he might well learn (and produce) only /š/ or only /kʷ/. On the other hand, the difference between Flathead /m/ and /m̓/ is easy to hear, but not very easy for an English speaker to produce; so the learner may learn to produce only /m/. The effects of such learning difficulties, spread over a population of learners, result in contact-induced change—in this particular example, change from imperfect learning, as in language shift.

In general, because they are harder to learn, universally marked features are less likely than unmarked features to be transferred in language contact, including pidgin genesis. In shift situations, this works two ways: shifting speakers are likely to fail to acquire marked features of the TL, and marked features carried over by shifting speakers from their original language are relatively unlikely to spread by imitation to the TL as a whole. Both of these tendencies may result in a decrease in the overall markedness of a (sub)system, and the frequency of such effects probably accounts for the commonly held view that substratum interference is largely simplificatory. But, as we saw in chapter 2, some interference through shift results in grammar complication—an increase in markedness. This probably occurs only in cases of moderate to heavy interference, and it may always begin with the carryover of contrasts and patterns from the shifters' original language into their version of the TL—that is, with their failure to learn that these patterns do **not** exist in the TL. (We should emphasize here that by "failure to learn" we do not mean "inability to learn, under the circumstances"; the lack of acquisition may just as well be due to a refusal to learn.)

In the maintenance situations, it is harder to generalize about the role of markedness. In casual contact situations, structural borrowing is unlikely to occur. But in intensive contact situations, which involve much bilingualism among borrowing-language speakers, we must know something about the type of bilingualism before we can make any predictions about the borrowing of marked features. If a large subgroup of borrowing-language speakers is fully (perfectly) bilingual, then the source-language structures have already been learned, and differences in learnability will not be particularly relevant to the question of borrowing: marked features, at least in the phonology and syntax, can be incorporated into the borrowing language as readily as unmarked features. In such cases, typological distance may be more important than markedness per se for predicting what will be borrowed.

The morphology presents a somewhat different problem. Since inflectional systems, in particular, tend to be highly structured and thus relatively closed, the integration of borrowed features into such systems may be difficult. We therefore find more cases of syntactic borrowing to replace a functionally congruent morphological feature than the reverse. We would agree with the general view that an elaborate inflectional morphology is (usually) more highly marked than corresponding syntactic structures,[7] so in this domain markedness is a significant factor in borrowing, as it is in interference through shift.

The other possibility, in a borrowing situation, is that borrowing-language speakers have achieved only a partial command of the source language. In such a case, if strong cultural pressure leads to structural borrowing, the borrowers can only adopt source-language features that they have learned, and they might not have learned all the marked features. But all the borrowing cases we have studied that have resulted in significant structural interference involve full (perfect) bilingualism among some or all borrowing-language speakers.

If we consider markedness alone as a factor in contact-induced change, then, we expect its effects to be important for interference through shift but less important for borrowing. In this respect the process by which a pidgin crystallizes in a contact situation resembles interference through shift more closely than borrowing (although a pidgin language, once it has crystallized, can of course borrow from other languages just as any other language can): as we will show in chapter 7, the only marked features that are likely to appear in an emerging pidgin are those that are shared by all or most of the languages whose native speakers are developing the pidgin.

The other linguistic factor that must be considered in predicting kinds of interference is typological distance. Unlike markedness, typological distance seems to be as important for borrowing as it is for interference through shift. Numerous writers on language contact have commented on its relevance. Perhaps most notably, Weinreich (1953) emphasizes the importance of functional congruence in facilitating morphological interference in particular. Similarly, Vildomec observes that "it is really not the linguistic difference between two languages that fosters mutual interference, but, on the contrary, the similarity" (1971:78). (We would of course disagree with Vildomec's implication that typological similarity **promotes** interference; social factors do that.) Ultimately, we believe, Meillet's point (1921*b*:87) about grammatical loans occurring only between very similar grammatical systems is based on the notion of typological distance.

The evidence we have collected that bears on this point does not permit a firm conclusion about the validity of the general hypothesis. Certainly it is true that—as shown by, for instance, the example in chapter 2 of Standard Serbocroatian suffixes and patterns replacing those of čakavian Serbocroatian dialects—dialect interference seems to be extremely common and without any noticeable tendency to simplification. That is, structures in one dialect seem to be replaced by corresponding structures from another regardless of any difference in complexity between the two. But most cases of dialect interference that we have examined involve standard-dialect pressure on a nonstandard dialect, and the social factors are so important in these cases that any inhibiting force exerted by linguistic factors would probably be overridden. In addition, we have solid evidence from cases of heavy structural borrowing (e.g., Ma'a, Asia Minor Greek) and even moderate structural borrowing (e.g., various contact situations in India) that features can and do get borrowed regardless of their typological fit with borrowing-language features. Specifically, in all such cases some of the borrowed features do not correspond closely in a typological sense to any previously existing feature in the borrowing language. Examples are the development of vowel harmony in Asia Minor Greek, Bantu noun-class prefixes and concord in Ma'a, the development of an inclusive/exclusive 'we' distinction in Kupwar Urdu, and complications in "have to" and abilitative constructions in the Nāgpuri dialect of Hindi under the influence of Marathi (Pandharipande n.d.; see chap. 4 for discussion). Similarly, in cases of moderate to heavy interference through shift, some transferred features represent a significant typological innovation in the target language. Examples are the partitive genitive construction in Russian (from Uralic influence; see 9.5) and the morphological distinction between future and present tense in some Ethiopic Semitic languages (from Cushitic influence; see Leslau 1945, 1952, and chap. 5).

In cases of heavy borrowing and shift interference, at least, the effects of typological distance on the expected kinds of interference features seem limited, if not negligible. Ma'a, for instance, has borrowed all kinds of grammatical features from Bantu, with no visible differentiation according to typological or markedness factors.

Nevertheless, although we have no definitive evidence to support it, our tentative hypothesis is that in cases of light to moderate structural interference, the transferred features are more likely to be those that fit well typologically with corresponding features in the recipient language. That is, we believe (with Meillet, Weinreich, Vildomec, and others) that one structure will more readily replace another if they already match rather closely in function.

In phonology, interference in these cases very ofen results in the phonemicization of previously nondistinctive phones. Examples are the phonemicization of [v z] in Middle English, which was caused at least in part by French influence (see 9.8 for a fuller discussion); the phonemicization of [č ǰ] for younger Japanese speakers under English influence (Takano 1985); and, if those who argue for previously existing phonetic retroflexion in Indic are correct (see below, 5.2.4, for discussion), the development of phonemic retroflexion in Indic, under Dravidian influence. Of course, entirely new phones and phoneme types also appear as interference features, but if our hypothesis is correct these will be rarer in light to moderate interference than the innovations that fit better with the receiving language's preexisting phonetics and phonology.

In morphology and syntax it seems likely that most interference, except in cases of heavy influence, will involve either new means of expressing functional categories already present in the receiving language or (for morphology) loss of previously existing categories (Thomason 1980b discusses this point in detail). Most morphological influence in Ethiopic Semitic (from a Cushitic substratum) and in Asia Minor Greek (through borrowing from Turkish) fits this pattern, for instance, though exceptions do occur in these and in most other cases we know of. Examples of the replacement of functionally similar morphological structures are the development of a causative formation with a double prefix in Ethiopic Semitic and the replacement of certain flexional suffixing constructions by agglutinative ones in Asia Minor Greek. Loss of previously existing categories is exemplified by the disappearance of the dual number in Ethiopic Semitic and of gender distinctions in Asia Minor Greek.

Syntactic examples that fit the pattern vary considerably, but they may be most prevalent in word order changes. The evidence we have collected does not support the often implicit assumption, in the literature on word order change, that word order patterns constitute a fundamental "deep" structural feature relatively impervious to foreign influence. On the contrary, word order seems to be the easiest sort of syntactic feature to borrow or to acquire via language shift. This is not surprising when it is considered from the viewpoint of functional congruence: dominant SVO and SOV word order patterns, after all, typically perform the same basic syntactic function—identification of subject and object by their position relative to each other and to the verb. The literature is full of examples, among them the change from SOV to SVO in Finnish (under Indo-European influence), SOV to SVO in Ma'a (under Bantu influence), VSO to SOV in Akkadian (under Sumerian influence; S. Kaufman, 1974:132), and SVO to SOV in Austronesian languages of New Guinea (under Papuan influence; Bradshaw 1979, cited by Bickerton, 1981:292). There are, in addition, many syntactic examples that involve features other than word order. One is the replacement, in the Dravidian language Gondi, of the characteristic Dravidian relative participle by an adopted Hindi construction with a relative pronoun (Sridhar 1978:205).

In contact-induced morphosyntactic replacements of this general type, the functional congruence very often links a morphological feature with a syntactic one, so that the changes are not confined to one or the other subsystem. So, for instance, the addition of third-person possessive suffixes to nouns partially replaces a typically Indo-European analytic possessive construction in some Asia Minor Greek dialects. The replacement of morphological patterns by corresponding syntactic patterns is usually claimed to be more common; and (as noted above) our evidence supports this view (this point will be discussed further in chap. 4).

Here is a typical example, an Asiatic Eskimo borrowing from the Paleosiberian language Chukchi. According to Menovščikov (1969:124–130), the Eskimos of northern Asia had to learn the language of the economically powerful Chukchis during many centuries of intensive contact. Among the many words borrowed into Eskimo from Chukchi were numerous function words, and these included coordinating and subordinating conjunctions. The borrowing of these conjunctions led in turn to a partial loss of the native Eskimo morphological means of expressing coordination and subordination, for instance by gerunds and loosely bound postpositional elements. Thus the Eskimo comitative clitic/suffix -*łju*, which was originally obligatory, became optional and finally (at least sometimes) disappeared entirely after the Chukchi conjunction *inkam* 'and' was borrowed into Eskimo. Menovščikov says that the following three sentences are all currently possible, depending on individual style and on the situation (1969:128):

(1)   Nunivaɣmi kijaxtaqut tiɣiɣat-łju qawaɣɛt-łju.   'On the tundra
       on the tundra live beasts-COM birds-COM   live beasts and
                                                             birds.'

(2)   Nunivaɣmi kijaxtaqut tiɣiɣat-Tju inkam qawayit-łju.

(3)   Nunivaɣmi kijaxtaqut tiɣiɣat inkam qawayit.

The greater likelihood that morphological means of expression will be replaced by syntactic ones for particular categories is explained, we believe, by the interaction of markedness considerations with typological distance. If two languages in contact share a given morphological category, then interference from one language to the other with respect to that category is more likely than not to result in replacement of a particular kind of morphological expression by another of the same type. If the source language expresses a given category syntactically and the recipient language expresses it morphologically, the recipient language is quite likely to adopt the syntactic means of expression. But, in the reverse case, the recipient language is relatively less likely to replace its own syntactic expression with a corresponding morphological one from the source language.

Scales of interference probabilities or possibilities that have been proposed generally emphasize, usually implicitly, the markedness aspect rather than the interplay between markedness and typological distance. The most comprehensive scale we have seen recently is Heath's list of "factors favoring diffusability" of morphosyntactic features (1978:105). All the factors in his "favoring" list (except "analogical freedom," which we find to be vaguely defined and of dubious potential usefulness) fit well with the notion of markedness as connected with ease of learning: "syllabicity [capable of being pronounced in isolation, e.g., a suffix -*um* as opposed to a suffix -*m*], sharpness of boundaries, unifunctionality, categorial clarity." In a similar vein, Comrie (1981a:203) argues that it is "more likely that clearly segmentable affixes will be borrowed than fusional morphology." In effect, these proposals spell out the reasons for the oft-claimed greater markedness of morphology as opposed to syntax, and therefore for the even more widespread view that the morphology is relatively impervious to contact-induced change. Heath's approach is likely to be especially fruitful in further research, since it avoids overgeneralization. That is, it is not morphology itself that is marked and unlikely to be transferred from one language to another; rather, it is certain common features of morphological structure that often, but not always, make morphology hard to learn.

One refinement that is necessary in Heath's approach, in our view, is the addition of a typological dimension: close matching of categories, as we have argued, is likely to facilitate replacement through interference even if the structures display features that would otherwise tend to impede diffusability.[8] An example is the replacement of case + number noun suffixes in čakavian dialects of Serbocroatian by the functionally equivalent suffixes of Standard Serbocroatian, even though both sets of suffixes are typologically flexional and hence not clearly segmentable (see 2.3 for discussion; see also chaps. 4 and 5 for further examples, e.g., interference in Ethiopic Semitic from Cushitic).

3.3. EXPLAINING LINGUISTIC CHANGES: WHEN IS AN EXTERNAL EXPLANATION APPROPRIATE?

We already observed, in chapter 1, that historical linguists have traditionally been strongly prejudiced in favor of internal explanations for linguistic changes. In particular, the methodological inclination has been to consider the possibility of external causation only when all efforts to find an internal motivation for some change have failed (see, e.g., Martinet 1955:194, Polomé 1980:196). Aside from the fact that a weak internal motivation is less convincing as a cause than a strong external motivation, the possibility of multiple causation should be kept in mind. We would agree with Ohala, for instance, that to explain sound change "one should first try all the phonetic explanations" (1974:268); but we disagree with his added comment that "only if they don't work [one should] seek an explanation in terms of social, psychological, or historical facts." In our view, an explanation should be as complete as possible. It may well be that, as some have argued, phonemic retroflexion in Indic arose in a series of phonetically plausible stages, but the original stimulus or trigger for that series of changes was surely the Dravidian substratum influence. In other words, even if Vogt were correct in believing that structural changes **can** always be described "in terms of the system in which they take place" (1954:372–373), it would not follow that the best explanations for them will always be achieved through such descriptions.

Similarly, interference through shift in particular may even be responsible sometimes for **lack** of change. This means that, since retention as well as innovation may be externally motivated, the presence of inherited features is not always adequately explained once one determines their genetic origin. For example, the elaborate systems of noun inflection in most Balto-Slavic languages resemble reconstructed proto-Indo-European noun inflection (or, at least, one common reconstruction which rests heavily on the evidence of Indo-Iranian) in a number of striking ways. The possibility should at least be considered that the Balto-Slavic case systems were retained under the conserving influence of a Uralic substratum, because the relevant Uralic languages have some of the most elaborate case systems in the world (see 9.5 for further discussion of shift-induced Uralic influence on Baltic and Slavic languages).

The problem remains, however, of developing criteria for establishing external causation. A negative criterion that is frequently invoked runs like this: a feature x cannot (or should not) be ascribed to external influence in language A because language/dialect B has also developed feature x, without the same foreign contact(s). A typical example of this line of reasoning is Polomé's argument (1980:192) that the loss of phonemic tones in Swahili need not have occurred through Arabic influence, because (for instance) the language Tumbuka in Malawi "has lost tone though no dialect mixture or impact of another language can be adduced to account for the phenomenon." The implication is that Arabic influence therefore should not be adduced in the Swahili case. Similarly, Hock (1975, 1984) argues against the emergence of retroflex consonants in Indic through Dravidian influence by citing languages that have developed retroflex consonants without Dravidian influence. And some scholars argue that Afrikaans cannot have arisen through a process of creolization because every structural change that has occurred during its history is also attested in one or another Dutch dialect in the Netherlands (though not, significantly, the whole package of changes in **the same** Dutch dialect; see 9.6 for discussion of Afrikaans).

The flaw in this type of argument is its assumption that a given change that arises through internal motivation in one language can and should automatically be ascribed to the same sort of cause when it occurs in another language. Since even the most natural changes often fail to occur, it is always appropriate to ask why a particular change happened when it did. In cases of interference through shift, naturalness plays an important role in determining the results of change—perhaps as important a role as in internally motivated change. And though it is less important in borrowing situations, many structural borrowings correspond to changes from m̂ to m̂. We should therefore expect the same natural changes to arise sometimes through internal causes and sometimes through external causes, and it is no more reasonable to extrapolate a particular internal motivation from one case to another than it would be to extrapolate an external motivation from one case to another. Natural internally motivated changes very often begin with structural imbalances such as opaque morphophonemic or syntactic alternations, and we have no right to **assume** that any other language had analogous imbalances. If a reasonable external explanation for a change is available, it must not be rejected merely because similar changes have occurred under different antecedent conditions.

Nevertheless, given the historical linguist's traditional prejudice against hypotheses of external causation, external explanations for isolated changes that strike people as natural tend to be unconvincing. There is a suspicion—sometimes well founded, to be sure—that possible internal causes have not been sufficiently explored, and multiple causation is rarely suggested. Probably for this reason, some scholars have argued that a claim of external causation should be made primarily (or only) for changes that are demonstrably not "natural," or common. For instance, Heath (citing Meillet as the source of the idea) believes that "the sharing of a typologically rare category is much better as an indication of indirect diffusion [i.e., transferred structure without actual transferred morphemes] than is the sharing of a recurrent feature" (1978:124). However, though adopting this criterion is useful as a methodological strategy for convincing skeptics, it is not promising as a general theoretical approach to the analysis of linguistic change, because—as we pointed out above— there is every reason to suppose that external causation is responsible for common and natural changes as well as for uncommon changes.

We need a methodological criterion that matches better with theoretical considerations. Here it is. As with the establishment of genetic relationship, a successful criterion for establishing external causation is possible only when we consider a language as a complex whole—a system of systems, of interrelated lexical, phonological, morphosyntactic, and semantic structures. Instead of looking at each subsystem separately, we need to look at the whole language. If a language has undergone structural interference in one subsystem, then it will have undergone structural interference in others as well, from the same source. Not necessarily in all other subsystems: as we have argued above, lexical interference may be negligible in cases of interference through shift; and considerable structural interference may occur without including externally-motivated changes in the inflectional morphology. But we have found **no** cases of completely isolated structural interference in **just one** linguistic subsystem.

In interference through shift, if there is phonological interference there is sure to be some syntactic interference as well, and vice versa. In borrowing too this is probably generally true, though limited phonological restructuring apparently can occur without concomitant syntactic restructuring (and possibly vice versa). But we can at least predict confidently that in such cases there will be heavy lexical borrowing. One dramatic example is the borrowing of clicks from Khoisan into certain southern Bantu languages, notably Nguni (including Zulu). Lickey (1985) points out that in Nguni most clicks occur in Khoisan loanwords. In native vocabulary, clicks are found primarily in ideophones and in **hlonipha** (lexical avoidance, or taboo) terms. Lickey was, however, unable to find any syntactic interference from Khoisan in Nguni. (This case is discussed briefly below, in 5.2.4—i.e., under language shift. Apparently Nguni has been influenced by Khoisan both through borrowing and through shift. We claim clicks as a borrowed feature because they seem to have entered

Nguni primarily with loanwords, and because their penetration into native vocabulary is confined to lexical categories that are phonetically peculiar in other Bantu languages too.)

The appropriate methodology, then, requires examination of a contact situation as a forest rather than as a collection of isolated trees. In order to support a claim that feature x arose in language A under the influence of language B, we need to show that features a, b, c, y, z—at least some of which belong to a subsystem different from the one x belongs to—also arose in A under the influence of B.[9] Examination of the case studies in chapter 9, in addition to many of the examples given in chapters 4 and 5, will show why we believe this to be an adequate criterion for establishing external causation in the explanation of linguistic changes.

Note that this criterion also applies in cases of multiple causation: it does not commit us to the untenable position that an external cause excludes an internal one. So, for instance, the French loanwords that flooded Middle English after French speakers shifted to English certainly contributed to the phonemicization of English voiced fricatives, but this change was also partly motivated internally, e.g., by the loss of final schwas during the thirteenth and fourteenth centuries, and by the simplification of geminate consonants in the late fourteenth century (see 5.2.3 and 9.8 for discussion). Notice also that adopting this criterion permits us to offer a single unified explanation for a variety of structurally independent changes, e.g., the emergence of retroflex consonants and agglutinative noun morphology in Indic (Emeneau 1964 [1956]). Such an explanation is clearly preferable to a variety of unconnected, exclusively internal explanations for the separate changes, even when each hypothesized internal explanation is in itself quite reasonable. Since modern historical linguistics (like other historical sciences) has always emphasized the greater value of unified explanations as opposed to atomistic ones, our criterion is supported by a tradition even stronger than the one that has tended to favor internal explanations.[10]

One final caveat must be added before we turn to a detailed consideration of the two main types of contact-induced change. It has sometimes been claimed that a particular change cannot be due to foreign interference because the putative source language does not exhibit exactly the same structure that has been innovated. This claim has been popular in the recent literature on pidgin/creole genesis, especially in criticisms by Bickerton of what he calls "substrato-maniac" views on the origins of creole grammar. Although language genesis cannot be absolutely equated with interference through shift in an already existing language, the two processes have so much in common that Bickerton's proposal would also be relevant for shift-induced change and even, perhaps, for borrowing in our narrow sense. Bickerton believes that a claim of sub- or superstratum influ-ence on the development of creole grammar must rest on a "point-by-point identity" of the relevant source-language and creole structures (e.g., 1977:61). This is a mistake, both in creole history and in contact-induced change. As Alleyne points out in arguing against Bickerton's view, "in dealing with the input source for first language transfer in SLA [second language acquisition] and for creolization, we have to make allowances for plausible processes of change analo-gous to what in anthropology are called reinterpretations, remodel-ings, of such a nature and to such a degree that the relationship between the new form and the input source becomes difficult to decipher" (1979:100). In other words, many interference features will in fact **not** be exactly the same as the source-language features that motivated the innovations. Lack of "point-by-point identity" must therefore not be taken to mean that an innovation is not due to foreign influence.

Here is a typical example of reinterpretation in substratum change to illustrate this point. Most dialects of Serbocroatian have phonemic stress, which they inherited from Pre-Serbocroatian. But in one dia-lect spoken in northern Yugoslavia near the Hungarian border, stress has become fixed on the penultimate mora of the word. Ivić (1964) explains this innovation in the following way: Hungarians living in this area shifted from Hungarian to Serbocroatian. They failed to learn the complex Serbocroatian accent patterns; instead, they as-sumed that stress was predictable, as it is in Hungarian. But they perceived enough of the accentual differences between Serbocroatian and Hungarian to realize that the stress was not fixed on the initial syllable, as it is in Hungarian, so they adopted a kind of average stress place—on the penultimate mora. Their influence was strong enough to spread the innovation throughout the dialect, via imitation by original Serbocroatian speakers. Similar examples can be adduced from cases of borrowing. Heath (1978), for instance, discusses cases of phonological borrowing that leads to language-specific chain shifts, with results that differ from source-language phonological structure.

Comparable examples in other grammatical subsystems can easily be found both in interference through shift and in borrowing. A probable instance is the absence of the verb 'to be' in certain sentence types in Russian, as a result of Uralic substratum influence. Décsy points out that this verb is missing in more contexts in Russian than in the relevant Uralic languages, and concludes from this fact that the loss of 'to be' in Russian cannot be due to the Uralic substratum (1967:158), though various other features of Russian in various grammatical subsystems are certainly the result of Uralic interference. The fallacy in this reasoning is the same as in Bickerton's: an exact correspondence between source-language structures and target-language structures is not even very likely, much less inevitable. For an example from borrowing, consider the case of literary Kannaḍa, which, according to Sridhar (1978:213), was claimed by a thirteenth-century grammarian to have extended a passive construction borrowed from Sanskrit to intransitive verbs. Another type of example is reported by Heath (1978:76–77): the Arnhem Land language Ngandi has acquired an ergative-instrumental suffix from Ritharngu, but without the suppletive allomorphy displayed by the source morpheme in Ritharngu.

We can sum up this section by answering the question posed in its title in the following way: an external explanation for a particular structural change is appropriate, either alone or in conjunction with an internal motivation, when a source language and a source structure in that language can be identified. The identification of a source language requires the establishment of present or past contact of sufficient intensity between the proposed source language and the recipient language. Sufficient intensity (especially in a past contact situation for which little sociolinguistic information is available) may be inferred from the presence, in different grammatical subsystems of the recipient language, of structural innovations that may reasonably be attributed to that source language. The proposed source-language structures need not be, and frequently are not, identical to the innovated structures in the recipient language, but a successful claim of influence must of course provide a reasonable account of any reinterpretation or generalization that has occurred as a result of the interference.

This section concludes the outline of our overall approach to the analysis of contact-induced language change. In the next three chapters we will expand on our discussion of interference through borrowing (chap. 4) and shift (chaps. 5 and 6). Then, in chapter 7, we will show how these findings, in particular those of chapters 5 and 6, are related to the peculiar kind of language learning that occurs during processes of pidgin genesis. Finally, we will consider the products of language contact from a retrospective viewpoint, in particular their implications for hypotheses of genetic relationship and for comparative reconstruction (chap. 8). Chapter 9, as already mentioned, contains studies of especially interesting and/or much-cited cases.

4
Language Maintenance

Asia Minor Greek is a language in which "the body has remained Greek, but the soul has become Turkish."

—Dawkins 1916:198

4.1. INTENSITY OF CONTACT AND TYPOLOGICAL DISTANCE

A language as profoundly altered by borrowing as Asia Minor Greek presents a striking contrast to more familiar instances of borrowing, such as cultural loanwords in a few semantic domains (e.g., food and music) from Italian in American English. Although the adoption of a handful of loanwords may be the most common manifestation of borrowing—especially in the modern world, where a few languages of international status provide all the technological vocabulary—extensive structural borrowing is more common than has generally been recognized. Predicting just when it will occur is difficult (or perhaps impossible), since attitudinal and most other social factors that affect the linguistic outcomes of contact situations vary in ways that are, at least at present, beyond prediction. Nevertheless, some generalizations can be made—on the basis of a few social factors, such as relative population sizes, length of contact, and degree of bilingualism—about the recorded cases in which structural borrowing has occurred, and these in turn permit us to make limited predictions in this area.

The traditional prerequisite for structural borrowing—that is, for structural interference initiated by native speakers of the recipient language—is the existence of a bilingual group within the borrowing-language speaker population.[1] In a typical statement of this prerequisite, Oksaar (1972:491) emphasizes "the fact that a bilingual group is the condition necessary for any large-scale borrowing—as already pointed out by Paul (1909:391 ff.)." Moreover, it is "commonly admitted doctrine that extensive borrowings from one language into another can only occur through the agency of a bilingual section in the joint community" (Emeneau 1980 [1962]:45). (This standard view presumably accounts for Lightfoot's criterion for establishing external influence on syntactic change; see chap. 3 n. 10.)

Ironically, this generally uncontroversial prerequisite can be accepted only with qualification: it is not valid as a condition on structural or heavy lexical borrowing if by "bilingual group" we mean a group of people who speak the language fluently. Of course the source language must be known to some of the borrowing-language speakers. But most cases of slight structural borrowing that we have found involve borrowing from a prestigious literary language, and in these cases the source language is often known to the borrowers primarily or only in its written form. The structural interference is therefore primarily or only syntactic—not phonological. (We have found no cases of this type that involve morphological borrowing.) And since contact through writing need not be face-to-face, there is often no joint community of source-language speakers and borrowing-language speakers, at least not in the geographical sense. Interference of this specialized sort is usually confined to educated borrowing-language speakers (or writers)—but not always, as we will show in chapter 4.2. Examples can be found in various parts of the world, e.g., in Persian and Turkic languages from Arabic, in Standard English from Latin, in Yiddish from Hebrew, in Japanese from Chinese, and in literary Dravidian languages from Sanskrit. In cases like these, if we were to maintain the traditional criterion, "bilingualism" would have to be defined in a way that includes literary competence without oral competence (but we do not in fact recommend such an extension of the meaning of "bilingualism").

By contrast, all cases of moderate to heavy structural borrowing that we have found involve a group of active bilinguals who speak the source language fluently and use it regularly for at least some ordinary communicative purposes. The contact in these cases is intimate enough that we can reasonably speak of a joint community.

The more intense the contact situation is, the more likely it is that extensive structural borrowing will occur. As we noted in chapter 3.2, two crucial parameters of intensity of contact in a borrowing situation are time and the level of bilingualism: long-term contact with widespread bilingualism among borrowing-language speakers is a prerequisite for extensive structural borrowing. A high level of bilingualism in turn reflects the more nebulous factor of cultural pressure: a population that is under great cultural pressure from another speech community is likely to be largely bilingual in the language of that community (see Weinreich 1953, especially pp. 64–65, for a more detailed outline of potentially relevant social factors). Cultural pressure is most obviously exerted by a politically and numerically dominant group on a subordinate population living within its sphere of dominance; this is the classic situation that promotes structural borrowing, as (for instance) in nonliterary Dravidian languages in northern India from Indic, Asia Minor Greek from Turkish, some kinds of Romani and Yiddish from various Slavic languages, and various Mexican Indian languages from Spanish. Even in cases like these, other factors can and do influence the amount of structural borrowing: in Asia Minor Greek, for example, Greek underwent less interference from Turkish in villages with well-established Greek schools (where a literary variety of Greek was taught) than in villages without Greek schools.

In other cases, however, cultural pressure is not clearly a function of political dominance. Ma'a speakers, though surrounded and outnumbered by Pare and Shambaa speakers, are not under Bantu political sway; here, the cultural pressure is more intimate. Similarly, Warndarang was influenced by Nunggubuyu in Australia without its speakers being politically dominated by Nunggubuyu speakers—but the fact that all the Warndarang speakers eventually shifted to Nunggubuyu may indicate cultural pressure of some sort.

The relative sizes of the speaker groups of two languages in contact may contribute in part to a negative prediction about the likelihood of bilingualism: a politically superordinate group is unlikely to become bilingual in a nonprestigious subordinate group's language unless the superordinate group is much the smaller of the two. This accounts, we believe, for the fact that the only reported cases of extensive structural borrowing by a superordinate group are those in which the dominant group is quite small relative to the subordinate group.

Where there is neither a clearly asymmetrical dominance relation nor a large discrepancy in population sizes, cultural pressure leading to structural borrowing is determined by factors that may be impossible to establish for most past contact situations. In such a case, we will not be able to explain why, for instance, language A borrowed from language B but not vice versa (unless we can eventually extrapolate from similar settings in current contact situations). In all the directly observable cases in this category that we have found, the two populations intermingle through mixed marriages and/or have other intimate social connections. Perhaps the best-known example is the village of Kupwar in India, where, according to Gumperz and Wilson (1971), all the languages converged grammatically. Since the four speaker groups were rigidly separated by caste, religion, and profession, interference through recent shift can presumably be ruled out. The modern convergence must therefore be due to borrowing, under circumstances which, as Gumperz and Wilson explain, require constant contact and bi- or multilingualism. (Kupwar is not, of course, the only place in India where extensive convergence has occurred; other instances elsewhere in India, in fact, involve some of the same languages.)

The most troublesome cases of this type are past contact situations whose linguistic results could have come about either through borrowing or through shift, or (perhaps most likely) through a combination of the two processes. As we pointed out in chapter 3, interference through shift need not include lexical transfer. But sometimes it does, especially when the shifting population is not subordinate to the target-language speaker group. The extensive lexical influence of French on English partly as a result of the shift by superstrate French speakers to Middle English is the most famous case, but there are others too, among them Cushitic interference in Ethiopic Semitic (see chap. 5 for discussion). In cases like these, lexical and even structural borrowing may have been going on before and during the process of shift: that is, English speakers were probably borrowing from French while French speakers were shifting to English. More significantly, since there was more eventual structural interference, Ethiopic Semitic speakers may have borrowed vocabulary and structure from Cushitic speakers while Cushitic speakers were shifting to, and incorporating their learners' errors into, Semitic.

In cases of light to moderate interference that include transferred words, the types of structural interference features will help to indicate the mechanism of interference. The reason is that syntactic and phonetic changes, which are among the most expected shift-induced changes, will be among the last borrowed features. But in moderate to heavy interference of both types, structural features of all kinds are likely to be transferred.

In retrospect, then, in a case where we find lexical as well as structural interference but lack sociolinguistic information, we may not be able to tell which group introduced the interference features into the affected language.[2] If we know that contact was intimate enough to make shift as well as borrowing probable, then there is no reason to suppose that one process operated to the exclusion of the other, barring established social or numerical asymmetry that would enable us to rule out one of the mechanisms. Since we do not want to ignore interesting cases of interference simply because of complexities and indeterminacies in the way they developed, we will divide problematic cases between this chapter and the next according to the following criterion: if we can be reasonably sure that a large-scale shift has occurred, we will discuss the case in the chapter on shift-induced interference, even though extensive borrowing may also have taken place; the Norman and Angevin French-to-English and Cushitic-to-Semitic cases therefore belong in chapter 5, along with Burushaski-to-Shina and cases of "pure" shift—i.e., those without much lexical tranfer. If we have no evidence for shift by an entire group, but at most by individuals in (say) mixed households, then we will discuss the case in this chapter, assuming that borrowing played a large—if not the major or only—role in the introduction of the interference features.

Here are two examples of such socially complex cases. The northernmost Dravidian language, Brahui, has undergone extensive interference from the Iranian language Balochi, and perhaps some from neighboring Indic languages as well, especially Sindhi. Basing his account primarily on Bray's (1909, 1913) comments and figures, Emeneau observes that Brahui, with about 200,000 speakers, is "surrounded and interpenetrated by Baloches" (1980 [1962]:46). He goes on to say that mixed marriages between Brahuis and Baloches were very common, and that many speakers in both groups reported that they spoke the other group's language. For nearly 300 years, starting in the mid-seventeenth century, the Brahuis enjoyed political ascendancy in the Kalat region of Baluchistan. Presumably as a result of this, Emeneau concludes that "at one time in the history of the Brahui Confederacy there must have been more nonnative speakers of Brahui"—mainly people with Balochi as their first language—and descendants of nonnative speakers, than original native speakers and their (exclusive) descendants (60).

In other words, thanks in part to the many mixed marriages, considerable interference in Brahui could have come about through imperfect learning by nonnative speakers. But since a great many native speakers of Brahui were bilingual in Balochi (or in some other local language; see Emeneau 1962:53 for discussion), and since the Brahuis were surrounded by Baloches, conditions were also ripe for extensive structural borrowing. Emeneau's assessment of the linguistic results of this situation is that the Brahui evidence "will . . . bring to the attention of linguistic scholars clear instances of structural borrowings such as I know of in large numbers nowhere else" (1962:55). As we will see in 4.3.2, the Brahui case is indeed impressive, though not as extreme as, for example, Asia Minor Greek or Ma'a. By contrast, Brahui influence on Balochi is said to be confined to loanwords (Emeneau 1980 [1965]:130).

The second example of a complex contact situation in which borrowing and shift together may account for the interference is the Uzbek-Tadzhik contact in the Soviet Union. This contact was established, or at least intensified, by heavy continuing migration of Turkic tribes into what had been Iranian territory after the downfall of the Iranian Sassanid Empire in the seventh century (Menges 1945:190). According to Menges (189), the Turkic language Uzbek was strongly iranized among town-dwellers, less so among half-settled peasants, and not at all among nomadic Uzbeks. The Uzbek spoken in Tashkent in Uzbekistan (which by 1945 was mostly Uzbek-speaking) has undergone particularly heavy Tadzhik (New Persian) influence. As with the Brahuis and Baloches in Baluchistan, the Uzbeks and Tadzhiks here developed close ties, including mixed marriages and much bilingualism (Comrie 1981*b*:51). Unlike the Brahui-Balochi case, however, in this situation both languages were affected: as we will see in chapter 4.3.1, northern dialects of Tadzhik were turkicized while—in other parts of the contact area, to be sure—town dialects of Uzbek were iranized. In the Uzbek-Tadzhik case too, it seems likely that borrowing and shift-induced interference were going on simultaneously.

In a number of other cases, we can be sure that structural interference has occurred, but we have no evidence at all about the social circumstances. For convenience, we will discuss examples from cases of this sort in this chapter, for instance interference in Quiché from Cakchiquel (both are Mayan languages), interference in Chinook from one or more Salishan languages, and interference in the Turkic language Gagauz from Slavic (and perhaps also Rumanian).

We should note here that we have found no linguistic criteria, other than the absence of extensive lexical transfer, that would enable us to decide whether or not a past contact situation that resulted in moderate to heavy interference involved large-scale shift. In particular, our data does not support Whinnom's (1980:206, 209) proposed quasi-dichotomy—substratum influence, he argues, leads to simplification in morphology and perhaps syntax, while borrowing almost always enlarges the phonological inventory. (He does not say whether he also expects phonological simplification in substratum interference and morphosyntactic expansion in borrowing.) Numerous examples of morphosyntactic and phonological complication introduced through shift will be given in chapter 5; examples of phonological and morphosyntactic simplification through borrowing will be given in later sections of this chapter. To mention just two here, Turkish borrowing into Asia Minor Greek caused the loss of the phonemes /θ ð/ as well as the addition of a few phonemes; and borrowing from Bantu into Ma'a caused the loss of glottalized and labialized consonant phonemes as well as the addition of prenasalized stop phonemes and /v ɟ ɣ/. It may be that Whinnom's prediction about phonological complication in borrowing will hold for cases of slight interference—

we have no definite counterexamples in this category—but it is not valid for cases of moderate to heavy interference.

Let us sum up our comments on intensity of contact and its relevance for predicting how much borrowing will occur. Greater intensity of contact in general means more borrowing, though attitudes (especially, maybe, those fostered by a well-established standard dialect of the would-be borrowing language) can hinder structural borrowing, at least to some extent. The major factors that promote greater intensity of contact, or greater cultural pressure on borrowing-language speakers, are these: length of time—enough time for bilingualism to develop and for interference features to make their way into the borrowing language; many more source-language speakers than borrowing-language speakers; and either sociopolitical dominance of source-language speakers over borrowing-language speakers or intimate contact in mixed households and/or other social settings. In the latter situation, the source language is likely to contribute structural features to the affected language both through borrowing and through shift. (In cases with an asymmetrical dominance relation, of course, shift and borrowing are also likely to be occurring simultaneously—but shift only to the dominant language, and borrowing mainly from the dominant language.)

In addition to these social factors, one linguistic factor seems to be relevant for predicting how much, and what kinds of, interference will occur in a borrowing situation: typological distance. As we observed in 3.2, typological distance does not appear to have an effect on the linguistic results of the most intense borrowing situations, i.e., those involving heavy to extreme borrowing; but in slight to moderate borrowing, source-language features that fit well typologically with functionally analogous features in the borrowing language tend to be borrowed first. This hypothesis, we emphasize again, must remain tentative; the evidence provided by our data supports it to some extent but is not conclusive. The evidence is sufficiently strong, however, that it seems worthwhile to use it in constructing a tentative borrowing probability scale.

We should explain the interpretation we give here to the notion of typological distance. It is, in our view, a measure of structural similarity that applies to linguistic categories and their combinations, including ordering relations. The more internal structure a grammatical subsystem has, the more intricately interconnected its categories will be (see Weinreich 1953:35); therefore, the less likely its elements will be to match closely, in the typological sense, the categories and combinations of a functionally analogous subsystem in another language. Conversely, less highly structured subsystems will have relatively independent elements, and the likelihood of a close typological fit with corresponding elements in another language will be greater. Since most or all languages have adverbial particles, for instance, it is fairly easy for a language to borrow a negative particle even if negation is already expressed in the borrowing language by a verbal affix; but it is harder for a language that expresses negation by a particle to borrow a negative verb affix which, in the source language, is integrated into a morphologically elaborate verb complex. Morpheme orderings are in general more readily borrowed than grammatical categories, since rearranging existing categories causes less typological disruption than adding (or subtracting) categories. When Heath (1978:105) and Comrie (1981a:202–203) argue that sharpness of boundaries makes affixes easier to borrow, they are ultimately appealing to a typological criterion: affixes in a flexional language are more closely bound to their surroundings than are affixes in an agglutinative morphology. Similarly, Heath's unifunctionality factor is relevant here because the fewer functions a structural element has, the more likely it is to match some element in the borrowing language.

Our argument that typological similarity between two languages is likely to vary according to the structuredness of a particular subsystem links two important structuralist lines of thought about borrowing. Meillet (1921b:84) represents one with his argument that it is easy to borrow words, since the lexicon is not a system, but hard to borrow into a closed system like phonology or grammar (i.e., morphosyntax). Weinreich (1953:33) expresses the other when he says that "it stands very much to reason that the transfer of morphemes is facilitated between highly congruent structures." Our tentative borrowing probability scale, then, is a hierarchy determined by the relative degrees of structuredness of various grammatical subsystems: the more internal structure a subsystem has, the more intense the contact must be in order to result in structural borrowing. We propose that, in the absence of a close typological fit between particular source-language and borrowing-language structures, features lower on the scale will not be borrowed before features higher on the scale are borrowed. Typological barriers increase as we go down the list; we know of no exceptions—and would be astonished to find any—to the rule that nonbasic vocabulary is always borrowed first.

The borrowing scale below of course applies only to cases of borrowing in our narrow sense, not to cases that involve language shift.

BORROWING SCALE

(1)   Casual contact: lexical borrowing only
      Lexicon:
           Content words. For cultural and functional (rather than typological) reasons, non-basic vocabulary will be borrowed before basic vocabulary.[3]
(2)   Slightly more intense contact: slight structural borrowing
      Lexicon:
           Function words: conjunctions and various adverbial particles.
      Structure:
           Minor phonological, syntactic, and lexical semantic features. Phonological borrowing here is likely to be confined to the appearance of new phonemes with new phones, but only in loanwords. Syntactic features borrowed at this stage will probably be restricted to new functions (or functional restrictions) and new orderings that cause little or no typological disruption.
(3)   More intense contact: slightly more structural borrowing
      Lexicon:
           Function words: adpositions (prepositions and postpositions). At this stage derivational affixes may be abstracted from borrowed words and added to native vocabulary; inflectional affixes may enter the borrowing language attached to, and will remain confined to, borrowed vocabulary items. Personal and demonstrative pronouns and low numerals, which belong to the basic vocabulary, are more likely to be

borrowed at this stage than in more casual contact situations.

Structure:

Slightly less minor structural features than in category (2). In phonology, borrowing will probably include the phonemicization, even in native vocabulary, of previously allophonic alternations. This is especially true of those that exploit distinctive features already present in the borrowing language, and also easily borrowed prosodic and syllable-structure features, such as stress rules and the addition of syllable-final consonants (in loanwords only). In syntax, a complete change from, say, SOV to SVO syntax will not occur here, but a few aspects of such a switch may be found, as, for example, borrowed postpositions in an otherwise prepositional language (or vice versa).

(4) Strong cultural pressure: moderate structural borrowing

Structure:

Major structural features that cause relatively little typological change. Phonological borrowing at this stage includes introduction of new distinctive features in contrastive sets that are represented in native vocabulary, and perhaps loss of some contrasts; new syllable structure constraints, also in native vocabulary; and a few natural allophonic and automatic morphophonemic rules, such as palatalization or final obstruent devoicing. Fairly extensive word order changes will occur at this stage, as will other syntactic changes that cause little categorial alteration. In morphology, borrowed inflectional affixes and categories (e.g., new cases) will be added to native words, especially if there is a good typological fit in both category and ordering.

(5) Very strong cultural pressure: heavy structural borrowing

Structure:

Major structural features that cause significant typological disruption: added morphophonemic rules; phonetic changes (i.e., subphonemic changes in habits of articulation, including allophonic alternations); loss of phonemic contrasts and of morphophonemic rules; changes in word structure rules (e.g., adding prefixes in a language that was exclusively suf-

fixing or a change from flexional toward agglutinative morphology); categorial as well as more extensive ordering
changes in morphosyntax (e.g., development of ergative
morphosyntax); and added concord rules, including bound
pronominal elements.

All these changes can and do occur without disruption of normal
transmission in a borrowing language. Borrowing in category (1) is
characteristic of casual contact. Borrowing in categories (2) and (3)
constitutes slight structural interference. Our distinction between
these two categories is based on evidence from varying degrees of
Spanish influence on Latin American Indian languages, which undoubtedly has parallels in other parts of the world. Category (4)
borrowing is moderate and occurs under conditions of reasonably
intense cultural pressure on borrowing-language speakers. The heavy
borrowing in category (5) reflects more intense cultural pressure.[4]
The linguistic difference between category (5) borrowing and the
kind of extreme borrowing that does lead to a break in normal
transmission is a matter of quantity, not quality. In heavy borrowing
of type (5), interference features are still scattered among the various
grammatical subsystems, so that typological disruption in any one
subsystem is limited: the inherited structures, including the morphemes that express them, are still largely intact.

But in the most extreme instances of borrowing, borrowed structures and borrowed morphemes to express them are so pervasive in
one or more grammatical subsystems that inherited structures and
morphemes have largely or entirely vanished. In such a case there
has been a break in transmission—the inherited structures and morphemes have not been passed on intact from one speaker group to
the next. (There may, however, be another type of extreme borrowing that leaves inherited structures partly intact in all subsystems: see
the discussion of Cypriot Arabic in 4.4.)

In 4.2 and 4.3 below we will illustrate slight to heavy borrowing
with normal transmission, in situations of casual to intense contact.
Section 4.4 will be devoted to a discussion of the two possible nongenetic linguistic results of overwhelming long-term cultural pressure: extreme, that is, pervasive borrowing; and language death.

4.2. CASUAL TO NOT-SO-CASUAL CONTACT: EXCLUSIVELY LEXICAL TO SLIGHT STRUCTURAL BORROWING

The boundaries between any two borrowing categories on our scale are of course fuzzy. In this section we will concentrate on categories (1), (2), and (3), but it is often hard to be sure (since detailed case studies are generally lacking) whether we are dealing with a category (3) or a category (4) case: isolated examples of structural borrowing are not diagnostic unless we know enough to gauge the overall systematic effects.

4.2.1. CATEGORY (1): LEXICAL BORROWING ONLY

With a minimum of cultural pressure we expect only lexical borrowing, and then only in nonbasic vocabulary. (By "cultural pressure" we mean, here and elsewhere, any combination of social factors that promotes borrowing, e.g., prestige or economic forces that make bilingualism necessary. The notion is of course vague; making it more precise—i.e., giving relative weights to various kinds of social factors in an effort to predict structural borrowing—is a task that falls into the domain of the sociolinguist rather than the historical linguist, and is therefore beyond the scope of this book.) Nonbasic lexical borrowing is the norm both with prestige borrowings between separated populations—without widespread bilingualism among borrowing-language speakers—and with borrowings into the languages of superordinate groups from those of numerically inferior subordinate populations (who may or may not be shifting to a superordinate group's language). In the former category are Modern English borrowings from Modern French (as opposed to Middle English interference from Old French), e.g., *chaise* (compare the old borrowing *chair*), *ballet*, *pâté* (compare the old borrowing *pasty*), and the like.[5] In the latter category are typical borrowings of names for local objects into victorious invaders' languages, e.g., the Algonquian words *skunk* and *wigwam* in American English, and also cultural items from immigrants' languages, such as American English *kosher* from Yiddish (whose speakers borrowed it from Hebrew), *sauerkraut* from German, or *spaghetti* from Italian.

These are all cases involving relatively few loanwords. One can also find cases where loanwords flood into the borrowing language without, apparently, bringing structural borrowings along with them. We have already noted, in 3.1, Deshpande's (1979:258) point that hundreds of Indic loanwords entered Southeast Asian languages without introducing any new phonemes or other structural interference (though we have not searched any Southeast Asian literary languages for possible syntactic borrowing). Similarly, uneducated Moslems who are native speakers of Urdu nativize the pronunciation of the numerous Arabic loanwords borrowed into Urdu, and have no syntactic features borrowed from Arabic either. Large numbers of English loanwords in scientific and technological areas occur in many languages and are not accompanied by structural borrowing.

4.2.2. Categories (2) and (3): Slight Structural Borrowing

The more interesting borrowing cases are those which do include some structural interference. As we observed above, minor structural influence from a prestigious literary language sometimes occurs through the written medium alone, without actual oral bilingualism among borrowing-language speakers. Several syntactic features borrowed into Standard English from Latin would certainly fall into this category. Vachek (1962) attributes to Latin influence the Standard English rule that restricts negatives to one per clause; this rule, he says, was not fixed in Standard English until the eighteenth century, and it does not occur in nonstandard dialects. Another Standard English rule (now almost dead) that is said to be based on a Latin pattern—and provided by eighteenth-century grammarians—is the prohibition against split infinitives: since Latin infinitives are morphologically marked by a suffix, the infinitive marker cannot be separated from the verb stem by adverbial morphemes.[6]

The structural influence of Classical Arabic on the languages of various Moslem peoples apparently falls into this same category, except that Moslems also hear spoken (or at least recited) Arabic in religious services. So, for instance, though Hindi speakers (i.e., Hindu speakers of Hindi-Urdu) and uneducated speakers of Urdu (i.e., Moslem speakers of Hindi-Urdu) use Arabic loanwords but no Arabic phonemes, educated Moslems used borrowed Arabic phonemes in speaking Urdu, e.g., among others, /z/ and /ʔ/. A number of Turkic languages spoken by Moslems have undergone similar phonological changes as a result of Arabic influence, and borrowed Arabic function words have also led to minor syntactic changes in some of these languages. For instance, the Arabic coordinating conjunction *wa* 'and' (pronounced [ve] in Turkish) has come to be used "where Turkic languages would otherwise normally use . . . parataxis" (Comrie 1981*b*:48).

In India, Sanskrit, the sacred language of the Hindu religion, is said to have influenced literary Dravidian languages both phonologically and morphosyntactically, in the speech and writing of educated Dravidian-speaking Hindus. Sridhar (1978:202–206) says that Brahman Dravidian speakers avoid making the usual Dravidian substitutions to nativize Sanskrit loanwords, such as deaspiration of aspirated stops and voicing of intervocalic obstruents; instead, they retain the Sanskrit pronunciations in loanwords and even extend some of them, for example, aspirating stops in borrowed Sanskrit words that did not originally have aspirated stops (Sridhar, 208; cf. also Sjoberg 1962). (However, not all Brahman Dravidian communities avoid nativization of Indic loanwords.) Syntactic borrowings from Sanskrit in literary Dravidian—some of them restricted to medieval texts—include, according to Sridhar (citing other authors' analyses), a passive construction that is said to be used even with intransitive verbs in Kannaḍa; a relative construction using a finite verb and a relative pronoun (beside a typical Dravidian participial construction), also in Kannaḍa; and, in several of the literary languages, a tendency to replace negative verbs with an analytic negative construction. Lexical borrowings from Sanskrit in literary Dravidian languages include quantifiers, intensifiers, conjunctions, many derivational affixes, and even a few derivational prefixes (Sridhar, 202).

This last feature is startling, given the fact that the southern Dravidian languages, including all those with literary dialects, are exclusively suffixing. Moreover, according to Sridhar, these prefixes are even added occasionally to native Dravidian roots. This suggests strong enough influence to count as moderate rather than slight; compare the discussion of Indic influence on nonliterary Dravidian languages in 4.3.

A final example of (primarily) literary-language interference is, apparently, Chinese influence on Japanese. Chinese loanwords in Japanese are very numerous, including an entire set of numerals. In addition, according to Miller (1967:245), "imitations of Chinese word order introduced significant changes into the word order of Japanese, some of which eventually found their way into the spoken language." An example is the placement of verb forms in *-ku* meaning '[he] said, it is said' before the quoted material, as in Chinese, rather than after it, as in spoken Japanese. Miller (246) also notes an example of lexical semantic borrowing that is based on a "spelling pronunciation" of a Chinese character that is used in Chinese to denote two homophonous words, one meaning 'grass, straw, herbs' and the other meaning 'draft, written sketch'.

There are also cases of minor structural borrowing through bilinguals, under social circumstances that do not promote extensive structural borrowing, because of attitudinal barriers to borrowing, or an insufficiently high level of bilingualism among borrowing-language speakers, or any of many other reasons.

In Mexico, some instances of borrowing from Spanish into Amerindian languages range from category (2) to category (3). One dialect of the Mayan language Huastec has borrowed Spanish conjunctions (*por* 'but' ← *pero, kom* 'as, since, because' ← *como*) and the Spanish phonemes /d g/ (in loanwords only); this seems to be category (2) borrowing. Another Huastec dialect has borrowed conjunctions in minimally nativized form (e.g., *pero, komo,* and *porke* 'because' ← *porque*), the phonemes /f ř/, the pronoun *otro* 'other', and perhaps some inflectional affixes used on Spanish loanwords. Since this dialect has no borrowed prepositions and no derivational affixes abstracted from borrowed words, it looks like a borderline case between (2) and (3). Borrowing into some dialects of the Uto-Aztecan language Nahuatl from Spanish clearly falls into category (3): numerous function words and basic vocabulary, including conjunctions and the pronoun *otro;* borrowed phonemes /b d g f ř/; borrowed derivational suffixes *-ero, -tero* (used to derive nouns meaning 'person who works with a thing' from nouns); and a plural suffix *-es* that is used with Spanish loanwords.

The famous Sprachbund in the Pacific Northwest region of the United States and Canada provides some examples of category (3) borrowing (as well as examples of more extensive borrowing, whose directionality is often unclear; see section 4.3.3 for discussion). Often our synchronic and diachronic knowledge about relevant languages is too scanty to permit us to give more than isolated examples. The presence of first person pronouns borrowed from the genetic isolate Kutenai in several Interior Salishan languages, for instance, would suggest the possibility of minor structural borrowings too (and, of course, other loanwords), but no systematic comparison has been carried out yet, and in any case Kutenai grammar has not been thoroughly studied (though Garvin [1948, 1951] made some preliminary analyses).

For other languages we have more information. Thompson (1979:750) observes that there is "obviously a great deal of borrowed material" between Chimakuan and Wakashan languages, and Jacobsen (1979:795, citing Powell 1975) provides an example of minor phonological interference from Wakashan in the Chimakuan language Quileute. Quileute, like most languages of the area, originally had only two lateral obstruent phonemes, a (voiceless) glottalized affricate and a voiceless fricative, though other glottalized consonants have nonglottalized counterparts. But Wakashan languages also have a voiceless nonglottalized lateral affricate (in addition to other plain : glottalized pairs of voiceless stops), and Quileute has acquired a nonglottalized lateral affricate phoneme through Wakashan loanwords. This phoneme now appears also in native vocabulary as a result of coalescence of sequences of /t/ + the lateral fricative /ɬ/. This change filled in a gap in the Quileute phoneme inventory and thus represents a type of change that also commonly arises through internal motivations (as Prague structuralists predicted).

Another Northwest phonemic borrowing is similarly "easy" in terms of typological fit: Twana, according to Drachman (1969:208), has acquired voiced stop and affricate phonemes in loanwords from another Salishan language, Lushootseed. These fill in gaps in the Twana inventory, which already had /b d/ from older /*m *n/ (as opposed to most Pacific Northwest languages, which have nasals and lack voiced obstruent phonemes).

Examples of slight structural borrowing can also be found in immigrants' languages, particularly—at least in the United States—in those spoken in relatively isolated nonurban settings. Bender (1980) gives examples of English syntactic borrowing in a Low German dialect spoken in Nebraska. The borrowed features involve changes in several German word order rules in constructions that are otherwise syntactically similar to corresponding English constructions. In particular, past participles and separable prefixes sometimes occur in midclause in this dialect rather than, as in German, clause-finally; and there is sometimes no subject-verb inversion where it is required by the German verb-second rule for main clauses, e.g. [dɛn hɛe fəkɔopt dɛe] 'then he sells them' (83; compare Standard [High] German *dann verkauft er sie*).

A comparable example, perhaps, is a gender assignment rule in the German spoken in some rural Australian communities. According to Clyne (1981, cited by Heath 1984:192), this rule, like the syntactic changes just discussed, builds on a similarity between English and German: because of the phonetic similarity between the German feminine article *die* [di] (as opposed to masculine *der* and neuter *das*) and the English article *the*, these dialects tend to assign feminine gender to borrowed English nouns. The extent to which this tendency changes the structure of the German dialects is debatable, but at least it changes the relative frequencies of the three gender categories, and it might constitute partial erosion of the German gender system.[7]

Other immigrants' languages have undergone more interference. Yiddish borrowings from Slavic might possibly belong in category (4) rather than in (2) or (3), but the examples given by Comrie (1981*b*:185) seem to fit within the parameters of our slight borrowing category: lexical borrowing is heavy and includes basic vocabulary and function words; phonemically distinct palatalization (in some dialects) and an affricate /ǰ/ have been introduced, but (though Comrie does not mention the point) the new phonemes are confined to loanwords; a Slavic derivational suffix that forms feminines, -*ka* (Yiddish -*ke*), tends to replace the corresponding native German suffix -*in*, as in *šnájder* 'tailor' : feminine *šnájderke* (cf. Standard German *Schneiderin*); yes/no question formation makes use of the sentence-initial question particle *ci*, borrowed from Polish *czy* [čɨ]; and the German third person reflexive pronoun *zix* (cf. Standard German *sich*) is used for all persons and numbers, like Polish *się* and corresponding reflexives in other Slavic languages—an example of functional change that represents structural borrowing without (though not **before**) morpheme borrowing.

If we try to categorize the changes mentioned in this section according to whether they constitute grammatical simplification or complication, or neither, we find a considerable amount of indeterminacy. Most of the phonological changes expand the phonemic inventory. Of these, however, only the addition of phonemic palatalization in some Yiddish dialects and of phonemic aspiration in Brahman dialects of some Dravidian languages are clear systemic complications. The new nonglottalized lateral affricate in Quileute, the new voiced stops and affricates in Twana, and the new affricate /ǰ/ in Yiddish all fill in gaps in the borrowing languages' inventories: they exploit already existing distinctive features (glottalization, voicing) and make the system more cohesive, in Trubetzkoy's terms. One other phonological change—the suppression of the obstruent voicing rule in some Brahman dialects of Dravidian—might count either as a simplification or as a slight complication, depending on one's views of natural processes and partial regularities. Another rather commonly borrowed type of rule, stress placement, also constitutes a simplification when it replaces phonemic stress.

As for the morphosyntactic changes cited above, few clearly complicate the system. The addition of clauses with finite verbs through borrowing of conjunctions, as in some Turkic languages, might constitute a complication, depending on the interrelations between these clauses and the previously existing nonfinite clauses. The same is true of the relative clauses with finite verbs in some literary Dravidian languages, and also of their borrowed passive constructions. But the no-split-infinitive and no-multiple-negative rules in English, the minor word order changes in Japanese, and the feminine suffix -ke in Yiddish look like simple replacements of previously existing structures. The remaining morphosyntactic changes arguably led to systemic simplification: demorphologization of verbal negation in Dravidian, word order changes in Nebraska Low German that include suppression of the rigid verb-second rule, possible erosion of gender marking on articles in some dialects of Australian German, and morphological simplification in the Yiddish reflexive pronoun.

4.3. INTENSE CONTACT: MODERATE TO HEAVY STRUCTURAL BORROWING

4.3.1. CATEGORY (4): MODERATE STRUCTURAL BORROWING

In this section we will discuss borrowing changes characteristic of category (4). Weinreich's (1953) Romansh case probably fits into category (4); the social situation, which he describes in some detail, is one in which almost all Romansh speakers are bilingual in the socially dominant language of their region, German, and in which there is no standard dialect of Romansh to hinder structural borrowing. Unfortunately, his examples of structural borrowing in Romansh from German are too few to permit definite classification of the case. But the interference features he mentions are characteristic of category (4): loss of gender in predicate adjectives (39); (partial) replacement of noun-adjective word order by adjective-noun word order (38); and the future tense formation (41).

Another case of extensive structural borrowing from a prestigious language is that of Estonian interference from German, which was the language of the Baltic German elite in Estonia in the nineteenth century (see chap. 7 for some discussion, with reference to Halbdeutsch). Among the structural features Estonian has borrowed from German are an analytic possessive construction to replace its original Uralic possessive pronominal suffix (Weinreich 1953:41), a passive construction (Weinreich, 41), and a syntactic rule placing the verb at the end of a subordinate clause (Sandfeld 1938:60). (If Sandfeld is right about this last feature, it must have appeared in Estonian **after** Estonian changed—under earlier IE influence—from an SOV to an SVO language.)

However, in most of the cases we have found with category (4) results, the reason for the cultural pressure is not so obvious as in the Estonian and Romansh instances. For Ossetic (Iranian) borrowing from Caucasian languages, for instance, the social background is not entirely clear, but the linguistic results, as reported by Comrie (1981*b*:167, 171, 179), are not in doubt: lexical borrowing from Caucasian languages (e.g., Georgian) is heavy; through these loanwords Ossetic has acquired a series of glottalized stop phonemes that have also spread to native Iranian words; it has developed a declensional system more elaborate than the one inherited from Proto-Iranian (or Proto-Indo-European), with nine cases that include absolute, interior-locative, and exterior-locative categories; not only are the cases themselves similar to those of neighboring Caucasian languages but the system is agglutinative—noun stem (+ plural) + case—like the corresponding Caucasian systems, but unlike the flexional case/number structure of IE declension; and, in syntax, Ossetic is more typically SOV and has a better-developed system of postpositions than other Iranian languages of the USSR.

Structural borrowings in various nonliterary Dravidian languages have no doubt occurred under a variety of social conditions. All the examples we have found are either in Dravidian languages spoken in central and northern India and surrounded by Indic speakers, especially Pengo, Gondi, and Kurukh, or in languages which (like those of Kupwar, as reported by Gumperz and Wilson 1971) are spoken along or near the border area that separates the Dravidian-speaking south from the rest of India. The examples given here, unless otherwise noted, are from Sridhar (1978, often citing other authors).

In phonology, Kurukh has acquired nasalized vowels of the Indic type, and Pengo has borrowed aspirated stop phonemes, though they are very rare except in loanwords from the Indic language Oriya. Also as a result of Oriya influence, Pengo has lost an inherited distinction between /j/ (with allophones [dẓ] and [ǰ]) and /z/ (Burrow and Bhattacharya 1970:5).

Among the Oriya loanwords in Pengo are function words of various kinds, including several postpositions in regular and widespread use and a number of particles, some of them used as conjunctions. As in some other instances we have mentioned, the borrowing of such words can bring about syntactic changes—for example, in Pengo, the use of the borrowed particle *ki* as a sentence-final question marker. Gondi and Kurukh have borrowed infinitive suffixes from Indic (Andronov 1964), a morphological change that fits well typologically with the suffixing morphology typical of Dravidian. Pengo makes occasional use of a genitive and a locative suffix borrowed from Oriya, another morphological change that fits Dravidian typology, since Dravidian generally has suffixed case markers that correspond closely to postpositional clitics in Indic. (Burrows and Bhattacharya [1970:41] give several examples of lexical items with these suffixes; in at least one of them, the borrowed suffix is added to a loanword from Indic. We do not know the etymologies of the others, but we can find none of them in the *Dravidian Etymological Dictionary* [Burrow and Emeneau 1961], so it may be that these suffixes are used only with loanwords.)

Another Indic-to-Dravidian example, apparently, is the borrowing of a system of numeral classifiers, i.e., classifier morphemes used when nouns are counted. Emeneau (1980 [1965]:131) describes these systems, which have up to six classes where they are most developed, in eastern Indic languages of the Maghadan group—Bengali, Assamese, Oriya, and some dialects of Bihari. Farther to the west, e.g., in Marathi and Hindi, there is just one classifier, used with personal nouns. Now, Indic did not inherit such a system, which, as Emeneau observes, is characteristic of languages to the east of India, in East and Southeast Asia. But the other languages of India that exhibit this pattern—not only Dravidian but also the Austro-Asiatic languages of the Munda branch—seem to have borrowed it from Indic. Emeneau does not venture a guess as to where Indic acquired it. In any case, he says, the Dravidian languages Kui-Kuwi, Kurukh, and Malto borrowed it from northeastern Indic languages; Malto has the best-developed system among the Dravidian languages, making use of some borrowed Indic classifier morphemes but using others of Dravidian origin.

As a final Indian example of category (4) borrowing, we should discuss the Kupwar situation, as described by Gumperz and Wilson (1971). All three of the Kupwar languages discussed in the article—Marathi (Indic), Kannada (Dravidian), and (Hindi-)Urdu (Indic)—may fit in this category, though Kupwar Urdu has undergone so many changes that it might belong in category (5) instead. However, the widespread view that the Kupwar dialects arose through radical restructuring in all the languages strikes us as incorrect, at least on the evidence provided by Gumperz and Wilson. Kannada, Marathi, and Urdu are already typologically similar in a number of ways, thanks partly to old shift-induced influence by Dravidian on Indic (see chap. 5 for discussion). The Kupwar changes do indeed make the languages even more similar, but there are no wholesale replacements of structure, unlike the cases discussed in 4.4 below. Moreover, the equally widespread view that most or all of the convergent changes are simplificatory is not clearly justified by the examples given.

Gumperz and Wilson discuss sixteen features in all. Kupwar Marathi has changed (toward Kannada) in four of these features; Kupwar Kannada has changed toward Marathi, and usually toward Urdu too, in five or six features;[8] and Kupwar Urdu has changed toward Kannada and/or Marathi in twelve features. All sixteen features are morphosyntactic: gender categories; the exclusive/inclusive

'we' distinction; subject-verb agreement rules in four different constructions; a head noun-modifier agreement rule; two word order
features; an equational construction (NP-is-NP); three features involving case functions; yes/no question marking; use of demonstrative and possessive forms in attributive and predicative constructions;
and the form(s) of past tense nonfinite verb forms in two constructions. Only one change involves borrowed morphemes: this is the
borrowing by Kannaḍa of an Indic subordinator *ki*, with part of its
syntactic relations, for use in quotations and questions. In all the
other changes (as far as we can tell from the examples given), structure
alone is borrowed. Examples are the extension of copula use to
equational sentences in Kupwar Kannaḍa, and the restriction of subject-verb agreement to the auxiliary verb only in verb + auxiliary
sequences in Kupwar Urdu and Kupwar Marathi. (This matches
Kannaḍa; other Urdu and Marathi dialects have agreement on both
the main verb and the auxiliary.)

Deciding whether a given change simplifies the grammar, complicates it, or has neither effect is not always easy. Reducing the scope
of a rule, for instance, decreases the instances in which the rule must
be applied, but it might increase the difficulty of learning where to
apply it. We therefore feel confident in our categorization of just a
few of the Kupwar changes. Only one change clearly complicates the
grammar of one of the Kupwar languages. This is the development
of an inclusive/exclusive 'we' distinction in Kupwar Urdu (but
perhaps also in Kupwar Kannaḍa; see n. 8).

Several changes look clearly simplificatory. Noun modifiers in
Kupwar Marathi and Kupwar Urdu have lost gender agreement with
their head nouns under Kannaḍa influence. Kupwar Kannaḍa has lost
a distinction between attributive and predicative forms of demonstratives and possessives, under the influence of the other two languages.
Kupwar Urdu has lost a distinction between past nonfinite verb
forms in two constructions; like the other two languages, it now has
the same form in both constructions. And the yes/no question marker
in Kupwar Urdu, which originally occurred in various positions in
the sentence, now occurs only in sentence-final position, as in
Marathi.

Some of the other Kupwar changes may be simplificatory, but
none is obviously so. For instance, changes in the semantic range of
pronominal gender categories in the two Indic languages, such as the

restriction of feminine gender to human females in Kupwar Urdu, are arguably neutral as far as the overall complexity of the system is concerned. Other changes are more obviously neutral, e.g., the word order changes in Kupwar Kannaḍa from quote or question sentence + subordinator + matrix sentence to matrix sentence + subordinator (*ki*, borrowed from Marathi and/or Urdu) + quote or question sentence. Still other changes cannot be categorized without further knowledge of relevant syntactic patterns in the languages. Kupwar Kannaḍa, as a result of Indic influence, now uses the copula in NP-is-NP sentences; but, though this may look at first glance like a complicating change, it might actually have simplified (by generalizing) the language's copula placement rules.

Other cases that might represent category (4) borrowing are more sketchily studied, so that we have only isolated examples of interference features. The Salishan language Comox, for instance, has acquired a Kwakiutlan syllable-structure constraint prohibiting syllable-initial consonant clusters (Thompson 1979:732; Davis 1971 says that there are initial clusters in two Comox words recently borrowed from other Salishan languages); this is a striking change in a family with some of the most elaborate consonant clusters in the world.

The various dialects of Romani comprise another set of cases. These dialects have undergone changes through borrowing that range from moderate to heavy (and even to extreme, in the case of Anglo-Romani, which is discussed in 4.4). Kaufman (1973:12) and Comrie (1981*b*:157) have given examples of borrowed features in various Romani dialects. These include lexical items of all types; borrowed phonemes, including entire contrastive sets such as palatalized consonants in dialects spoken in Russia; development of a typical Balkan periphrastic future construction using a reduced form of the verb meaning 'want' before the main verb; prefixes borrowed from Baltic and Slavic languages; near-total loss of the definite article in some Baltic dialects; and a plural suffix borrowed from Rumanian in what are known as Vlach dialects. All dialects of Romani have developed special paradigms (modeled on Greek) for inflecting borrowed nouns, adjectives, and verbs.

Another case that probably belongs here, but whose details are unclear because of insufficient historical information about the languages, is that of borrowing from Nunggubuyu into Warndarang in Arnhem Land, Australia (Heath 1978). Heath does not mention any examples of phonological or purely syntactic diffusion into Warndarang, but Warndarang has borrowed several suffixes from Nunggubuyu, e.g., an instrumental suffix -*miri* (144). A native Warndarang locative suffix has been reinterpreted as an absolute suffix, at least partly because it was phonologically similar to a Nunggubuyu absolute suffix; this absolute suffix is used as a third singular possessive with kin terms in Warndarang and also displays some allomorphy borrowed from Nunggubuyu (Heath, 134–136). (Another feature Heath [87–91] identifies as a likely borrowing from Nunggubuyu is a set of noun-class prefixes; however, the historical picture described by Heath strikes us as insufficiently clear to establish these prefixes as borrowings in Warndarang.)

For contact between the Turkic language Uzbek and Iranian (mainly Tadzhik) in the Soviet Union we also have rather sketchy evidence of interference, but what we do have seems to put this case in borrowing category (4), though the possibility of simultaneous shift and borrowing interference should be kept in mind here. According to Menges (1945) and Comrie (1981*b*), phonological interference in urban Uzbek dialects has led to the loss of the characteristic front rounded and high back unrounded Turkic vowels through merger (/ɨ/ with /i/, /ü/with /u/, and /ö/ with /o/), resulting in a six-vowel inventory "almost identical down to phonetic detail to Tadzhik," but with partial preservation of rounding as a distinctive feature (Comrie, 51 f., 66). Thanks to this change, the Turkic vowel harmony rule has been completely lost.

Menges observes that, next to the phonology, the most iranized Uzbek dialects show the greatest amount of interference in the syntax. His main syntactic example is the "intrusion of subordination," i.e., clauses with subordinating conjunctions and finite verbs in place of characteristic Turkic participial or gerund constructions. But Comrie (84) suggests that the borrowed Iranian clause types have never been used in ordinary speech in Uzbek (and so have been stylistically marked), though in Azerbaidzhani, another Turkic language with a long history of close contact with Iranian, such clauses have apparently been in frequent use since the thirteenth century.

Borrowing in the other direction, from Uzbek to Tadzhik, has affected northern Tadzhik dialects heavily enough to include the following features (Comrie 1981*b*:167 ff.): borrowed derivational suffixes and nonfinite verbal suffixes; a definiteness distinction marked by postpositions (Turkic languages distinguish definite from indefinite direct objects by means of a suffix); and extensive influence in the verbal tense/aspect/mood system, including both semantic and morpheme borrowings such as new presuppositional and inferential mood categories.

Two current contact cases in western China that have been studied by Li (1983, 1984) seem to straddle the borderline between moderate (category [4]) and heavy (category [5]) borrowing interference. Borrowing from Chinese into the Mongolian language Baonan probably belongs on the moderate side of the borderline, though the very high proportion of Chinese loanwords—50–55 percent of the vocabulary of Baonan—is striking. Structural interference features from Chinese include lexical semantics, e.g., new functions for the native Baonan verb meaning 'hit', to match the functions of the corresponding verb in Chinese (1983:43–45); phonemic stress in Chinese loanwords, with the position of the stress determined by the tones of the source-language words (this contrasts with a word-final stress pattern in native words); verb-medial copula sentences using a borrowed Chinese copula, beside verb-final copula sentences using the native Baonan copula; a comparative construction that uses both the borrowed Chinese comparative morpheme in the position appropriate for Chinese and the native Baonan comparative suffix[9] (beside a complete native construction with only the suffix); and the development of resultative compounds that match the corresponding compounds in Chinese both semantically and syntactically, and contrast with the native Baonan construction that uses a suffixed causative marker.

Before turning to heavy borrowing (and to Li's second borrowing case from China), let us sum up the illustrations of moderate structural borrowing that we have cited in this section. Five of the phonological changes produced systemic complications: the development of glottalized stop phonemes in Ossetic, of nasalized vowel phonemes in Kurukh, of aspirated stop phonemes in Pengo, of palatalized consonant phonemes in some Romani dialects, and of phonemic stress in Chinese loanwords in Baonan. But almost as many of the phonological changes are simplificatory, though the two interrelated Uzbek changes—loss of several vowel phonemes and the consequent loss of vowel harmony—may be due primarily to shift.

The loss of the /j/ : /z/ contrast in Pengo, however, is surely due to borrowing rather than shift, and the loss of syllable-initial consonant clusters in Comox is more likely to be due to borrowing than to shift.

In morphosyntax, about half of the changes may constitute overall systemic complications: the Estonian rule placing the verb at the end of a subordinate clause (assuming this is not a retention); the Pengo rule for marking yes/no questions; the numeral classifiers in Kui/Kuwi and several other Dravidian languages; finite subordinate clauses beside nonfinite ones in Uzbek; a new definite/indefinite marking system and new verbal moods in Tadzhik; and double comparative marking and the development of verb-medial copula sentences (beside verb-final ones) in Baonan. The development of new cases in Ossetic and perhaps Pengo, and of a periphrastic future in Balkan dialects of Romani, may or may not have been complicating changes, but they certainly caused no typological change in the borrowing languages. Several other morphosyntactic borrowings are arguably simplificatory (though we would need to have much more information about their wider systemic effects to be sure): loss of grammatical gender in predicate adjectives in Romansh; loss of the definite article in some Romani dialects; development of agglutination in Ossetic declension (replacing a flexional case/number suffixing declension); and a change from suffixed possessives to an analytic means of expressing possession in Estonian. Still other changes, particularly the partial change from NA to AN word order in Romansh and the development of an absolute case and more consistent SOV syntax in Ossetic, seem likely to be replacements that neither complicate nor simplify the overall system.

As with structural borrowings in the category we have labeled "slight interference," then, we find no clear pattern here of simplifying or complicating changes for any grammatical subsystem. When we move on to heavy interference, category (5), we can no longer detect any typologically-based tendencies that control the kinds of features that will be borrowed. In category (5) borrowing, literally anything goes.

4.3.2. CATEGORY 5: HEAVY STRUCTURAL BORROWING

The second western Chinese case Li discusses (especially in Li 1983) involves borrowing from Tibetan into Wutun. Li observes that

"Wutun belongs to the Chinese language family, but it is so heavily influenced by the local Tibetan language, both lexically and grammatically, that one may easily mistake it, on first impression, for a Tibetan dialect" (32). According to the Wutun speakers' own oral history, they are descendants of Chinese immigrants to the region who were forced to assimilate to the surrounding Tibetan culture. Few now speak another Chinese language, but many (most?) speak Tibetan as their second language (33). The lexicon, though mostly Chinese, includes many Tibetan loanwords. These loanwords have non-Chinese segments and consonant clusters; in addition, Wutun has entirely lost phonemic tones (according to Li [32], the local Tibetan language, Anduo Tibetan, lacks tones and has elaborate consonant clusters). The most striking morphosyntactic features borrowed from Tibetan are rigid verb-final word order; strictly postpositional ordering, with no co-verbs; use of a causative suffix instead of resultative compounds; development of several cases; and almost total reduction of the classifier system to one classifier.

The complex Brahui case seems to belong in this category, but it is possible that it fits into category (4) instead: the actual interference features that have been identified in Brahui are neither as numerous nor as obviously disruptive typologically as, for example, borrowing in Wutun or Asia Minor Greek. In spite of Bray's and Emeneau's careful analyses of the Brahui situation, the main language from which Brahui has borrowed—Balochi—has not been thoroughly studied, and the amount of available information about Brahui itself is limited, particularly in syntax. So it seems likely, especially given the nature of some of the structural features that Brahui has borrowed, that more information about the two languages would lead to the discovery of more borrowed structure in Brahui. Tentatively, then, we classify Brahui as a case of category (5) borrowing.

Emeneau (1962), while emphasizing the high proportion of non-Dravidian vocabulary in Brahui (53), also says that the language's "morphological and syntactic system is still quite unmistakably Dravidian" (61). The Dravidian nature of the phonology, at least the vowel system, may be in some doubt: Emeneau refers to "the almost complete . . . conversion of the Dravidian vowel system into one like that of Balochi" (55), including the loss of the characteristic Dravidian vowel phonemes /e o/, which do not occur in Balochi. (Sridhar [1978:203] mentions that Brahui has developed nasalized vowel phonemes of the sort one finds in Indic languages; these could have arisen through the influence of Indic languages spoken in Baluchistan, but not, apparently, from influence of the neighboring Indic language Sindhi or of Balochi, since these languages are said to lack phonemic nasalization.)

In morphosyntax, Brahui has lost the characteristic Dravidian distinction between exclusive and inclusive 'we' (Balochi never had such a distinction), and also the old Dravidian gender system (Balochi, like most other Iranian languages, has entirely lost its inherited Indo-Iranian gender system) (Emeneau 1962:56). Brahui has borrowed a Balochi subordinating conjunction *ki*, whose syntax is similar to that of the corresponding (and cognate) Persian conjunction (Emeneau, 59; Emeneau has no detailed information about the syntax of *ki* in Balochi itself); other Dravidian languages have no such conjunction or usage. Brahui is the only Dravidian language to develop (from native morphemes) enclitic or suffixed pronominal elements that function as possessives when added to nouns and as objects when added to verbs. Emeneau observes that such a feature occurs quite generally in Iranian and in northwestern Indic languages, so that the Brahui pattern could come from either source (1962:60, but cf. 1980 [1962]). Since several other interference features can only come from Iranian, however, and since Balochi is clearly the best Iranian candidate, the best guess is that Balochi contributed this feature to Brahui too—though Indic influence may have helped fix it in Brahui. And finally, Brahui has borrowed one aspectual verbal prefix directly from Balochi (Emeneau 1962:56–58) and has developed two or three derivational verbal prefixes with locative meanings, on a Balochi model, from native Dravidian morphemes (Emeneau 1980 [1971]:176)—a striking innovation for a language belonging to the exclusively suffixing Dravidian family.

A final and extensively documented case of heavy structural borrowing is Asia Minor Greek. Dawkins's 1916 study of this dialect group is the most useful case study (for our purposes) that we have found in the literature for any contact situation: Dawkins gives copious linguistic examples and detailed information about the linguistic and religious affiliations and other cultural attributes of the populations of the villages he studied. Most Asia Minor Greek dialects clearly retain enough inherited Greek grammar to count as Greek dialects in the full genetic sense; a few dialects may be close to or even over the border of nongenetic development. As is typical of heavy borrowing, the Asia Minor Greek case shows no typologically constrained patterns of development: Turkish cultural pressure is so pervasive that structural features of every kind are borrowed, including morphophonemic rules (e.g., vowel harmony and spirantization of a stem-final velar stop after a vowel and before a suffix -i; see Lewis [1967:10] for a description of the more general Turkish rule); the syntax of the copula (in Turkish the copula is a sentence-final enclitic); various word order features; drastic adjustment of the definite/indefinite distinction to match the Turkish pattern; and loss of several grammatical categories that Turkish lacks, such as gender and adjective-noun agreement. (See 9.1 for a discussion of the kinds of borrowing Dawkins cites, and for examples of borrowed structures.)

Promising sociohistorical generalizations that might help to distinguish cases of moderate structural borrowing from those of heavy borrowing are hard to establish, because the available sociohistorical information about past contact situations is scanty in the extreme. The growing body of research on current, directly observable contact situations should contribute to a data base for generalizing about the linguistic results of contact. But with current contact situations we often don't know what the eventual linguistic outcome will be. This is particularly true when we only have detailed information about the linguistic repertoire of a few individuals; extrapolating from the behavior of individuals to the norm of an entire speech community is no simple matter. The difficulty, then, is to correlate known results of past contact situations with known facts about current contact situations. (This is, of course, the same difficulty that arises in all attempts to correlate studies of ongoing linguistic change with the much greater store of information about completed changes.)

In spite of these difficulties, we can at least observe that two of our three cases of heavy borrowing—Wutun and Asia Minor Greek—demonstrably involve long-term intense cultural pressure in a context of resistance to total cultural assimilation. Li's report of Wutun speakers' oral traditions and the pressure toward bilingualism in Turkish on Asia Minor Greek speakers at least since the mid-fifteenth century (Dawkins 1916:1) attest to the intensity of the contact. The pressure of Balochi on Brahui was clearly more intimate, as we have already indicated. Among the cases of moderate borrowing, German cultural pressure on Estonian was not so long-lived as in the heavy borrowing cases, and the other moderate borrowing cases did not (at least not obviously) involve any long-term domination of source-language speakers over borrowing-language speakers. Beyond this we can say little of substance about the respective social situations for moderate and heavy borrowing. For instance, if Balochi-Brahui contact was more intense than, say, Pengo-Oriya or Uzbek-Tadzhik contact, we do not know why.

4.3.3. SPRACHBUND

Two other issues need to be discussed briefly before we consider extreme cases of borrowing that, in our opinion, reflect abnormal transmission. First, readers will no doubt have noticed that we have hardly mentioned the world's most famous contact situation: the Balkan Sprachbund. Moreover, we have given only scattered examples from two other well-established linguistic areas, the Pacific Northwest and MesoAmerica, and from a third that has recently been well described, Arnhem Land in Australia (Heath 1978, 1981). The reason for these omissions is that our interest in unraveling the causes, effects, and mechanisms of contact-induced language change has led us to focus on two-language contact situations in which the direction of interference can be definitely established. Sprachbund situations are notoriously messy.

In the Balkans, the long period of widespread back-and-forth migrations of small groups, caused by the Turkish invasions, resulted in mutual bilingualism and multilingualism rather than the one-way bilingualism that is common, though not universal, in two-language situations. Although the sources of the various linguistic Balkanisms are much disputed and probably varied (despite Sandfeld's [1968 (1930)] and others' arguments for a Greek origin), it is at least clear that they did not arise through massive borrowing by all the Balkan languages from a single source language in which most speakers of the other languages were bilingual. The Balkan languages—Greek, Rumanian, Albanian, Bulgarian, Macedonian, and southeastern dialects of Serbocroatian—constitute a Sprachbund without asymmetrical dominance relations or large-scale shifts, and with multilateral rather than one-way bi- and multilingualism. The linguistic results, as is well known, include features characteristic of moderate to heavy structural borrowing, such as a quite specific periphrastic future construction, the replacement of morphological infinitives by a particular kind of clausal construction, and the development of post-posed articles.

What a long-term multilateral Sprachbund seems to promote, in fact, is the gradual development of isomorphism (equivalence of form) in all areas of structure except the phonological shapes of morphemes. Thus we find, for instance, comments such as Capell's about the languages of the central highlands of New Guinea—that adjoining languages have very different vocabularies, but their grammatical features "recur with almost monotonous regularity from language to language" (cited by Wurm 1956:451). The case of Kupwar in India seems similar in kind to this one, though the evidence presented by Gumperz and Wilson (1971) for the Kupwar languages, as we argued above, does not suggest extreme morphosyntactic convergence. Our interpretation of the Kupwar changes discussed by Gumperz and Wilson indicates systemic results that are comparable to those of much-studied Sprachbund cases like the Balkan one, because the best established Balkan developments in the various languages are not obviously simplificatory. Nor, certainly, are the structural features characteristic of the Pacific Northwest Sprachbund, another case apparently involving widespread mutual bi- and multilingualism. Jacobs (1954) cites areal phonological features such as glottalized phonemes, labialized dorsal phonemes, uvulars (or back velars), and lateral obstruents. Thomason (1983a) exemplifies areal morphosyntactic features such as yes/no question markers, possessive affixes, and (citing Boas) a periphrastic imperative construction (see also Sherzer [1976] for a list of selected Pacific Northwest areal features).

It seems likely that convergence in a multilateral Sprachbund situation proceeds along the lines proposed by Pfaff (1979) for bilingual code-switching, with bi- and multilingual speakers favoring structures (including ones that are less popular stylistically to begin with) that are common to some or all of the languages. This strategy cannot account for all of the results, but we would expect it to be an important mechanism of convergence, especially in morphosyntactic convergence. Joseph's analysis (1983) of the Balkan infinitive developments supports this supposition.

Besides the problem of directionality, multilateral Sprachbund cases usually have only a few area-wide features, together with many

instances of localized diffusion. Sometimes we can establish directionality for local diffusion, but often we cannot, especially, as in cases
like the Pacific Northwest, when the histories of the language groups
are not (yet?) well known. We do not know, for instance, where the
limited areal change from nasal to voiced oral stops first occurred in
the Northwest, or where the limited areal feature of pronominal
gender first arose in the region.

Other well-established linguistic areas were apparently never multilateral in our sense, and we can therefore establish both the source
of interference features and the direction and mechanism of diffusion.
This is true for old Dravidian-to-Indic interference in India (a shift
situation; see chap. 5 for discussion) and for some more recent local
cases there, e.g., Pengo borrowing from Oriya. The Uralic/Balto-
Slavic Sprachbund arose partly through shift by Uralic speakers to
Slavic and Baltic (see chaps. 5 and 9.5), and partly through borrowing
by Uralic languages from Baltic and Slavic.

4.3.4. Typologically Favored Borrowing

The other topic that we should touch on before going on to the
next section is the question of typologically favored borrowing, that
is, structural borrowing at a higher level than the intensity of contact
might seem to warrant, thanks to a close typological fit between
source-language and borrowing-language structures. The classic cases
of this type are those of dialect borrowing, where the typological fit
is close for all grammatical subsystems, including the lexicon (see 2.3
for an example of borrowing from Standard Serbocroatian into a
nonstandard dialect).

Similar examples can be found in borrowing between closely
related languages, where again both lexicon and typological structure
match to a great extent. This process surely accounts in large part for
much of the interference from Norse in the Old English of northern
England (see 9.8 for discussion). Campbell (1976:184–185) gives examples of a neutralization rule and a borrowed allophonic rule among
Mayan languages: some Quiché dialects borrowed from Cakchiquel
a rule that neutralizes word-final /m/ and /n/ as [ŋ]; and western
dialects of Quiché and other languages borrowed from Mamean languages a dissimilation rule that palatalizes the velar stops /k/ and /k'/
before a vowel followed by /q/, /q'/, or /x/. Comparable morpholog-

ical examples involve borrowing from the Bantu languages TshiLuba and ChiBemba into KiNgwana (Lubumbashi Swahili) (Bokamba 1977:198, citing Polomé 1968): Lubumbashi Swahili has lost syllabic nasal prefixes and has replaced two noun-class prefixes—*ji-* by *li-* (Bantu Noun Class 5) and *u-* by *bu-* (Bantu Noun Class 14).

In syntax, various borrowings between the Indic languages Hindi and Marathi belong to this same type. Bombay Hindi, for instance, has switched its question particle from sentence-initial to sentence-final position under Marathi influence (Apte 1974:33). Bombay Hindi has also added an additional suffix, borrowed from Marathi, to the main verb root in forming the past perfect: compare ordinary Hindi *pīyā thā* '(he) had drunk' (cf. *pīnā* 'to drink') with Marathi *pīlā hotā* and Bombay Hindi *pīyelā thā* (Wagle 1981 MS). Still other morphosyntactic examples are given by Pandharipande (n.d.) for mutual interference between Marathi and Hindi (but mostly from Marathi to Hindi) in the village of Nāgpurī in central India; these include word order changes, changes toward more analytic structure, and changes toward less analytic structure.

Less closely related languages may also be sufficiently similar typologically to permit borrowing of otherwise hard-to-borrow features under conditions of moderate cultural pressure. Weinreich (1953:32), for instance, argues that close structural similarity in verb inflection permitted the borrowing of Bulgarian inflectional verb endings into Meglenite Rumanian. Sandfeld (1938:59) exemplifies this change: Meglenite Rumanian *aflum* 'I find' and *afliš* 'you(sg.) find', with the Bulgarian person/number/tense suffixes *-m*, *-š* added to the original Rumanian forms *aflu*, *afli*.

Another large class of changes that belongs at least partly in this category comprises the process of decreolization, in which the language of a substrate creole-speaking population gradually changes through structural and lexical borrowing from the superstrate vocabulary-base language. In many of these cases, the intensity of contact is sufficient to warrant any amount of structural borrowing, so that typological factors need not be invoked to account for the transfer of hard-to-borrow features; in other cases, however, typology may be a relevant factor in promoting the borrowing of particular features. (We should note that, although some authors use the term in more general ways, in the standard usage that we employ decreolization involves convergence toward vocabulary-base language structure.)

As in borrowing between dialects, especially into nonstandard from standard dialects, the percentage of shared vocabulary in cases of decreolization is very high indeed. But unlike the dialect cases, a basilectal creole often does not, initially, match its vocabulary-base language closely in the typological sense, as is shown, for instance, by the well-known differences in their tense/aspect systems (see chap. 6 for discussion). It would therefore not be surprising to find fairly significant differences between the processes of decreolization and dialect borrowing; and Bickerton's claim that "decreolization proceeds by acquiring new forms first and new functions later" (1981:193) suggests some such difference. He supports this claim by giving examples of function words which, when they are borrowed into the creole, are used at first in the same ways as the original creole function words that they replace.

But, although we do not doubt Bickerton's examples, it seems extremely unlikely that this is the only kind of change that occurs in decreolization. For one thing, some structural changes, such as changes in word order, do not involve the acquisition of new forms at all. More importantly, creole speakers who are even partly bilingual in the vocabulary-base language will surely borrow structure as well as lexicon, just as other borrowers do: we see no reason (and none is given in any of the literature on decreolization) to suppose that creole speakers are any less likely to borrow structure than speakers of languages with different sorts of historical origins. It is important to remember here that a number of the examples given above involve borrowing of structural features **without** the morphemes that express them; for instance, the new Brahui enclitic/suffixed possessive-object marking construction uses native Dravidian pronominal morphemes, and the native Baonan verb meaning 'hit' has acquired new functions through borrowing from Chinese. We would expect comparable changes to occur in decreolization too, and they would be counter-examples to Bickerton's prediction.

We realize, of course, that these comments are programmatic. The literature on decreolization contains examples of changes that might support our position, but we have not found sufficient historical information about the relevant creoles to decide whether such changes represent early or late stages in the decreolization process. However, since decreolization certainly involves some borrowing interference, the burden of proof should lie on anyone who claims that it is wholly different in this aspect from other types of borrowing, and a few examples of "new forms first" borrowing should not shift the burden of proof.[10]

4.4. OVERWHELMING CULTURAL PRESSURE: REPLACEMENT OF LARGE PORTIONS OF THE INHERITED GRAMMAR

Cultural pressure so intense that all the pressured speakers must learn the dominant language of the community usually leads to one of three linguistic outcomes. First, a subordinate population may shift fairly rapidly to the dominant language, abandoning its native language so that the abandoned language (at least as spoken by that group) dies a sudden death. Second, a shift may take place over many generations, in which case the language of the shifting population may (as long as it is maintained) undergo the slow attrition process known as language death. The third possibility is that, for reasons of stubborn language and cultural loyalty, the pressured group may maintain what it can of its native language while borrowing such large portions of the dominant language's grammar that they replace all, or at least sizable portions of, the original grammar. The first of these three possible outcomes is probably rather common. The second, though little studied until recently, may also be common. But the third outcome, as far as we know, is very rare indeed.

We will concentrate on the third result in this section, because that is the most interesting one from the viewpoint of contact-induced language change. First, however, some discussion of the place of language death (i.e., slow death) in our view of language contact results is in order.

Probably the most famous early description of language death as an individual phenomenon (and also of the "semi-speaker" phenomenon—when a person knows no language well) is Bloomfield's comment about White Thunder (1970 [1927]:154):

> White Thunder, a man round forty, speaks less English than Menomini, and that is a strong indictment, for his Menomini is atrocious. His vocabulary is small; his inflections are often barbarous; he constructs sentences on a few threadbare models. He may be said

to speak no language tolerably. His case is not uncommon among younger men, even when they speak but little English. Perhaps it is due, in some indirect way, to the impact of the conquering language.

The standard view of language death for a whole community of speakers indicates the nature of the indirect impact of the conquering language, to which the group is shifting (even if some members fail to learn it well). According to a typical definition, language death is a "process involving the simplification of language form along with the restriction of language function" (Knab 1980:230). It is the loss of domains of usage that leads to loss of stylistic resources and, ultimately, to loss of grammatical structures, as new generations of speakers fail to learn forms their elders never or rarely use.

Here is an example to add to those provided in various studies of language death (e.g., Dressler 1972, Dorian 1973, 1981). Flathead, an Interior Salishan language spoken in northwestern Montana, is fairly healthy for a language of this family: it still has several hundred fluent speakers, some of them in their thirties, and it is still spoken in households where there are elders. In working with younger speakers (under sixty years old) on grammar lessons for their community-college language classes, Thomason has elicited most paradigms without difficulty, including some for which a stage-setting story is necessary to motivate a particular form (e.g., the optional distributive third person plural verb form). But she has had difficulty eliciting any verb forms with first plural subect + second plural object, or vice versa, either through translation or through recognition of forms she constructs on the basis of descriptions of closely related languages. These particular forms are especially complex in Salishan, with transitive and pronominal suffixes that differ from those of all the other forms in the elaborate paradigm. It is a structure point that seems to be missing for fluent younger speakers. Though the elders probably still have the forms, there may be few occasions for using them, and younger speakers may never, or rarely, have heard them.

As all analyses of language death have emphasized, a structural loss of this type has nothing to do with borrowing from English. It does have to do with the fact that all Flathead speakers, including the elders, have native-speaker fluency in English and can thus say anything in English that they cannot say in Flathead. (Even if the elders do not need to resort to English themselves, they can understand it when younger speakers do so. We ignore here the question of language and culture compatibility: of course Flathead is needed to discuss some Indian cultural topics, but the language is not the only part of the culture that is being lost.) Flathead, in fact, has apparently borrowed nothing from English except a few words, as we would expect, given that the shift to English will have been completed within a few generations from the onset of intense cultural pressure from English speakers.

Where language death results from a slow shift process, by contrast, structural borrowing from the dominant language is likely to occur in addition to the loss of structure characteristic of language death. For instance, some southern dialects of Welsh—most of whose speakers also speak English—seem to be undergoing both processes. Thomas (1982) mentions several structural borrowings into Welsh from English, probably amounting to category (4) borrowing on our scale: heavy lexical borrowing; phonemicization, in southern Welsh dialects, of a formerly allophonic distinction between /s/ and /z/; borrowing of a plural suffix -s, which is added to native Welsh words as well as to English loanwords (this borrowing causes no typological disruption, since Welsh already had several plural suffixes); and the development of an entire system of modal auxiliary verbs, using native Welsh verb roots but paralleling English modals very closely in both semantics and syntax. Besides these borrowings, which are within the range of undisturbed transmission, Thomas notes that the kinds of Welsh in question have undergone (or are undergoing) simplifying changes, such as stylistic shrinkage, elimination of redundancies, and analogical leveling, which are in no sense borrowing of English structure. These latter changes are certainly not extreme manifestations of the language death phenomenon, but they may constitute some first steps along the way.

The language death situations that have attracted the most scholarly attention are those in which the process is in its final stages, when a whole group is in the linguistic position, with respect to the language of its ethnic heritage, of White Thunder. Complete shift, for the group, is only a short step away: the dominant language is the main language for all but the oldest members, and the original language is not used regularly by the least fluent speakers for any purpose, except perhaps for an occasional phrase or word thrown into conversation in the dominant language. In a case like this it may actually be necessary to consider the phonology as borrowed from the dominant language: if words are to be pronounced at all, phonemic contrasts must be used, and if the speakers never learned those of the original language, then the only ones available are those of the dominant language. Thus Bloomfield, for instance, says that younger Menominis who speak English often anglicize their Menomini pronunciation (1970 [1927]:154). Linguists who study American Indian languages have long been familiar with the difficulty of eliciting vocabulary and grammatical structures from a language's few remaining speakers, who may not have used their native language regularly for years.

But what if, in spite of the most intense pressure to shift to the dominant language, speakers nevertheless maintain their ethnic group's original language for some regular purposes, e.g., as a home language? As we have seen, the most common result is moderate to heavy borrowing from the dominant language. There is another possibility, however: the borrowing may be so extensive as to constitute complete grammatical replacement in at least some subsystem. Consider the case of AngloRomani. All English Gypsies speak English natively, but they maintain part of the lexicon of their original ethnic language, Romani, for use—with English grammar—as a secret code (Ian Hancock, personal communication, 1980). (Probably nobody ever learned AngloRomani as a first language or had it as the only language.) To the extent that it is part of the ordinary linguistic repertoire of all members of the English Gypsy community, it is a speech form distinct from Romani itself, as spoken in (for instance) Russia and elsewhere in Europe, with Romani grammar and Romani lexicon both preserved.

AngloRomani is a mixed speech form: the group's original language was not ultimately passed on as a coherent set of interrelated lexical and grammatical structures. Currently, AngloRomani is the product of two entirely distinct historical processes: inherited vocabulary, borrowed grammar. Its origin is thus nongenetic in the historical linguistic sense, since vocabulary and grammar cannot be traced to the same source.

But what distinguishes AngloRomani from a case of language death? The obvious linguistic difference is that AngloRomani is not grammatically impoverished. It has all the grammatical complexity that English has; in fact, its grammar is simply that of English. Still, unless the shift was sudden, there may have been a stage when English Gypsies retained a few Romani grammatical structures, and these may well have been simplified in ways similar to those found in some dialects of Welsh and, at a much later stage in the process of language death, some kinds of Scots Gaelic (Dorian 1973, 1981). Why did AngloRomani speakers replace the vanishing Romani structures with English ones, while speakers of other threatened languages replaced their vanishing grammars with nothing, so that what was left of their original language was no longer stylistically and grammatically rich enough to be used for most purposes? The answer seems clear: AngloRomani continued to serve important communicative functions, and for those functions it needed adequate structural resources. This answer does not, of course, explain the difference; it merely shifts the focus of the puzzle. We have no answer to the main question: why does one fully bilingual speech community lose its ethnic language by concomitant functional and linguistic attrition, while another exhibits a stubborn resistance to cultural assimilation so strong that its ethnic language is partially preserved functionally, though not grammatically?

Although we cannot explain or predict such an outcome, we can at least exemplify it. Aside from the AngloRomani case, we have found one other linguistically similar example and one borderline case, on the way to total grammatical replacement (if complete shift does not cut the process short).

The case that most closely resembles AngloRomani linguistically is Ma'a (Mbugu), a Tanzanian language which has perhaps 50 percent Cushitic vocabulary (including most of the basic vocabulary) and a few Cushitic structural features, while its remaining vocabulary, together with almost all its grammar, is of Bantu origin, in fact borrowed from Bantu. Socially, the Ma'a case differs considerably from the AngloRomani case. Though they are all bilingual in one or two Bantu languages and surrounded by Bantu speakers, the Ma'a are still a people apart, and they apparently speak Ma'a to one another regularly. Moreover, a major source of bantuizing pressure is their continuing connection with their Bantu-speaking kinfolk—Ma'a clans that have shifted to Bantu. (This case is discussed in 9.2; see also Thomason 1983b.)

We mentioned above, in discussing Asia Minor Greek, that a few dialects may have undergone so much structural borrowing from Turkish that normal transmission must be considered interrupted. Some other cases of heavy borrowing also seem to be near the border-line dividing ordinary borrowing from near-total grammatical replacement.

In addition to cases like these, we have two examples in which borrowed grammatical structures are confined to particular grammatical subsystems. One of these is the (ex-?)dialect of Aleut that is spoken on Mednyj, one of the two Commander Islands off the northeastern coast of the USSR. Menovščikov (1969) describes briefly the social setting that led to intermarriage and bilingualism between Aleuts and Russians on this island, and he reports the following startling linguistic result: although other Aleut grammatical subsystems remain largely intact, including the elaborate noun declension and nonfinite verb morphology, the entire Aleut finite verb morphology has been replaced by Russian finite verb morphology, including flexional person/number/tense suffixes. Russian affixes, particles, and pronouns are used with native Aleut verb roots (and also, presumably, with borrowed Russian verbs).

The other case is Michif, an (ex-)dialect of Cree that retains the elaborate Algonquian verb morphology but has borrowed French noun morphology and noun-phrase syntax along with French nouns. That is, Michif uses Cree morphology with its verbs, which are all native Cree forms, but its entire nominal system (both the noun roots themselves and their grammatical patterns) is French, including, to a great extent, the phonological structure. (This is something of an oversimplification; there is some leakage between the French and Cree components of Michif. See 9.3 for more detail on Michif, and 9.4 for discussion of Mednyj Aleut.)

Finally, before we comment here on the significance of these languages for genetic linguistics and language contact effects generally, we will describe briefly the sixth and final dramatic example of language mixing that we have found: the (ex-?)Arabic dialect spoken in Kormakiti on Cyprus, as described by Newton (1964). Kormakiti Arabic is spoken by Maronite Christians whose ancestors apparently migrated to Cyprus in 1191. It is the main home language in Kormakiti, but all members of the community are completely fluent in Cypriot Greek too. Kormakiti Arabic is not a written language, and all formal schooling in the community uses Greek as the medium of instruction. In a list of 630 common words that he elicited from Kormakiti Arabic speakers, Newton found that 38 percent were Greek loanwords, including some kin terms, numerals (all the ordinals are Greek), body parts, and basic color terms, as well as function words. Newton describes the language's structure this way (43): "Words of Arabic . . . origin retain the full morphological apparatus of Arabic while those of Cypriot-Greek . . . origin appear exactly as they do in the mouths of monolingual speakers of the Greek dialect." Borrowed Greek nouns, verbs, and adjectives thus inflect with Greek affixes and according to Greek patterns, while native Arabic words have Arabic inflection. There are a few exceptions to this rule, such as Greek masculine and feminine diminutive suffixes added to native Arabic words.

In the phonology, borrowed Greek features have penetrated into the Arabic morphemes, including a borrowed morphophonemic rule changing /j/ (=[i̯]) to [ç] after a voiceless stop /p/. The Arabic and Greek parts of the lexicon basically have a single shared phonological structure, thanks partly to loss, in the Arabic lexicon, of non-Greek features such as emphatic consonants and distinctive vowel length. Only a few phonological differences, in syllable structure and the Arabic voiced pharyngeal fricative, separate the different lexical sets.

In the syntax, the compartmentalization of Arabic and Greek structures is not so rigid. As in Michif, where Cree demonstratives are used in construction with borrowed French nouns, Arabic demonstratives are used here with borrowed Greek words. But the syntactic behavior of the native Arabic definite article *l* is either very similar or identical to that of the Greek definite article, whether it is used with Arabic or with borrowed Greek nouns. Attributive adjectives, too, follow Greek syntactic patterns; so do a number of other constructions.

Newton concludes his discussion of Kormakiti Arabic structure by observing that "there is something slightly amiss with the common assumption that mixed languages simply do not exist" (51).

We agree with Newton that Kormakiti Arabic is a mixed language. The type of mixture it exhibits is an extreme version of a pattern described earlier in this chapter, the borrowing of morphology (and phonology) along with lexicon—for example, English Latinate plurals such as *alumni* and *alumnae*. In the extreme Kormakiti form, even though the borrowed Greek morphology is largely confined to Greek loanwords, it does not seem reasonable to view Kormakiti Arabic as a whole as a changed later form of Arabic: too many of its structures, including numerous syntactic patterns used with Arabic lexicon, are borrowed from Greek, and the original Arabic-origin structure has simply disappeared.

Kormakiti Arabic resembles Ma'a in that all its grammatical subsystems are equally, and heavily, influenced by borrowing. In fact, it looks like an earlier stage in a process that could end in a Ma'a-like structure, with Greek morphology replacing Arabic morphology in Arabic words too. Since we lack historical documentation for Ma'a, we cannot tell whether Ma'a followed a route of development more like that of Kormakiti Arabic, where borrowed structure would at first have been confined to Bantu loanwords, or more like that of Asia Minor Greek, where borrowed Turkish structure is used with Greek words as well as with Turkish loanwords (though some features, e.g., vowel harmony, are more widely and consistently used with Turkish words).

These cases differ significantly from the Mednyj Aleut and Michif cases. The borrowed Mednyj Aleut finite verb morphology is similar, in the scope of borrowing, to borrowed Bantu verb morphology in Ma'a, and the wholesale takeover of French morphosyntax with borrowed French nouns in Michif is similar to the borrowed Greek component of Kormakiti Arabic. But the categorial specificity of the structural borrowing in these two languages—only verb structure in Mednyj Aleut, only noun phrases in Michif—sets these cases apart from the ones with a uniform level of borrowing in all grammatical subsystems. In our view, a uniform level of borrowing is the norm; certainly it is so in more ordinary cases of contact-induced language change. So Mednyj Aleut and Michif are odd, even in the company of other highly unusual products of intense contact. In chapter 9 we offer guesses at possible linguistic causes of these odd results: borrowed verb morphology in Mednyj Aleut because Russians who learned Aleut found the even more elaborate Aleut verb morphology beyond them (in which case the result has to do with imperfect learning as well as with borrowing); borrowed noun phrases in Michif because foreign noun phrases were fairly easy to fit into the verb-centered Cree sentences.

We can find only one social factor that distinguishes the two sets of cases: Ma'a, Asia Minor Greek, and Kormakiti Arabic have all developed through centuries of intense contact involving very extensive bilingualism and strong pressure to shift to the dominant language. Michif and Mednyj Aleut speakers are (or were) also bilingual—otherwise they could not have borrowed complete grammatical subsystems—but in these two cases the length of time was shorter than in the others, and there does not seem to have been any strong pressure on either group to shift to the dominant language. (We should add that we have little sociolinguistic information about either situation, so that we do not know to what extent Michif and Mednyj Aleut are fully crystallized languages with some stability over time. Commentary on Michif indicates that some speakers, at least, do have strong views about how Michif should be spoken, and that it is in fact learned as a language by its speakers. We would like to know more about the social contexts of both cases.)

But whatever factors may account for their varying histories, Ma'a, Kormakiti Arabic, Michif, Mednyj Aleut, and a few dialects of Asia Minor Greek all arose, in our view, through a process of abnormal transmission. Even though they all retain some grammatical structures inherited from their original ethnic languages (though only very few in Ma'a), they share the historical feature of interrupted transmission with speech forms like AngloRomani. Their grammars and lexicons (especially basic vocabulary), as whole entities, are not primarily derived from a single historical source.

Their potential value for comparative reconstruction varies, however. AngloRomani is worthless for reconstructing Proto-Romani structure; structural features of Ma'a can be used for comparative reconstruction of Proto-Southern Cushitic only with the greatest caution, and with constant attention to the necessity of considering the structures in light of Bantu as well as Cushitic structure. But the Arabic, Cree, and Aleut portions of the grammars of Kormakiti Arabic (at least its morphology), Michif, and Mednyj Aleut may be usable—with due caution—for purposes of reconstruction (see chap. 8 for further discussion of this point).

The development of these languages, then, was nongenetic. They share this feature with abrupt creoles (chap. 6) and nativized pidgins (chap. 7). But they differ from these better-known kinds of mixed languages in an important respect. Abrupt creoles and pidgins almost always arise in multilingual settings in which no linguistic group achieves full bilingualism in the language of any other. As a result, no large part of their grammar (as opposed to their lexicon) is derived intact from any single language. But the languages discussed in this section all arose in two-language contact situations with full one-way bilingualism, and their grammars reflect this fact. The most noticeable linguistic difference is that these languages, unlike pidgins and creoles, have elaborate morphological systems. (This is not, of course, a necessary result; it would not occur in a mixture of two isolating languages.) The fact that particular structures can be traced to particular source languages also has an important retrospective consequence: given a total lack of sociohistorical information, it should be easier to discover the route by which a language like Ma'a developed than to unravel the history of, say, Saramaccan.

5
Language Shift with Normal Transmission

The Sauromatae speak the language of
Scythia, but have never talked it correctly,
because the Amazons learned it imperfectly
at the first.
—Herodotus, *The Persian Wars,*
Book IV, chapter 117.

5.1. PROBLEMS IN DEMONSTRATING INTERFERENCE THROUGH SHIFT

Herodotus' linguistic observation about a community established by a group of Scythian men and their Amazon wives was written in the fifth century B.C.; it is the oldest mention of contact-induced language change known to us. It also points indirectly to the major difficulty besetting the study of linguistic interference that comes about through language shift: solid, well-documented historical examples are hard to find. Herodotus' case is, to be sure, an extreme instance of the problem; although the Scythians are believed by Iranian specialists to be the linguistic ancestors of the Middle Iranian

Sakas, whose language is reasonably well documented, we don't even know what language the Amazons (assuming they even existed as a people) spoke originally, much less what it was like structurally. So Herodotus' report is worthless for an investigation of the linguistic phenomenon, except perhaps as an indication that he (unlike some modern linguists) was aware of the potential effect of a group's imperfect learning on the structure of a language.

The problem arises primarily from the fact that a completed language shift results in the disappearance of the shifting group's original language from the community. Unless that language is still spoken in some other area(s), or its structure is known from historical documents or by inference from related languages, we cannot study its possible effects on the language that replaced it. A similar problem arises in those cases where, although the abandoned language is well known, we cannot establish that any changes have occurred in the target language, because there is no information about what its structure was like before the shift. These are cases in which we have no historical documentation and no close relatives of the target language available for study, so we can at most establish typological similarities between the two languages (except, of course, when actual morphemes from the shifting group's original language have been acquired by the target language). The worst cases are those in which we have no structural information either about the abandoned language or about the target language before the shift. These all-too-common situations impose strict methodological limitations on the study of interference through shift: in order to make educated guesses in this area, we must be able to identify a substratum language or language group (some of) whose speakers shifted to the target language at the relevant time period; we must have information about its structure; and we must have information about the structure of the target language before the shift.[1]

These methodological prerequisites have frequently been ignored by substratum enthusiasts, and this fact probably accounts in large part for the widespread suspicion with which historical linguists tend to view substratum explanations of language change. It is possible, for instance, that Celtic languages of the British Isles owe their un-Indo-European-like system of initial-consonant lenition, and other features too, to a pre-Indo-European substratum; but since we have no information about what language(s) the pre-IE inhabitants spoke, we cannot establish such a cause for these changes (even if we were to agree that an external explanation is needed). All the hypotheses that have been advanced about such a substratum, for instance some Berber language (cf., e.g., Wagner 1959, Adams 1975), rest on such tenuous historical and linguistic evidence that the chances for a convincing proposal in this area seem remote. And an argument that the changes must be due to substratum interference because they cannot have arisen "naturally" from internal causes is circular, at the present stage of our knowledge: for the vast majority of attested changes there is no established cause or route of development, so claims about what is and is not possible are at best premature.

In other cases, the relative timing of the shift and the proposed resultant substratum changes is off. This is the difficulty with the "mystical" (thus Bloomfield, 1933:386) explanation involving Celtic substratum influence on changes in Germanic or Romance languages that occurred hundreds of years after all the speakers of Continental Celtic had shifted to Germanic, or to Vulgar Latin or incipient Romance. (One such change, the lenition of postvocalic [p t k] to [b d g], occurred in both Brythonic and western Romance at about the same time—maybe ca. A.D. 600—so that the language of origin of the trait is hard to determine. In any case, it is not an old trait in Celtic.)

It is also easy to find examples of cases in which too little is known about the structure of the target language before the shift to make definite statements about the linguistic effects of the shift. In India, for instance, investigation of possible 'indianization' of Munda languages (as in, e.g., Snyder 1984)—via shift or borrowing, or both—is greatly hampered by lack of knowledge about the structure of proto-Munda (and of the language from which it descended, Proto-Austro-Asiatic). (Of course, in this instance we can confidently expect eventual progress in the reconstruction of the proto-language, so that investigations of possible contact-induced changes in Munda will be feasible in the future.) Another example is Jacobsen's discussion (1966) of changes in Washo that were apparently motivated by contact with Uto-Aztecan. The situation Jacobsen describes suggests that any Uto-Aztecan interference in Washo came about through language shift, since Washo has few loanwords from Uto-Aztecan languages. But the claim that Washo has changed, e.g., in acquiring a new phoneme /ɨ/, rests on comparison of Washo with other Hokan languages; and if, as Campbell and Mithun observe (1979:42–43),

Hokan is not firmly established as a genetic grouping, then in fact there is no evidence that Pre-Washo lacked /i/.

We do not mean to imply that the difficulties with demonstrating interference through shift do not arise in borrowing situations as well. They do. The Bolivian language Chipaya is a case in point: it is surrounded by Aymara and has clearly been losing ground to it for centuries. Chipaya has adopted large numbers of Aymara loanwords, and its structure, e.g., certain morphological processes involving suffixation, strongly suggests that there has been borrowing interference in its grammar. In particular, Chipaya has apparently borrowed a plural suffix -naka from Aymara; this suffix is used in Chipaya with both nouns and pronouns. However, we do not know what Chipaya was like before it came under Aymara influence, so we cannot say with confidence that it has **changed** in the direction of Aymara except with such borrowed morphemes. (We do at least know that Chipaya cannot be shown to be genetically related to Aymara, and that it is typologically very similar to Aymara in a number of respects. But typological similarity is not enough to prove diffusion. Proposals have been made about wider genetic affiliations of Chipaya, especially with Mayan, but none of them is generally accepted by specialists.)

Nevertheless, though claims of structural borrowing are also hard to establish sometimes, they are in general easier to argue for than claims of interference through shift, for two main reasons. First, a borrowing situation is one in which both the source language and the receiving language are maintained, at least for a considerable period of time. And second, structural borrowing is invariably preceded by lexical borrowing. So it is more likely in borrowing instances that the source language or language group will be identifiable from the loanwords, and therefore that information about the structure of that language will be available. The problem of discovering what the borrowing language was like before it borrowed remains, but this problem will usually arise only with languages which, like Chipaya, have no known close relatives. (This situation is, however, quite common in the New World, where there are many more unaffiliated languages than in the Old World.)

Shift and borrowing situations also differ in the extent to which we can safely draw inferences from linguistic structure about a past contact situation. If two languages are known to have been in contact in the past, the presence of noninherited universally marked features in one of them may (given appropriate structural conditions) provide good evidence of interference from the other. If the interfered-with language has adopted few or no words from the source language, then the mechanism of the structural interference must have been shift; if many words have been adopted, the mechanism was probably either borrowing alone or a combination of shift and borrowing. But, as we argued in 3.2, marked features are more likely to be transferred in borrowing than in shift. If we are looking for interference in a long-past contact situation for which only limited sociohistorical and linguistic information is available, we are therefore more likely to find it if the mechanism was borrowing. Light to moderate interference through shift, since it more often results in grammatical simplification, will be harder to distinguish from simplificatory internally motivated changes.

So, for instance, the addition of new cases in the declensional systems of Russian and Lithuanian provides good evidence of Uralic substratum interference (since there are few Uralic loanwords in these languages; see below and 9.5 for discussion). Even a simplificatory change like the loss of grammatical gender in the Livlandish dialect of Latvian can easily be established as an interference feature if we also have non-simplificatory changes from the same source, e.g., the so-called relative (inferential) mood and the nominative object, also from the Uralic language Livonian (Comrie 1981*b*:152, 154).

But if all the candidates for interference features are simplificatory, such as the loss of gender in rural Brazilian Portuguese, it is harder to establish substratum influence (*pace* da Silveiro Bueno 1963)—in this case from Tupí and Guaraní—because these changes may well have developed either independently through internal means or through other external influences, e.g., from a Portuguese-based creole (see Holm, forthcoming, for a fuller discussion of the history of Brazilian Portuguese). Or, of course, the changes could have been caused by a combination of internal and a variety of congruent external factors. Since, especially in an ancient case of light to moderate interference through shift, some formerly present interference features are likely to have been lost or obscured through later changes, a remaining handful of simplificatory changes may be too insubstantial to support a claim of shift-induced change.

An added difficulty is that, while borrowed morphosyntactic structures are more often expressed by actual borrowed morphemes, morphosyntactic interference through shift more often makes use of reinterpreted and/or restructured TL morphemes.[2] These tendencies are too weak to have predictive value, but they are strong enough to make it harder, in retrospect, to detect past interference through shift. The new Uralic-influenced cases in Russian and Lithuanian, for instance, are expressed by inherited Russian and Lithuanian morphemes, developed from suffixes taken from a vanishing noun class and from postpositions, respectively; similarly, the Indic quotative *iti* is a native morpheme, though its use to mark direct quotations is usually attributed to Dravidian substratum interference. For restructuring of native morphemes, an argument can almost always be made for an internal motivation, although the weight of the evidence is on the side of substratum influence as soon as we can point to several unrelated features from the same source language. But no one will try to argue for an internally motivated change from agglutinative to flexional finite verb morphology in Mednyj Aleut when all the suffixes are of Russian origin, or for internal causation in the change from flexional suffixes to agglutinative prefixes in Ma'a verbs when all the prefixes are borrowed from Bantu.

All these factors, historical and linguistic, no doubt contribute to the fact that we have found more good cases of moderate to heavy structural interference in borrowing than in shift situations. For several promising shift situations we have only isolated examples of structural transfer. Of the solid cases we have found, some are accompanied by little lexical transfer, e.g., Uralic interference in Baltic and Slavic, and older Dravidian interference in Indic. Others, notably Cushitic interference in Ethiopic Semitic, show such extensive adoption of words from the source languages (Leslau 1945:79–81) that borrowing and shift interference must have been occurring simultaneously.

5.2. SOME LINGUISTIC RESULTS OF SHIFT

5.2.1. PRELIMINARY REMARKS

In this section we will discuss and exemplify results of interference in different kinds of shift situations, following the outline in the shift column of table 3 (3.2), above the double line. Before we begin, though, some general remarks are in order.

First, there is the matter of terminology. So far we have mainly used the socially neutral but cumbersome phrase "interference through shift" to cover the phenomena known as substratum, superstratum, and adstratum interference. The trouble is that different authors define these terms, often implicitly, in different ways. Compare, for instance, the Russian translation of the entry for "substratum" in Marouzeau's dictionary of linguistic terms (1960:302) with the Russian editor's note, and see also the discussion in Vildomec (1971:116). The examples given by various authors, however, seem to fit best within a framework of relative social and political status: superstratum languages are typically those of victorious invaders who then shift to the language of the conquered people; substratum languages are those of conquered, or at least sociopolitically subordinate, indigenous populations and immigrants; and adstratum languages are those of invaded or invader groups that are neither dominant nor subordinate in the contact situation. In addition, some linguists seem to reserve the term 'adstratum' for situations in which the (nondominant, nonsubordinate) shifting speakers constitute only a part of the speech community of the language they are shifting from, so that some parts of that speech community maintain their original language. In particular, adstratum interference is often claimed in cases of Sprachbund, though sometimes (and thus inappropriately) without evidence that any shift has occurred.

Only one significant linguistic consequence seems to depend on the substratum/adstratum/superstratum distinction: superstratum interference is more likely to include lexical items than substratum interference is.[3] The masses of French loanwords in English, for instance, would indicate that shifting French speakers constituted a superstratum even if we had no sociohistorical information at all beyond the fact of the shift. This conclusion would be strengthened by certain semantic domains in which French words cluster, such as the language of the law. Similarly, the lack of many old Dravidian loanwords in Indic, or of old Uralic loanwords in Slavic, indicates that shifting Dravidian and Uralic speakers were not sociopolitically dominant over their respective groups of Indo-European invaders.

Caution is required when we draw such conclusions, however, because here too complications arise from a variety of sociohistorical factors. According to Fowkes (1973:195, in a review of Ternes 1970), both the Breton and the non-Breton speakers of Ile de Groix, France, think that Breton is "no earthly good," suggesting that any Breton interference in the local French would be substratum interference. But, says Fowkes, the local French is "markedly affected by Breton in its phonology, morphology, syntax, and lexicon, even when the speaker does not actually know Breton—which, in general, is spoken fluently by only the oldest inhabitants." Fowkes gives no examples, so we cannot tell what semantic domains the loanwords occur in. They would have to be examined before an interpretation according to the model we offer would be possible. Nevertheless, this is a case in which a language that is now a substratum language has apparently contributed numerous loanwords to the target language.

For many past instances of shift there is even less social information for the period in which the shift occurred. Although Lorimer (1937) does not present examples, the structural features contributed by shifting Burushaski speakers to the Indic (specifically Dardic; cf. Emeneau 1980 [1965]:143) language Shina were apparently accompanied by numerous loanwords. In discussing the two main castes into which Shina speakers are now divided, Lorimer (1937:69) says that one caste claims social superiority, while the other claims that it "formerly supplied the ruling family" in the region of Gilgit in the Karakoram (a mountainous section of present-day northern Pakistan). If, as Lorimer seems to be suggesting, the former caste represents the invading Shina population and the latter derives from the indigenous population that once spoke Burushaski, a simple identification of shifting Burushaski speakers as either socially subordinate or socially dominant is obviously not justified. The same might be said, though the evidence is exclusively linguistic, of the Cushitic speakers who shifted to Ethiopic Semitic, since Leslau (1945:79–81) cites numerous Cushitic loanwords in semantic domains that include (among others) animals, vegetation, tools, body parts, numerals, kin terms, and astronomical terms. Only the first three of these categories are typical for vocabulary contributed by indigenous substrata.

Such cases indicate that we can be confident about only one retrospective generalization in this area: if the language of a shifting population did **not** contribute lexicon to the target language, other than a few words for local natural and cultural items, then we can conclude that the shifting population did not enjoy much social or political prestige. ("Prestige" is a trait recognized by the fact that people behave as if they thought it was either **useful** or **necessary** to have some of it, i.e., by imitation.) This may mean, though it need not mean, that the shifting group was a true substratum, i.e., socially and politically subordinate. It should also be noted that when a shifting group is prestigious to some extent, as with the superstrate French in England or, apparently, Burushaski in Gilgit, words are likely to be borrowed by speakers of the target language in addition to being introduced by the shifting population.

All this means, in our opinion, that the traditional superstratum/adstratum/substratum distinction is of limited usefulness for the interpretation of most past shift situations. We will continue to use the terms in the following sections, especially in clear cases, i.e., for an invading superstratum or for an indigenous substratum that contributed few or no loanwords to the target language. But we will in general avoid the term 'adstratum', since its linguistic effects are not obviously distinguishable from those of superstrata and substrata. Since some languages traditionally called substrata were no doubt adstrata, judged on the criterion of relative social status of their speakers, the terminology in this area is, necessarily, historically imprecise. (We ignore the even more obvious difficulty that "relative social status" is hopelessly inadequate as a sociolinguistic criterion; we know of no way to improve on it for the kinds of past contact situations we are focussing on.)

Aside from the terminology, one other general point must be mentioned before we begin our survey of results of interference through shift. As we mentioned in chapter 3, it has frequently been claimed that syntax is relatively impervious to external influence. Mühlhäusler (1980:36), for instance, considers syntax (along with morphology) to be "relatively independent of substratum or superstratum influences." Similarly, Polomé views interference through shift as "limited essentially to phonology and the lexicon" (1980:192). We have seen no explicit justification of this widespread view, but we suspect that it arises from a belief that—as Nadkarni (1975:673) implies—syntax is in some way the "deepest" level of the grammar. While there may be some aspects of a language's syntax which, because of internal structural cohesion, are especially resistant to foreign interference, the evidence we have collected indicates that syntactic interference is as common as phonological interference. In particular, the statistical links among various word order features are easily broken by interference through shift (though subsequent changes, both internally and externally motivated, may of course reestablish statistically predicted "harmonious" patterns). We will exemplify such syntactic changes, and others too, in the following sections.

It is nevertheless true that examples of phonological interference are easier to find in the literature than examples of syntactic interference. There is, we believe, one major reason for this discrepancy. In every language family, more is known about sound change than about any other kind of structural change; therefore, theories of sound change are much more fully worked out, and the methodology in this area is more reliable. So it is easier to demonstrate past interference in this structural subsystem than in others. Still, the best-documented case studies—notably Uralic influence on some Baltic and Slavic languages, Cushitic influence on Ethiopic Semitic, Dravidian influence on Indic, and Burushaski influence on Shina—show comparable amounts of structural interference in phonology and syntax. The only class of exceptions we have found are cases in which educated speakers shift to, or use as a second language, a major international literary language such as English. In such cases we occasionally find, as in India, a local variety of the international language that is phonologically, but not necessarily morphosyntactically, influenced by the indigenous substratum.

5.2.2. Shift Without Interference

Many processes of language shift leave no linguistic traces in the target language (TL) as a whole, or even in an isolated part of the TL speech community. As we observed in chapter 3.2, there seem to be two main circumstances that are likely to produce this result: a small shifting group relative to the numbers of TL speakers, and a slow shift, i.e., one that takes at least several generations to complete. These are not absolute predictions, however; exceptions can be found. Even a small shifting group can contribute structural features to a TL if the shifting speakers are a superstratum, although (as we will argue in 5.2.3, and in 9.8) in such cases nonlexical interference is likely to be slight.

The timing of the shift is relevant to the extent that it correlates with the level of command of the TL. If an entire large population shifts to the language of a much smaller group of conquering invaders over one or two generations, the shifting speakers are unlikely to be fully bilingual in the TL before they abandon their native language, so we can expect to find extensive substratum interference in the TL. But if, before they shift to the invaders' language, the substrate population first becomes fully bilingual ("accent-free") during a long period of constant contact with TL speakers, then substratum inter- ference is not a probability. Sometimes, however, exceptions are found in the latter category; for example, the Breton-to- French shift mentioned in 5.2.1 has been taking place over many generations, and yet has resulted in extensive interference in the TL. Exceptions prob- ably won't be found in the other category, though: we do not believe that a very rapid shift by a large population, in a new contact situa- tion, could fail to alter the TL. In other words, full access to native TL speakers during the shift process is a necessary condition for achieving full bilingualism, but it is not a sufficient one. The relative sizes of the shifting and TL speaker groups therefore offer a more reliable criter- ion for predicting whether or not structural interference will occur.

One of the most typical cases of shift without interference is that of urban immigrant groups of European origin in the United States. Many of these groups maintain their own languages for some time, but when the original immigrants' children or grandchildren shift to English, there is usually no carryover from the original languages into the English of the community as a whole. Rayfield (1970:101), for instance, describes the linguistic assimilation of Yiddish-speaking immigrants in the following way:

> Interference is strong in the English speech of the first-generation Jewish immigrants. Their children use an occasional Yiddish idiom and perhaps retain a trace of Yiddish intonation. Their grandchil- dren speak American English as native speakers.

That is, the grandchildren speak English with no hint of Yiddish interference, beyond a few loanwords.

In some cases, however, some structural features of the original language may remain in the speech of an ethnic group. The probabil- ity of this sort of localized interference is a function of the group's cohesion and isolation from other sections of the community. Not surprisingly, examples are easiest to find among immigrant groups that settled originally in rural areas.

Shift by a very small superstrate immigrant group will probably have the same structural results as shift by a small substrate immigrant group, though superstrate immigrants are of course more likely to contribute numerous loanwords to the TL. An example is the shift by conquering Germanic-speaking invaders to the medieval Romance languages (or dialects) of southern France and Spain. In these areas the conquerors quickly abandoned their native Germanic languages (Gothic and Burgundian) but Germanic influence on the Romance target languages was confined to loanwords, especially military terms and the like. This contrasts with the case of Frankish in northern France, where the Germanic-speaking presence was larger and lasted longer. The linguistic results of this situation are much disputed, but it seems clear that they included at least some minor structural interference from Frankish on northern Gallo-Romance (i.e., French) (see 5.2.3 for discussion).

As for indigenous populations that shift to the languages of invaders, here too cases of shift without interference can be found. North American Indian languages, whose speakers were overwhelmed numerically as well as militarily by English speakers, left only minor lexical traces in English when their speakers shifted to English. There are some groups, notably the Navaho, that are reported to speak varieties of English influenced structurally by the native language, but on many reservations most Indians are native speakers of the variety of English spoken by their non-Indian neighbors.

5.2.3. SLIGHT INTERFERENCE

In cases of language shift, the continuum between slight interference and moderate to heavy interference has no sharp dividing lines. Slight interference will include phonological and syntactic features; moderate to heavy interference will have more examples of these and, in addition, some interference in the inflectional morphology. (Derivational morphology is, we believe, more likely to accompany lexical interference and possibly syntactic interference.) We have found relatively few examples in the literature of interference in lexical semantics (except in abrupt creoles; see chap. 6), but we would expect this subsystem to pattern with phonology and syntax rather than with inflectional morphology. The reason is that the inflectional morphology owes its special position to its relatively high degree of structural cohesion, and the lexicon has a less closed internal structure than the various inflectional systems of a morphologically complex language.

We should emphasize the impossibility of making specific predictions about the outcome of interference, even in comparable shift situations. When, in different cases, the respective source-language structures and target-language structures match closely, we still find different linguistic results. Several cases in which Uralic speakers shifted to Baltic or Slavic languages present an interesting set of contrasting prosodic interference features. Uralic languages, including Livonian, Hungarian, and Karelian, have fixed word-initial stress; Balto-Slavic languages inherited phonemic accent (either pitch or stress, or a combination of the two). Interference from Livonian, whose speakers shifted to the Baltic language Latvian, has led to a pattern of fixed initial stress in Latvian (Comrie 1981*b*:149). We discussed in chapter 3.3 the case of a Serbocroatian dialect in which shifting Hungarian speakers innovated a pattern of fixed penultimate stress, which then spread to the entire dialect. And finally, Karelian substratum influence on certain Russian dialects of the Olonets region has led to a system in which, though stress is still phonemic, all original word-final stresses have moved to the first syllable of the word (Jakobson 1962 [1938]:239). Now, it may be that Livonian exerted more overall influence on Latvian than did Hungarian and Karelian on the two Slavic languages, and this may account for the precise match between the Livonian and the new Latvian stress rules. Certainly Livonian interference in Latvian, to judge by Comrie's examples, is extensive. But we have too little information about the other two cases to make such a judgment, and we also have no indication that Hungarian influence on the Serbocroatian dialect differed in intensity from Karelian influence on the Russian dialects. In any case, even with much fuller social information we would not expect to be able to predict the extent and precise types of influence in such cases.

If we are right about the importance of the relative sizes of the two groups of speakers for predicting the extent of interference through shift, then we would not expect to find much structural interference in simple cases of superstratum shift. When the size of a superstratum group, especially a group of conquering invaders, approaches a large fraction of the entire community—say, a third—then surely a shift to the substrate language is rather unlikely. In fact, we know of no clear case in which a relatively large invader group has shifted to the language of the indigenous population. But if a shifting superstrate group is quite small in comparison to the subordinate population, then it seems relatively unlikely that many of their learners' errors, no matter how prestigious, will eventually be imitated by the entire TL speech community. Moreover, in such a case the shifting speakers are likely to have all the access they need to native speakers of the TL, even from near birth; so, even in the absence of a strong motivation to achieve perfect control of the TL, their learners' errors will probably be limited in influence.

This prediction about the probable extent of superstratum interference must remain tentative, because we have found very few clear instances of pure superstratum shift. In most successful invasions that have led to shift with interference, it is the language of the invaders that survives, not the language(s) of the newly subordinate population: this was the case with the Russians in formerly Uralic-speaking territory, Indic speakers in northern India, the Shina in (apparently) former Burushaski territory, and Semitic speakers in parts of Ethiopia. There are, of course, well-known cases of conquerors being absorbed linguistically, but very few of these involve languages that are well enough documented to permit the study of possible structural interference. There are also complicated cases in which the invaders may not have constituted a clear superstratum; as mentioned above, the Burushaski and the Cushitic speakers in Ethiopia may not have been subordinate to the invading Shina and Semitic speakers, respectively. Of the relatively simple cases, the ones that have received the most attention are the Frankish (Germanic) shift to Romance in northern Gaul and the Norman French shift to English in England.

The latter case, in particular, has given rise to claims of extreme superstratum interference. Several authors (Domingue 1975, Bailey and Maroldt 1977) have claimed that English was creolized under French influence. (These three authors also consider Norse influence in their proposals that English has been creolized; we discuss both contact situations in detail in chapter 9.8. Note also that Bailey views every case of significant structural interference as creolization, whereas we draw a line between ordinary interference and interference so extreme as to disrupt genetic continuity.) All these authors, and others as well, consider French superstratum influence on English to be extensive. In terms of relative speaker numbers, the case of French in England would not have been promising (in our view) for extensive structural interference through shift: at any time between 1066 and 1250, out of a total population of perhaps one and a half to two million, there were probably never more than 50,000 native French speakers in England. And, in fact, though French lexical influence on English was very heavy—and somewhat more so in Southern dialects than in the Midland dialects on which modern Standard English is based—the lexical influence was rather light in the basic vocabulary, amounting only to about 7 percent.

Demonstrable structural interference from French does exist, but it is not at all extensive. Some derivational affixes have been abstracted from French loanwords and added to stems of Germanic origin. Phonological interference features are few: the formerly allophonic distinction between [f] and [v] was phonemicized in Middle English when French loanwords with initial Old French /f/ and /v/ retained their distinctive pronunciations; the formerly allophonic distinction between [i̯] and [ǰ] was similarly phonemicized when initial Old French /ǰ/ kept its obstruent pronunciation in French loanwords; and a new diphthong, phonemically /ui/, was added to the system (see Thomason and Kaufman 1976 for a fuller discussion of these features). Significantly, French influence generally anticipated or reinforced internal processes that might have led to the same phonological results even without the French loanwords. Most notably, two internal English sound changes, the loss of word-final schwa and the degemination of medial C_1C_1 clusters, helped to erode the allophonic voiced/voiceless alternation in fricatives. And French loanwords did not introduce any new phones at all into English.

A few other phonological changes have sometimes been claimed as simplificatory and thus due to the disruptive influence of the French superstratum. One such change, the centralization of unstressed vowels to schwa, was completed by the middle of the eleventh century (see, e.g., Moore 1928:238–266 and A. Campbell 1959:161), too early for the Norman Conquest of 1066 to have affected its progress. Another, the merger of /ü/ and /i/ through the unrounding of /ü/, began as early as the ninth century in some parts of West Saxon territory, too early for French influence, and much later in the rest of southern England (1350–1400), too late for French influence to be relevant. Moreover, since French had a phoneme /ü/ as well as /i/, this merger is hardly a likely candidate for interference through shift.

Only one phonological innovation that is clearly both non-simplificatory and not in line with internal developmental tendencies can be ascribed to French influence. This is the so-called Romance stress rule (Chomsky and Halle 1968). But even if this is a genuine phonological rule of English (and its status continues to be disputed), it is confined to words of Latin and French origin. For the historical linguist concerned with problems of genetic relationship and linguistic reconstruction, phonological (or morphological) features that appear only in nonbasic vocabulary of demonstrably foreign origin are of limited interest. The extent to which loanwords are assimilated to the native phonology is of course an important issue, but even numerous unassimilated loanwords represent the most superficial type of structural interference as long as their foreign phonological features fail to spread to the native vocabulary.

The morphosyntactic evidence is harder to evaluate, though here too some proposals for French interference are anachronistic and others relatively superficial. Some linguists believe that French influence contributed to the development of exclusive SVO word order, which replaced an Old English system that included optional clause-final finite verbs in dependent clauses.[4] This influence would be roughly equivalent in degree to the phonemicization of former allophonic variants.

Other morphosyntactic claims are more dubious. The replacement of grammatical gender by natural gender in third person pronoun reference had already occurred by 950 throughout England, and reassignment of gender to nouns on this principle was well under way by 1066. Since French had (and has) a well-established system of grammatical gender, its influence is not likely to have contributed to the loss of grammatical gender in English, unless, as has been claimed, the normal transmission of English as a whole was so greatly threatened or disrupted by the Norman Conquest that the wholesale simplification typical of language death resulted. But such a scenario seems very improbable in view of the fact that no suppression of spoken English or influx of numerically overwhelming invaders occurred in the wake of the Conquest. A comparison of the English situation with well-documented cases of language death—where the few speakers of the dying language are, typically, bilingual in the dominant language—shows how far England was, in 1066–1250, from the conditions necessary for such extensive loss of structure. Comparisons between the situation in England and the development of early-creolized creoles or pidgins seem equally farfetched: English speakers in England never lacked a common means of communication, so they had no reason to develop a pidgin or creole; and modern

English can hardly be considered a French-based creole (as Bailey and Maroldt 1977 suggest) when the basic vocabulary is still mainly English.

Similarly, simplifications in nominal and verbal inflection do not appear to have been influenced by the French superstratum. The degrees of simplification in various Midland and Southern English dialects at relevant periods do not correlate with the degrees of French lexical influence: lexical influence from French was greatest in the South, but the inflectional simplifications in English occurred earliest in the North, and next in the Midlands. In the South, in fact, the late Old English (OE) nominal inflectional systems remained largely intact until 1250 and, in some areas, until at least 1350. And except in the North, English verbal inflection underwent no simplification at all until after 1350. Since French speakers had all shifted to English by about 1265–and since the process of shift must have begun much earlier—the shift was too late to have had a strong effect on inflectional simplifications. (French was, of course, maintained for some time in England for various official and cultural purposes, but not as any large group's native language.)

In this context it should be noted, finally, that inflectional simplification in some or all morphological subsystems is characteristic of the histories of all modern Indo-European languages. Establishing a positive French influence on these processes in English would therefore require showing isomorphism between specific French and Middle English structures. This cannot be done; to see what such a demonstration would be like, compare the clear instances of morphosyntactic interference through shift cited in the following sections of this chapter. Aside from the word order change mentioned above, we know of only one type of minor syntactic change that can be ascribed to French influence, namely, the choice of particular prepositions in certain constructions (e.g., *of* in geographical expressions like *the city of London*).

The case of the Franks in northern France is even more controversial than that of the Normans in England, and it is complicated by the fact that the structure of northern Gallo-Romance before the Franks arrived in 486 is not well known. From what is known of the two sociolinguistic situations, Frankish seems to have been in a better position to influence its TL. We have seen no estimates of the sizes of the two speaker groups in the territory conquered by the Franks, but the period before the superstratum shift was completed was longer in northern France than in England: 486–ca. 850 vs. 1066–ca. 1250 (Berndt 1965). In addition, the Frankish conquerors were not the only Germanic speakers who shifted to northern Gallo-Romance during that period. There was also a sizable minority of Frankish-speaking free peasants who immigrated to northern France and maintained their Frankish for several centuries before shifting to Romance (Wartburg 1969:67). This is therefore not a simple case of superstratum shift. It seems reasonable to suppose that the linguistic separation of French and Provençal owes its existence to the Frankish settlement in Gaul, since that settlement area, as observed mainly from place names, is practically identical with the linguistic zone of northern Gallo-Romance, the precursor of French.

Unfortunately, however, very few undisputed structural interference features from Frankish can be found in French, though the presence of numerous Frankish loanwords is obvious. The best phonological candidates are, like the putative Romance stress rule in English, largely confined to loanwords. Romance languages in general lack both /h/ and (at least word-initially) /w/, since Latin /h/ > Ø, and Classical Latin /w/ > [v] or [β] already in Late Latin. But medieval French had—and modern French dialects of Picardy, Wallonia, and Normandy still have—word-initial /h/ in Germanic loanwords. Similarly, /w/ appears word-initially in medieval and modern French dialects in Picardy, Wallonia, and Lorraine. In other French dialects, this [w] was strengthened to [gw] and then simplified to [g]. A few Romance words, moreover, acquired /h/ and /w/ through Frankish influence: Old French (OF) *halt* 'high' ← Vulgar Latin (VL) *altus* (influenced by Frankish *hôh* 'high'); OF *waste* 'waste' ← VL *vastus* (influenced by Frankish *wōsti* 'waste'); and OF *waïne* 'sheath' ← VL *vagina*.

Another phonological feature that is often claimed as a Frankish superstrate interference feature is the weakening and/or loss of certain unstressed vowels and the lengthening and diphthongization of stressed vowels. Although heavy word stress is characteristic of both Germanic and Romance languages (and French lost distinctive stress relatively late), it is only in Germanic languages and in those Romance languages with significant Germanic superstrata that diphthongization of certain stressed vowels and dropping of unstressed vowels occur. The relevant Romance languages are French, Rhaeto-Romance, and northern Italian dialects.

Two French syntactic features that are sometimes claimed to be due to Germanic influence also look promising as candidates, since both are present in Germanic, directly attested in French, and not inherited by French from Latin. First, Old French had an obligatory verb-second rule in prose, and such a rule is unknown elsewhere in Romance. The placement of other sentence constituents was relatively free, so that we find sentences like *les deniers prendrons nos* 'we will take the money' (literally 'the-PLU money-PLU take-FUT-we we') and *biaus estoit et gens* 'he was handsome and kind' (literally 'handsome was-he and kind') (Wartburg 1969:66, 103). Modern Standard French has replaced this rule with an SVO word order pattern. The second feature is the use of 'be' instead of 'have' as the perfect auxiliary with certain intransitive verbs of motion and change of state. Rumanian, Spanish, and Portuguese (as well as most Low German dialects!) use only 'have'; Italian follows the French pattern, but this feature, along with so much else in Italian, was undoubtedly borrowed from French, probably during the twelfth century (and possibly reinforced by Lombard influence in northern Italy).

Internal explanations have also been proposed for these and other features claimed to be of Germanic origin. It is of course possible that some or all of the changes arose through a combination of external and internal causes, but there seems to be no consensus among scholars on these points. As a result, the question of whether or not the Frankish superstratum, plus peasants, produced significant contact-induced changes in northern Gallo-Romance remains open (and attracts evaluations that often seem to be politically motivated). But if the two syntactic features discussed here do turn out to be due to Germanic interference, then this influence is more extensive than French morphosyntactic influence on Middle English.

As for slight interference from substrata, we have generally found only isolated examples reported in the literature—no comprehensive case studies. We can therefore only guess at the total amount of interference in these languages, though sometimes extensive interference can probably be ruled out.

One class of examples of this general type is found in the speech of people who, though isolated from the main TL speech community, have shifted to, or use as a second language, an established literary language. In some of these cases, especially where use of the TL is confined to educated people who write it regularly, interference is very slight or nonexistent in the morphosyntax but more extensive in the phonology. In fact, these are the only cases we have found in which significant phonological interference is not accompanied by morphosyntactic interference. The English spoken by Indians in India is a classic example, with Standard English syntax but phonological features like these: trilled /r/; uniform unaspirated pronunciation of voiceless stops; lack of a contrast between /v/ and /w/ (in some versions); and realization of English /θ ð/ as dental stops [t̪ʰ d̪], contrasting with the realization of English /t d/ as retroflex stops (Kelkar 1957, Pandit 1964:202–205). All these features, as well as certain characteristic intonation patterns, can be explained by reference to typological features common to most or all languages of India. In other cases, however, such as Irish English, we find considerable morphosyntactic and phonological interference, but little lexical interference (that is, the lexical borrowings of Irish Gaelic origin in Irish English are not really numerous, and were in many cases plausibly introduced into it by English speakers).

5.2.4. MODERATE TO HEAVY INTERFERENCE

In this section we will examine languages in which a number of structural interference features are to be attributed to the effects of language shift, but in which enough inherited grammatical patterns remain that genetic continuity has clearly not been disrupted. Sets of interference features in various grammatical subsystems fall into three different categories as far as their systematic effects are concerned.

First, there are simplificatory changes that result from the learners' failure to learn TL structures that are more complicated than functionally corresponding structures in the shifting speakers' original language. The clearest examples in this category are phonological changes involving phonemic mergers or replacement of more marked by less marked features, and morphological changes involving mergers of categories of their replacement by syntactic expressions. Most purely syntactic interference seems to involve simple replacements, neither simplificatory nor complicating; this is particularly true of word order changes, e.g., SOV to SVO or vice versa. It may well be that some apparently neutral syntactic replacements actually do lead to overall simplification or complication, but in almost every case we lack sufficient evidence to make judgments on this issue: not only is too little known about the syntactic structures of the languages involved, but syntactic theory has not progressed to a stage where it is possible to define "simpler" or "more complex" uncontroversially.

Phonological examples of simplificatory shift-induced changes are the development of fixed initial stress in Latvian under Livonian influence, and the merger of /l/ and /lʸ/ in Czech through German superstratum interference (Jakobson 1962 [1938]:240). Elimination of allophonic alternations probably also falls into this category. An example is the general pronunciation of all English voiceless stops as unaspirated, in the English of India (Pandit 1964) and the English of Papua New Guinea—and the hypercorrection, especially by highly educated women, to exclusively aspirated pronunciation in Papuan English, as in [stʰaːpʰ] 'stop' (Crowley 1983:182). Depending on one's view of naturalness, the devoicing of final obstruents in the English of some German and Czech immigrants in the United States (Winter 1973:144) may also be a simplificatory change. Examples of simplificatory morphological changes include the loss of gender in Latvian (Livonian influence), and the loss of the dual in Ethiopic Semitic (Cushitic influence).

The second category of changes includes those which, as far as we can tell, neither complicate nor simplify the system. The English interdental fricatives, for instance, are rather highly marked, but the Irish English "intensified dentals" (Sommerfelt 1960:323–324) that replace them do not look like less marked segments. The same is true of the glottalized emphatic consonants which, thanks to Cushitic influence, have replaced inherited pharyngealized emphatic consonants in Ethiopic Semitic.

In morphology, the replacement in Indic of typically Indo-European flexional case/number noun suffixes by agglutinative number + case suffix sequences, presumably under Dravidian influence (Emeneau 1964 [1956]), may belong in this category, though in general flexional morphology is more highly marked—because it is less easily segmentable—than agglutinative morphology. Another morphological example is the formation of noun plurals by reduplication of one of the root consonants in Ethiopic Semitic (under Cushitic influence), a process that replaces inherited Semitic plural formations in Semitic words in some of the languages (Leslau 1945, 1952; cf. Hetzron 1975:109).

Most shift-induced syntactic changes, as noted above, fall into this category. Examples are the changes in Ethiopic Semitic from VSO, Aux-Verb, Noun-Adjective (probably), and Head Noun-Relative Clause word orders with prepositions to SOV, Verb-Aux, Adjective Noun, and Relative Clause-Head Noun word orders with postpositions to match the patterns of the substrate Cushitic languages. (There are, however, variations in some of these patterns among the Ethiopic Semitic languages: some of the languages use combinations of prepositions + postpositions, a more complicated system than the inherited prepositional one; similarly, a few languages have variant NA and N-Rel orders in addition to the AN and Rel-N orders. See Leslau 1945, 1952 for discussion.) Other examples are the use in Indic of the quotative particle *iti* (Dravidian structural influence, though *iti* is of IE origin) and the optional use of the ablative case of verbal and temporal nouns to denote 'after' in Shina (Burushaski influence).

In the third category are changes that seem to complicate the TL grammar. Although, as we have argued, interference through shift is in general more likely to simplify the TL grammar than to complicate it (at least in cases of slight to moderate interference), we have more clear examples of complicating changes in the phonology and the morphology. We retain (at least for the present) our general prediction in the face of this counterevidence because we suspect that the preponderance of complicating changes is due to the greater difficulty of establishing interference as the cause of simplificatory changes (see above, 5.1, for discussion; see also Thomason 1986*b*). It is often harder to find plausible internal motivations for changes that complicate the grammar, so external explanations for them tend to be more readily accepted. The singulative suffix of Burushaski, for instance, is unusual enough typologically that the appearance of the structural feature in Shina, with identical patterning (though with a native Indic morpheme) and usage, is certainly due to Burushaski influence. A related morphosyntactic development in Shina, though more complex, also falls into this category: in Shina, as in Burushaski, the indefinite/interrogative pronoun takes a plural verb. In Burushaski, the pronoun itself, *mɛn*, is plural; the singulative suffix -ʌn must be added to make it singular. Now, Shina has inherited singular and plural forms for this pronoun, *ko* and *kɛ* respectively; nevertheless, *ko* is used with a plural verb, and the singulative suffix -ʊk is added to it to make it specifically singular (see Lorimer 1937 for discussion).

Here are a few more examples of complicating changes. In the

Ethiopic Semitic case, Cushitic influence has led to the development of labialized dorsal phonemes opposed to plain dorsals. The morpho-syntactic influence of Cushitic for the most part involves new means of expressing already existing functional categories; some of these, such as the negative perfect formation with a prefix-plus-suffix combination, result in minor morphological complications. Only one, the development in some Ethiopic Semitic languages of a future tense in opposition to the present, creates a new morphological category. The emergence of new morphological case distinctions seems to be a rather common complication that arises through shift interference. Examples occur in Russian and Lithuanian under Uralic influence. And in India several modern Indic languages, e.g., Marathi, have developed a negative conjugation whose formation (verb stem + NEG suffix + personal suffixes) is "startlingly like the Proto-Dravidian and general Dravidian negative conjugation type" (Emeneau 1962:56; cf. Southworth ms.).

When we turn from categorization of isolated examples of structural interference to a consideration of specific shift situations, we run into difficulties of interpretation almost immediately. There are, as we have already pointed out, few well-documented cases. Some of the cases for which adequate information is available, such as Irish English, are represented in the literature only by scattered examples, not by thorough case studies. Gaps in our knowledge of interference in a case like Irish English can be filled in rather easily; meanwhile, the interference features we do know about are common enough in interference through shift. Examples are the replacement of English /θ ð/ by "intensified" dental stops (Sommerfelt 1960:323–324); intonation patterns; the development of a recent past construction using 'after', as in *he's after singin'* 'he has just sung', corresponding to Gaelic *tá sé indhiaidh ceól a dheanamh* (literally 'BE he after music [a-] making') (Todd 1975:16); and the development of new aspect distinctions, including a habitual usage of *be* to match the usage of the cognate Irish Gaelic verb *bi* (Todd 1975:16, Sommerfelt 1960:322–323). Although some authors suggest that Irish English also has many loanwords and calques from Gaelic, the data we have indicates that lexical interference is actually relatively slight.

Other cases, too, look promising for further investigation. The stage was set for such a study of Khoisan influence on southern Bantu as early as 1846, when Horatio Hale made this observation about the sociolinguistic situation in southern Africa (1846:659):

> The [Hottentots] are said to have formerly occupied much of the country now in possession of the [Caffre tribes (i.e., Bantu)]. Isolated families and bands of them are still found by travellers in this region, and are supposed to be the remnants of the original population, of which the greater part has been either absorbed or driven southwards by the advancing hordes of Caffres.

A particularly striking interference feature from Khoisan, the presence of phonemic clicks, was observed in Zulu and other Nguni dialects of Bantu quite early (cf., e.g., Boas 1911:43–44; see also Campbell 1976, Louw 1962). However, Lickey (1985) found no evidence of other nonlexical interference features from Khoisan in Nguni, and she also notes that Khoisan/Nguni contacts were, and are, varied, so that both borrowing and shift-induced changes may have occurred. The explanation she proposes for structural interference in the phonology alone involves southern Bantu cultural patterns that promote phonological distortion—ideophones and, more importantly, **hlonipha**, a system of lexical avoidance (or taboo) that requires phonetic alteration of words that resemble a tabooed term.

Of the cases that have been more thoroughly investigated, almost every one is controversial in one way or another. An exception is the Ethiopic Semitic case, in which extensive Cushitic substratum interference is well established. The major studies of this case are Leslau's two articles (1945, 1952); some details of his analyses have been disputed (cf., e.g., Moreno 1948, Hetzron 1975), and further examples of Cushitic interference have been proposed (e.g., Little 1974, Hetzron 1975). A broader view of the Ethiopian Sprachbund, with lists of widely shared features but without historical discussion of how they spread, is provided by Ferguson (1976). Not all the Cushitic interference features occur in all of the Ethiopic Semitic languages: the southern languages, especially those of the Gurage region, have undergone more Cushitic interference than the northern languages.

As mentioned above, this case does not seem to represent a "pure" instance of **sub**stratum interference, because many Cushitic loanwords, as well as Cushitic structural features, are found in Ethiopic Semitic. The social conditions that encouraged the adoption of so many loanwords from Cushitic might have encouraged structural borrowing too; in that case, not all the Cushitic structure in Ethiopic Semitic can be attributed to the shifting speakers' imperfect learning. Nevertheless, the shift itself is a historical fact, so in spite of this complication we can be confident that much of the structural interference resulted from the shift.[5] Leslau's catalogue of loanword categories (1945) includes some that one would expect to find in the language of successful invaders new to an area: animals, vegetation, and geographic terms. Tools are not surprising, either. But other kinds of Cushitic words adopted by Ethiopic Semitic are not typical of loanwords from indigenous subordinate populations: body parts, numerals ('one', 'hundred', 'ten thousand'), astronomic terms, kin terms, and (in some languages) a verb meaning 'to bury'. A few other items, such as derivational suffixes that form abstract nouns and a vocative particle, are functional morphemes that could have been introduced by original Semitic speakers through borrowing.

Leslau lists a number of phonological features introduced into Ethiopic Semitic through Cushitic influence. At least two of these, the development of labialized dorsal phonemes and of homorganic glides before /e o/, complicate the system. The replacement of (presumably) pharyngealized Semitic emphatic consonants by glottalized ones is, as mentioned above, a neutral change in terms of its systemic effect. Another change, the development of several alveopalatal consonants (e.g., /č č' ǰ ñ/) cannot be classified without information about what, if anything, they replaced in Semitic; the same is true of the two other phonological changes Leslau mentions.

As for morphology, it should be noted that Cushitic and Semitic already shared many or most of their functional categories, presumably due to inheritance from Proto-Afro-Asiatic, their common ancestor. The only Cushitic-induced categorial innovation in Ethiopic Semitic, as mentioned above, is the future tense, which is opposed to the otherwise typical Semitic "imperfect" (including present + future). But Hetzron also emphasizes the development of a "shared morphological distinction between main and subordinate verbal forms" (1975:106). Simplificatory changes include the almost total loss of the dual number (Cushitic has no dual); the erosion of consistent gender distinctions in South Ethiopic (gender is a less prominent category in most Cushitic languages than in non-Ethiopic Semitic languages); and the (partial?) loss of plural marking in nouns in western Semitic dialects of the Gurage (number is an optional category in most Cushitic languages).

Other morphological changes involve new means of expressing already existing categories, bringing the Semitic systems closer to the Cushitic ones. Two of these were mentioned above: the prefix-suffix combination to form the negative perfect, using Semitic morphemes but deviating from the prefix-only negative formation in other Semitic languages; and the formation of certain noun plurals via reduplication of the last radical. Other examples are formation of a frequentative stem with a vowel plus reduplication of the penultimate root-conso-nant, formation of intensive or attenuative adjectives by reduplication (Hetzron, 109), and formation of the causative by a double prefix. This last feature provides a nice example of interference that does not produce an exact copy of the shifting speakers' structure: Cushitic has a productive causative formation via a double **suffix**, and the Ethiopic Semitic causative contrasts with the (single) prefix causative marker found in other Semitic languages (as well as in at least two of the other three branches of Afro-Asiatic, Berber and Egyptian). Shift-ing Cushitic speakers presumably learned that the Semitic TL formed the causative by prefixing, but followed their native languages' method of doubling the affix.

Cushitic-influenced syntactic changes, besides the word order changes described above, include the development of 'converbial' (gerund) constructions, which are widely used instead of finite coor-dinate or subordinate verbs, and of compound verbs, especially X + 'say' (Hetzron, 113). Other areal features noted by Ferguson, such as "quoting" clauses with the direct quote followed by 'say' and the use of singular nouns with numerals, may also belong in this category, since they are absent in at least some other Semitic languages—notably Arabic.

The case reported by Lorimer (1937), from the Karakoram Range in what is now northeastern Pakistan, seems to be similar in some ways to the Ethiopian case. The languages involved are Burushaski, a genetic isolate, and Shina, an Indic (specifically Dardic) language belonging to the Indo-Iranian branch of Indo-European. Burushaski, according to Lorimer, is now spoken in the more remote and less accessible parts of the region, while Shina invaders have taken over the major portion of the Gilgit valley. Lorimer argues, from his own field work in the area, that the present-day contact between the two populations is probably not sufficient "to affect the structure of either language as spoken by the main bodies of the two linguistic commu-nities" (70); he also believes that, before the Shina invasion, the lan-guage of the region was probably Burushaski (69), and that the invad-ers mixed with the invaded population.

If this is correct, then many Burushaski must have shifted to

Shina, since Shina is now the major language of the area Lorimer believes to have been previously Burushaski-speaking, and since the Shina now dominate there. As mentioned in 5.2.1, this hypothesis is supported by the existence of two main Shina-speaking castes, one of which claims to have descended from the former rulers of Gilgit. The linguistic evidence supports this historical picture. Lorimer concludes his discussion of Shina-Burushaski structural similarities by commenting that "most of these resemblances seem to be the result of the adoption by Shina of Burushaski methods and technique" (97)—that is, native Shina morphemes combined and used in Burushaski ways, as is typical in interference through shift. This fits the Cushitic/Ethiopic Semitic pattern. And, though Lorimer explicitly avoids discussing lexical interference, he indicates that Burushaski has influenced Shina heavily in this area too; this would also fit the Ethiopian situation, in that here too the shifting Burushaski speakers were apparently not completely subordinate during the transitional period.

The historical picture thus seems clear enough, and the conditions for studying interference between Shina and Burushaski are met here. We know, to a considerable extent, what kinds of structures Shina inherited from Proto-Indo-Iranian, though we have little information about specifically Dardic features. (Shina itself could, of course, have undergone innovative changes after separating from other Indic languages, and it could have passed some of those innovations on to Burushaski.) Moreover, since Burushaski is still spoken in areas that were and are outside the sphere of Shina speakers' dominance, we know what its structure is like. The only remaining question is the possibility of Shina influence on Burushaski as a whole at the time of the invasion: since Burushaski has no known relatives, this possibility cannot be ruled out on comparative evidence. Nevertheless, Burushaski certainly has some striking grammatical features that are not found in any of its neighbors—notably its noun class system, its elaborate system of pronominal prefixes on verbs, and a "curious medial and final y sound" (72)—so its structure has obviously not been swamped by Shina. We believe, therefore, that the presence in Shina of numerous non-Indo-Iranian structural features that match Burushaski features precisely provides solid evidence for a Burushaski-to-Shina direction of interference. (Such interference, of course, does not exclude the possibility of interference in the other direction too, If, as Lorimer's description suggests, Shina speakers did not shift in numbers to Burushaski, any Shina-to-Burushaski interference would have resulted from borrowing.)

Some of the shared phonological features that Lorimer mentions are suggestive, but none provides definitive evidence for phonological interference. He observes (72) that both languages have generally similar phonological systems, including series of retroflex consonants ("cerebrals" in his terminology) and voiceless aspirated stops. The presence of the latter series in Indo-Iranian languages has long been a puzzle for Indo-Europeanists; however, since they occurred in native vocabulary already in Proto-Indo-Iranian, Burushaski influence is not likely here.[6] Lorimer does suggest that the intervocalic and final /ŋ/ in Shina may be due to Burushaski influence, since (he believes) other nearby Indic languages have only [ŋg]. Otherwise, the shared phonological features he discusses seem inconclusive.

The situation is quite different in the morphology and the syntax. Two striking interference features in this domain have already been mentioned: the singulative suffix and the use of a plural verb with the indefinite/interrogative pronoun. The morphosyntactic behavior of the singulative suffixes matches closely in the two languages, and Burushaski must be the source, because such constructions are not native to Indo-Iranian. When added to a singular noun, this suffix functions rather like an indefinite article; when added to a plural noun, it denotes a number of individuals "considered as constituting a unity or group" (74). The order of affixation is Noun stem (+ PLU) + SGV (+ CASE), e.g., Burushaski *hi·r-ʌn-ər* 'to a man' (man + SGV + DAT), Shina *čhom-ɛk-ɪšʊ* '(in) to a skin' (skin + SGV + DAT). Besides nouns, the suffix is added to adjectives, the indefinite/interrogative pronoun, numerals, passive participles of verbs, and verb stems (to form agent nouns). Finally, in both languages the suffix is derived from the word for 'one' (Burushaski *hʌn*, Shina *-ɛk*), but 'one' itself may occur in construction with the singulative suffix; for instance, it optionally precedes the noun in constructions like the ones exemplified here.

Shina has acquired a number of other morphosyntactic features from Burushaski. Lorimer's own choice of 'the most significant illustration of linguistic contagion' (79) in his data is the ablative ('away from') case suffix used with nouns. In both Burushaski and Shina (and in striking contrast to functionally comparable suffixes or postpositions in other Indic languages), the noun ending is composed of a suffix meaning 'on, upon' followed by an ablative suffix that is used alone only with adverbs: Burushaski -tsɛ 'upon' + -ʊm ABL (with adverbs only) → -tsʊm ABL (with nouns); Shina -ɛ'j 'upon' + -o ABL (with adverbs only) → -ɛ'jo ABL (with nouns). Lorimer believes that this formation originated in Burushaski, "which regularly adds an ablative in -ʊm to a number of other suffixes" (80), while Shina does not. However, he notes, at least one Indic language, Hindi/Urdu, does sometimes add its ablative postposition sē to other case markers.

Other morphosyntactic interference features are the reduplication of 'one' to form reciprocal pronouns (vs. the use of 'other' for this purpose in other Indic languages); a vigesimal numeral system (vs. the decimal systems typical of Indic); reduplication of the nonverbal element in a compound verb to indicate continuously repeated action; addition of a question suffix -a to the end of the verb, but only to the verb of the first clause in a sentence containing two alternative questions; addition of a particle meaning 'and, also' after an indefinite pronoun that is used with a negative verb; formation of an indefinite relative by means of a simple pronoun and, after the verb, a particle meaning 'if, when'; addition of case suffixes to the verb stem to express subordination; and the optional use of the ablative case of verbal nouns and temporal nouns to denote 'after'.

A final example (though this does not complete Lorimer's list) is a device used frequently in narratives: the use of an infinitive with an added case ending to begin a sentence, where the infinitive is that of the verb of the preceding sentence. The case in the Burushaski construction is the dative, whose suffix is -ər; it is probably no accident, as Lorimer points out, that the Shina construction uses the locative suffix -ər, which happens to be homophonous with the Burushaski dative.

Now, while some of the above examples may not represent actual complications in Shina morphosyntax, none of them looks remotely like a simplification; and all are clearly too specific to be plausibly attributed to accidental similarity. In the examples Lorimer gives, both languages use native morphemes in the various constructions. It may be that further typological study of Indic languages (and of their Dardic subdivision, a genetic grouping Lorimer did not specifically recognize[7]) will show that one or more of these shared features are inherited in Shina. Further research might also reveal simplificatory changes in Shina which—especially given the non-simplificatory changes that can surely be attributed to Burushaski influence—can be established as Burushaski interference features. But even if details of the picture change, Lorimer's case is strong as it stands: Shina shares with Burushaski an impressive number of features that were clearly not inherited from Proto-Indo-Iranian, and few of them are likely to have arisen spontaneously in Shina. The argument that the mechanism of interference was shift can be disputed; but we find Lorimer's discussion of this point cogent, and the fact that the relevant grammatical morphemes themselves are native to Shina suggests interference through shift rather than borrowing.

In better-known cases (perhaps **because** they are better known) claims of interference through shift meet with stiff opposition. Probably the most famous example is the Indian Sprachbund. This case has been widely discussed; Emeneau's influential 1956 article (reprinted as Emeneau 1964 and also in Emeneau 1980) is the starting point for most of the recent discussions (e.g., Emeneau 1980, Kuiper 1967, Masica 1976, Hock 1975, 1984). The controversy centers on the claims made by Emeneau and others for early Dravidian influence on Indic as a whole. As mentioned earlier, Emeneau's argument clearly indicates interference through shift rather than borrowing.

Claims about more recent interference among various languages of India are less controversial, and a comparison between the earlier situation and the recent ones shows why this is so. First, some of the modern interference is indeed borrowing interference or, at least, it includes transferred morphemes to express transferred structural features. In the Dravidian language Pengo, for instance, phonemic aspiration is said to occur mainly in loanwords from the Indic language Oriya (Sridhar 1978:103); Gondi has replaced its typical Dravidian relative participle with a typically Indic clause structure that includes a borrowed Hindi relative pronoun (Sridhar, 205); and the Indic language Bengali has acquired Dravidian noun plural suffixes -ra (human) and -gulō ~ -guli (nonhuman) along with the Dravidian personal/impersonal noun class distinction (Andronov 1964:124). By contrast, none of the proposed old interference features from Dravidian in Indic involve transferred morphological material.

Second, modern contacts are still directly observable, but ancient contact between Dravidian and Indic, or between Munda or even Burushaski and any other Indian group as a whole, cannot be established historically: we can only infer old contacts from geographical, archeological, and linguistic evidence. The claim for old Dravidian-Indic contact, and for large-scale shift by Dravidians to Indic, has received the widest acceptance. Some available historical hints indicate that Dravidian speakers were once much more widespread in northern India than they are now, and the linguistic map of India— with a solid Dravidian-speaking south and Dravidian islands surrounded by Indic in the north—supports this hypothesis, since there is no evidence of scattered northward migration of numerous small groups of Dravidians. Accepting this claim does not, of course, exclude the possibility of ancient contact between either or both groups and Munda, and/or Burushaski. But, since there is better evidence for old Indic/Dravidian contact, and since the history of Munda is much less well understood than that of Indic or Dravidian, attention has focused on Dravidian-Indic interference.

Third, simply because of the great time depth of any ancient Dravidian interference in Indic as a whole, determining its possible effects is hampered by questions of relative chronology and by the fact that there is almost sure to be much less detectable influence now than there would have been (say) two thousand years ago. By contrast, the current contact situations have produced obvious and specific interference features, and these have not yet been obscured by subsequent changes.

And finally, since the proposed ancient TL in India is an Indo-European language, hypotheses of structural interference inevitably bump into the Indo-Europeanist's traditional prejudice against external explanations for change, especially the view that a plausible internal motivation is preferable to, as well as exclusive of, an external motivation. This prejudice is particularly difficult to overcome when all the proposed interference takes place without actual transfer of grammatical morphemes.

Nevertheless, in spite of the extraordinary complexities of the Indian situation, we believe (with Emeneau and most other scholars) that there is clear evidence of extensive interfernce in the region, and that at least some of it is ancient Dravidian-to-Indic substratum interference. Starting with the directly observable contact situations, we find large amounts of structural interference from Dravidian to Indic (apparently through both borrowing and shift) and from Indic to Dravidian (mostly through borrowing). There is also interference from Indic and Dravidian to Munda and from language to language within both the Indic and the Dravidian groups. When we focus our attention on situations where Dravidian shift to Indic is hypothesized, we find, first of all, a group of features that occur in most or all Dravidian languages but only in those Indic languages that are supposed to have been spoken in areas where a Dravidian substratum was strongest (see, e.g., Southworth MS), and/or where Dravidian still is spoken. The most striking features in this group are the development of an inclusive/exclusive 'we' distinction, for example in Marathi (Southworth MS) and Sindhi (Emeneau 1962:56), and of negative conjugation in verbs, e.g., in Marathi (Emeneau 1980 [1971]:175–176) and Bengali (Klaiman 1977). Neither of these features, certainly, was inherited from Proto-Indo-European or Proto-Indo-Iranian, and neither is a particularly likely spontaneous innovation. Extending our view to Indic as a whole, we find several shared features which, again, are not demonstrably inherited in Indic but are pan-Dravidian. The examples are well known (and all are discussed by Emeneau in various writings, collected in his 1980 book): a series of retroflex consonants opposed to dentals; agglutination in noun morphology, with case markers added to distinct singular and plural stems; a system of echo-word formation; the quotative construction with *iti*; absolutive constructions whose form and syntax differ from comparable constructions elsewhere in Indo-European; the syntax of the particle *api* (Sanskrit and later Indic), corresponding to Dravidian *-um*; and rigid SOV word order accompanied by other statistically expected ordering features, such as postpositions. To this list Emeneau tentatively adds the second causative, or causative of causative (e.g., 'cause to be killed' vs. 'kill' vs. 'die'), which is formed by doubling the causative suffix (1980 [1971]:171–174). The interpretation of this feature, however, is complicated by the fact that it is missing from a few Indic languages, e.g., Marathi.

These features provide, in our view, strong prima facie evidence of old Dravidian-to-Indic interference; and given the near-total absence of old Dravidian loanwords in Indic, any such interference must have come about through shift. Three different sorts of arguments have been offered against this position. First, and most prominently, the claim is made that these features were either all inherited in Indic or developed through drift, via changes whose seeds can be found in Proto-Indo-European. There are two main problems with this claim. First, the fact that scattered retroflex phones and even phonemes occur in various other IE languages hardly accounts adequately for the stable and consistent phonemic distinction, in all Indic consonant systems, between a complete retroflex series and a complete dental series. Positing retroflex pronunciation of certain sounds and sequences in pre-Indic may suggest some ways in which shifting Dravidian speakers might have exerted their influence, but it cannot provide an argument against Dravidian influence. The same is true of the fact that the retroflex phonemes have a less restricted distribution in Indic than in Dravidian. Similarly, Proto-Indo-European (PIE) may have had a dominant SOV word order, but (*pace* some enthusiasts of typologically-oriented reconstructions) the old syntactic attestations show too much variation to support the claim that PIE was a rigid, completely consistent SOV language. Attributing Indic features like strings of nonfinite verb stems in constructions closed by a finite verb to direct inheritance is thus surely unjustified, given the rarity of such constructions elsewhere in IE.

But the major problem with the claims that all these features were inherited by Indic is that they are all separate (i.e., atomistic) claims: they constitute (in, e.g., Hock 1975, 1984) a set of independent internal explanations, often rather shakily supported, opposed to a single external explanation. It simply is not true that an external explanation, to be accepted, must be established "beyond a reasonable doubt" (Hock 1975, 1984).[8] The best historical explanation, internal or external, is the one that accounts best for all the facts, historical and linguistic. If two hypotheses account equally well for the facts, then the simpler one is to be preferred. In this case, not only is the external explanation as a whole simpler, but it accounts for several of the facts much better than any internal explanation that has been proposed.

The second line of anti-Dravidian-influence reasoning goes like this: many of the features in question could have arisen spontaneously through drift, so no external influence is required to account for them. The evidence offered in favor of this view consists of similar developments in other IE branches and similar features, or combinations of features, in other language families. But the relevant question is not whether we can find languages outside of India with features like SOV word order and retroflex consonants; the question, rather, is how the appearance of these particular features in Indic is to be explained, if they were not inherited. As we argued in 3.2, unmarked features are transferred from one language to another more readily than marked features, so a criterion relying on uniqueness is hardly likely to lead to historically accurate results in this domain. And the Dravidian/Indic situation meets the criterion we have proposed: there are several examples of noninherited Dravidian-like features in Indic, from several linguistic subsystems and thus independent of each other. (We should also point out that, where other IE languages have developed some of these same features, other external sources can often be established; examples are the agglutinative number + case suffix sequences on nouns and common SOV word order in Asia Minor Greek, under Turkish influence.)

The third kind of counterargument cites possible external sources other than Dravidian for some of the features. These proposals also ignore the fact that the features as a set match Dravidian, while other explanations are necessarily atomistic (except, of course, for the inter-linked features to be expected with SOV syntax). More seriously, some of them lack any historical justification. Altaic languages, to be sure, have SOV syntax, but how is that relevant to the history of Indic? The observation that Chinese languages have retroflex conso-nants is even less interesting in this context, because in addition to the lack of any demonstrated old contact between Indic and Chinese, the fact is that most of the Chinese retroflex consonants are phonet-ically and phonologically quite different from those typical of the languages of India. Claims of Burushaski or Munda influence are geographically reasonable, but they cannot be established in the ab-sence of evidence about the precontact structures of these languages and, for Burushaski, about old contact with all of Indic.

Snyder (1984) has made a start at identifying features that link Munda with other Indian languages, as opposed to the Austro-Asiatic relatives of Munda. She rightly considers her results to be highly ten-tative, since other Austro-Asiatic languages themselves belong to the Southeast Asian Sprachbund, and reconstruction of Proto-Austro-Asiatic is in its infancy; still, among the features are several of the same ones often proposed for Dravidian-to-Indic interference. Unlike Austro-Asiatic in general, Munda has retroflex consonants, extensive agglutination with many suffixes (though it also has some prefixes and infixes, as do other Austro-Asiatic languages), negative verbs, and SOV syntax with postpositions. If Munda does indeed stand opposed to other Austro-Asiatic languages in these features (and others discussed by Snyder), then it looks very much as if Munda, like Indic, has undergone "indianization," to use Emeneau's terminology. Even if this happened so early that Indic got these features from Munda rather than directly from Dravidian—or, for that matter, even if both Dravidian and Munda got them from some other source, say a now extinct relative of Burushaski—the typological links between Dravidian and Indic would still be historically relevant. From what is known now, in any case, Dravidian is by far the best candidate for the source of the features in Indic. We cannot, at present, look elsewhere for a different source, since supporting historical evidence is lacking. More important, we do not need to, because the Dravidian hypothesis accounts for the facts very well.

In chapter 9.5 we consider a case that in many ways parallels the Indic one: Uralic substratum influence in Baltic and Slavic languages. Claims that have been made for early Uralic interference in late Proto-Slavic have run into the same difficulties as have the Dravidian-to-Indic claims. Contact between the two groups must be inferred for the early period, since neither group is attested in documents that early; although the time depth is much shallower (ca. A.D. 500) than in the Indian case, there has been quite enough time for shift-induced changes to be obscured by later changes. Furthermore, perhaps even more than in the Indian case (because the Neogrammarian tradition was arguably most rigidly developed in Balto-Slavic linguistics, starting with August Leskien), the Indo-Europeanist's prejudice against external explanations has worked against the development of hypotheses in this domain.

As in India, the linguistic map of the Soviet Union shows relic speech islands—in this case Uralic languages surrounded by Slavic—and current contact situations can reasonably be interpreted as a continuation of earlier ones. Here too there is indisputable evidence for Uralic-induced changes due to recent (often attested) shifts; the problem is to decide whether it is possible to extrapolate backward in time to late Proto-Slavic. Since Slavic languages were separated geographically by Hungarian intruders at a relatively early period, the time limits within which Uralic influence could have affected all of Slavic are narrow. Some of the proposed old interference features, like some of the ones in India, show an inexact correspondence with the source-language features. The palatalized consonant series in

Slavic is similar in this respect to the retroflex series in Indic and, because of the inexact correspondence, some scholars have argued here, too, that the distinction cannot be due ultimately to imperfect learning by shifting Uralic speakers. (The flaw in this argument is discussed in 3.3.) Overall, we believe that the case for old Uralic interference in Slavic is fairly strong, though fewer interference features have been identified here than in Indic from Dravidian (see 9.5 for detailed discussion).

So far we have not dealt with a potentially valuable source of information about interference through shift. This is the field of second language acquisition where, though they may not actually shift to the TL, learners certainly display imperfect learning as they study a second language. To a considerable extent these learners' errors are directly comparable to shift-induced language change, as we noted above in discussing Yiddish-to-English interference in the speech of bilinguals. Numerous other examples can be found in the literature—for example in the English of Bantu-speaking learners, where Bokamba (1982) reports constructions like these: *I met the teacher our new* (cf. the frequent Bantu orders NA, N-POSS-DEM) and *My daughter she is attending the University of Nairobi.* Unfortunately, we have found few systematic studies of such phenomena. This is partly due to the sociology of the field: studies of this sort would most likely be carried out under the approach known as contrastive analysis, where first-language interference in the TL is emphasized; but contrastive analysis has been out of fashion in recent decades, replaced by approaches like error analysis, which emphasizes similar errors made by learners with diverse first languages, and Schumann's pidginization hypothesis (e.g., Schumann 1978), which emphasizes simplification of TL structures by learners. (The latter corresponds to the common belief among historical linguists that substratum interference usually or always simplifies the TL grammar; we have argued against this view as a general doctrine in 2.3.)

Another problem with studying first-language interference features in the speech of active learners is that these "interlanguage" phenomena are ephemeral, so there is hardly time to investigate the ways in which they are systematically embedded (if they are) in TL grammar. Fossilized intermediate or advanced stages in second language acquisition, such as the English spoken by Rayfield's (1970) group of Yiddish-English bilinguals, or even Irish English, provide better opportunities for the study of systematic effects of first-language interference.

Still another difficulty that arises in attempts to compare learners' errors with shift-induced language changes is that the bulk of the literature on second language acquisition focuses on individual learners. Since learners will surely differ from each other in unpredictable ways, caution is needed in extrapolating from what one person does in learning a second language to what a whole group of learners does in shifting to another language. There must be a close connection between the two processes, but the nature of this connection is unlikely to be a simple one-to-one correspondence between an individual's learning errors and incorporation of a group's shared learning errors into the grammar of the TL.

In all the cases discussed in this section, shifting speakers have acquired the bulk of the TL grammatical structures along with the TL vocabulary. Some of the grammatical features they have carried over from their original native languages have caused significant changes in the TL grammar, but the TL as a whole still reflects its genetic background in most respects: it has been transmitted normally, though the acquisition of a new speaker group has left a number of linguistic traces. In the next chapter we will examine shift situations in which the shifting speakers acquire so few of the TL grammatical structures that transmission must be considered abnormal: the TL has not been passed on to the new speaker group as a set of interrelated lexical, phonological, morphosyntactic, and semantic structures.

6
Shift without Normal Transmission: Abrupt Creolization

All the shift situations that we have discussed so far involved only two languages at a time. Even in those situations where there were obviously several substrate languages—e.g., Dravidian in India, Cushitic in Ethiopia, and Uralic in various parts of current Baltic and Slavic territory—we assume that each shifting speaker group shared the same original native language. This may, of course, be an over-simplification of the actual (but unrecoverable) historical facts. In particular, the disruptions caused by foreign invaders may have led to population movements that in turn caused mixing of speakers of different languages. This happened in the Balkans, for instance, as a result of the Turkish invasions (though no resulting mixed groups, as far as we know, shifted to Turkish). Nevertheless, we have no evidence against the hypothesis that the substrate populations discussed in chapter 5 remained more or less in place and shifted as separate groups to the respective TL's. Since we have emphasized typological features that are characteristic of the various substrate language groups in discussing interference in the TL's, the fact that different languages with the group constituted the substratum in a particular case does not weaken our claim for interference. There are, to be sure, examples—e.g., in Leslau's discussion of Ethiopic Semitic—where one or more features from a particular language turn up in only one dialect of the TL, or one language of the TL group. But these examples are readily distinguishable from features common to all the substrate languages that appear in the entire TL group.

The situation is different when we turn our attention to creoles, especially those creoles for which no fully crystallized pidgin stage is attested—namely, primarily, creoles that arose in the context of the European slave trade in Africa, the Caribbean area, and several islands in the Indian Ocean.[1] It sometimes happened that enslaved Africans in a given plantation colony came from linguistically diverse backgrounds. (However, this situation may have been less common than many scholars have assumed. In particular, it was only during later stages in the slave trade that newly acquired slaves were sometimes deliberately and systematically split into linguistically diverse groupings so that they had no common language in which to plot rebellion; see Craton 1982, as cited by Singler 1984. In some Caribbean colonies a stable pidgin must have been used; see the discussion later in this chapter.)

In the Indian Ocean, for instance, the early nonwhite population of Mauritius consisted of speakers of at least two West African languages, in addition to Malagasy speakers, Bantu speakers, and East Indians (see Baker's half of Baker and Corne 1982 for details). In the Caribbean, the slaves' languages comprised several West African branches of the Niger-Congo family, together with Bantu languages. In many or most slave contexts, the slave population would not have been entirely from one language background. In such cases an emergent creole developed in a multilingual setting that included at least one European language and two or more non-European languages. The English-based creole Pitcairnese presents a different picture: after the mutiny on the Bounty in 1790, the nine English-speaking mutineers settled on Pitcairn with sixteen speakers of Tahitian, so only two languages were involved in the development of Pitcairnese. (And, unlike the slave contexts, the society on Pitcairn was egalitarian.) Nevertheless, Pitcairnese certainly developed immediately as a creole, without a definite pidgin stage. (However, its linguistic features make it similar in type to Afrikaans [9.6]—that is, it may be best classed as a semicreole.)

In addition to the substrate groups' native languages, various maritime (pre-?)pidgins and the early Portuguese-based pidgin must be considered part of the linguistic milieu in which at least some of these creoles arose. But the evidence for the traditional view that a full-fledged pidgin language, relexified or not, was the major direct source for every plantation creole (not to mention Pitcairnese) strikes us, as it has struck others, as thin.[2] One version of this traditional view, the monogenesis hypothesis, will be discussed below, in chapter 7. The strong appeal of the hypothesis that all creoles are nativized pidgins lies in the linguistic similarities that link pidgin and creole languages, and in the fact that both arise primarily in multilingual settings. We will argue that these similarities (which are often somewhat exaggerated; see chap. 7) can be explained by their partly parallel routes of development, so that there is no need to claim an unattested pidgin for every creole, and we should therefore not make this claim, since to do so commits us to an unnecessarily complicated historical picture.

Aside from the lack of historical justification, the universal pidgin-to-creole claim does not seem very plausible in light of what is known about the social setting in which the European slave-trade creoles arose. Some linguistic diversity among slaves generally existed even when it was not deliberately sought, and it seems likely that, at the outset, a large proportion of newly arrived slaves did not already know a preexisting pidgin, in some slave communities. (However, as Hancock [1985] argues, there may have been rather widespread knowledge of an English-based pidgin or creole among enslaved Africans in Africa before they were transported to the Caribbean.) To develop a fully crystallized pidgin language takes time, because some degree of conventionalization is required (as, for instance, Sankoff 1980:140 points out), so that speakers learn it as a language. Since a pidgin is by definition a second language, such a development presupposes the availability of two or more (usually more) first languages that continue to be spoken by the pidgin developers. But in the uprooted and mixed speech communities of the slaves, a person might have few or no people to talk to in his or her native language. Such a person would need a primary language for communicating with his or her fellows, not merely a secondary language to use for limited purposes of intergroup communication. That is: as various authors have emphasized (e.g., Alleyne 1971, Chaudenson 1977), the process of linguistic deculturation from the native languages must have been rapid in many cases, virtually immediate, in fact, for those slaves who were completely isolated linguistically and therefore could not continue to use their native languages.

Even where there were several or many native speakers of particular languages, it seems likely (though direct evidence is lacking) that social conditions in the new speech communities often demanded rapid replacement of most of the native languages by a single shared medium of communication. In such cases some newly enslaved people may have been able to use their native languages; but probably they also needed to acquire some competence in the emerging contact language, and their children (if any) would be unlikely to continue using the parents' native language, even if they learned it first. This situation contrasts sharply with the two-language shift situations discussed in chapter 5: there, no matter how intense the pressures for shift might have been, a single substrate language was in each case available for use as long as it was needed, that is, until all members of the shifting group had become reasonably fluent in the TL.

We therefore hypothesize for the creoles under discussion, for example Isle de France Creole and probably some of the Caribbean creoles, a process of abrupt creolization (whose products correspond to what Bickerton calls early-creolized creoles). In this process the emerging contact language at once becomes the primary language of the community and is learned as a first language (though not necessarily as their only first language) by any children born into the new multilingual community. That contact language therefore expands rapidly into a creole rather than stabilizing as a functionally and linguistically restricted pidgin, though its formative period, before it crystallizes as a language, corresponds to what is generally called a prepidgin stage. As with limited-function pidgins, the new creole would require time for stabilization, i.e., crystallization (to use Weinreich's term) as a language that is learned as such by each new speaker group—namely, newborn children and/or immigrant adults. But since it was needed immediately for a much wider range of functions than is the case with most pidgins, and since children, the best language learners, were sometimes among its developers, crystallization may have occurred sooner than with most pidgins.

Before continuing with our discussion, we should emphasize again that the historical development we have outlined is not the only route by which creoles emerged in the slave communities. Alleyne

(1980a:141–142), Singler (1984), and Goodman (1985) observe, as have other authors, that in some Caribbean colonies African languages continued in use for a long time. For instance, Singler (1984) argues convincingly that in Jamaica most slaves were adult males; that the slave population was replenished primarily by new importations of adults, not by the raising of children; that concentrations of slaves from a single linguistic background often enabled the slaves to continue using their native languages; and that nativization of the emerging contact language was, in fact, slow and late. If Hancock (1985) is right, at least some slaves may have arrived in Jamaica already speaking an English-based creole. But if Singler's picture is essentially correct, the first contact language in Jamaica must have been an elaborated pidgin, and Jamaican Creole must have arisen out of this pidgin. The linguistic outcomes of situations like the one in Jamaica are, obviously, very similar to the outcomes of slave situations in which no crystallized pidgin had time to develop. This is not accidental; it will be discussed further in chapter 7. In this chapter, however, we will concentrate on what happened in cases where a large proportion of the slave population shifted rapidly, so that creolization began at once.

The idea of creoles without prior pidgins is hardly new, though it is by no means universally accepted. We emphasize it here because of its implications for the study of interference through shift: whatever happened next, it seems clear that, in the cases under consideration, the shift away from the native languages was abrupt.[3] The interesting question is, what did the slaves shift **to**?

In one sense, of course, the slaves in a given community shifted to the European language of the slavemasters. As in any shift situation, they first learned the vocabulary of the TL. With few exceptions (Angolar on São Tomé is one; see Ferraz [1974]), African lexical items constitute only a small portion of the vocabulary of these languages; this is predictable from the fact that in many slave communities no one African language was numerically dominant, and probably also from the fact that the deculturation process obviously involved more than one language. As far as the lexicon is concerned, then, these are typical instances of shift.

The grammar is another matter. If we consider these creoles from the viewpoint of the European TL, we will have no difficulty at all in establishing imperfect learning of that TL. The slaves had no opportunity for social integration into the TL community, and for many or most of them the TL was only minimally (i.e., lexically) available: field slaves on large plantations, in particular, typically had little access to native speakers of the TL. Moreover, unlike two-language shift situations, the slaves' greatest need was for a medium of communication to use among themselves. Under such circumstances, neither the motivation nor the opportunity to learn the TL as a whole—grammar as well as lexicon—was likely to be present.[4] In fact, the evidence is that plantation slaves did not learn the European languages as whole languages. The amount of European grammar in various creoles is still disputed (see Thomason 1980a for discussion of part of the controversy), and certainly marked features of European-language grammar can be found in many creoles, such as Haitian (see, e.g., Baudet 1976 for examples). But no one, as far as we know, views them as just moderately modified European languages.

Given the paucity of definite, generally agreed-upon features of European-language grammar in the least decreolized creoles, e.g., Saramaccan and São Tomé Creole, we see no real room for doubt that these languages resulted from a sharp break in transmission. And since marked European typological features are relatively few even in those creoles that have been decreolizing—converging structurally toward a European vocabulary-base language—for two hundred years or more, we claim that all early-creolized creoles also have a nongenetic origin. That is, the African languages were abandoned, but the European languages were not acquired as whole languages by the slave populations. This removes all these creoles from consideration for genetic classification: they are not changed later forms of any parent language. They did not, in our view, arise through any sort of direct transmission from one speaker group to another, either by generation-to-generation/peer-to-younger-peer enculturation or by shift involving acquisition (perhaps with modification) of the grammar of a TL. Instead, they were created in various multilingual communities by the first generations of slaves.

By making explicit an assumption underlying our entire previous discussion of shift, we can gain some insight into the development of these creoles. In ordinary two-language shift situations, the learners make guesses at the structure of the language they are learning and shifting to. Sometimes they guess wrong and miss or reinterpret TL structures, or carry over structures from their native language that the TL lacks.[5] Under certain circumstancs, as described in chapter 5, these learners' errors may persist in the speech of the shifting group after the shift, and even spread to the TL as a whole. Now, in a multilingual slave context, lack of access to the TL may have prevented the shifting speakers from making testable guesses about the TL per se. Nevertheless, the principle should be the same: thrown into a new multilingual community and given a new vocabulary which they must learn, people will make guesses about what their interlocutors will understand as they try to talk to one another. Those guesses that promote intelligibility will be the "right" guesses. To begin with, the grammar of the emerging creole will be a direct reflection of the shared "right" guesses made by the shifting speakers.

What makes a guess "right"? The same factors, we would argue, as in other shift situations. The reason shifting Uralic speakers were able to introduce a partitive case into their version of Russian (and later into everyone's Russian) was that their "wrong" guess about the function of a particular Russian noun suffix—i.e., wrong from the viewpoint of original native Russian speakers—was understood by, and thus right for, all members of the shifting group. Or, to put it another way, the Uralic speakers did not learn the original Russian distinction between two suffixes (the distinction was certainly opaque, if not semantically empty, by the time of the shift), but they did learn the two suffixes, and attributed to them a functional distinction that made sense from their Uralic viewpoint. Examples of this exact type (though not, usually, morphological ones) can be found in all creoles. Perhaps the most obvious are the examples from lexical semantics reported by various scholars, e.g., Huttar (1975a) and Ferraz (1975). An example given by Ferraz for São Tomé Creole is typical: the Portuguese words *pé* 'foot' and *mão* 'hand' turn up in the creole as *ɔ'pɛ* 'foot and leg to knee' and *mõ* 'hand and arm', respectively, reflecting the semantic ranges of the corresponding lexical items in the Bantu and Kwa substrate languages. In fact, this particular difference from the various European vocabulary-base languages is repeated in pidgins and creoles in many parts of the world, and for the same reason. For instance, the Bislama word *han* 'arm, hand' reflects the structure of Tangoan and other local Austronesian languages (Camden 1975:5), and Pitcairnese *hand* 'hand, arm' and *leg* 'leg, foot' reflect Tahitian lexical structure.

If this is the pattern for shifting speakers' efforts to communicate, as we believe, then the structure of the emerging creole will be a function of the structures of its developers' native languages. The learners' strategy we have outlined will produce a grammar that is a cross-language compromise; to the extent that the learners' languages are typologically similar, this compromise should include numerous features shared by the various original native languages. This is true of pidgins, too; but (as we will illustrate in chap. 7) pidgin structures vary more widely than structures of early-creolized creoles, partly because almost all abrupt creoles developed on a similar typological base: westernEuropean vocabulary-base language, Niger-Congo substrate languages. (See Alleyne 1980*a*, chap. 6, and Singler 1984 for a discussion of typological similarities among relevant Niger-Congo languages of West Africa.)

A number of studies have suggested the mechanism of the cross-language compromise we are positing. Le Page (1977:236) states the principle in this way: " . . . any kind and degree of coincidence between the features of linguistic systems in a contact situation is likely to favor the retention of those features in the pidgin." Or, we would add, in the abrupt creole. Several authors have provided data that support this prediction. Pfaff's (1979) study of Spanish/English language mixing is a particularly valuable investigation of such compromise in code-switching in a current contact situation. Her demonstration that "surface structures common to both languages are favored" (315) offers insight into processes of creole genesis in new slave communities, especially since Spanish and English (like Niger-Congo languages) are typologically similar in many respects. The case she describes is a two-language situation with a higher level of bilingualism than we are assuming for the new creole communities. Still, the analogy seems reasonable, because the strategy we hypothesize is a general one that is used in ordinary shift as well as in bilingual code-switching and, we suggest, in creole and pidgin genesis. A probable multilingual example corresponding to Pfaff's bilingual one, but displaying completed changes in the three major languages, is the famous Kupwar case (Gumperz and Wilson 1971).[6] At least one study of pidgin structure draws the same conclusion: Camden (1975) shows that Bislama has tended to develop structures that are common both to English and to relevant New Hebridean languages, though he also presents examples of Bislama structures that are found in New Hebridean languages but not in English.

This last example raises an important point. In the above discussion, we assumed a new slave community with certain characteristics, namely, (almost) no access to the TL as a whole and a slave population so heterogeneous that no substrate languages could be used widely within the group. Such communities presumably existed, but there were, as is frequently pointed out, many different numerical combinations of TL speakers and speakers of specific substrate languages. Detailed historical studies of who was where when are being carried out with increasing frequency for the Caribbean and elsewhere; see, for instance, various writings of Ferraz on the Portuguese-based Gulf of Guinea creoles (e.g., 1983) and Baker's half of Baker and Corne (1982:131–259). We would expect such population differences to affect the structures of the resulting creoles, and, though evidence for variation according to substrate populations is still scanty, we have good evidence of structural differences according to the proportion of TL speakers. Where the proportion of TL speakers to substrate speakers is high, we would expect shifting speakers to learn some (more) TL grammar, given the dominant position of the TL. That is, increased access to the TL should promote better learning of it, even without the motivation that might be provided by (among other things) an opportunity for social integration into the TL community.

There are several reports in the literature of cases in which this prediction is borne out. First, and most detailed historically, is Baker's and Corne's (1982) description of the historical and linguistic contrast between the crucial early periods of colonization on Réunion and Mauritius in the Indian Ocean. On Réunion, Baker says, native speakers of French actually outnumbered slaves during the formative period for Réunion Creole; but on Mauritius, during the relevant period for the development of Isle de France Creole, the proportion of native French speakers was much lower (as it was in Haiti, for instance, in the Caribbean). Moreover, the slave population at that period on Mauritius—but not during the analogous period on Réunion—included enough West Africans to have influenced the developing creole. As a result of these demographic differences, according to Corne's linguistic analysis, Isle de France Creole grammar rather closely resembles that of (say) Haitian Creole, where demographic conditions were comparable, but Réunion Creole grammar displays a significant number of French grammatical categories and processes. In fact, Corne argues, the language of Réunion is perhaps best viewed structurally as a semi-creole, rather than as a true creole like Isle de France Creole and Haitian Creole.

In his Preface to Baker and Corne (1982), Le Page comments on a Caribbean parallel to the historical and structural contrast between the two Indian Ocean languages: "the proportion of Whites to Blacks in Barbados was far higher in the crucial formative years than in Jamaica, where Blacks rapidly outnumbered Whites by 10 to 1" (vii), and this accounts (in part?) for the fact that Bajan, the creole of Barbados, is much closer linguistically to English than is Jamaican Creole.

A possible third example is the contrast between the Portuguese-based creole of the Cape Verde islands and those of the Gulf of Guinea islands São Tomé, Príncipe, and Annobón. Ferraz (1983:125) emphasizes that "in having a strong African substratum, the Creoles of the Gulf of Guinea contrast with such other Creoles as that of the Cape Verde islands, which is much closer to Portuguese in phonology, lexicon and grammar." Ferraz ascribes the difference to the smaller number of Portuguese speakers on the Gulf of Guinea islands, and to the fact that the slave population there was more homogeneous linguistically than in other creole contexts. But Bickerton (1981:47) remarks that the "presence [of decreolization] in Cabo Verdiense . . . is quite apparent." Decreolization would, of course, account for the apparent linguistic closeness of this creole to Portuguese as well as Ferraz's demographic argument does. The point we wish to make here, however, is that there is no need, on linguistic grounds, to make the appeal to decreolization, since other instances show the relevance of demographics to the linguistic outcome of a creolization process.

In any case, Bickerton's view that decreolization **must** be invoked here may be explained by a creole analogue to his comment about how vocabulary-base language structures may enter a pidgin (1981:122):

> For a superstrate feature to be accessible to a pidgin, that feature must be more or less unambiguous with respect to meaning, more or less free from mutation with respect to phonological structure, and as close as possible to the canonical form of CV(CV).

Since these attributes are part of what makes an unmarked structure unmarked—that is, easier to learn—they may well help language developers to learn TL structures. But to give them as **constraints** on TL contribution to a pidgin (or creole) suggests an odd notion of language learning capabilities and probabilities. Acquisition of TL structures is primarily determined, for any language learning situation, by access to the TL and by motivation to learn it, and only secondarily by markedness and by the typological fit between TL structures and structures in the learners' language(s). (Consider, as one counterexample to Bickerton's substantive claims, the highly marked Chinookan consonant clusters that are preserved faithfully by Indian speakers of Chinook Jargon; see chap. 7 and 9.7 for discussion.) Moreover, Bickerton's constraint does not allow for partial learning, i.e., reinterpretation, which is so common in interference through shift and in second language acquisition in general.

In any event, contrasting cases like these pairs of languages—one pair each from among the abrupt creoles with French, English, and (possibly) Portuguese vocabulary—make it clear that, if we want to account for creole structures, we must consider possible access to the TL as a whole in addition to the structures of the slaves' native languages. Equally clearly, that is not all we need to consider. Ferraz's second reason for the greater number of African structures in the Gulf of Guinea creoles points to another vital factor: the diversity and especially the typological range represented by the various substrate languages.

The Gulf of Guinea creoles, which were developed by the least diverse substrate population of any Atlantic creole we know of, also have, probably, the largest number of African substrate features of any Atlantic creole. (Saramaccan might be a potential rival.) The two main sources of slaves for these islands were apparently speakers of the Kwa language Bini and of western Bantu languages, especially KiKongo. Ferraz's list of African features includes several that would not be predictable on grounds of markedness: palatalization of /t d s z/ → [č ǰ š ž] before high front vocoids, and depalatalization of /š ž/ in Portuguese words to /s z/ in other environments, corresponding to a rule in some KiKongo dialects (the former is a rather common phonological rule in languages of the world); implosive phonetic realizations of /b d/, as in a number of West African and Bantu languages; negative constructions with one negative particle before the verb and another at the end of the sentence, as in western Bantu; disjunctive pronouns after prepositions in questions and relative clauses; several word order features characteristic of both Kwa and western Bantu but not of Portuguese; and, among the numerous Kwa and Bantu lexical items, Kwa- and Bantu-style ideophones. Other features he mentions, such as lack of a distinction between /l/ and /r/ (only /l/, in Annobonese Creole), loss of syllable-final consonants, and lack of a passive voice, are unmarked features which could easily have arisen spontaneously, though an African origin seems probable for these features too.

Not surprisingly, more diversity among original substrate languages means fewer marked features in the emerging creole that are to be attributed to the substrate languages. If shifting speakers tend to exploit those structures that they already share with their interlocutors, and if unmarked features in general occur more freely, then most shared features will be unmarked (or at least not universally marked)—unless, as in São Tomé Creole and its neighbors, the substrate languages are very close typologically.[7]

Unmarked shift-induced features, as we noted in chapter 5 in discussing ordinary shift situations, are harder to pin down to a substrate source, because internally-motivated change—or, in abrupt creolization, spontaneous emergence—can also be invoked as a possible source.

The most prominent appeal to spontaneous emergence of such features is Bickerton's bioprogram proposal (1981; see also, among other sources, 1977, 1979, and 1980). In arguing that certain features of early-creolized creoles are due to a process of biological evolution that resulted in (literal) genetic programming, Bickerton relies on four main premises, which he claims to have established: first, all these features appear in all early-creolized creoles; second, they cannot be accounted for by reference to vocabulary-base language structures (which, if the first premise is correct, would have to be the same in all the European vocabulary-base languages); third, they cannot be accounted for by reference to shared substrate-language structures; and fourth, they cannot be accounted for by direct diffusion, because some of the languages, in particular Hawaiian Creole and Caribbean creoles, are totally independent of each other historically. Of these four premises, only the second has not (as far as we know) been seriously challenged; although the relevant European languages are indeed typologically similar, they lack some of the most famous of Bickerton's proposed bioprogram features, notably the preverbal tense/aspect markers.

The fourth premise is in doubt if, as many scholars believe, some knowledge of the same maritime (pre-)pidgins could have been present in both the Pacific and the Atlantic. As for the first premise, criticisms of some of Bickerton's specific structural analyses and cross-creole structural comparisons have appeared recently, but so far no consensus has emerged as to the accuracy and import of these criticisms. In any case, structural similarities in early-creolized creoles with different lexical bases, particularly in their tense/aspect systems, have been a focus of historical discussion at least since Taylor's early work (e.g., 1956, 1960).

It is Bickerton's third premise that we wish to address here. If he cannot make his case on this point, then his bioprogram loses most of its appeal, because structural contribution by languages known to have been spoken in the right places at the right times provides a much simpler historical explanation than reliance on a specific unobservable bit of genetic programming. (Bickerton's other line of evidence for the bioprogram, from child language acquisition, is admittedly less fully worked out, and we cannot judge its ultimate value.) He offers two arguments against substrate explanations. The first is that some early-creolized creoles—for instance (at least on his analysis), Hawaiian Creole and Caribbean creoles like Guyanese—have totally different sets of substrate languages, so that shared features in the creoles cannot be due to direct diffusion or to shared substrate features. There is an important flaw in this argument—namely, in his implicit assumption that different sets of substrate languages cannot have similar shared structural features.

This is not a promising prediction on the face of it, since (as mentioned earlier in this chapter) most shared features in a diverse group of languages will be unmarked, and universally unmarked features appear in historically unconnected language families all over the world. In this connection, a remark made by Camden (1975:26) about syntactic similarities in pidgins—and, by implication, in creoles too—is worth noting:

> In discussion of the origin of the "European-language-based pidgins" attention is frequently drawn to . . . syntactic features in common. At the level at which these common features are usually discussed, they are almost all features of most of the languages of the New Hebrides [i.e., Austronesian languages] . . . had the pidgin so introduced not had these features, the local language structure would have exerted pressure on it for it to include them.

At the least, this casts doubt on an a priori assumption that shared features in one set of substrate languages will not resemble shared features in another set. In a preliminary effort to test the hypothesis that shared pidgin/creole features might be due to typological similarities between different sets of substrate languages, Rollins (1978) compared Tok Pisin, which had primarily Austronesian substrate languages, and Gullah, which had African substrate languages. She found that most structural similarities in these two languages (which have very different histories, though both have mainly English vocabulary) can be accounted for by shared similarities in the two sets of substrate languages. Among her examples are the SVO word order and the use of the third person plural pronoun as a nominal pluralizer.

Bickerton's other argument against hypotheses of primary substrate contributions to emerging abrupt creole grammars rests on a serious misunderstanding of the nature of these hypotheses. Although he is not the only scholar to make this particular mistake, Bickerton's defense of his bioprogram hypothesis depends so heavily on successful refutation of substrate explanations that misunderstanding is especially harmful to his case. Here are two representative comments on the subject:

> In the highly unlikely event of some African language's being found that showed point-by-point identity with the creole model, "substratomaniacs" would still be faced with the problem of explaining how that language . . . could have won out against all competing models, sub- and superstrate, during the period of creole formation. Bickerton 1977:61

> Let us suppose that a very common structure in Caribbean creoles is also attested for Yoruba and perhaps one or two other relatively minor languages. . . . To most substratomaniacs, the mere existence of such similarities constitutes self-evident proof of the connection. They seldom even consider the problem of transmission. Bickerton 1981:48

These two comments, made four years apart, reflect the same basic position (though by 1981 Bickerton has removed the shudder quotes from his mocking term "substratomaniac," and he refers to it [1981:48] as the 'traditional name' for those who offer substrate explanations).[8] Bickerton has not, so far, dealt with criticisms, e.g., by Alleyne (1979), of his characterization of substrate explanations.

Our previous discussion, in chapter 5, has already provided answers to the charges Bickerton makes against substrate explanations. Point-by-point identity with a substrate feature, in interference through shift, is by no means to be expected; see the examples given in chapter 5, such as Hungarian interference in the stress system of a Serbocroatian dialect, and the development of a causative formation with a double prefix in Ethiopic Semitic under the influence of a corresponding Cushitic construction with a double suffix. Note also, in this connection, Alleyne's (1979:100) response to this part of Bickerton's argument (quoted above, in 3.3).

As for Bickerton's belief that substrate explanations rest on the predominant influence of one (or two or three) particular languages, this isn't so. It is true that claims have been made (at least implicitly) along these lines, for example in the early work of Sylvain (1936), who compared Ewe and Haitian Creole structures. But even authors who use one language as representative of a whole group often point out that the features they cite are in fact typical of the group. And some authors who have written on the subject, e.g., Alleyne (1980a), Holm (1976, 1978), and Baudet (1976, 1981), have emphasized relevant typological similarities among the substrate languages as groups. The approach we take here certainly relies on typological overlap among substrate languages. If shifting speakers have sufficient access to the TL as a whole, then TL structural features can be expected to appear in the creole; and an important single group of substrate speakers, such as western Bantu speakers on São Tomé, may well contribute features from their own language(s) to the creole. But with minimum access to the TL and maximum linguistic diversity among substratum speakers, substrate contribution should be largely confined to features common to most or all the substrate languages.

As mentioned above, in most abrupt creoles these shared structures include few or no universally marked features. Phonetically, West African and Bantu languages are for the most part not particularly exotic, from a European viewpoint. The non-European features that many of them do have occur only in a few of the creoles, e.g., Saramaccan and the Gulf of Guinea creoles: phonemic tones, phonemic nasalized vowels (these do occur in some European languages, of course, but not in English), prenasalized stops, and double-articulated stops, all in Saramaccan (Voorhoeve 1961); and implosive stops in the Gulf of Guinea creoles.

Some of the relevant African languages do have elaborate morphological systems, but these often do not match closely, especially between the West African and the Bantu groups. The lack of typological overlap here would ensure absence of much morphology in the creoles, but there are exceptions. Saramaccan, for instance, has vestiges of a noun class system of the Niger-Congo type (Alleyne 1980*b*:2). More interestingly, the widespread use of a third person plural pronoun (e..g, *dem* in English-based creoles) as a postposed noun pluralizer and, with proper names, to mean 'and others' (Holm 1980:59) is sometimes analyzed in the last two uses as a noun suffix. These three uses, Holm says, correspond exactly to the uses of the third plural pronoun in Yoruba and many other relevant Niger-Congo languages. The lexical semantics, as we have observed, offers more evidence for African substrate contribution to the Atlantic creoles, in the form of numerous calques of common African lexical structures. Besides the examples given by Huttar (1975*a*), note Holm's examples (1980:58) of color terms whose usage parallels that of West African color terms.

The syntax, however, provides the most-discussed examples of possible substrate features, especially in the Atlantic creoles. Although none of these features is obviously marked (and we have already discussed the difficulty of establishing markedness in syntax), the typological fit between numerous syntactic structures in Atlantic creoles and corresponding structures in most or all relevant Niger-Congo languages is surely too close to be accidental. The features cited include, among others, the famous preverbal tense/aspect markers (see, e.g., Alleyne 1980:162 ff., Holm 1980:60), as well as quite specific uses of, and variation in, the copula (Holm 1976, 1984); serial verbs (Huttar 1975*b*; see the response by Holm [1982:113] to Bickerton's [1981] effort to explain away this resemblance); and reduplicated numerals functioning as distributives (Baudet 1981:113). (See Boretzky 1983 for the most thorough discussion to date of African substrate influence in Atlantic creoles.)

All these features in the various grammatical subsystems, or close analogues of them, can be found as interference features in ordinary shift situations, so they are demonstrably diffusable. The case for substrate contribution to early-creolized creoles (and to pidgins, as we will show in chap. 7) meets all the conditions we have set for establishing interference through shift, though the first is irrelevant where there was no access to the entire TL: the structure of the TL before the shift is known; the structures of the original native languages of the shifting speakers are known; the shift itself is an established historical fact; and the proposed structural contributions from the original native languages are independent of each other and belong to different grammatical subsystems (We have not discussed unmarked phonological features, e.g., a tendency toward CV syllable structure; but there are several of these, too.)

The mechanism of transmission that we hypothesize has been discussed above. However, our scenario for the formative period of early-creolizing creoles differs sharply from Bickerton's. Bickerton (1977:49) believes that "pidginization is second-language learning with restricted input, and . . . creolization is first-language learning with restricted input." On his view, it is the children born into the new multilingual community who are the primary (or only) developers of the emerging creole: since, he says (1979:16, 17), in this sort of contact situation the child receives no corrective linguistic input, the child's innate grammar, determined by the bioprogram, will persist into adulthood and thus comprise at least part of the new creole's grammar. Meanwhile, the adults in the new community will be developing, and speaking, an unstable, soon-to-vanish (pre-)pidgin (e.g., 1981:5). But the adults' speech, according to Bickerton, will be the most rudimentary and highly variable sort of prepidgin and will have no influence on the structure of the emerging creole.

This view of communication in a new contact situation embodies two claims that seem extremely improbable: adults' efforts to talk to one another when they have no common language will influence the development of a pidgin, but **not** of an abrupt creole; and even if the children talk and/or listen to the adults in the community, the adults' speech will have no effect at all on the grammar that the children construct. Since human infants are notoriously dependent on adult care until well beyond the initial stages of first-language acquisition, and since the caretakers are not likely to be silent, we find it difficult to see how the adults' pre-pidgin **and native languages** could fail to influence the emerging creole directly, even if we grant a special role to the children in its development.

Since we are concerned here with Bickerton's proposal from a theoretical viewpoint, we do not address the historical facts that also stand in its way in the case of Hawaiian Creole: if, as Takaki (1983) and Reinecke (1969) point out, plantation workers in Hawaii were mostly separated into ethnically homogeneous groups in their living quarters, then their children would certainly have learned the ethnic-heritage language first. Even if they were also exposed to the pidgin at an early age, those children would not bring a linguistic tabula rasa to the task of learning the pidgin and creating the creole. Bickerton's bioprogram theory requires a tabula rasa; the actual attested historical situation would still be compatible with his earlier theory about universally unmarked structures, but not with the bioprogram. The discussions of Caribbean plantation history by Singler (1984) and Goodman (1985) present equally devastating problems for Bickerton's hypothesis for that area.

In light of the evidence for early language mixing in the speech of children who are growing up bilingual (e.g., Leopold 1939–1947, 1948; but cf. Burling 1973), we feel strongly that Bickerton must bear the burden of proof for his claims about the mechanism of abrupt creolization. In our opinion, he has not provided convincing evidence for his strong claims about the communicative setting. It is far simpler, and more consistent with the evidence from directly observable multilingual communities, to assume that different generations constitute one speech community, not two, and that both adults and children contribute to the development of an early-creolizing creole. So we reject the claim that children in this context have restricted input for their language-learning task. The only way in which the children's linguistic input is likely to be truly restricted is with respect to the vocabulary-base language. When Bickerton poses the question of how a child can "produce a rule for which he has no evidence" (1981:6), he is, in our view, asking the wrong question. We prefer to ask how the child can create grammatical rules on the basis of input data which is much more variable than the input data received by a child in a monolingual environment. In any case, the child's learning will, we believe, be dependent on his elders' linguistic output to a crucial extent.

Given the evidence for African substrate influence on the structures of the Atlantic and Indian Ocean creoles, and for Tahitian influence on Pitcairnese, is there any role left for Bickerton's bioprogram? Perhaps, but his theory is a strong one, so the fewer features that remain for it to explain, the less attractive it will be.[9] There is at least a role for considerations of universal markedness, especially, probably, with respect to ease of learning. In addition, the foreigner-talk register which, according to Ferguson (e.g., 1971), is a normal part of a speaker's linguistic repertoire, needs to be taken into account, both for TL speakers and for shifting speakers. We do not mean to suggest, by our emphasis on substrate contributions to creole grammar, that other influences are to be excluded. We would, however, reverse the priority of the factors Corne (1983:75) cites in concluding his discussion of substrate contributions to the grammar of Isle de France Creole:[10]

> One can hypothesize that it is only where these two major substratal language groups [i.e., Malagasy and the Bantu languages] do coincide substantially, as in the case of their completives, that there is sufficient impetus to modify the "regular" operation of the bioprogram.

Our version would read like this: the bioprogram, if any— or, at least, universal structural tendencies based on markedness—will be important only where the structures of the substrate languages do **not** coincide substantially. Where the substrate language structures do coincide typologically, the shifting speakers will tend to retain them, unless pressure from a readily available TL pushes in another direction.

We would look first, then, to the grammars of the shifting speakers' native languages to account for the structure of an early-creolizing creole. The evidence we have seen indicates that shift in a new multilingual community resembles ordinary two-language shift in the types and range of features contributed by the shifting speakers' original languages. But the number of clearly identifiable substrate-language features in a creole is inevitably limited by the fact that only typologically shared marked features are likely to appear in the creole, so we must look to other factors to explain other aspects of creole grammar.

In spite of the similarities in the two kinds of shift situations, we cannot agree with the various authors who argue that, historically, the "process of creolization is 'not very different except in intensity' [i.e., speed] from change in any language" (Hancock [1980:63], citing Goodman [1964:135]). The reason is that we do not believe that an abrupt creole can reasonably be viewed as a changed later form of its vocabulary-base language; there is, in fact, no language that has changed. Instead, an entirely new language—without genetic affiliation—is created by the first members of the new multilingual community, and further developed and stabilized by later members, both children born into the community and (in many or most cases) newcomers brought in from outside.

This discussion of creole genesis not done justice to the complexity of the subject. Those aspects of the historical issue that are more relevant to pidgin genesis will be discussed in chapter 7; that will leave a large residue of questions that we have not addressed. For instance, we have omitted systematic discussion of grammatical differences among early-creolized creoles that might be due to the influence of different substrate populations, though a few relevant examples are cited above (e.g., Ferraz's anlysis of the Gulf of Guinea creoles [1973, 1976, 1983], and Corne's 1983 analysis of the Isle de France completive). We have also omitted discussion of decreolization, primarily because convergence toward the vocabulary-base language is ordinary contact-induced language change, akin (for both social and linguistic reasons) to dialect borrowing from a standard to a nonstandard dialect (see 4.3.4 for discussion). Still, for all that we have left out, we hope to have established that abrupt creolization should be dealt with as a special case of language shift, and that both the process and its linguistic results combine characteristics of ordinary language shift (where the TL as a whole is available and is, for the most part, acquired by the shifting group) with characteristics unique to the context of abrupt creolization.

7
Pidgins

Moja på tvoja: another name for Russenorsk
—(Broch 1927:220)

7.1. DEFINITIONS AND THEORIES OF PIDGINIZATION

The current boom in pidgin/creole studies has produced an enor-
mously increased body of data on the history and structures of pidgin
languages, and a rash of new and revamped old theories about how
they arise and develop. A thorough consideration of the theories
alone would require a book-length format. In this chapter, therefore,
we will concentrate on the historical questions that bear most directly
on the general topic of contact-induced language change. Our goal,
ultimately, is to elucidate the ways in which pidgin genesis resembles,
and the ways in which it differs from, change in an existing language
that comes under foreign influence.

The phrase *moja på tvoja* consists of the Russenorsk first person
singular pronoun, its all-purpose preposition, and its second person
singular pronoun. The phrase may be translated as 'me according to
you' or—more freely—'I [talk] in your [way]'. It provides a useful
reminder of one important aspect of pidgin genesis: the process of
linguistic negotiation by which members of the new contact community develop a common means of communication. We will argue that

the crucial factor in this process is simplification, by their speakers, of the various languages in contact—not only, or even primarily, simplification of the vocabulary-base language—and that the outcome of the mutual simplifications is determined primarily by a combination of universal markedness considerations and typological distance among the specific languages involved. (Social factors such as the relative size and status of the speaker groups of the various contact languages will of course also affect the outcomes of particular cases of pidginization. But, although we cannot generalize about these effects, the evidence we have collected suggests that the best starting point is mutual simplification.) Before presenting the arguments for our position, we will review briefly some background points about pidgins and theories of pidginization.

Since both Norwegians and Russians reportedly believed that, in speaking Russenorsk, they were speaking the other group's language, the phrase *moja på tvoja* also points to one of the three oldest and best-established diagnostic features for identifying a speech form as a pidgin language: lack of mutual intelligibility between the pidgin and any of the languages whose native speakers use the pidgin (see, e.g., Sankoff 1980:140).[1] If Russenorsk were immediately intelligible to Russian speakers, Russians could hardly have believed it to be Norwegian—and similarly for Norwegians. The argument for this criterion is that a speech form that is mutually intelligible with its (primary) lexical source language—for example, English—is usually considered by speakers of English to be "broken English" or "foreigner-talk English," not a separate pidgin language.

There are at least three kinds of cases in which this criterion might lead to a mistaken identification. First, there must be a period in the history of any pidgin when the speech form has not fully crystallized, and during this period the version used by lexical source-language speakers may be mutually intelligible with the lexical source language. That is, the historical borderline between "pidgin" and "foreigner-talk" may be fuzzy, as in other historical linguistic processes involving change from one sort of language to another (and we have noted a number of instances in preceding chapters). Second, even if a stable speech form is to some extent intelligible to native speakers of its lexical source language, it may reasonably be considered a pidgin if its sphere of usage expands until it serves as a contact medium for speakers of other languages. For instance, even if Chinook Jargon

was partly mutually intelligible with Lower Chinook on the Columbia River in Oregon, it would be classed as a pidgin once it was
learned and used by English and French speakers with other groups
of Indians, and among the Indians themselves, as far south as California and as far north as Alaska. And third, if all the languages whose
speakers are developing a contact medium are both typologically and
genetically close, the contact medium may stabilize at a point so close
to one or more of these languages that it may remain mutually
intelligible with them. (Other authors have also identified this type
of case as a problem.) In such cases, even when speakers of the lexical
source language are constant users of the speech form, it is probably
appropriate to call it a pidgin. An example is the African pidgin
Kituba, which arose in the early 16th century as a trade language
among the various Bakongo tribes (Nida and Fehderau 1970). Its
main lexical source is the Manianga dialect of KiKongo, and it is
mutually intelligible with all KiKongo dialects, but is apparently not
a mere simplification if KiManianga. In any case, according to Nida
and Fehderau, its one and one-half million speakers are not now all
KiKongo speakers.

The second traditional criterion for status as a pidgin language is,
as Sankoff (1980:140) puts it, some degree of conventionalization—
or, in Weinreich's terms, crystallization. A pidgin language must be
learned (Hymes 1971:79); it cannot be produced by a speaker of any
other language simply as an *ad hoc* simplification of his or her own
language (with or without some lexical substitutions), any more than
any other language could be produced in such a way. Here again
borderline cases can be imagined during the early stages of pidgin
genesis, because grammatical norms take time to develop. But if
Bickerton (1981) were right about the extreme variability of what he
calls Hawaiian Pidgin English, then we would claim that there never
was a genuine pidgin English in Hawaii. On Bickerton's account (an
account which receives some support from the data presented in
Nagara [1972]), each speaker used his or her own native-language
grammar, with considerable simplification, in speaking "Hawaiian
Pidgin English"; but "Hawaiian Pidgin English" had no grammar of
its own.[2]

The third diagnostic feature of pidgins, also traditional, is that a
pidgin is nobody's native language. By "nobody" we mean "no community," i.e., no sizable group of native speakers; if a few isolated

children acquire a pidgin as their native language, it remains a pidgin. It follows, then, that the borderline between a pidgin and a creole resulting from nativization of a fully crystallized pidgin will be fuzzy too.

This third diagnostic feature is a social criterion whose linguistic implications have often been exaggerated. There is, in our view, no **necessary** correlation between richness of linguistic resources and exclusive second-language status. (This view is not exclusively ours; Sankoff [1979], among other authors, has made the same claim.) The crucial point is this: the range of linguistic resources correlates rather with the range of uses of a language. The best illustration is Tok Pisin, a long-lived pidgin which, before it began to creolize, had achieved major lingua franca status and was used in such official spheres as government publications and the recording of proceedings in village courts. As Sankoff (1979:25) observes, "creolization per se has been responsible for fewer of the developments in Tok Pisin than might have been expected according to the thories of a decade ago." During its attested history Tok Pisin has undergone many grammatical changes, but most of the ones that resulted in grammatical expansion, e.g., in the number category (Mühlhäusler 1981), took place well before creolization began.

Nevertheless, though a small vocabulary and severely restricted grammatical and stylistic resources are not a diagnostic feature of pidgins, they are certainly typical of pidgin languages, including nineteenth-century Tok Pisin. The reason is historical: all attested pidgins arose as socially and (therefore) linguistically restricted contact languages, and very few have significantly expanded their sphere(s) of usage. Since pidgins whose range of usage remains restricted also remain linguistically restricted, we would reject claims of inevitable "natural" grammatical expansion, for instance Mühlhäusler's argument that the "grammar of a pidgin is constantly expanding" (1980:41). The grammar of Tok Pisin did indeed expand dramatically. But the grammar of Chinook Jargon, whose attested history is as long as that of Tok Pisin, did not, except conceivably when it creolized on the Grand Ronde Reservation (Zenk 1984). Nor, apparently, did Chinese Pidgin Russian expand during its 150-year history (Neumann 1966).

In considering the mechanism by which pidgins arise, we start with Hymes' characterization (1971:81) of the process of pidginization as learning and adaptation, a *selective* acceptance of lexicon and grammar, so far as any one source is concerned, in a context of limited opportunity, limited need, and, as adults, of more limited ability. From the standpoint of the community or group, the process . . . is one of sharing in the *ad hoc* adaptation and creation of a novel means of speech.

The question is, what determines the particular features that turn up in the pidgin grammar in a given instance? That is, what do the pidgin developers learn, and what do they adapt? Three different processes of pidgin formation have been proposed, and vigorously advocated, by various authors over the years: simplification of the vocabulary-base language; grammatical contribution from substrate languages;[3] and the operation of universal structural tendencies to produce a maximally simple grammar. (Other processes have also been proposed, of course, but these are the only three that have attracted much support.)

None of these processes in principle excludes either of the others—indeed, our own proposal combines all three—and in practice few proponents of any of them argue for an exclusive role for one process. Nevertheless, it is commonly assumed that one of these processes is **the** starting point for the development of a pidgin. The most popular choice has traditionally been simplification of the lexical source language. Ferguson (1971:147–148), for instance, suggests that "the initial source of the grammatical structure of a pidgin is the more or less systematic simplification of the lexical source language which occurs in the foreigner talk register of its speakers, rather than the grammatical structure of the language(s) of the other users of the pidgin." He goes on to say that the other language(s) might also have influenced the emerging pidgin grammar, but that a universal simplification process "would help to explain some of the otherwise surprising similarities" in distant creoles (and pidgins).

The hypothesis that the grammar of a pidgin is determined by the grammars of the substrate languages is implicitly reflected in recurrent references to "the characterization of pidgins and creoles as having the lexicon of one language and the grammar of another" (Traugott 1977:73; see also Rickford 1977:196). Traugott (like Rickford and others who make such references nowadays) remarks cautiously that this view is "highly oversimplified," but believes nevertheless that it "captures an important generalization." A more extreme version of the substratum hypothesis in pidgin formation is apparently advocated by Bickerton and Givón (1976:12) when they argue, with reference to Hawaiian Pidgin English, that "in the classic contact situation, the average speaker begins by gradually relexifying his original grammar." They then go on to argue for later grammatical adaptation in the direction of the vocabulary-base language.

The third proposed process, the manifestation of universal structural tendencies, has attracted considerable attention in recent years. Some authors, for example Schumann (1979), argue for a strong version of this position; Bickerton (1981:123–124) seems to belong to this group when he assumes that "pidgins begin with nouns, verbs, and very little else."[4] A major advantage claimed for the universals hypothesis is that it would account both for the structural similarities often noted in geographically separated pidgins and for the typical absence in them of large numbers of universally marked features.

All three hypothesized processes, separately and in combination, are usually linked in discussions of pidgin genesis by a common thread of directionality: pidginization is viewed as simplification of a target language, as substratum/first-language interference in learners' versions of a TL, and/or as a TL stripped down to the bare bones of universal grammar. A typical (and much cited) instance of this emphasis on TL's is Bickerton's claim (1977:49) that "pidginization is second-language learning with restricted input."

One implicit assumption here is that all features of the pidgin's grammar which are not found in the supposed TL have resulted from changes in that TL as it was pidginized. Another implicit assumption in the claims of directionality is that, given the opportunity, the developers of a contact language would learn the TL itself, not create a pidgin—or, at least, that their goal is in fact to learn the TL to some extent. In discussing abrupt creolization in chapter 6 we tacitly adopted this viewpoint for those languages, because if a linguistically mixed population shifts rapidly away from various native languages it seems reasonable to suppose that the lexical source language constitutes a genuine target language, even if it is a remote target. One piece of evidence that supports this assumption is the demonstration that such creoles incorporated significant portions of the grammars of their lexical source languages when speakers of those languages were present in sufficient numbers during the formative period of the creoles. (Even in these cases, we argued that differences between the creole and the TL are not a result of changes **in the TL**, because there was no normal transmission of the TL as a whole language, and therefore no single language that was undergoing changes.)

But we do not believe that the assumption of directionality is justified as a general proposition in the case of pidgin genesis. We agree that the goal of speakers who are creating a pidgin is language learning, but not that their shared goal is necessarily the learning of a particular language (namely, the one that may provide up to 90 percent of the pidgin's vocabulary). Sometimes, to be sure, a claim of directionality is justified, as in the case of Pidgin Arabic among newly converted Moslem non-Arabs in Africa, where access to the language of their religion was probably an important factor in promoting the crystallization of an Arabic-based pidgin (Thomason and Elgibali, 1986). To judge by Sankoff's account (1980), Queensland Plantation Pidgin is another case where there was a definite TL.

In other cases, however, the claim that "in the incipient stages, the learners' goal is to acquire the language of some other group" (Sankoff 1980:145) is not supported by any substantive evidence and is, on the contrary, opposed by a few social and linguistic indications. Surely a process of linguistic negotiation need not presuppose a target language; the desire for a common means of communication strikes us as an adequate motivation, in principle, for the development of a compromise grammar with a single agreed-upon lexicon. One piece of evidence that supports our position is found in the reports that speakers of two languages believed that they were speaking the other group's language: it does not follow that they tried to learn each other's languages, but rather, as noted above, this phenomenon suggests joint efforts to make linguistic accommodations to the other group's linguistic behavior. Another bit of evidence is Hall's observation that the Chinese who learned and used Chinese Pidgin English refused to "stoop to learning the foreigners' language in its full form" (1966:8).

The most interesting linguistic evidence that bears on the general question is found in pidgin structures that differ from, but are not less marked than, corresponding vocabulary-base language structures. We have a number of suggestive examples, but one of the clearest we have found is the SOV word order in Chinese Pidgin Russian: unless one wants to argue that SVO word order is somehow more marked than SOV order, it is hard to account for this pattern on the hypothesis that the people who developed the pidgin were in any sense trying to learn Russian, which is an SVO language (as is Chinese; see 7.3 for discussion of the source of this feature).

7.2. PIDGIN GENESIS AS A RESULT OF MUTUAL LINGUISTIC ACCOMMODATION

The process of pidgin formation that we envision is basically the same as the one described in chapter 6: members of the new contact community make guesses about what their interlocutors will understand, and "right" guesses are incorporated into the grammar of the developing contact language. As with abrupt creoles, when the contact medium crystallizes into a pidgin language its grammar will be a function of the structures of the languages spoken by its developers. There are, however, two important differences between pidgin genesis and abrupt creolization. First, since abrupt creoles are needed to serve as an entire community's primary language, and needed immediately, they are likely to crystallize faster than pidgins, which are needed (at least at first) only for restricted purposes in intergroup communication. This may mean that universal markedness plays a greater role in determining the linguistic outcome of abrupt creolization than of pidginization, since in the latter case the process of compromise can be more leisurely. The evidence on this point is inconclusive, however, mainly because all the abrupt creoles we know of have typologically similar European vocabulary-base languages and almost all have typologically similar groups of substrate languages, so that the potential amount of typological diversity reflected in these languages is limited.

The second developmental difference between pidgins and abrupt creoles is that significant participation by speakers of the lexical source language will not, in pidgins, necessarily have a disproportionate effect on the grammar of the resulting pidgin. This is to some extent a result of the fact that pidgins need not have a TL. One major reason for the lack of a TL for many pidgins probably is that—unlike abrupt creoles, almost all of which arose under conditions of extreme social asymmetry—trade and work-group pidgins often emerge among speaker groups of more or less equal status. Another reason is that in cases of pidginization speakers of the lexical source language sometimes deliberately use a simplified version of their language as a social distancer. In such cases increased participation by them in the process of pidgin development will **not** lead to the incorporation of increased numbers of structural features from their own language in the developing pidgin, because they are withholding their full range of native-language structures from the other participants in the pidginization process. Although this phenomenon is mentioned occasionally in the literature, its importance has not been emphasized by writers on pidgin/creole genesis, so we will give some examples here.

At least two North American pidgins with Indian lexicons provide illustrations. One was the seventeenth-century Delaware-based pidgin that was used between the Delaware Indians and various groups of European traders and settlers—Dutch, Swedish, and English. (It may also have been used between Algonquian and Iroquoian Indians; there is, however, only slight and indirect evidence to support such a hypothesis. See Thomason 1980c for discussion.) Although some Europeans, notably William Penn and the Swedish missionary Campanius, believed that this pidgin was Delaware itself, others recognized the difference. The Dutch minister Michaëlius, for instance, commented in 1628 (Jameson 1909:128) that the Delaware Indians

> rather design to conceal their language from us than to properly communicate it, except in things which happen in daily trade; saying that it is sufficient for us to understand them in that; and then they speak only half sentences, shortened words . . . ; and all things which have only a rude resemblance to each other, they frequently call by the same name.

The other Amerindian pidgin that functioned as a barrier to access to the Indians' own native language(s) was Mobilian Jargon. According to Drechsel (1984:160–161), many Louisiana Indians used Mobilian Jargon as a "social and cultural barrier against non-Indian outsiders in particular," so that most non-Indians believed that they were learning Choctaw or Chickasaw, or some other Indian language, when actually they were only learning the pidgin.

A strikingly similar case is reported by Lydall (1976:397) in a discussion of field work in the early 1970's on the previously undescribed Ethiopian language Hamer, a member of the Omotic branch of Afro-Asiatic:

For the next seven months we lived in Hamer villages without any interpreter or intermediary between ourselves and the Hamer. We learned through listening and practice until, at the end of the seven months, we felt we had achieved a working knowledge of Hamer. . . . Today we realize that the language which we had learned in the first seven months was a kind of "Pidgin Hamer" which is used only for and by policemen, traders, and non-Hamer settlers. In the past year we have succeeded in having our Hamer friends and companions talk to us in proper Hamer.

A fourth example, separated geographically from the other three by thousands of miles, is mentioned by Dutton and Brown (1977:760–761, citing Chatterton 1970:95–96) in their historical and linguistic description of Hiri Motu, the trade pidgin whose lexical source language is the Austronesian language Motu of coastal New Guinea:

The first references of any sort to any "unusual" language spoken by the Motu is that contained in references to W.G. Lawes' early attempts to learn Motu from villagers in Port Moresby harbour where he and his wife first settled in 1874. According to several recent reports, the Motu were never keen on teaching him their "true" language but instead attempted to communicate with him and later to teach him "a simplified form of their language." . . . However, it was not until some time later that his son, Frank, who played with the boys of the village and learned the "true" language from them drew his father's attention to the deception. Even so it was only with difficulty that Lawes was able to learn the true language, because many of the villagers were still opposed to imparting this knowledge to strangers.

A slightly different motive for promoting social distance is suggested by Baron's observation (1975:23) that "there are numerous instances in the literature . . . in which 'native' populations have received ill treatment for addressing the dominant population in the dominant language rather than in pidgin." Although her examples involve dominant Europeans and subordinate non-Europeans, analogues can be found among Indians in the Americas. Bruce Rigsby (personal communication 1981) has pointed out that slaves in some Amerindian communities were obliged to adopt a humble posture and, perhaps, a similarly "humble" pidginized version of their Indian slavemasters' language; following this suggestion, Thomason (1983a) has proposed master-slave communication as one possible component of the context in which Chinook Jargon arose (see also Hymes [1980:417]).

These and other documented examples show that speakers do indeed simplify their native languages for specific social purposes in contact situations.[5] As we have said, such instances provide one reason for the absence of many marked vocabulary-base language structures in newly crystallized pidgins. Although these examples suggest that the ability to simplify one's native language is, as Ferguson and others have argued, a common (or perhaps even a universal) learned skill, we have no documentary evidence of concomitant simplification by speakers of languages other than the lexical source language in pidginizing contexts. Given the nature of the evidence just cited, this is not surprising: in each of these instances, except for the last one, foreign visitors or settlers were trying to learn an indigenous language. There was therefore a definite target language, and no motive for the foreigners to simplify their own languages or to arrive at a compromise contact medium. None of the situations in which known pidgin languages arose is recoverable historically. (Current work on Gastarbeiterdeutsch and other guest-worker languages is relevant and fascinating, but these situations are not, in our opinion, a close analogue of the conditions under which pidgin languages arose in the past.)

All the evidence that we have to offer in support of our hypothesis of mutual simplification is therefore indirect. Our case rests on three kinds of indirect evidence, two of which have already been discussed in part. First, people who come into regular contact with speakers of other languages can and do have well-developed ways of communicating with such people, including simplification of their native languages. This is what LePage calls "the learned expectancies of how to behave in a contact situation" (1977:229); an example is found in Dutton's description (1983) of the Motu speakers' linguistic behavior on their *hiri* expeditions, which provides a glimpse of sophisticated strategies for intergroup communication. (Anyone who has traveled in foreign countries can provide personal anecdotes of learned strategies for talking to people who share no common language with the traveler; the obvious example is the tendency to try using some other language one knows slightly, even when it is certain that no one else present knows that language.)

Second, the social contexts in which many pidgins apparently arose do not support the hypothesis that the lexical source language constituted a target language in any serious sense. If other speakers were not trying to learn the vocabulary-base language, then simplification of it by its speakers could play only a limited role in the formation of the eventual pidgin grammar. And—to comment on an all-too-frequent misconception—simplification of the lexical source language by people who did **not** know it could play no role at all, because you can't simplify what you don't know. Even in cases where there is clearly a target language, only its speakers can simplify it; the learners' **intake** from the TL speakers' **input** will no doubt be simpler than the input, but the process surely differs from simplification by TL speakers, and the results will often differ too. To take a well-known example from first-language acquisition, the child who hears a passive sentence *The boy is hit by the girl* (input) and understands it as an active sentence *boy hit girl* (intake) is not simplifying known structure but rather ignoring unfamiliar structure, and interpreting the sentence in a way that no fluent adult speaker would interpret it.

The third kind of evidence is found in the structures of attested pidgins. Our main argument here has to do with what kinds of features each proposed mechanism can explain. Simplification of the lexical source language can account for pidgin structures that match those of the lexical source language, and, in conjunction with the hypothesis of universal structural tendencies, it would also account for pidgin structures that can be viewed as simplified versions of structural features found in the lexical source language. By itself, the hypothesis of universal structural tendencies can account only for universally unmarked structures in pidgin languages.

But both of these hypotheses, separately and together, fail to explain the presence in pidgins of features that are neither universally unmarked nor derivable from structures of the lexical source language. More significantly, while they offer explanations for widespread structural **similarities** among pidgins (and creoles), they cannot account for structural **differences** among these languages, except where those differences can be ascribed to structural differences in various lexical source languages. An approach that rests on mutual linguistic accommodation, by contrast, can account for differences among pidgins that arose in different linguistic contexts. Together with the notions of universal structural tendencies and typological distance, it can also account for the presence of universally marked features in pidgins whose source languages are typologically similar, as well as for the structural similarities found in all pidgins—namely, features predicted because they are unmarked, and because even typologically similar languages will differ in many grammatical structures.

To the extent that pidgins differ from each other in ways not predictable from differences in their lexical source languages, therefore, a primary emphasis on TL simplification and/or structural universals loses credibility as a general claim about the origins of pidgin grammars. And if we find in pidgins universally marked features that are not present in the lexical source languages, the argument against these two hypotheses as exclusive or primary ones is strengthened. Below, in sketches of portions of diverse pidgin grammars (7.3), we will give examples of both types. Before doing so, however, we need to comment on objections that have been raised, and will surely be raised again, to any theory of pidgin genesis that includes contribution from substrate languages as a major component. These objections fall into two main categories.

One type of objection is really a subcategory of the general suspicion with which explanations involving substratum interference are viewed by historical linguists. We have already discussed such views in chapters 5 and 6; here is one further example that is relevant specifically to pidgins. Naro (1978:339), in discussing the origin of the first Portuguese-based pidgin, comments that, once we bring in what he calls Eastern Sabir as a possible influence on the developing pidgin, we have

> given substratum enthusiasts all the languages of the eastern Mediterranean [as well as all West African languages] in which to search for models of the pidgin features. . . . It would be rather surprising if one were not able to find a source for just about anything, given such a large portion of the world's languages to work with.

However, Naro has missed the crucial point about reasonable explanations involving substratum contribution to pidgin grammars. As we have argued above, the goal is not to search, language by language and feature by feature, for a source for each of the pidgin's features individually; rather, one must first identify the typological features of the pidgin and of all the languages spoken by the pidgin's developers, and then check to see if, and where, the typological profiles match. If many of the pidgin's structures are also found in the substrate languages **as a group,** then contribution from substrate languages is a reasonable explanation, though not necessarily a complete one, for their appearance in the pidgin. If the typological profiles do not match, then contribution from one or more particular substrate languages is a reasonable hypothesis only under the conditions we outlined above, in chapter 3 (for contact-induced changes in general) and in chapter 5 (for shift-induced changes in particular).

In this respect (among others) the methodological requirements for identifying substrate contribution to initial pidgin grammars are the same as the requirements for identifying shift-induced changes in already existing languages. One case in which such an explanation is needed and justified is the SOV word order of Chinese Pidgin Russian, which cannot be due to Chinese contribution any more than it can be derived from Russian; the source of the feature is surely to be found in the SOV Altaic languages whose speakers are thought to have helped in creating the pidgin (see 7.3 for discussion).

The other type of objection is specific to the problem of pidgin genesis. Numerous authors have dismissed substrate features from consideration in this context on the ground that they entered the pidgin only after the period during which the language was crystallized. That is, in this view demonstrable substrate features are taken to be later additions to an early pidgin grammar that lacked them. A major recent statement of this position is in Mühlhäusler (1980:41):

> The fact that the grammar of a pidgin or a creole is similar to substratum and/or superstratum languages supports neither common-core nor substratum theories of pidginization, since structural expansion, particularly at the morphological and syntactic levels, proceeds of its own accord.

Mühlhäusler's rationale for this view is that "developing systems of restricted complexity are incapable of integrating complex structures from the languages with which they are in contact" (1981:71).[6] Since Mühlhäusler believes that initial pidgin grammars are maximally simple, it follows for him that (in our terms) such grammars can contain no universally marked features. His evidence for this position is in changes in Tok Pisin grammar from its earliest attestations until the present, for instance in the category of number (Mühlhäusler 1981).

While we do not dispute Mühlhäusler's analysis of the Tok Pisin data, we do not believe that he is justified in generalizing from one set of data to pidgins in general. There are certainly marked morpho-syntactic features in a number of pidgin languages; we will give examples in 7.3. The fact that Tok Pisin has expanded grammatically does not mean that other pidgins with marked features must have done so; in fact, as we noted 7.1, Tok Pisin is quite unusual among pidgins in its degree of expansion in social functions and, conse-quently, in linguistic resources. Similarly, though any long-lived pidgin is likely to have undergone changes during its history, this fact does not in itself carry any implications about the specific sorts of changes to be expected. Both internally and externally motivated changes will no doubt occur, just as they do in non-pidgin languages.

The problem Mühlhäusler raises is a difficult one: since we have no adequate records of the actual formation process for any pidgin, and since very few pidgins have undergone significant structural changes during their attested history, how can we determine what features were in a given pidgin when it first crystallized as a language? The answer is that we usually can't, at least not directly. This means that historical hypotheses about initial pidgin structures are subject to the same methodological constraints as historical hypotheses about any other unattested language states: **the historical account which best fits the attested data and which requires the smallest number of unattested steps is to be preferred.** Of course linguists will con-tinue to argue about theories of languages structure and language change, and theoretical differences will affect what one sees as the best fit with the data. Nevertheless, a theory that depends crucially on unattested changes after a pidgin's undocumented period of origin suffers from a considerable initial handicap, and this handicap in-creases with each instance that requires such a scenario. Our model is simpler, and it accounts for the data at least as well as Mühlhäusler's and other hypotheses that rely on unattested changes.

7.3. EXAMPLES: DIVERSITY IN PIDGIN STRUCTURES

Let us turn now to some illustrations of diversity in pidgin struc-tures. We concentrate here on lesser-known pidgins, because these are the ones that provide the best examples of diversity. The most familiar pidgins (and creoles) are those which occupy a prominent position in the colonial history of major European powers; all of them have European lexicons and African or (more rarely) Austronesian substrate languages. Since the languages of major European powers share many typological features, and since relevant African and Austronesian languages also fall into well-defined typological groupings, a restricted range of features is found in pidgin and creole languages arising out of these contacts. Some of these features have been claimed as typical of pidgins in general. But when we look at pidgins outside the major European trade and colonial routes—and even at a few within them, notably Chinese Pidgin English—we find much greater typological diversity. Our examples come from one Amerindian pidgin, Chinook Jargon; two African pidgins with Bantu lexical source languages, Kituba and Fanagalo; three Pacific pidgins, Hiri Motu, Chinese Pidgin English, and Bislama; and the central Asian pidgin Chinese Pidgin Russian.

Chinook Jargon, which has now almost vanished from use, was widely used in northwestern North America during the second half of the nineteenth century. Its attested history goes back at least to the 1830s, but we believe that it was already in existence as an intertribal contact language along and near the Columbia River before the period of extensive European settlement in the region. (Chinook Jargon is discussed in Thomason 1983*a*; see also Hymes 1980 for a more detailed sociohistorical analysis.) Whether or not it predated European contact, its structure is clearly derived from the structures of the numerous Indian languages whose speakers helped to create the pidgin. One problematic feature is the dominant SVO word order: except for Kalapuya, none of the relevant Amerindian languages has this pattern. Otherwise, however, Chinook Jargon reflects its Amerindian milieu faithfully.

Systematic phonological features of Chinook Jargon include glottalized stops, labialized dorsal stops, lateral obstruents, separate series of velar and post-velar stops, a glottal stop phoneme, and consonant clusters consisting of two stops. Among the syntactic features are a variant VS word order, used especially with adjectival predicates; pleonastic subject and possessive pronouns, as in *Kakwa yaka wawa t'alap'as kapa lilu* 'thus the coyote spoke to the wolf' (literally 'so 3.sg. speak coyote to wolf'); a NEG SV word order; and an optional question particle *na*, as in *na ulu mayka?* 'are you hungry?' (literally

'Q hungry you?'), which occurs in about a third of the attested yes/no questions in the older Chinook Jargon materials (and much more often in mid-nineteenth-century catechisms). All the phonological features mentioned are highly marked in universal terms. None of the syntactic features is especially unusual in languages of the world, but none of them is common in the better-known pidgins and creoles, either. All these phonological and syntactic features are shared between Lower Chinook, the primary lexical source language, and virtually all the other Indian languages of the region, so Chinook Jargon grammar may reasonably be claimed as a cross-language compromise—but emphatically **not** as the result of the operation of universal structural tendencies (see 9.7 for a fuller description of this case).

Kituba, as mentioned above, is based lexically on the Manianga dialect of the Bantu language KiKongo. Nida and Fehderau (1970) suggest that the pidgin arose in the early sixteenth century as a means of communication among various BaKongo tribes participating in the slave and ivory trade. The Bantu languages and dialects whose speakers developed the pidgin are all very similar typologically; accordingly, the cross-language compromise in Kituba grammar is much more complicated morphosyntactically than the structures of pidgins that arose on a more diverse typological base. Thus, although Kituba has independent subject pronouns instead of the verbal subject prefixes that are characteristic of Bantu languages, it also has (according to Nida and Fehderau) nine preposed tense/aspect particles (vs. seventeen tense/aspect prefixes in KiManianga); four non-alliterative plural noun-class prefixes (vs. six alliterative prefixes in KiManianga); and some tonal distinctions, though not as complex a system as in KiManianga. Kituba differs sharply in these respects from Chinook Jargon and from other pidgins and creoles as well.

Fanagalo, another Bantu-based pidgin, apparently arose in Natal, South Africa, in the nineteenth century. (This and other information about Fanagalo comes from Cole 1964 [1953] and from Heine 1975.) Its creators spoke several Bantu languages, English, and perhaps (East) Indian languages. The main lexical source language is Zulu. Fanagalo spread inland from the coast for use in the mines of South Africa and Rhodesia. Like Zulu and other Bantu languages (and English), Fanagalo is an SVO language; unlike Zulu and Bantu in general, but like English, it has Adjective-Noun word order.

Fanagalo lacks the Bantu concord system but has pleonastic third person subject pronouns. It also lacks Bantu noun classes entirely, but plural is marked on nouns by a Bantu prefix *ma-*, e.g., *skatul* 'shoe' : *maskatul* 'shoes'. Fanagalo does have three typical Bantu suffixal constructions, a passive formed with the suffix *-wa*, a causative formed with the suffix *-isa*, and a past suffix *-ile;* all three suffixes are of Zulu origin. Examples are *penta* 'paint' (an English-origin word) : *pentwa* 'be painted', *figa* 'come, arrive' : *figisa* 'bring', and *shefa* 'shave' (another English-origin word) : *shefile* 'shaved'.

Cole comments that Zulu clicks (which Zulu acquired through interference from Khoisan) are 'frequently replaced' in Fanagalo by /k/. This suggests that the clicks sometimes remain in Fanagalo; if they do, they represent a highly marked phonological feature. Clicks do not, of course, occur in English or in Indian languages, but they are common in a few other Southern Bantu languages besides Zulu, and they occur in Bantu languages as far north as Rhodesia. Prefixed plurals are typical of Bantu but not of most other languages in the world. Suffixed tense, causative, and passive markers are rather common in the world's languages, but none of these morphological features occurs in the better-known pidgins and creoles. More importantly, Fanagalo differs grammatically from Kituba in ways that are not predictable from the differences in the grammars of Zulu and KiManianga. Both Zulu and KiManianga have typical elaborate Bantu morphological structures, including verb concord systems, prefixal noun classes, and tense/aspect markers. But only Kituba, with its much more homogeneous group of input languages, reflects the Bantu structures to a significant degree; Fanagalo arose in a context of greater typological diversity and therefore shows much less Bantu morphosyntax than Kituba.

Hiri Motu is spoken in an area that stretches along coastal Papua New Guinea for considerable distances east and west of Port Moresby. Its lexical source language is the Austronesian language Motu, which is spoken in and around Port Moresby, and the pidgin apparently arose before European contact in the context of Motu trade with peoples who speak, for the most part, non-Austronesian (NAN) languages (Dutton and Brown 1977:760, 764).[7] According to Wurm (1964:20), Hiri Motu and Motu "are not readily mutually intelligible in full, . . . though individual words in the utterances may be recognized."

The comparative sketch we give here is based on information in Dutton and Brown (1977), Wurm (1964), Wurm and Harris (1963), and Dutton (1983). Phonologically, neither Motu nor any of the relevant NAN languages is particularly exotic; all of them have small phonemic inventories, mainly CV syllables, and other unmarked features. Hiri Motu does have (on some accounts) a labialized velar stop phoneme, like Motu; but unlike Motu, it has an /s/ phoneme, which it shares with at least some of the relevant NAN languages. Wurm and Harris observe that, though pronunciation of Hiri Motu varies from place to place, there is apparently some norm of "correctness" for the pidgin, so that good speakers make distinctions that do not occur in their native languages.

Hiri Motu lacks the object suffixes characteristic of Motu verbs, but it does have transitive verb suffixes that distinguish the number of the direct object, singular -(i)a and plural -(i)dia. This pattern—the marking on a transitive verb of the number, but not the person, of the direct object—matches the suffixal pattern in one relevant NAN group, the Eleman languages. The only other regular morphological features of Hiri Motu are the causative prefix ha- and the common adjective suffixes -na (sg.) and -dia (pl.). These constructions all match Motu; we have no information about corresponding constructions in the NAN languages of the region. One feature of the Hiri Motu pronominal system should be noted here: the pidgin distinguishes between inclusive and exclusive 'we', just as Motu and many of the NAN languages do.

Word order patterns in Motu, as in other Austronesian languages of New Guinea, resemble those of neighboring NAN languages, thanks to interference from the NAN languages on the Austronesian ones. (At least, this is the commonly held view; we have not investigated the matter independently, though certainly SVO, and also VSO and VOS, are the dominant patterns for Austronesian languages elsewhere.) All the relevant languages are SOV with postpositions; they also have determiners and relative clauses preceding the head noun, but Noun-Adjective (NA) word order. This last feature may be statistically surprising, since according to Greenberg's well-known study (1963) we should expect AN order in SOV languages.[8] To the extent that Greenberg's statistical universal represents a genuine universal tendency, the NA word order of Hiri Motu is a marked feature in the context of its frequent SOV sentence structures and its DET and REL + head noun orderings; but it is easily explained in the typological context in which the pidgin arose.

Probably the most interesting feature of Hiri Motu syntax, however, is its variation in sentential word order between SOV and OSV, with the latter especially common when the subject is a pronoun. (SVO sentences also occur, but rarely.) Now, dominent OSV word order occurs in some South American Indian languages, but in general it is a rare pattern in the world's languages. Its presence in Hiri Motu is presumably to be explained by the fact that Motu has subject particles that are preposed to the verb; a full-noun object precedes these in a sentence. (Drechsel gives a similar argument for the OSV word order of Mobilian Jargon; see also Thomason 1980c:191–192 for discussion.) The NAN languages may also have influenced this development, but we do not know what their corresponding patterns are.

Hiri Motu has two tense markers, a postverbal past tense particle and a preverbal future particle, whose position corresponds to Motu usage. The pidgin also has a continuous aspect particle whose syntax is said to resemble corresponding constructions in the NAN language Toaripi rather than the suffixal Motu construction (Dutton and Brown 1977:763). Hiri Motu, like Chinook Jargon and Fanagalo, has pleonastic subject pronouns, which correspond functionally to the semantically redundant pronominal subject markers of Motu and of at least some relevant NAN languages. In two syntactic features Hiri Motu clearly matches the NAN languages but not Motu. The first is the position of the negative particle *lasi,* which follows the verb phrase, as do the corresponding particles in the NAN languages. Motu, by contrast, has a complex system of combined negative and subject markers preceding the verb. The second feature is a sentence connective whose form is Motu but whose function is similar to that of constructions in NAN languages.

Hiri Motu thus has a number of features, most notably its most frequent word order patterns, that distinguish it from most other pidgins and creoles. It has a few inflectional affixes, including one pattern, the singular and plural transitive verb suffixes, which would not necessarily be predicted as an independent simplification of its lexical source language, although it is quite reasonable as a compromise between mutually simplifying Motu and NAN speakers. Two syntactic features, the sentence connective and the syntax of the negative particle, would certainly not be predicted as simplifications of Motu itself. And the OSV word order is arguably more highly marked than corresponding patterns in the source languages, especially since it introduces sentential ambiguity;[9] but this feature too is reasonable when viewed as a cross-language compromise.

Chinese Pidgin English arose some time after the English first established a trading post at Canton in the late seventeenth century (Hall 1966:8; Shi 1986). Its possible connections with a prior Portuguese-based pidgin in the area have been debated. It could be at least in part the result of relexification from such a pidgin, but the social circumstances of its development, as described by Shi (1986), make this rather unlikely: Shi argues convincingly that Chinese Pidgin English arose through contact between a small and constantly changing group of visiting English traders and a stable resident population of their Cantonese-speaking servants. Since contacts between the English traders and other people in China—that is, other foreigners as well as Chinese—were rigidly controlled by the Chinese government during the relevant period (1699–1748), most other possibilities can be ruled out with confidence.

Shi presents a systematic comparison of Chinese Pidgin English with Cantonese structure. He concludes that, while many Chinese Pidgin English structural features "are shared by both English and Cantonese, or can be considered simplifications from both languages," a sizable number of features "can only be seen as contributions from Cantonese" (1986:112). The most striking of the numerous Cantonese structural contributions that he identifies are the different treatments in Chinese Pidgin English of English labial fricatives, with *v* (which Cantonese lacks) replaced by *b* but *f* (which Cantonese has) maintained; the obligatory use of the numeral classifier *piece* between a numeral and its head noun; the use of the copula in construction with predicate nouns but not with predicate adjectives; the use of a Cantonese yes/no question pattern; and the deletion in discourse of a topic-connected noun phrase from a comment sentence. Significantly, Shi finds no structural features in pre-twentieth-century Chinese Pidgin English that can be viewed as contributions from English alone.

It is also important to note that none of the specifically Cantonese features of Chinese Pidgin English can be explained by any theory of universal structural tendencies, and none of them is common in pidgins or creoles around the world; the numeral classifier, in particular, is unique among pidgin and creole languages and must be considered a universally marked feature.

Another unusual feature of Chinese Pidgin English, both among pidgins and creoles and in languages in general, is its lack of plural personal pronouns. Mühlhäusler (1981:61) ascribes this feature to a universal pidgin base on the ground that it cannot be due to simplification from English or to substratum influence. We would agree that English speakers would be unlikely to drop plural pronouns spontaneously in simplifying their language, but the possibility of contribution from Chinese cannot be dismissed so easily. Mandarin, Cantonese, and other Chinese languages do have regular plural pronouns, but these are secondary forms derived by the addition of a suffix to the singular pronoun, e.g., Mandarin *wǒ* 'I, me' : *wǒmen* 'we, us', *nǐ* 'you(sg.)' : *nǐmen* 'you (pl.)' (Tewksbury 1948:1), Cantonese *ngǎw* 'I, me' : *ngǎw-dǎy* 'we, us' (Bruce 1970:23–24), and so forth. Possessive pronouns are often identical to the personal pronouns (Tewksbury, 22; Bruce, 34). Simplification from a system like this to a set of personal/possessive pronouns that show no number distinctions does not seem improbable, especially when the other speakers involved—that is, English speakers—have pronouns built on a quite different organizing principle. (It should also be noted that the Shanghai dialect has a pronoun *ala* which means 'I, me, we, our' [Dingxu Shi, personal communication, 1985]; however, we know of no such homophony in any other Chinese language, so this fact is probably not relevant to the question of Chinese Pidgin English pronoun origins.)

Bislama, one of the three official languages of Vanuatu (formerly the New Hebrides), is an English-based pidgin which, like Tok Pisin, developed among speakers of Austronesian languages. Camden (1975:64) remarks that it may have originally developed from, or at least under the influence of, Chinese Pidgin English and Australian Aboriginal Pidgin English in the nineteenth century; but if so, he says, it diverged rapidly from those pidgins after it crystallized. Camden is cited in chapter 6 on the subject of exploitation in Bislama grammar of constructions shared by English and Austronesian languages of the New Hebrides. He also notes that Bislama is closer structurally to the local languages than to English and, further, that the various non-English features of Bislama cannot be viewed as simplifications from English. One obvious example that Camden gives is the presence in the pidgin of an inclusive/exclusive 'we' distinction and dual and trial numbers in the pronoun system. Syntactic movement rules for emphasis, such as moving a constituent into clause-initial position (Camden, 51; cf. 55–56) are also typical. Another example is the construction in which a noun is followed by a modifying noun, e.g., *boks tul* 'tool box'. Other examples are found in the lexical semantics, e.g., *papa blong mi* 'my father; my father's brother' vs. *angkel blong mi* 'my mother's brother'. A few of these features, especially the dual and trial pronouns, are highly marked in universal terms, and all of them can be explained by reference to the Austronesian languages whose speakers helped to develop the pidgin.

Chinese Pidgin Russian is so named because of its use in Chinese-Russian trade, particularly in the border town of Kjaxta, south of Lake Baikal, starting some time after the establishment of a trade treaty between the two governments in 1728 (Neumann 1966:237). Russian is the lexical source language. The most interesting thing about this pidgin, in the present context, is that some of its structural features can be attributed neither to Russian nor to Chinese, and they are unlikely to be the result of mutual accommodation by speakers of these two languages alone. Nichols (1980) argues that the Ussurian dialect of the pidgin reflected strong influence from Altaic languages of the Tungusic branch; in fact, several features of the Kjaxta dialect also suggest participation by Altaic speakers in the formation of the pidgin. This would not be surprising, since Kjaxta and its counterpart on the Chinese side of the border attracted sizable populations, and since many of the peoples on both sides of the border region are speakers of Altaic languages of all three major branches—Tungusic, Turkic, and Mongolian. Published sources on Chinese Pidgin Russian are limited; the main ones are nineteenth-century Russian publications. One of these reports that the Chinese used the pidgin even in talking to each other (cited by Neumann 1966:238). This would be possible with Chinese alone, because the major so-called Chinese "dialects" are mutually unintelligible; but it is even more likely if some of the Chinese citizens in question were actually speakers of Altaic languages. Nichols cites Kozinskij (1974) as the source of a hypothesis that Chinese Pidgin Russian 'goes back to an early Russian-Uralic or Russian-Turkic contact language' (406), and observes that her data on the Ussurian dialect supports that hypothesis (as does Neumann's data). In any case, it is worth noting that both Neumann and Nichols emphasize the fact that Chinese Pidgin Russian is systematic, with a consistent grammatical norm.

Neumann identifies a number of structural features in the Kjaxta dialect. Phonological features include mostly CV syllables, with few consonant clusters (like Chinese and Altaic, unlike Russian) and no closed syllables (unlike Russian). The pidgin has a few suffixes: a reflexive one of Russian origin, an imperfective aspect suffix from Mongolian (!), and a gerund-forming suffix. Altaic languages are almost exclusively suffixing languages, with extensive use of nonfinite verbal forms (such as gerunds). Russian is also primarily suffixing, and it has aspect suffixes in addition to aspect prefixes. More interestingly, the Ussurian dialect of the pidgin has a verbal inflectional category based on evidentiality, another feature typical of Altaic languages, including Tungusic ones. Nichols cites Tungusic as the probable source of this feature and of the use of specific types of reduplication which are characteristic of Tungusic.

In (at least) the Kjaxta version of the pidgin, the occasional tense/aspect particles follow the verb, like Altaic morpheme order but unlike Russian. Like many other pidgins, Chinese Pidgin Russian has an "all-purpose" preposition, the Russian-derived preposition *za*. But the language also uses postpositions in specific locative meanings; the adpositional elements themselves are derived from Russian prepositions. The use of postpositions is characteristic of Altaic languages, and of SOV languages in general. It is not surprising, therefore, to find that Chinese Pidgin Russian is an SOV language. This word order pattern is completely consistent in the brief Kjaxta texts Neumann gives, and Nichols says that it is also typical of the Ussurian dialect. One other ordering feature is worth noting: Neumann's texts show a predominant V NEG word order (five examples) and a rarer NEG V order (two examples, both in sentences spoken by a Russian woman). Nichols does not discuss this feature, but her examples suggest that the Ussurian dialect may also have a dominant V NEG order. This feature is interesting because, like the SOV word order, it is non-Russian and non-Chinese: in both Russian and Chinese, the negative particle precedes the verb. The situation in Altaic is complicated. Most Tungusic languages have prefixed or preposed negative elements, but the prominent language Manchu has innovated with a negative verb that follows the main verb (Miller 1971:254). Negative sentences in Mongolian have negative particles preceding the verb and postposed negative particles after nouns, including the very common verbal nouns (Grønbech and Krueger 1955, Sanzheyev 1973). In Turkic languages negative elements typically follow the verb.

Like the other pidgins described in this section, then, Chinese Pidgin Russian has features that are unusual among the better-known pidgins and creoles with European lexical source languages: SOV word order, postpositions as well as preposition(s), V NEG word order, and a few inflectional and derivational suffixes. Only the last of these features could possibly be viewed as the result of simplification of Russian, and even that possibility is shaky in light of the fact that the categories do not all occur in Russian. None of these features could be predicted as the result of the operation of universal structural tendencies alone, because the suffixes represent marked constructions, and the word order features are different from the ones found in other contact languages. The presence of both preposition(s) and postpositions is itself rather highly marked in universal terms. So the hypothesized contribution from Altaic participants in the pidginization process (and, if Kozinskij is right, perhaps also from speakers of Uralic languages, which are typologically similar to Altaic in many respects) is necessary to account for a number of the structural features of the pidgin.

We should emphasize, finally, that the examples given in this section do not by any means exhaust the instances of pidgin structures that are not promising candidates for simplified lexical source language features or features of universal grammar. Others can be found in the Delaware-based Traders' Jargon of the northeastern United States, in Mobilian Jargon of the southern United States, in Pidgin Eskimo, in Juba Arabic and Bantu-based pidgins in Africa, and elsewhere. Our goal here has been to demonstrate that origin theories based solely on evidence from well-known, well-documented mainstream pidgins and creoles are inadequate to the extent that they fail to predict the kinds of features we have illustrated.

7.4. PIDGIN GENESIS AND CONTACT-INDUCED LANGUAGE CHANGE

Our own theory does predict that pidgins with different source languages—lexical and substrate—will differ from each other in structure. The previous linguistic experience of members of a new contact community will determine, to begin with, the guesses they make about what their interlocutors will understand. They will use whatever strategies they have learned for simplifying structures of their native languages and, no doubt, of other languages they know. The degree of simplification will depend, we believe, on the degree to which marked features of languages they already know are shared with marked features of their interlocutors' languages: if other members of the community are familiar with, for instance, suffixal causative constructions or prefixed plural markers, then a given speaker will be understood when s/he uses such grammatical devices. And s/he is likely to do so, because the task of linguistic accommodation will be easier if s/he can continue to use structures as close as possible to ones s/he already uses in his/her native (and other) languages.

When a given speaker does simplify native-language structures, the results of that process will be determined by universal structural tendencies. When the pidgin crystallizes, its grammar should therefore contain only those marked features that are widely shared among the source languages; it will also contain numerous unmarked features, and in pidgins whose source languages are typologically dissimilar these may comprise all or almost all of the pidgin's grammar. Some structural features of a pidgin will not, of course, differ from functionally equivalent features on any scale of simplicity. Word order features are the obvious example, except possibly where statistically incongruent features co-occur (e.g., SOV and NA orderings).

We should repeat that this view of pidgin origins can only provide a full explanation for an initial pidgin grammar (that is, the grammar of a pidgin soon after it has crystallized as a language) when it is combined with relevant social information: if there is clearly a TL, or if speakers of one language or language group are especially numerous or prestigious—to give just two examples—then the grammar of the pidgin will reflect those social facts by having a disproportionate number of features from one or more particular source languages. And, as we emphasized above, limitations in the range of communicative functions for which a pidgin is needed will inevitably lead to limitations in the range of linguistic resources (e.g., stylistic variants and other kinds of grammatical complexity) in the emergent pidgin.

When we compare pidgin genesis to contact-induced language change, we find some obvious differences. As with abrupt creoles, most pidgins arise in multilingual settings; shift and borrowing situations, by contrast, typically involve only two languages at a time.

Unlike cases of language shift, pidgin genesis does not occur as a result of speakers' giving up their native language in order to adopt another one; as we have argued, pidgin genesis sometimes does not even involve an attempt to learn another language, quite apart from giving up the original native language. Unlike cases of structural borrowing into a maintained language, pidgins do not arise under conditions of full bilingualism. In fact, the notion of borrowing seems inappropriate as a label for the process of incorporating lexical or structural features from different languages into an emerging pidgin: to us, "borrowing" suggests the addition of features from a secondary language into a primary one; and, if there is no TL for an emerging pidgin, then—in our opinion—no valid distinction can be made between "primary language" and "secondary language." Moreover, until the pidgin crystallizes fully, there is no language to borrow features into; rather, all features that become part of the emerging grammar have the same primary grammatical status.

Nevertheless, in spite of these and other differences between pidgin genesis and contact-induced change in an already existing language, the two processes are also similar in important respects. Specifically, pidgin genesis as a process shares a number of features with imperfect group learning during a process of language shift. In both cases, speakers are engaged in a learning process whose ultimate goal (at least in part) is to talk to speakers of some other language(s). The strategies employed are comparable: a large group of shifting speakers will learn some or most TL structures but keep some of their native-language structures, which in turn are learned by original TL speakers; pidgin creators will learn a vocabulary and some foreign structures but, at the same time, will simplify and adapt their native-language structures only as much as they have to to arrive at a form of speech that is mutually intelligible with the similarly simplified and adapted speech of other participants in the process. Though the shifting speakers are trying to learn a particular language, while pidgin speakers often are not, both situations involve learning that is "imperfect" in the sense that the end point is not the acquisition of the entire grammar of any particular language.

Finally, the linguistic results of shift-induced language change and of pidgin genesis are similar in kind—though not in degree, because the differences between the two processes, and the sociolinguistic differences between a community's primary language and a multilingual community's functionally restricted secondary language, dictate major differences in the resulting system's overall resources and in the level of complexity in any of its grammatical subsystems. In both cases, markedness considerations and typological distance are the major linguistic factors that determine the linguistic results, as attested by the examples given in this chapter and in chapters 5 and 6. Universally marked features are less likely than unmarked features to be retained from the original language by a group of shifting speakers, less likely to be acquired from shifting speakers by original TL speakers in cases of language shift, and less likely to constitute part of the cross-language compromise in pidgin genesis. But if the TL and the shifting group's original language are typologically similar in a case of language shift, then marked features may well be transferred from the latter to the former, and if most or all of the languages of the pidgin's creators share particular marked features, then those features may be kept by the various speakers and turn up in the initial grammar of the crystallized pidgin. Similarly, a proportionately large shifting group may introduce features of the original native language into the TL, just as an especially large (or prestigious) group of pidgin developers may contribute features of their native language to the emerging pidgin grammar.

In the last section of this chapter we will address one other important question that is often raised in discussions of pidgin and creole genesis: how likely is it that a pidgin will arise in a new contact situation? Although not all scholars who disagree with our approach would subscribe to the monogenesis hypothesis, the prominence of monogenesis in pidgin/creole studies in the recent past makes it an appropriate context for our comments.

7.5. MONOGENESIS AND THE PROBABILITY OF PIDGINIZATION

Proponents of the monogenesis hypothesis in its strong form take the original western European trade pidgin—i.e., the Portuguese-based pidgin thought by some scholars to be an outgrowth of Sabir—to be the direct historical source of all later pidgins and creoles with European vocabulary-base languages. The suggestion is that when other European powers took over bits of Portuguese trading and colonial territory in Africa and Asia, the Portuguese-based pidgin was relexified by indigenes and/or the new European traders and

sailors, and then transplanted to new territories. Relexification has
been documented in cases where a new superordinate group has
replaced an earlier one whose language provided the lexicon for a pidgin or creole; this is said to have happened in the Philippines and in
Papiamentu in the Caribbean, in both cases with Spanish vocabulary
replacing an earlier Portuguese lexicon. The monogenesis hypothesis
is a generalization from the documented cases to cases in which there
is no attested earlier pidgin or creole in the relevant location. Sometimes it is even extended to include pidgins with non-European lexical
source languages and with different grammars, on the ground that
stimulus diffusion is responsible for the emergence of a pidgin.

We believe that the monogenesis hypothesis is such a strong one,
with so little historical evidence to support it, that it will be attractive
only if it is the only hypothesis that accounts adequately for the
linguistic and social facts of pidgin nature and origin. But, as our
arguments in earlier sections of this chapter indicate, we do not think
this hypothesis is needed to account for structural similarities among
the various European-vocabulary pidgins and creoles, and
monogenesis, like TL simplification and universals, fails to account
for grammatical differences among pidgins and creoles.

In this section we will consider the main sociolinguistic argument
that has been offered in support of monogenesis. That argument rests
on the claim that the sociolinguistic conditions required for pidgin
development are so specific that they are likely to have occurred only
very rarely in history (see Whinnom 1971), and maybe only in the
context of the social upheavals and population displacements that
accompanied European exploration and colonialism (see, e.g., Sankoff 1980:154 and R. Andersen 1983:4–5). There are two kinds of
responses one can make to this argument.

The first is an easy one: some pidgins demonstrably did not arise
in the context of European expansion, and others that did involved
no social upheavals or population displacement. Chinese Pidgin Russian arose in a trade situation, as far as we can tell, but the only significant displacement was the gathering of traders in Kjaxta and in its
counterpart city across the border in China. Russenorsk involved no
population displacement at all, apparently. Juba Arabic arose in the
southern Sudan as a result of Arab expansion, not European; and the
Arabic-based creole Ki-Nubi emerged among ethnically diverse sol-
diers, probably at first in the Sudan, but later to the south in Uganda.
(Moreover, since Thomason and Elgibali [1986] have documentary

evidence of a pidginized form of Arabic dating from the mid-eleventh century A.D., the usual nineteenth-century starting point posited for Arabic-based pidgins may be much too late.) There is some controversy about the periods of origin for Hiri Motu and Chinook Jargon, and even more doubt about the starting dates for Mobilian Jargon and the Delaware-based Traders' Jargon. But it would at least be rash to conclude that all of these pidgins arose after European contact, and there are other Motu-based trading languages (Dutton 1983) that are surely precontact. None of these, moreover, involved significant population displacements, at least not at first. Some of the Bantu-based pidgins may predate the Europeans' arrival on the scene, and population displacements are doubtful for Kituba (at least). Other examples of possible or certain exceptions to the exclusive European-expansion-and-displacement claim can be found, too.

The second kind of response is a methodological one. For the vast majority of past contact situations, there is no reason to expect to find any direct evidence about the existence (or nonexistence) of pidgins. In general, before Europeans arrived in the relevant areas, nobody was writing about language (or about anything else). Even if Europeans found indigenous pidgins in place when they did arrive, such languages are likely to have disappeared before the newcomers realized that they were pidgins. Remember that Lydall spent seven months learning a form of speech that turned out to be a pidginized variety of Hamer (though not, perhaps, a fully crystallized pidgin language) rather than Hamer itself (see 7.2); and other such cases are reported in the literature, in addition to the ones cited in this chapter. This means, in our view, that the general claim about the rarity of pidgins in history relies too heavily on an accident of history—namely, on the fact that most information on the subject comes from Europeans. If this historical accident is not to bias our theories, we must not take silence on the subject of precontact pidgins around the world as proof that there were none. We do know that linguistic responses to various kinds of contact situations are extremely varied; and if we find such bizarre artifacts as Mōkkī, the secret language formed by systematic metatheses and spoken by the Lōṛīs of Baluchistan (Bray 1913:139–140), what justification is there for **assuming** a priori that pidgins are rare?

In this connection, we want to examine the frequent claim that at least two languages besides the lexical source language are needed before a stable pidgin can develop. Whinnom (1971:106), for instance, holds this view; so do Sankoff (1980:143) and R. Andersen (1980:290). Whinnom (1971:194) assumes that, in a two-language contact situation,

> (a) there cannot be any really effective withdrawal of the target language, and the substrate speakers will continue to improve their performance in it; (b) a second-degree secondary hybrid dialect (a 'stage-Irish' type) is not actually employed as a medium of communication from superstrate to substrate; and (c) even where such a dialect existed it is very difficult to see how it could have . . . stabilized the dialect at all.

Moreover, says Whinnom, the substrate group in such a situation will not develop a pidgin for communication among themselves, because they have a "much more viable system in common, namely their mother tongue" (105).

Whinnom's position makes a good deal of intuitive sense, and we agree that most pidgin situations do indeed involve more than two groups of speakers. But intuitive sense and linguistic reality (as we have mentioned before) do not always coincide, and there are a number of cases which suggest that his sociolinguistic assumptions about two-language contact situations are too simplistic. First, as we pointed out in 7.2, in some cases speakers of the lexical source language deliberately withhold their language from other members of the contact community; in such cases, in two-language situations, substrate speakers cannot continue to improve their performance in the TL (if it is a TL), and the superstrate speakers will use only the simplified form in speaking to members of the substrate group.

Stabilization is a trickier question. Some scholars argue that Tây Bôi, the French-based pidgin of Vietnam, is best viewed as foreigner-talk French, not a true pidgin. But at least it seems to be clear that French masters did "deliberately simplify morphology and syntax and use scraps of VN [Vietnamese] in speaking to their servants" (Reinecke 1971:48); and it seems equally clear that, for the Vietnamese servants, the target language **was** effectively withdrawn: the substrate speakers of Tây Bôi probably heard French spoken very frequently, but they were not encouraged to improve their performance in it. Withdrawal of a TL, in other words, may be social rather than physical. This case suggests that, as one would expect, a two-language contact situation can lead to the development of a pidgin only when there is profound social separation of the two groups of speakers.

In any case, although the status of Tây Bôi remains controversial, Chinese Pidgin English is universally acknowledged as a fully crystallized pidgin. Until the eighteenth century the social separation between English-speaking traders at Canton and their Cantonese-speaking servants was even more profound than in the Vietnamese servant/French employer contact, so that the early English/Cantonese contact met this crucial social condition for the development of a pidgin in a two-language contact situation. Shi's careful historical analysis (1986) convincingly demonstrates that all the Chinese who could have participated directly in the development of Chinese Pidgin English were servants who spoke Cantonese; and since neither the servants nor their English-speaking masters were permitted freedom of movement outside the Englishmen's compound, speakers of other Chinese dialects would have had no opportunity for exposure either to Chinese Pidgin English or to English itself until the end of the eighteenth century (when the legal opium trade ended in China and the English took to smuggling). Chinese Pidgin English, therefore, is a clear case of the emergence of a pidgin among speakers of just two languages.

One other case should also be mentioned in this connection. This is Halbdeutsch (literally, "half-German"), the form of Baltic German spoken in the nineteenth century by Latvians and Estonians. Mitzka refers to this speech form as a colloquial form used between groups, i.e., between Latvians and Estonians and Germans (1943:101). But Lehiste (personal communication, 1975) suggests that Halbdeutsch may have been created independently, at least by the Estonians, and used for some communicative purposes **among Estonian speakers** who constituted an emerging Estonian middle class in the cities and towns. The situation, as she outlines it, was as follows. German was, in the nineteenth century, the language of the Baltic German elite in Estonia. The Germans deliberately kept their language to themselves, and avoided speaking it to Estonians. For Estonians who lived in cities and towns, however, some knowledge of German carried a high degree of prestige and offered a chance of assimilation into the German-speaking middle class; therefore, those Estonians who managed to acquire a smattering of German—the Halbdeutsch—actually used it as a means of communication among themselves, even though they had, in their native Estonian, "a much more viable system in common."[10]

Many of the linguistic features of Halbdeutsch that Lehiste (1965) describes are pidgin-like characteristics, such as a general absence of noun inflection and of adjective-noun agreement. Probably Halbdeutsch was not stable enough to be considered a fully crystallized pidgin. But this case does suggest that it is ill-advised to assume that attitudinal factors could not promote the development of a true pidgin, even in a two-language contact situation.

We are not convinced, therefore, by the arguments that pidgins are inherently a rare linguistic phenomenon. We suspect that they have arisen rather frequently in history. We may be mistaken in this belief, but at least the evidence we have given here may convince other scholars not to prejudge the question when faced with a situation in which a pidgin might reasonably be looked for.

8
Retrospection

8.1. GENETIC RELATIONSHIP AND THE PRODUCTS OF CONTACT-INDUCED LANGUAGE CHANGE

In the preceding chapters we have discussed various kinds and degrees of contact-induced changes, starting from the claim that such changes have important implications for genetic linguistics. In this final chapter of our general exposition we will explore those implications. The most important one has to do with the historical methodology of comparative reconstruction that is embodied in the Comparative Method.

We have argued that the most extreme products of linguistic interference are not genetically related to any of the languages that contributed to their lexical and structural systems, because they did not arise through a process of normal transmission—that is, the transmission of an entire single set of interrelated lexical and structural features. We have also argued that the presence of interference features in a language does not in itself mean that the development of that language was nongenetic, because genetic relationship can be established as long as systematic correspondences can be found, to a comparable degree, in all grammatical subsystems. Throughout our discussion, we have concentrated on this distinction between genetic and nongenetic development because we believe that it is crucial for the application of the Comparative Method in reconstructing prehistoric linguistic states. We do not intend to suggest that this particular formulation of genetic vs. nongenetic is the only important parameter in the historical analysis of a group of languages, or that it is the only point of interest in a discussion of specific aspects of social and linguistic continuity. Rather, we are interested in identifying, retrospectively, languages that **cannot** be used in the reconstruction of any proto-language. (This is oversimplifying our position to some extent. As we will point out below, parts of some of these languages can indeed be used for reconstruction purposes, just as one can use the evidence of structures borrowed from a particular proto-language into a neighboring language. But these languages as wholes are not appropriate objects for comparative reconstruction.)

The languages in question are of two main types: those that resulted from massive grammatical replacement through borrowing, such as Ma'a, AngloRomani, Michif, and Kormakiti Arabic (chap. 4), and those that resulted from abrupt creolization (chap. 6). Creolized pidgins would belong with the second group, from a retrospective viewpoint. Languages of both types are of course natural languages (as are pidgins; but a pidgin, since it is nobody's native language, will cause no problems for after-the-fact identification). If one of them becomes the main speech of a community, it can then diversify through time and space; that is, it can have dialects and descendants. If such languages arose in the past (and they may have done so), long enough ago that sociohistorical information about their origins is completely lacking, how can we recognize them? How can we keep them—and their modern analogues whose histories we do know in part—from skewing the results of our reconstructions by introducing alien elements into the comparison? To answer these questions, we need to consider the Comparative Method itself and the ways in which it is used.

The Comparative Method is often described as comprising two different tasks, the establishment of genetic relationship for a group of languages and then the reconstruction of features of the proto-language from which those related languages arose. In practice, this description is approximately correct: historical linguists first arrive at a hypothesis that two or more languages are genetically related and then try to reconstruct a common parent language from the proposed group of related languages. But when one looks at the criteria that are used to arrive at the initial hypothesis, the distinction between the two tasks breaks down. Hypotheses that rest solely on unsystematic sound/meaning correspondences in a moderate-sized list of words do not meet with much favor among historical linguists, and in fact much more evidence is required before a hypothesis of related-ness will be generally accepted. Properly applied, then, the Compara-tive Method is a means by which a hypothesis of genetic relationship is demonstrated through the following kinds of evidence: not only (1) the establishment of phonological correspondences in words of same or related meaning, including much basic vocabulary, but also (2) the reconstruction of phonological systems, (3) the establishment of grammatical correspondences, and (4) the reconstruction of gram-matical systems, to whatever extent is possible. Where more than two languages are involved, a thorough exploitation of the Comparative Method also includes (5) construction of a subgrouping model for the languages and (6) the elaboration of a diversification model.[1]

Implicit in the term "reconstruction" is the notion of regularity in the correspondences that are posited, because it is regularity that permits the formulation of a specific set of diachronic rules for each language which will derive the phonological shapes of attested mor-phemes from reconstructed morphemes and attested grammatical rules from reconstructed ones. For historical phonology, of course, this is possible only under the constraint that sound change is regular unless interfered with.

When one or more of points (1)–(4) cannot be attained, some doubt, ranging from minor to serious, can be cast on a hypothesis of genetic relationship. Since point (4) is currently feasible primarily for morphological correspondences,[2] we must ask whether these stric-tures of grammatical comparability might filter out some linguistic relationships that are undoubtedly genetic and are universally ac-cepted as such; certain languages of Southeast Asia, for instance, lack any significant amount of morphology. However, even in these lan-guages detailed correspondences according to grammatical conditions in consonantal, vocalic, and tonal alternation can be established that fulfill the requirements of (4). Our position is, therefore, that a hy-pothesis which is supported only by regular sound correspondences in basic vocabulary can be considered no more than "promising."

The questions we raised above can now be reformulated as fol-lows: is it possible for the data of a language to deceive a linguist applying the Comparative Method into believing it to be related to another language when it may in fact be a creolized pidgin, an abrupt creole, or the product of massive grammatical replacement through borrowing, somewhere back in the unwritten past? Well, if you can't reconstruct grammar, you can't prove genetic relatedness, although in historical fact the languages in question may be related (that is, they may be changed later forms of a single parent language).

Of the three nongenetic possibilities, the product of extreme borrowing is most likely to betray its mixed origin. Assuming that it is completely separated from the language that provided its grammar, the fact that the grammar is of an ordinary marked single-source type should prevent its being identified with the lexical source language. This will be true even if the grammatical source language itself is completely unknown, directly or (by way of its own relatives) indirectly. Ma'a is a good example: we certainly need evidence from Bantu languages to identify the source of its grammar, but not to show that its grammar is of non-Cushitic origin. In cases of this type, problems will arise only if the two source languages are very similar typologically, and even then, probably, only if they have little morphology.

An abrupt creole that forms part of a postcreole continuum will probably be in the process of converging with the language from which its lexicon is derived. (This would be true of a creolized pidgin in a comparable social situation too, but we know of no certain examples.) As we argued in 4.3.4, the process of decreolization is essentially a borrowing process. It may be that the creole will be shifted away from before it can be completely destroyed by convergence; but if not, a heavily decreolized creole might indeed be mistakenly identified as genetically related to (most likely a dialect of) its vocabulary-base language, since both lexicon and grammar will for the most part match in the two languages. The same is true of borderline cases resulting from other kinds of historical processes, specifically, borrowing or shift interference between very closely related languages, and nativized pidgins that originally arose among very closely related languages (e.g., many Bantu-based pidgins): some of these might be identified as relatives of their lexical source languages by the application of the Comparative Method. Although such an identification would do violence to historical fact, using these languages in reconstruction would cause little distortion in the results of that reconstruction, given the close structural similarities. This would then be just another instance of a problem familiar to all historical linguists: gaps in the historical record inevitably prevent us from reconstructing a complete, and completely accurate, historical picture.

The problems will be different in the case of abrupt creoles and nativized pidgins that have survived and **not** been reintegrated with their lexical source languages. A particularly subtle trap is that after a few hundred years with no documentation, a language like this might look like a distant relative of its lexical source language—that is, one that has undergone great changes in all grammatical subsystems and in lexicon as well. When the various languages of a putative family have a good deal of morphology, this may not be a serious problem, because the creoles will not agree morphologically with the lexical source language in the right way. But some areas of the world, as mentioned above, contain languages with very little morphology. Furthermore, after several thousand years, even a normally transmitted language that maintains much of the morphology inherited from its parent language may have changed considerably the functional categories and replaced many of the phonological shapes of the affixal material. Even so, an abrupt creole or nativized pidgin will probably not be mistakenly assumed to be related to its vocabulary-base language, because grammatical correspondences will be either missing or discrepant. That is, if the creolization was ancient, a modern language descended from a creole will probably not be identified as related to a modern language descended from the creole's lexical source language, since the grammatical and lexical correspondences will be out of phase.

It is a truism in historical linguistics that nonrelatedness can never be proved. We would like to modify that saying in one respect: if our analysis is accepted, nonrelatedness can be proved for languages which, like Ma'a, have basic vocabulary primarily from one source and some or all grammatical subsystems from some other single source. Nonrelatedness can also be proved, we believe, for nongenetic cases like Isle de France Creole or Tok Pisin, in which the lexicon is clearly derived mostly from one source but the grammar comes neither from that source nor from any other single language. Otherwise, however, nonrelatedness cannot be proved; in other words, such proof is confined to cases that can be definitely identified as nongenetic. For all other languages, only relatedness can be demonstrated, but to do this certain prerequisites must be met. If any of these prerequisites is not met, then, even though the languages in question may have a common genetic origin, the verdict must remain "unproved." The reason is that, given a great enough time depth, all the features needed to establish genetic relationship will change so much that few systematic correspondences remain in any part of the language—vocabulary, phonology, morphology, or syntax. We might therefore find it impossible, as Boas predicted, to tell whether the shared features we do find result from inheritance or from diffusion, including diffusion so extreme that a language has undergone nongenetic development.[3]

We can specify, then, several possible outcomes of a comparison between two languages. I: Vocabulary (especially basic vocabulary) matches and permits phonological reconstruction, and all grammatical subsystems match and permit grammatical reconstruction. Verdict: the languages are genetically related. II: Vocabulary matches closely and shows regular sound correspondences, but there are few or no grammatical correspondences. Verdict: the languages are not genetically related. If the grammar of one of the languages has little morphology and shows few universally marked features, then it is likely that that language is descended, in the not too distant past, from an abrupt creole or a nativized pidgin; that is, it is the result either of rapid shift (probably in a multilingual situation) without acquisition of much of the lexical source language's structure, or of the nativization of a pidgin created (most likely) in a multilingual contact situation. If, on the other hand, the grammar of one of the languages matches that of a different language or language group, then the first language is the product of massive grammatical replacement through borrowing. (The same is true if just one grammatical subsystem matches that of some other language or group.) III: Grammar matches closely but (basic) vocabulary does not match. Verdict: the languages are not genetically related; one of them is the product of grammatical replacement through borrowing. IV: There are some regular correspondences in basic vocabulary—not very many or very close ones—and few or no systematic grammatical correspondences. Verdict: The languages may well be distantly related genetically, but the relationship cannot be established. Alternatively, one (or even both) of them may have arisen in the distant past by any of the three nongenetic routes of development, or they may have undergone structural interference without losing genetic continuity. In such a case we have no basis for choosing between these two alternatives. V: Nothing matches. Verdict: none possible.

The two main theoretical points to be made here are these. First, since time will obscure the results of inheritance and of diffusion alike, the most that can be said about cases of type IV is that the languages had some historical link at some time in the past. And second, if there is a significant discrepancy between the degree of lexical correspondence and the degree of grammatical correspondence—in some or all grammatical subsystems—then abnormal transmission, or at least extensive diffusion, is more likely than direct inheritance to account for the discrepant correspondences. The reason is that no part of a language is so stable that it will remain largely intact over time while other subsystems change drastically through internally-motivated changes alone. (See Thomason 1980*b* for a discussion of this point with reference to the Na-Déné hypothesis.)

8.2. COMPARATIVE RECONSTRUCTION AND CONTACT-INDUCED LANGUAGE CHANGE

We must still ask, however, whether we can make any use of data from such discrepant cases in carrying out comparative reconstruction. That is: even when we know that one or more of a language's subsystems come mainly from some other source(s), can we use evidence from the subsystems that **are** shared in reconstructing a proto-language for a particular group? Examples would be using the English-origin words of Tok Pisin in reconstructing "Proto-English" phonology, using the Cushitic-origin words of Ma'a in reconstructing Proto-Cushitic phonology, and using the Bantu-origin affixes and constructions of Ma'a in reconstructing Proto-Bantu. The answer to this question is a qualified yes, depending on the type of case we are dealing with and on the typological nature of the features we are comparing.

In all such cases, the process of historical interpretation is comparable to the use of borrowed elements in an attested neighboring language for drawing conclusions about the structure of an unattested language one is trying to reconstruct. The strategy is well known in historical linguistics; one classic example is the set of old Germanic loanwords in Finnish which preserve sounds that were lost in Germanic by the time of the earliest direct Germanic attestations. The main interpretive constraint is that all the evidence must be considered in light of the structures of the other language(s) involved as well as of the language in which the evidence is found. The same constraint applies in cases of nongenetic development: we can never **assume** that any structural feature in a nongenetically affiliated language arose in a simple straight-line development from a single source.

This is easiest to understand when the features in question are clearly not retentions from the ancestral language of the speech community. Tok Pisin speakers, for the most part, do not speak English themselves and are not descended from people who spoke English, so their English-derived lexicon cannot have developed gradually (or even rapidly) through internally-motivated changes in normally transmitted English; and Ma'a speakers, although they do speak one or two Bantu languages, are descended from Cushitic speakers and have retained in their native language some features of their ancestors' original Cushitic language, so that the Bantu elements they use are definitely foreign borrowings.

But even features for which there is historical continuity within the speech community—such as most of the basic vocabulary of Ma'a, which is of Cushitic origin—must be treated with great caution in reconstruction. The reason is that extensive diffusion from a foreign language is likely to penetrate into all subsystems, causing phonological changes in inherited vocabulary, some of them irregular; morphosyntactic changes, with and without the diffusion of actual morphemes; and changes in the lexical semantic structures of retained morphemes.

In practice, using great caution means drawing firm conclusions mainly about structural features—especially universally marked ones—that are present in only one of the groups involved in the contact situation. In Ma'a, for instance, the voiceless lateral fricative /ɬ/, which is rather highly marked in universal terms, occurs only in words of Cushitic origin, corresponds regularly to /ɬ/ in Southern Cushitic languages, and does not occur in relevant Bantu languages. We can therefore be confident that it is possible to use Ma'a data in reconstructions involving this phoneme. However, given the frequently irregular effects of contact-induced phonological change, we need to be careful even here, because some original Cushitic /ɬ/'s in Cushitic vocabulary may well have been replaced by other sounds. In such instances, Ma'a itself would not be a reliable guide to the **distribution** of /ɬ/ in Proto-Southern Cushitic.

Similarly, the five-part system of basic color terms in Ma'a can be used in reconstructing Proto-Cushitic lexical semantics, because it matches other Cushitic systems and differs from the corresponding three-part system that is typical of Bantu. But the absence in Ma'a of pharyngeal fricatives and labialized dorsal stops can tell us nothing about the phonological structure of Proto-Cushitic, because Bantu also lacks these characteristic Cushitic features; and the prenasalized stop phonemes of Ma'a are surely due to Bantu influence, not to internally motivated changes from earlier Cushitic phonological structures.

Note that data from cases of massive borrowing is more likely to be useful for reconstruction than data from cases involving multilingualism and cross-language compromise, because in the former type the structures are much more likely to be marked and assignable to a particular source. The highly marked Bantu inflectional structures of Ma'a could be used in reconstructing Proto-Bantu (in, say, a hypothetical case in which all the Bantu languages of the region had vanished), but we could discover little about Chinese systems of numeral classifiers from the very limited evidence of Chinese Pidgin English alone.

Although in this section we have concentrated on languages that evolved through abnormal transmission (because those are going to be the most troublesome cases), the same problems of historical interpretation arise in languages that have undergone moderate to heavy interference **without** having their historical continuity completely disrupted in any of their subsystems. In these cases it will usually be easier to distinguish inherited material from structures of foreign origin, but not always; making this distinction will be particularly difficult when the language's closest relatives are quite distantly related. It is therefore necessary, in our opinion, to consider the areal situation as well as the genetic picture in carrying out any comparative reconstruction.

Participants in the ongoing controversy about the dominant word order pattern of Proto-Indo-European, for instance, often ignore the fact that some of the ancient SOV languages—notably Hittite, Old Persian, and Sanskrit—were spoken in the vicinity of non-IE SOV languages, some of which may well have exerted structural influence on their IE neighbors (e.g., Sumerian and/or Akkadian on Hittite, Dravidian on Sanskrit) before the earliest period of IE attestations. This means that evidence from SOV IE languages that were **not** demonstrably in contact with non-IE SOV languages should carry more weight in the comparative reconstruction; Celtiberian might be such a case.

Another interesting example is the problem of what to reconstruct for Proto-Salishan for the regular correspondence between Straits Salish *č, č'* and other Salishan languages' *p, p'*. Thompson (1965; 1979:715) argues that Proto-Salishan labialized velars are the source of both sets, while Suttles (1965, cited in Thompson 1979:715) derives the Straits alveopalatal affricates from Proto-Salishan labial stops. Thompson (716) observes that his labiovelar reconstruction would yield a Proto-Salishan consonant system without any labials at all, and that this system would fit well with those of the many non-Salishan languages in the area that lack labials. We have not examined all the evidence independently, so we offer no judgment on which reconstruction is the correct one. We want to point out, however, that the areal argument works just as well the other way: Straits Salish could have lost inherited Proto-Salishan labials under the influence of labial-poor languages in the region. (A phonetic change from labial stops to alveopalatal affricates is not as peculiar as it may look at first glance; see Thomason 1986*a* for discussion.) To the extent that the decision in this case depends on the areal context, therefore, it cannot be decided without a careful investigation of that context, in an effort to determine directions and types of interference features in the densely clustered and genetically diverse languages of the region.

We would like to consider, finally, a special case of diffusion and its implications for reconstruction: language standardization. Language standardization can be defined as whatever processes are involved in the elevation to preeminence in official, learned circles of a particular form of speech and/or writing out of dialects of a single language, which may be numerous. The processes are various; they may or may not involve dialect mixture (or diffusion), and they may be evolutionary (natural) or revolutionary (artificial). Most of the standard languages of Europe arose through evolution and dialect mixture: we can cite English, French, German, Spanish, and Italian. In each case, somewhere between 1200 and 1500, when a particular region or city became pre-eminent for nonlinguistic reasons, its speech became a model for official and other general use; but the pre-eminence of the region attracted large numbers from outlying regions, many of them bearing their own prestige for economic or social reasons, and some or many of their habits of speech became grafted onto the developing standard language. Elsewhere, Persian is a case of standardization of this type in the middle centuries of the first millennium A.D.

As a result the languages mentioned above, though internally rather homogeneous, abound with examples of irregular sound correspondence when compared with cognate languages, or even with nonstandard dialects of the same language. It is by no means impossible to apply the Comparative Method to these standardized languages, but the process is quite bewildering to the beginner who is not presented with pre-cooked data, such as between English and German, or between Spanish and Italian. To be sure, the failure of regularity of sound correspondence is precisely what encourages linguists to seek other explanations for similarity between apparent cognates, but the proportion of apparent cognates that fail this test is rather high in the cases mentioned, perhaps as high as 25 percent.

It is also a real question whether discrepancies in sound correspondence as a result of dialect mixture are really cases of noncognacy. They would indeed be noncognate if we define as belonging to the main line of development only those items which have been subject to a particular set of diachronic phonological rules, and as borrowed those items which have been subject to a partially-to-totally different set of diachronic phonological rules. Of course, within a single language, many to most such changes will have been the same for all dialects. The same is true of nonphonological correspondences.

In other cases of standardization, more readily characterized as revolutionary (or artificial) than evolutionary, the speech of a particular region may be selected for standardization and no significant mixture with other dialects may occur, although some aspects of structure of the regional dialect chosen for standardization may be simplified if such simplifications are typical of other dialects. Such cases as Indonesian, Serbocroatian, and a number of languages of Africa and the New World have been standardized in this way to meet modern demands of centralization and nationalism, usually with the collaboration of linguists who dislike the kinds of patchworks produced by "natural" standardization. But it must be agreed that almost all standardized languages show some form of marked dialect mixture, and even the artificially standardized language, once it is standardized, is liable to become mixed lexically (at least) through dialect borrowing. It may be that all languages show some dialect borrowing, but personal experience by Kaufman with a number of preliterate languages suggests that high levels of it are relatively uncommon in such languages.

8.3. CONCLUSION

We have tried, in our discussion of contact-induced language change, to make generalizations and theoretical proposals where they seem justified by the evidence, and to avoid doing so in the many areas where the evidence does not seem to us to support any general claims. In this last section we will sum up our major conclusions.

We have argued, first of all, for the existence of a class of languages whose developmental history involves abnormal transmission, by which we mean that a language as a whole has not been passed down from one speaker generation to the next with changes spread more or less evenly across all parts of the language. This class of languages is divided into three types, according to the particular route of nongenetic development: languages that have borrowed so massively from some other language that genetic continuity has been destroyed for some or all grammatical subsystems (though the basic vocabulary remains largely intact); abrupt creoles, that is, languages that arose in (primarily) multilingual situations in which speakers who shared no common language shifted rapidly away from their several native languages but learned only the vocabulary—not the bulk of the grammatical structures—of the target language; and pidgins, which also arose in multilingual situations in which speakers shared no common language, and which did not (at first) involve language shift, but rather the creation of a linguistically restricted contact language for restricted purposes of intergroup communication. From a retrospective viewpoint these three types can be collapsed into two, because a long-lived pidgin that becomes nativized, or creolized, will present essentially the same sorts of evidence for historical interpretation as an abrupt creole.

In the absence of direct sociohistorical information, a history of nongenetic development can be inferred, if not too much time has passed, from comparisons with proposed related languages: there will be, as Boas predicted in 1917, a lack of agreement between lexical and some or all grammatical subsystems. The specific nature of the disagreements will usually enable us to determine which route of nongenetic development a given language has followed. A language that has undergone massive grammatical replacement through borrowing will have grammatical structures that match those of some other particular language (and this will often be evident even when that language cannot be identified); creoles of both types will not have the bulk of their grammatical structures derived from a single source language. Most languages of all three nongenetic types will derive most of their basic vocabulary from a single source.

We have also emphasized the need to distinguish between the two main mechanisms of interference in any discussion of contact-induced language change: interference that results from imperfect group learning during a process of language shift, and interference that results from borrowing, by native speakers of a language, of features of some other language with whose speakers they are in contact. The reason for this emphasis is that the results of these two processes differ significantly, in principle and often in historical fact. Specifically, in shift-induced interference lexical diffusion may be negligible, and in any case phonological and syntactic interference will be more substantial than lexical interference, unless, as is sometimes the case, native speakers of the target language borrow features from the language of the shifting population while the shifting population is shifting to the TL. By contrast, lexical diffusion is always first and most extensive in cases of borrowing. One retrospective implication of this difference is that a case in which structural interference is firmly established, while loanwords are few or nonexistent, must be the result of language shift, not borrowing. Another implication, obviously, is that the absence of loanwords does not constitute counterevidence to a claim of structural interference. (However, as we noted in 5.1, establishing a claim of shift-induced interference is not an easy task, because one or more of the requisite kinds of information is all too often lacking.)

Finally, we have argued throughout this book that the major determinants of contact-induced language change are the social facts of particular contact situations, not the structural linguistic relations that obtain among the languages themselves. Language shift, for instance, is a social fact with linguistic implications. Linguistic factors do influence the linguistic outcome of a contact situation, but only secondarily. The main linguistic factors that must be considered in predicting the results of language contact are universal markedness and typological distance between corresponding grammatical subsystems of the languages in contact. But predicting the results of contact-induced change in any detail is far beyond our present ability, given the kinds of evidence now available about language contacts. To mention just two of the enormous gaps in our knowledge, we know too little about the interaction of social variables and too little about the parameters of markedness. Deterministic predictions will surely remain permanently beyond our grasp, and simplistic predictions in this domain (as in other areas of historical linguistics) are bound to fail. But at least we can look forward to refining the very general and rough predictions that the current evidence does permit.

Refining these predictions will require, as Paul Kroskrity (personal communication 1985) has suggested, "a particular type of scholarship which attends both to the linguistic details of diffusion and to the social circumstances in which it occurs." In particular, what is needed is research on current or recent contact situations that permit a more ambitious analysis of sociolinguistic context than we have attempted here. Even for older contact situations, however, it is possible to strike a better balance of linguistic and social analysis than most of the literature we have studied reflects. This book will have achieved its main purpose if it convinces readers that no case of contact-induced language change (or of pidginization, or of creolization) can be adequately explained **without** attention to sociolinguistic context.

The main part of our book ends here. In the final chapter we present eight case studies that provide illustrations of, and detailed evidence for, the various points we have made in our theoretical arguments.

9
Case Studies

Our reason for appending the eight case studies in this chapter to our main exposition is that we wish to avoid the pitfall so many discussions of language contact fall into—namely, the use of isolated examples from a given case to support theoretical claims. We have argued emphatically that, to make a case for extensive contact-induced language change, one needs evidence of interference in different linguistic subsystems. We also believe that isolated examples of interference often give a false impression of the nature of a particular historical situation. Accordingly, in the reports below we have tried to indicate the full range of interference features in each case and to interpret the linguistic facts in light of what we can determine about the social context.

However, the studies here vary considerably in scope and (therefore) in the firmness of our conclusions. The most extensive one is our study of French and Norse interference in English (9.8), a case about which extravagant claims have been made. In this case study our main theoretical goal is to demonstrate the importance of discovering the relevant linguistic facts and of correlating them with known social facts. The other two full-scale case studies represent the two mechanisms of linguistic interference: Asia Minor Greek, a case of borrowing (9.1), and shift-induced Uralic interference in Slavic and Baltic languages (9.5).

Besides these three studies, we have included five less comprehensive ones. Two of the five are based on published papers by Thomason: Ma'a (9.2), a case of massive grammatical replacement through borrowing, and Chinook Jargon (9.7), a pidgin. The remaining three sections are preliminary studies of two cases of extreme borrowing, Michif (9.3) and Mednyj Aleut (9.4), and one of possible semicreolization, Afrikaans (9.6). Our information about these last three cases is limited at present, but we include our tentative remarks on them because of their importance for theories of contact-induced language change.

The arrangement of the first seven case studies follows the general organization of the main body of the book: the first four studies are cases of heavy to extreme borrowing; the fifth is a case of moderate interference during language shift; the sixth involves shift with possible abnormal transmission; and the seventh is a pidgin. The final case is one in which both borrowing and shift-induced interference have occurred, and for which creolization has wrongly been claimed.

9.1. ASIA MINOR GREEK: A CASE OF HEAVY BORROWING

R. M. Dawkins' 1916 study of Modern Greek dialects spoken in Asia Minor provides one of the most comprehensive pictures of contact-induced language change that we have found. It is an excellent example of heavy borrowing—category 5 in the scale we presented in 4.1.

Dawkins investigated the dialects of the regions Sílli, Cappadocia, and Phárasa in Asia Minor and collected very detailed linguistic and sociolinguistic facts about each village he visited. Like Romansh vis-à-vis Swiss German (Weinreich 1953), these Greek dialects stand in a subordinate position to the surrounding Turkish, with very widespread (though not universal) bilingualism among the Greek speakers. Under these circumstances, it is not surprising to find that history records a steady shift of Greek speakers to Turkish (and, apparently concomitantly, from Christianity to the Moslem religion). The earliest evidence of this shift that Dawkins mentions (1916:1) is in a 1437 document, and relatively recent figures show that the shift was still going on after the post-World War I population exchanges: 1927 census figures showed 119,822 Greek speakers in Turkey, while in 1955 only 81,799 were recorded (compare 109,905 Greek Orthodox Turkish Christians in 1927 vs. 84,759 in 1955) (*Encyclopaedia Britannica*, 1966 ed., s.v. "Turkey"). There is no indication that

Turkish speakers have shifted in any significant numbers to Greek. Meanwhile, the remaining Greek speakers are no doubt incorporating more and more Turkish features into their native language. Turkish interference in Cappadocian Greek, the most affected of the three above-named dialect areas, was so great in Dawkins' time as to produce a language in which, in his view, "the body has remained Greek, but the soul has become Turkish" (198).

Asia Minor Greek presents no problems of historical interpretation, since both major sources of its structures and lexicon are apparent, and since the mechanism of interference is equally clear: if Turks did not shift to Greek, all the interference must be due to borrowing. We include the case in this chapter both as a detailed illustration of heavy borrowing and because this is a particularly effective counterexample to the still common view that contact-induced language change is always superficial.

The various Greek dialects in the region have undergone different amounts of interference from Turkish. Not only are Cappadocian dialects more turkicized than those of Sílli and Phárasa but, within Cappadocia, such factors as the presence in a village of a Greek school and the proximity of a large Turkish town have influenced the linguistic outcome of the contact situation. In the following discussion we will concentrate on the most-affected dialects.

The list of interference features is impressive. The examples we give here show that borrowings have penetrated into all parts of the language—lexicon, phonology, morphology, and syntax.

(1) *Lexicon: content words*

All dialects show heavy lexical borrowing. Dawkins mentions no restrictions on types of lexical items borrowed; in particular, verbs seem to be borrowed as freely as nouns, often completely replacing equivalent Greek verbs (197). Sample loanwords are Sílli *ojaqï* 'hearth, pyre' ← Turkish *ojak*, *kizméči* 'fate' ← Turkish *kismet*, *šaštô* 'be astonished' ← Turkish *šašmak* (-*mak* is the back-vowel variant of the Turkish infinitive suffix). Numeral systems in all the dialects remain Greek, but at least two borrowed Turkish numerals do occur: Sílli *seksénia* '80' ← Turkish *seksen* and *doksánia* '90' ← Turkish *doksan* (49). Compare also Cappadocian *üčünjü* ← Turkish *üčünjü* 'third', *onikiléri* 'the twelve' ← Turkish *on iki '12'* + *-ler* PLU (cf. common Greek *ðoðekáða* 'the twelve'), and even *bír* ← Turkish *bir* 'one'. All three dialect groups contain many calques on Turkish idioms, translated word by word from the Turkish originals.

(2) *Lexicon: function words*

Here is a list of some conjunctions and particles borrowed from Turkish: *eyer* 'if' ← Turkish *eyer* (Sílli, Cappadocia); *ki, gi* 'that', a conjunction used after verbs of saying, seeing, and thinking, ← Turkish *ki* (Cappadocia, Sílli); *hemki* 'also, and' ← Turkish *hem* + *ki* (Sílli); *án* ← Turkish *en*, a particle used to form the superlative (Cappadocia); *xíč* 'nothing' ← Turkish *hič* (Sílli); *kéšge, kéški* ← Turkish *keške*, a particle introducing a wish (Sílli); *ičin, ičün* 'because of' ← the Turkish postposition *ičin* (Cappadocia); *pék* 'very' ← Turkish *pek* (Sílli); *xaïr* 'no' ← Turkish *hayïr* (Cappadocia); *mí* ← Turkish *mi*, an interrogative particle (Cappadocia, Sílli); *madémki* 'because' ← Turkish *madamki* 'as long as' (Sílli); *meyér* 'but' ← Turkish *meyer* (Cappadocia, Sílli); *číp* ← Turkish *čep*, a particle used to strengthen the meaning of a word (Cappadocia, Sílli).

(3) *Phonological interference*

Several features that Dawkins discusss fall into the category of phonetic interference, including phonological simplification of Greek by the reduction of phonemic contrasts. Among them are the widespread elimination of Greek θ and ð, a change that constitutes a simplification of the Greek phonological system, since the two fricatives are almost always replaced by various already existing sounds. Examples are *ártupus* 'man' (Sílli; 44) vs. Common Greek *ánθrōpos*, *skórdus* 'garlic' (Sílli; 44) vs. Common Greek *skórðon*, *xerízu* 'mow' (Semenderé; 76) vs. Common Greek *θerízo*, *yávolos* 'devil' (Ulaghátsh; 77) vs. Common Greek *ðiávolos*. Turkish has no interdental fricatives. A point worth noting about these examples is that the original Greek interdental fricatives are not always replaced by the same sounds in the Asia Minor dialects.

Another Turkish phonetic feature that has influenced Greek pronunciation in the Asia Minor dialects is the articulation of the velar stop /k/: in Turkish this phoneme has a postvelar pronunciation [q] in back-vowel contexts, and Greek speakers preserve the Turkish pronunciation in Turkish loanwords (86).

Phonological processes like vowel harmony (especially in Cappadocia, in Greek suffixes added to Turkish loanwords) as well as new (taxonomic) phonemes—/ö/, /ü/, /ï/, /č/, and /ǰ/—have been added to the phonological systems of several dialects as a result of Turkish interference. We have discussed and exemplified these phenomena elsewhere (Thomason and Kaufman 1976), so we will give only two additional examples here to indicate the depth of Turkish penetration into Greek phonology. In Sílli, the normal plural suffix for nouns in -os is -iri. After nouns with the back stem vowels a, o, u, however, the plural suffix is often -uri, with an initial back vowel to harmonize with the stem vowel. Examples are ártupus 'man' : plural ártupuri, vs. kléfčis 'thief' : plural kléfčiri (but cf. ǰuvánus 'a youth' : plural ǰuvániri) (47). Note that ártupus and kléfčis are native Greek words; ǰuvánus is from Persian via Turkish. Dawkins remarks (68) that

> the fullness with which the vowel harmony is observed clearly depends on how far the individual speaker is accustomed to talk Turkish and has the Turkish ear for these distinctions. It [is] . . . more or less prevalent and thorough in proportion as more or less Turkish is spoken alongside of the Greek dialect.

Another Turkish morphophonemic rule that appears in Asia Minor Greek is one that spirantizes and voices stem-final postvocalic k before a suffix -i to ǧ, which is realized phonetically with varying degrees of velar constriction in Turkish dialects—from [γ] to mere lengthening of the preceding vowel (Lewis 1967:5, 10). This same rule is used in the Cappadocian dialects of Ulaghátsh, Malakopí, and Phloïta,[1] and the suffix vowel i is backed to ï.

Still another Turkish morphophonemic rule which, in Dawkins' view, has influenced these Greek dialects is the frequent devoicing of final obstruents (203). There is some doubt about the validity of Dawkins' claim here, since the change is not unique to Asia Minor Greek (see Thomason and Kaufman 1976, n. 5), but a concomitant analogic change that occurs only in some Cappadocian dialects seems quite likely to be due to the influence of the Turkish rule. This is the voicing of original final voiceless obstruents when, as a result of suffixation, they come into intervocoid position: Mistí *verkóč* (< *verikókkion*) 'apricot' : plural *verkójía* (91), Ferték nominative plural *nékes* 'wives' : the agglutinative genitive plural *nékezịu* (see below) (114).

(4) *Morphology*

Derivational Turkish suffixes are sometimes added to Greek verbs in Cappadocian dialects. More strikingly, some dialects of Cappadocia and Sílli use Turkish inflectional suffixes—borrowed personal suffixes—with Greek verbs. In the Cappadocian village of Semenderé,[2] for instance, the first person plural past tense form *kétunmistik* and the second person plural *kétunstiniz* contain the Turkish personal suffixes *-ik* 1.Pl. and *-iniz* 2.Pl.; note the lack of vowel harmony in these forms, and compare Turkish *geldik* 'we came' (*gel-* 'come', *-di* PAST, *-k*) and *geldiniz* 'you(pl.) came' (144).

Greek concord rules have been affected primarily in the area of adjective-noun agreement. Turkish has none. In the Cappadocian Greek dialects, only a very few adjectives inflect for gender or case, though an adjective used as a noun is declined like a noun (115).

Perhaps the most striking borrowed morphological feature is the adoption in several Cappadocian villages of partly agglutinative patterns of noun and verb inflection—a morphological organization that is startling in an Indo-European language, since Indo-European inflection is in general rather consistently flexional. Compare the following Turkish declensional forms with those of the Cappadocian village Ferték (114):[3]

		Turkish *qïz* 'girl'		Ferték *néka* 'woman, wife'	
Sg.	Nom.	qïz	girl	néka	wife
	Gen.	qïz-ïn	girl's	néka-yu	wife's
Pl.	Nom.	qïz-lar	girls	nék-es	wives
	Gen.	qïz-lar-ï	girls'	nék-ez-yu	wives'

Dawkins considers the loss of grammatical gender, which is almost complete in Cappadocia and occurs less extensively in Sílli and

Phárasa, to be due to Turkish influence; Turkish has no gender. In Cappadocia, for instance, third person pronouns and demonstratives have lost all gender distinctions, and adjectives are neuter in form and, with few exceptions, inflect for number only (115, 119, 125). The definite article, where it remains at all, has also lost all gender and case distinctions in Cappadocia (87). In any particular dialect, gender distinctions are better preserved in noun inflection than in modifier agreement.

A final morphological example is the occasional suffixation, in some dialects of Cappadocia, of a third person pronominal possessive marker on possessed nouns. For instance, Dawkins (201) gives this example from Ulaghátsh: *kanís qoqusú* 'the smell of a man' (literally 'man smell-his'), in which the second word consists of the borrowed Turkish stem *qoqu* 'smell' + the borrowed Turkish third person singular possessive suffix -*su*. What is noteworthy about this example is that the first word—an ordinary Greek word—lacks the genitive suffix that would be required in other dialects of Greek. Another type of example occurs in the Ulaghátsh sentence *írte na Devụú manayụú t to spít* 'he came to the house of a mother of a Dev' (literally 'came-he a Dev + GEN mother + GEN 3.sg.POSS the house'); here both nouns have the appropriate Greek genitive suffixes, but the redundant possessive *t* is added—either as a suffix or as a clitic—after the second noun, in a Turkish-style construction.

Other morphological interference features which Dawkins mentions, but which do not seem so clear to us (partly because Dawkins' analyses of the Turkish constructions do not correspond precisely to other accounts, e.g., that of Lewis 1967), occur in the formation of the pluperfect (Sílli, Cappadocia) and in the comparison of adjectives.

(5) *Syntax*

Dialects in all three groups have Turkish word order at least occasionally, though in Sílli this usage is rather restricted. In Turkish, a consistent SOV language, qualifiers always precede the qualified element: genitive before head noun, relative clause before head noun, and so forth. Common Greek permits either GN or NG order; however, if a construction includes two genitives of possession, they may not precede the head noun in Common Greek. They do so in Asia Minor dialects (201):

(a) Sílli:

$$quyumjí \quad enékas \quad oda \quad \text{'the jeweller's}$$
jeweller +   wife +   room   wife's room'
GEN(←T.)   GEN   (←T.)

(b) Common Greek:

tò ðomátion   tîs yinékas   tû xrisoxóu
the room   the wife   the jeweller
NEUT   FEM +GEN   MASC
              GEN   GEN

(c) Turkish:

kuyumjunun   karïsïn   odasï
jeweller   wife   room
 + GEN   + GEN   +3.sg.
                        POSS

Similarly, relative clauses frequently precede their head nouns in these dialects—as in Turkish, but in marked contrast to the Common Greek pattern (201):

(a) Sílli:

kját íra perí   'the boy who(m) I saw'
REL saw-I boy

(b) Common Greek:

tò   peðì pû   to   iða
the   boy REL   it   saw-I
NEUT   NEUT

(c) Turkish:

gör-düg—üm   oğlan
see+GERUND   boy(son)
 + 1.sg.   + 1.sg.POSS

The sentence-final position of the Turkish verb has also had some impact on Asia Minor Greek. When used as a copula, the local Greek verb *ími* 'to be' (Sílli), like its Turkish counterpart *dir*, appears as a sentence-final enclitic (61). Moreover, an examination of the dialect texts that follow Dawkins' analysis turns up a rather large number of other verb-final sentences. Since Common Greek word order, though predominantly SVO, is rather free, some of these sentences may well be quite normal for Common Greek. Most of them do not, however, seem to involve any special emphasis on the verb, the only reason for the uncommon verb-final

order in Common Greek, according to Thumb (1912:201). Below
are a few examples from Sílli:

(a) *ganinó*   *galají* *mí*   *frikisís*   'Listen to no man's
     of no   word   NEG   you listen   word!' (294). (*galají* is
     men   borrowed from Turkish
                                          keleži)

(b) *čin* *enékan* *du*   *xíč*   *ne* *pará* *ne* *xarčí* *či* *vémn'i*
     the +   wife   his nothing   money   letter the he
     ACC   neither   nor   sends
     FEM

                                'To his wife he sends neither
                                money nor letters' (292).

(c) *raxáčin*   *du*   *pék* *pol'í* *kaló* *iton* 'His pleasure was
     pleasure   his very much   fine   was   very great' (290)
                                                (*raxáčin* is bor-
                                                rowed from Turk-
                                                ish *rahat*; *pek* is
                                                also a loanword).

In subordinate clauses, in particular, the Common Greek verb
is said to be fixed in second position, immediately after the introductory conjunction or particle; also, almost always, the verb follows a relative (Thumb 1912:202). But compare this Sílli subordinate clause: *Madémki ší oz zaṛá xíč pará rén iripsis,* . . . 'Because
until now you have never asked for any money, . . . ' (literally
'because [← Turkish *madamki*] you[sg.] until now nothing [←
Turkish] not you-asked-for [aorist]') (292).
    Finally, in Sílli and in most Greek villages of Cappadocia, the use
of the definite article has declined drastically. Though Turkish lacks
a definite article, this change might be considered to have occurred
independently, if it weren't for the consistent retention of the Greek
article only in the single morphosyntactic context where Turkish
marks definiteness—on direct objects (i.e., in the accusative case)
(46, 87).

9.2. MA'A

This case study is based on Thomason (1983*b*).[4] In classifying Ma'a as a mixed language in 4.4—specifically, as the result of massive grammatical replacement—we observed that its mostly Cushitic basic vocabulary is combined with a grammar so heavily bantuized that only a very few systematic, productive Cushitic grammatical features remain in the language. For purposes of reconstruction, then, it is obvious (and presumably noncontroversial) that a comparison of the Bantu structures of Ma'a with structures of Bantu languages must take into account the fact that the relevant Ma'a structures are in fact borrowed, not inherited directly from a Bantu proto-language. More interestingly, we claim that even the Cushitic structures of Ma'a—which are indeed derived historically from the Cushitic language of the ancestors of the Ma'a people—must be treated, for purposes of reconstruction, as if they were, or might have been, diffused from a foreign language. The reason is that Ma'a has been so heavily bantuized in all its linguistic subsystems that we cannot **assume** that the remaining Cushitic nonlexical features were inherited intact from Proto-Southern Cushitic; rather, we must keep in mind the very real possibility that some or all of those structures have also been influenced, in form and/or in function, by Bantu.

We will cover three main points in this section. First, we will survey the structures of Ma'a to establish the point that the basic vocabulary and the grammar are not derived historically from the same source language. Second, we will sketch the social situation that gave rise to this language. And third, we will discuss the retrospective methodology Thomason originally used (in 1975) to make an educated guess about the history of Ma'a.

In its phonological inventory and syllable structure, Ma'a agrees typologically with Bantu—specifically, with the languages Pare and Shambaa—in most, but not all, of its typologically marked features. The only marked feature clearly inherited from Cushitic is the voiceless lateral fricative /ɬ/; the glottal stop and the voiceless dorsovelar fricative /x/ are also obviously good candidates for Cushitic-derived features, since they correspond regularly to similar phonemes in Cushitic languages, and since these phonemes are relatively rare in Bantu. Pare and Shambaa have few typologically marked phonological features, but they have contributed two (perhaps their only two) to Ma'a: a series of prenasalized voiced stop phonemes and allophonic implosive pronunciation of (oral) voiced stop phonemes. Other clear instances of Bantu phonological interference in Ma'a are the borrowed phoneme /v/, phonemicization of original Ma'a allophones [ǰ ɣ] as /ɟ/ and /ɣ/, and the elimination of syllable-final consonants.

In morphology, Ma'a retains only one systematic inflectional feature of Cushitic origin, namely, suffixed pronominal possessors; and even these differ only marginally from the Bantu possessive constructions, in which the independent possessive pronoun follows the possessed noun, to which the relational suffix -a has been added. Otherwise, Ma'a preserves just a few fossilized Cushitic inflectional features, while the entire productive inflectional apparatus is borrowed from Bantu—the functional categories, their ordering, and the affixes themselves. Where Cushitic is flexional in morphological type, Ma'a is agglutinative. Cushitic languages have primarily suffixed inflection, with a few prefixes, including reduplicative prefixes; Ma'a, like Bantu, has predominantly prefixed inflection, with some suffixes and no productive prefixed reduplicative affixes. Cushitic languages have a biologically-based gender system with two categories, masculine and feminine; Ma'a has a full-scale Bantu noun-class system, with paired singular/plural prefix sets that are added to nouns and (as concord markers, sometimes differing in form from the noun prefixes) to verbs and to adjectives and other noun modifiers.

In the category of number, Cushitic has a complex system with a distinction between singular and plural that is sometimes optional, and with a characteristic singulative category (e.g., á:dʒù 'lung fish' : singulative á:dʒùmè 'one lung fish' [Elderkin 1976:292]). Both Bantu and Cushitic languages have conjugated negation, but here too the Ma'a system agrees in form and precise function with Bantu; specifically, it has a regular distinction between the negative prefix used with a first person singular subject and the negative prefix used with other subjects. Ma'a also has Bantu subject and object markers for all three persons, both singular and plural, and various tense/aspect prefixes. In derivational morphology, the actual affixes of Ma'a are about evenly divided between borrowed Bantu suffixes and inherited Cushitic suffixes. But the productive derivational patterns, which are all suffixing, are no doubt themselves the result of Bantu influence, because Cushitic has a much wider range of affix types in its derivational processes, among them prefixed reduplication and infixation.

We have less information about Ma'a syntax, but enough to detect extensive Bantu influence. Cushitic languages are SOV, with postpositions; relevant Bantu languages, and Ma'a, are SVO, with prepositions. Ma'a has two different genitive constructions, one inherited from Cushitic and another borrowed from Bantu (using the Bantu relational particle -a); but the typological gap between Cushitic and Bantu is slight in this feature. The same is true of at least one syntactic feature in which Ma'a definitely agrees with Cushitic: the obligatory use of the copula in Cushitic and in Ma'a, vs. the optional use of the copula in Bantu. Similarly, Ma'a—like Cushitic—has a large class of adjectives, whereas Bantu languages generally have few adjectives. And finally, the expression of possession in Ma'a is of the Cushitic type, with an ordinary transitive verb 'have'; relevant Bantu languages, by contrast, use a construction involving '(be) with'.

Although most of the basic vocabulary of Ma'a, and much of the cultural vocabulary as well, are inherited Cushitic words, Ma'a has also borrowed many words from Bantu. According to Ehret, however (personal communication, 1982), Bantu lexical semantic categories have not penetrated into the Cushitic portion of the Ma'a vocabulary; Ma'a color terminology, for instance, preserves the five-part Cushitic system (cf. the three-part Bantu system of basic color terms).

As for the social background of Ma'a, different (and independent) sources present a picture of the Ma'a people as resisters of total cultural assimilation to their Bantu-speaking milieu. They are described as extremely conservative, uncommunicative, and reserved; their own oral traditions and those of the Pare and Shambaa people indicate that they deliberately sought (relative) isolation from their neighbors so that they could continue to follow their own customs. They did, however, have regular contacts with their Bantu-speaking neighbors, and Ehret (personal communication, 1982) believes that they are all fluent today in both Pare and Shambaa.

It has been estimated (from Pare and Shambaa traditions) that the Ma'a came to the South Pare mountains about three hundred years ago. Some time later the ancestors of today's Ma'a speakers abandoned the homeland in South Pare—and some of their Ma'a kin—and moved southward, settling in the Usambara mountains. The Ma'a clans that stayed in South Pare eventually shifted to the Bantu language Pare, but the Ma'a in the Usambaras kept their Cushitic tongue (or at least much of its lexicon). Nevertheless, the ties between the two groups remained strong, so that the Ma'a of the Usambaras traveled regularly to South Pare to participate in initiation rites; this practice continued well into this century and may still occur, though now irregularly. As a result, Ma'a speakers had continuing intimate contact with Pare speakers—namely, their own kinfolk—as well as with the alien Bantu-speaking peoples. This, then, is the context in which the Ma'a language has acquired its unusual mixed structure: the inherited Cushitic vocabulary has been maintained, but almost all of the inherited grammar has been replaced by Bantu grammar, under conditions of intense cultural pressure from both "foreign" and related Bantu speakers.

Enough is known about the history of the Ma'a speakers to establish firmly our claim that the mixture in this case resulted from borrowing in a situation of language maintenance, rather than from shift. An interesting methodological point can be made here, however: it is possible to arrive at the same conclusion from the linguistic facts alone, without any knowledge of the external historical or cultural context. In fact, that is how Thomason did originally arrive at this conclusion. She prepared a brief argument on this point (based solely on the linguistic evidence about Ma'a in Goodman [1971]), which appeared as a case study in Thomason and Kaufman (1975: 42–46). Between 1975 and 1982, as work on the present book progressed, it seemed advisable to try to find historical information and further linguistic data to test the hypothesis presented in the 1975 paper; the results of that research were published as Thomason 1983*b*. A number of details in the 1975 version turned out to be incorrect, but the main conclusion was fully supported. This outcome, of course, increased our confidence in the usefulness of our basic approach as a tool for uncovering unattested historical developments from synchronic linguistic facts. We will therefore review the 1975 argument here; a fuller version of it, though without the emphasis on its methodological importance, is given in Thomason (1983*b*).

In the first eight chapters of this book we have identified three different kinds of nongenetic development for languages in which vocabulary and grammar are demonstrably not from the same source. These are grammatical replacement through borrowing, in a maintained language; acquisition of vocabulary only, in a process of language shift where the target language is minimally available to the shifting population; and nativization of a pidgin that arose through a process of mutual simplification, with linguistic results similar to those of the second type. Abrupt creoles (the second type) and creolized pidgins usually arise in multilingual contact situations; borrowing is much more likely to occur in a simple two-language situation.

In the Ma'a case, we essentially have a two-language situation (if we are permitted a slight oversimplification from the chronologically layered Pare and Shambaa contributions to Ma'a structure): Bantu features come from one or two very closely related Bantu languages, and Cushitic features come from one Southern Cushitic language. We therefore have five possible lines of development for two languages A and B, depending on whether A is taken to be Cushitic or Bantu. The analysis sketched here is based on the arguments presented in chapters 4, 5, 6, and 7.

If Ma'a had arisen through shift from a Cushitic language A to a Bantu language B, then we would expect its basic vocabulary to be Bantu, not Cushitic; we can therefore eliminate this route of development. Similarly, Ma'a could not have resulted from massive borrowing from a Cushitic language B into a Bantu language A, because here again we would expect the basic vocabulary to be mainly Bantu, not Cushitic.

If Ma'a had arisen through shift from a Bantu language A to a Cushitic language B, we would expect to find—as indeed we do find—mostly Cushitic basic vocabulary. But all cases of abrupt creolization that we know of involve linguistically mixed groups who urgently need a common means of communication because they have none; in such cases, the shift is rapid for social reasons, and there is no time (or, usually, opportunity) to learn TL structures. Socially, it is hard to see how the Ma'a case could fit here. The fact that the grammar comes from just one source means that the putative shifting speakers must have shared a common language already; but then why would they shift to a TL that was available only minimally? This same basic argument would apply to a hypothesis that Ma'a is a nativized Cushitic-based pidgin in origin. No known pidgins have a single-source grammar, and—for social reasons—no functionally restricted pidgins have fully elaborated inflectional systems. Even the two-language pidgins Tây Bôi and Chinese Pidgin English (and perhaps the incipient pidgin Halbdeutsch) have much more restricted grammatical resources than Ma'a has. That is, it seems very unlikely that social conditions that might have favored the emergence of a pidgin would also have promoted the development of a language as complex grammatically and as uniform in its grammatical source as Ma'a.

The only remaining line of development is massive borrowing from a Bantu language B into a (minimally) maintained Cushitic language A.[5] This is what Thomason proposed in 1975, a retrospective prediction that was borne out by the evidence she subsequently collected.

9.3. MICHIF

This case study is an outline of a current research project of Thomason's. The results sketched here are preliminary and tentative; further research will probably not alter the main line of the argument, though details of the analysis will be greatly expanded and, no doubt, somewhat modified.

Michif is the language of some hundreds of residents of the Turtle Mountain Chippewa Reservation in north-central North Dakota. Most Michif speakers are descendants of Métis ('mixed-bloods') who came from Canada to settle in the Turtle Mountain area. Evans (1982) observes that the Métis "trace their heritage to Indian communities which have had extensive long-term contact with French or English-speaking peoples, such as French-speaking priests and trappers during the 18th and 19th centuries. . . . " The extent to which the Métis people arose from actual intermarriage between Indians and whites is a controversial question; it is likely that different Métis communities show different degrees of admixture. In Métis communities, members typically speak (and/or spoke) at least two languages, "their native language (usually Cree) and either French or English" (Evans 1982:158).

On the Turtle Mountain Reservation, English is now rapidly replacing Michif, but Michif is still rather widely spoken, along with French, Cree, and Ojibwa (Chippewa). Questionnaires filled out by Weaver's (1982) twelve consultants indicated that all twelve were fluent in English, eleven were fluent in Michif and had used it as a home language when they were young, six spoke passable or good French, five spoke at least a little Cree, and two spoke at least a little Ojibwa.

The historical picture, as described by Evans (1982) and Crawford (1981), shows a cohesive multilingual community with an Indian identity and a widely spoken prestigious European language, French. (The question of linguistic prestige, however, is not a simple one for Métis communities in general. For instance, Douaud says that, among the Métis of Lac la Biche in Alberta, none of the three languages—Cree, French, English—is prestigious now, and he doubts that "any of the Metis languages ever had a high status" there [1980:408].)

The structural sketch here is based primarily on the data and grammatical analyses given by Rhodes (1977), Evans (1982), and Weaver (1982). The most striking fact about Michif structure is the split between its nominal and verbal systems: almost all nouns and most adjectives in the language, together with some of their morphology and syntax, are French in origin; but almost all verbs, with their morphology and syntax, are derived from Plains Cree. Since in Cree, as in other Algonquian languages, "the verb with its internal elaborations is central" to the sentence (Teeter 1976:515), it is not surprising that Michif syntax as a whole has an Algonquian appearance. Algonquian nouns, as Teeter observes, "often do no more than give a more specific name to an entity already signalled within the verb as to its presence and function" (515). This suggests that the presence of French-derived noun phrases need not make a sentence with a Cree verb form look strikingly un-Algonquian.

The split between the French and Cree parts of Michif is in fact not as complete as it seems at first glance. It is true that the two sets of lexical items reflect different phonological systems, as Rhodes points out—French phonology for French-derived morphemes, Cree phonology for Cree-derived morphemes. But there is, as Evans shows, some leakage between the two systems; moreover, both components have been influenced phonologically by English, presumably recently. Most evidence of leakage that Evans cites is from the Cree component to the French component of Michif, a fact that would support the view that Michif is the result of French interference in Cree rather than vice versa.

In morphosyntax, the verb is all Cree, but noun phrases are by no means entirely French, either lexically or syntactically. The nouns themselves are mostly of French origin; so are all the numerals except 'one', and the definite and indefinite articles and possessive pronouns, all of which vary according to the French gender categories (masculine/feminine) and number (singular/plural). But Cree demonstratives are also used in construction with Michif nouns, often in addition to the French article. These Cree demonstratives show the usual Cree gender distinctions (animate/inanimate) as well as number (singular/plural) and location (proximate/intermediate/distant). Examples (from Fink [1983], with some normalization of the orthography) are *lɪ šiẽn šakwala ana* 'that brown dog' (literally 'the[MASC,SG] dog brown that [ANIM,INTERMED]'; the demonstrative is a Cree form) and *en bwet nema* 'that box over there' (literally 'a[FEM,SG] box that [INAN,DISTANT]'; the demonstrative is Cree).

Animate nouns take optional obviative suffixes—the so-called fourth person, a characteristic Algonquian marked category referring to a non-salient animate third person—in certain constructions, e.g., *la fam mičiminew lɪ pči(wa)* 'the woman is holding the child' (lit. 'the[FEM,SG] hold-3-4 the[MASC,SG] child-([OBV])'; both nouns and both articles are of French origin) (Rhodes 1977:10). This is the only instance in Michif in which a Cree affix, the obviative suffix *-wa*, is added to words of French origin, and the use of the obviative marking is more restricted than it is in Cree itself. In any case, the demonstrative and obviative patterns show that Michif nouns must be classified lexically for animacy as well as for masculine or feminine gender. Finally, some speakers use Cree possessive affixes with the few Cree nouns in Michif, while others use French-derived possessive pronouns or a combination of French and Cree possessive markers.

Syntactic connections between noun and verb follow the usual Algonquian pattern: verbs agree with subject and animate object nouns in animacy and number, and obviation is marked on the verb by most speakers (though one of Weaver's consultants failed to use any obviative markers).

Except for significant erosion of obviative marking for some speakers, Michif verb morphology shows no serious reduction compared with Cree. One indication of a tendency to simplify the Cree component is the near-total loss of the usual Cree exclusive/inclusive 'we' distinction in suffixes; however, the functional distinction is still marked by prefixes in the independent order (though it is lost in conjunct forms). Rhodes also notes the loss of an allomorph of a second person plural marker, but in this case no loss of functional distinctions results.

Outside the noun phrase, the only major French influence is in sentences with predicate adjectives and nouns. These optionally occur in construction with the French copula, beside alternative Cree predicate constructions.

It is certainly true, then, that Michif is mostly Cree, and that its Cree component shows no sign of overall simplification or reduction. It seems equally clear that the ethnic heritage of most Michif speakers is Cree: we know of no evidence that large groups of French speakers ever learned to speak good Cree, but many Cree speakers did (and still do) speak French. This means that the French part of Michif must have been incorporated into a Cree matrix by Cree speakers, through borrowing. French speakers did not shift to Cree in numbers, and if they had done so, we would expect any interference from imperfect group learning to produce changes in the Cree component of Michif, not just (or not at all) the replacement of Cree nominal structures by French ones. Similarly, if French speakers did not learn Cree, they could not have replaced native French verbal and syntactic structures with fully elaborated Cree substitutes. So Michif must have arisen by a process of wholesale grammatical replacement of native Cree nominal structures by French ones.

The resulting system cannot possibly be viewed, as a whole, simply as a changed later form of an Algonquian language, because a large component is not Algonquian at all: the French-derived nominal structures are completely discrepant with respect to the rest of the language. This means, among other things, that Michif data cannot be used in reconstructing Proto-Algonquian nominal structures. But if a significant portion of the language is excluded from Algonquian for purposes of reconstruction, then—in spite of the fact that the verbal structures are quite ordinary Algonquian—the development of Michif must be treated as nongenetic: Michif, like Ma'a and other languages discussed in 4.4, is a mixed language.

Also like Ma'a—but unlike abrupt creoles and creolized pidgins—the two main components of Michif could be used, with caution, in reconstructing "Proto-French" and "Proto-Cree" (or Proto-Algonquian), respectively. Using the Cree component would be relatively easy in this case—easier than using Cushitic portions of Ma'a in reconstructing Proto-Cushitic, because there seems to be no evidence that Cree portions of Michif have been significantly affected by interference from French. (The few simplifications that have been noted are of a type that one can find in other American Indian languages whose speakers use English most of the time; although the cause or causes of these changes are hard to determine, they resemble changes that occur in language death as much as changes that might result specifically from French influence.)

Using the French component of Michif in reconstructing "Proto-French" (in a hypothetical situation in which most other dialects of French had vanished) would cause more problems, because the French portions of the grammar have undergone some changes as a result—apparently—of Cree influence, and some of the basically French-derived constructions contain Cree elements. There is, then, an interesting difference between this case and the Ma'a case: in Ma'a, it is usually the borrowed parts of the grammar that more reliably reflect the language(s) of origin, while in Michif it is the inherited parts that are closest to the language of origin.

If we knew nothing about the history of Michif and nothing about its source languages, we would still have no trouble, probably, determining that its history involved extensive grammatical replacement. The reason is that both components of its grammar have morphosyntactically complex, but quite different, structures. If we had data from Algonquian languages other than Cree and/or from Romance languages other than French, then—even without any direct evidence of contact between an Algonquian and a Romance language—we could easily demonstrate exactly what mixture was involved in the development of Michif. The language could not be the result of either abrupt creolization or pidginization, because the people who created it must have been fully bilingual in both source languages; otherwise they could not have produced both the Cree and the French components correctly.

The next question is, under what circumstances would full bilinguals mix their languages in this way, rather than keeping the structures (and functions) of both languages basically separate? We can't answer this question until we know much more about the sociolinguistic history of Michif speakers than we do now, but we can at least mention one possible contributing factor: the tradition of their being a Métis "nation" might well have encouraged the emergence of a distinctive language to go with the distinctive culture.

In any case, we know of only one other mixed language that resembles Michif in having only one grammatical subsystem borrowed more or less intact from another language—namely, Mednyj Aleut, which is the subject of the next case study. However, if Muysken (1981) is right about the mixed Quechua-Spanish Media Lengua, which is said to have Quechua grammar but Spanish lexicon, that may be another example (see chap. 9 n. 5 for discussion). Michif is not unique, then, either in the degree or in the type of linguistic mixture it exhibits. The category to which it belongs has so few well-described members, however, that substantive historical generalizations—much less predictive historical explanations—must await further evidence.

9.4. MEDNYJ ALEUT

This section is based on a discussion of the Mednyj Aleut case in Thomason (1981 MS). The main original source of the linguistic and social information is Menovščikov (1969); Menovščikov (1968) gives a few additional examples.

Most Aleuts are U.S. citizens who live on the Aleutian Islands, an island chain that stretches westward across the Bering Sea from Alaska. But some Aleuts—now only 441 people, according to the 1970 USSR census (Comrie 1981b:252)—live on the Commander Islands, which are located off the eastern coast of the Soviet Union's Kamchatka Peninsula. These two islands, Bering Island and Mednyj (or Copper) Island, look on a map like the Soviet end of the necklace of islands whose greater part comprises the Aleutians. The Aleuts are not native to the Commander Islands; they first settled there in 1826, according to Menovščikov (and Comrie observes [252] that they were moved to the Commander Islands by the Russian authorities). Soon after the Aleuts arrived on Bering and Mednyj, Russians settled there too, to hunt for fur seals. On Mednyj, there were perhaps three hundred Aleuts and thirty Russians; on Bering, the Aleut population was much larger in proportion to the Russian population. Otherwise, Menovščikov says, the situations on the two islands were socially and economically similar. Most Russians married Aleut women, and bilingualism arose through intermarriage and through economic ties with Russia. This bilingualism was, however, functionally limited (Menovščikov gives no details on this point).

In the second half of the nineteenth century the fur seal trade declined, so there was no further influx of Russian hunters to the islands. There was thus no further need for the Russian language, and for a time Russian was no longer spoken there. This situation later changed dramatically: nowadays few Aleuts on the islands speak Aleut—only ninety-six people in all, according to Comrie (252)—so russianization must have proceeded rapidly over the last twenty or thirty years.

The Aleut spoken on Bering was apparently not heavily influenced structurally by Russian, a nice illustration of the importance of numbers in borrowing contexts, if Menovščikov is right in saying that the ratio of Aleuts to Russians was the only significant difference between the contact situation on Bering and the contact situation on Mednyj.

Mednyj Aleut is quite a different story. Its noun morphology and most other grammatical subsystems remained intact, but the elaborate Aleut inflectional patterns in finite verbs were replaced by Russian ones. This is particularly startling in view of the fact that Mednyj Aleut maintains Aleut nonfinite verb morphology. Below are examples of russianized Mednyj Aleut verb forms, from Menovščikov (1969:132), with functionally corresponding Bering Aleut and Russian forms for comparison:

		Bering Aleut	*Mednyj Aleut*	*Russian*	*gloss*
(a) sg.	1:	uŋuči-ku-q	uŋuči-ju	ja sižu	I sit
	2:	uŋuči-ku-xt	uŋuči-iš	ty sidiš	you sit
	3:	uŋuči-ku-x̣	uŋuči-it	on sidit	he sits
du.	1:	allax uŋuči-ku-s	allax uŋuči-im	my dvoje sidim	we 2 sit
	2:	uŋuči-ku-xt-xiðix	allax uŋuči-iti	vy dvoje sidite	you 2 sit
	3:	uŋuči-ku-x	allax uŋuči-jat	oni dvoje sidjat	they 2 sit

pl. 1:	uŋuči-ku-s	uŋuči-im	my sidim	we sit
2:	uŋuči-ku-xt-xičix	uŋuči-iti	vy sidite	you sit
3:	uŋuči-ku-s	uŋuči-jat	oni sidjat	they sit

(b) PRES:	uŋuči-ku-q	uŋuči-ju	ja sižu	I sit
PAST:	uŋuči-na-q	ja uŋuči-il	ja sidel (masc.)	I (m.) sat
FUT:	uŋuči-n aŋa-q	budu uŋuči-t'	ja budu sidet'	I will sit

(c)	awa-ða	aba-j	rabota-j	work!
	awa-lay-aða	niaba-j	ne rabota-j	don't work!
	saya-ða	saya-j	spi	sleep!
	saya-lay-aða	nisaya-j	ne spi	don't sleep!

(d)	saya-na-q	ja saya-l	ja spal (masc.)	I (m.) slept
	saya-na-xt	ti saya-l	ty spal (masc.)	you (m.) slept
	saya-na-x	on saya-l	on spal (masc.)	he slept
		tiŋ ayjaxčayu-ŋ	esli ja pojdu	if I go
		tin ayjaxčayu-n	esli ty pojdëš	if you go

In sets (a) and (b) we see that flexional Russian person/tense suffixes have replaced native Aleut agglutinative tense + person suffixes in Mednyj Aleut. The Bering forms show two tense suffixes in these sets, *-ku* PRESENT and *-na* PAST, as well as a periphrastic future construction with an auxiliary *aŋa-*. The Bering person suffixes, which follow the tense markers, are *-q* '1.sg.'; *-xt* '2nd person', which combines in the dual with a number suffix *-xiðix* that is used only with second person and in the plural with a similar number suffix *-xičix*; *-x* '3.sg.'; *-x* '3.du.'; and *-s* '3.pl.'. By contrast, the corresponding Mednyj Aleut suffixes combine tense and number and thus (though with some phonemic and morphophonemic differences) match the suffixes in the corresponding Russian forms: *-ju* '1.sg.pres.', *-iš* '2.sg.pres.', *-it* '3.sg.pres.', *-im* '1.pl.pres.', *-iti* '2.pl.pres.', and *-jat* '3.pl.pres.'.

A complication arises in the past tense, which in Russian is historically descended from a participial (i.e., an adjectival) form and does not inflect for person, but only for number and gender. Russian normally uses the independent personal pronouns even with present tense verb forms, where they are redundant. But in the Russian past tense, the pronouns are the only person markers. Mednyj Aleut has borrowed the Russian past tense suffix *-l* and its paradigm (added vowels for feminine and neuter genders and for plural masculine and feminine); more strikingly, it uses borrowed Russian pronouns to indicate person distinctions in the past. However, the borrowed Russian pronouns are used **only in the past tense of finite verbs**: in all other contexts, notably with nonfinite verb forms, native Aleut personal pronouns are used. Set (d) shows this difference, with Russian *ja*, *ty* 'I', 'you(sg.)' in the finite construction and Aleut *tiŋ*, *tin* 'I', 'you(sg.)' in the participial (or gerundive) nonfinite subordinate verb construction.

Another complication in the person/tense constructions is in the future. Both Russian and Bering Aleut have periphrastic constructions: Berin uses *aŋa-* with a nonfinite form of the verb 'sit', and Russian uses *budu* 'I will' in construction with the infinitive of the verb 'sit' (suffix *-t*'). In the Mednyj Aleut future construction, the entire Russian pattern is borrowed, including the nonfinite verb in *-t*'.

Mednyj Aleut has lost the dual number as a morphological category in finite verb inflection, a change that brings its number system into line with that of Russian verbs. This category is not distinguished throughout the Bering system, either, because in Bering Aleut the first dual form is simply the plural form combined with the numeral *allax* 'two'. But the second and third person dual forms in Bering are distinct from the plural forms. In Mednyj Aleut, the use of *allax* has spread from the 1st "dual" to the second and third persons, so that the constructions are similar to the corresponding Russian ones (though not identical, since the Russian word *dvoje* is a collective numeral meaning, roughly, 'twosome', derived from the numeral *dva* 'two').

Set (c) shows two other features of Russian verb inflection that have penetrated into Mednyj Aleut. One is the singular imperative suffix *-j*, which has replaced the native Aleut suffix (cf. Bering *-ða*). This replacement does not constitute a typological change in Mednyj Aleut. But the replacement of the native Aleut negative suffix *-lay* by the Russian negative particle *ne* (Aleut *ni*[-]) may represent a significant typological change: if, as Menovščikov's transcription suggests, the negative marker is a prefix, this is a noteworthy innovation in an otherwise suffixing language.

It should be noted that the Mednyj Aleut change toward flexional verb morphology from an agglutinative system mirrors changes in the opposite direction in Asia Minor Greek and in Ma'a. The Ma'a borrowings of Bantu verb prefixes are a closer analogue, since there too the phonemic shapes of the affixes are borrowed as well as the pattern, while in Asia Minor Greek the new agglutinative constructions are often made up of native Greek suffixes. The change in Mednyj Aleut from agglutinative to borrowed flexional morphology underscores an argument we made in chapter 4, namely, that in the most extreme borrowing situations there are no typological barriers to structural interference.

In Mednyj Aleut, as in Ma'a and Michif, the mechanism of the interference was clearly borrowing, not imperfect group learning in language shift. The fact that the Russian constructions are perfectly ordinary morphologically complete Russian patterns means that the Aleut speakers who borrowed the Russian constructions must have been completely fluent in Russian. Now, we have no detailed information about the communicative context in which Mednyj Aleut was spoken, or even about the stability over time of the Mednyj Aleut system presented here (though Menovščikov does say that Mednyj Aleut remained for some time as the only language of the island after the Russians left). But if, as Menovščikov's account seems to suggest, there was mutual bilingualism among Russians and Aleuts on Mednyj, then we can at least guess at a reason for the peculiar mixture we find in Mednyj Aleut.

A look at the inflectional categories of Aleut suggests a possible explanation. Aleut nouns are highly inflected, with five cases, three numbers, and a definite/indefinite distinction. But Russian also has case and number categories, even if the items in those categories do not exactly match those of Aleut, and definiteness is a syntactic feature of Russian. Aleut verbs are much less similar in their overall structure to the Russian verb system. An Aleut finite verb has over four hundred endings: three and one-half persons, three numbers, six tense-aspect categories, six moods, three voices, and two "degrees"; in addition, there are two verb classes (Geoghegan 1944). Functionally limited bilingualism in Aleut on the part of Russian traders—or, more likely, husbands—might include a reasonably good grasp of the somewhat familiar nominal inflectional patterns, but it is easy to imagine a failure to cope with the awe-inspiring array of finite verb forms. Aleuts bilingual in Russian might therefore have found it easier to communicate with Russians in Aleut if they used Russian endings on the verbs. In this context, it is worth noting that

Menovščikov observes that bilingual Bering Aleuts can manage to understand Mednyj Aleut to some extent, though with difficulty, because they know both the Russian and the Aleut patterns.

In any case, the extensive borrowing in just one grammatical subsystem puts Mednyj Aleut in the same class as Michif. There are also important differences between the two cases, however. In particular, Cree speakers borrowed French lexical morphemes along with a few French grammatical morphemes, while Aleut speakers borrowed only the grammatical morphemes. The relevant sociolinguistic difference here might be that French speakers did not learn Cree, while Russian speakers did, apparently, learn Aleut to some extent. Both languages are mixed in such a way that at least one grammatical subsystem cannot be used for purposes of reconstruction (to Proto-Algonquian or Proto-Aleut, respectively). In the Aleut case, the examples Menovščikov gives suggest that the borrowing has affected other subsystems besides the one that was primarily influenced; if so, then one must be very careful when using any Mednyj Aleut data for purposes of reconstruction. But the evidence for the nongenetic development of Mednyj Aleut lies in the massive grammatical replacement that has taken place in its finite verb system.

9.5. URALIC SUBSTRATUM INTERFERENCE IN SLAVIC AND BALTIC

As Baltic and, centuries later, Slavic speakers expanded northward and eastward from their original homeland, they encountered speakers of non-IE languages, including (but probably not confined to) Uralic. At least two kinds of historical evidence indicate that speakers of various Uralic languages shifted to Baltic and Slavic languages as the Indo-European groups took over new regions. The first kind of evidence involves inferences from linguistic geography: especially in Russia, Uralic languages are spoken in relatively small areas, isolated from each other. They thus present a classic picture of linguistic islands—relic areas in a sea of Russian. (There are exceptions, of course. In particular, the three major Uralic languages—Finnish, Hungarian, and Estonian—are geographically peripheral to Baltic and Slavic territory and are in no danger of being swamped by Baltic or Slavic.) The obvious historical inference, since small-group immigrations can be ruled out (before Soviet resettlings, at least) is that these speech islands are the remnants of a once widespread Uralic presence in northeastern Europe.

The second kind of historical evidence is documentary, though it is fragmentary for the older periods. Early chronicles show Slavic and Uralic peoples in contact by 862; Slavic expansion probably established such contacts at least by the sixth century A.D., and Baltic speakers came into contact with Uralic speakers even earlier (Veenker 1967:18). Décsy (1967:150–151) reports that Finnic speakers along the southern coast of the Finnish Gulf (between Narova and Leningrad) and near the White Sea coast began shifting to Russian in the thirteenth century. And, to give a final example, Comrie (1981b:100) says of the Finnic language Livonian that its 300 remaining speakers in Latvia are all bilingual in Latvian, and that "their inevitable absorption soon into the Latvians ethnically and linguistically can be viewed as the final stage in the merging of Baltic (IE) and Balto-Finnic substratum to give rise to Latvian." In fact, he observes, "to a large extent present-day Latvians can be viewed as linguistically assimilated Balto-Finnic speakers" (147).

Since language shift need not lead to interference in the target language, the question of possible linguistic consequences of these various shift processes remains open to investigation. Although it has received considerable attention (see, e.g., Décsy 1967, V. Kiparsky 1969, and Veenker 1967), the matter is still highly controversial. One reason for the controversy probably lies in the Indo-Europeanist's traditional reluctance to accept claims of substratum interference, especially when (as in this case) many or most of the hypothesized shifts are not directly attested. Other reasons, however, are more interesting.

First, it should be noted that not all the claims made in this area are disputed. Uralic influence on northern Russian dialects and on Latvian is, as far as we know, generally accepted. The most controversial claims are those made for Uralic influence on Slavic as a whole, since such interference would have to have occurred at a period before the final breakup of Common Slavic and thus before we have direct evidence of intensive Slavic-Uralic contacts. One common objection to any such hypothesis is that Slavic has no old Uralic loanwords, so that there cannot have been any other early interference from Uralic in Slavic either. We would of course argue that the absence of old loanwords means only that **if** there was early interference, it must have come about through shift, not borrowing. Since the historical evidence points to a shift situation in any case, the lack of loanwords is, in our opinion, not valid as an objection to claims of interference. (The fact that Slavic intruders entered Uralic territory from a nearby region may account for this lack: they may already have been familiar with flora and fauna in their new territories.)

Timing is a more serious problem. But if Décsy is right in believing that the ancestors of the Russians first came into contact with Uralic speakers about the end of the sixth century A.D. (1967:150), then there could have been time for some contact-induced changes to spread from northern to southern Slavic dialects, because communication between northern and southern Slavs was not finally cut off until several centuries later, in the tenth century in the west, later in the east (Jakobson 1955:5). The initiation of the last Common Slavic change—that is, the last single change to affect all the Slavic languages/dialects, namely, the fall of the jers ($ĭ,ŭ$)—is generally dated from the tenth century. It spread from south to north, and it was not completed in northern Russian dialects until the thirteenth century. It should therefore have been possible for changes to have spread from north to south before the tenth century. (It must be kept in mind, however, that the jer developments could possibly have arisen independently in the various languages, through drift.)

Even if some Uralic-induced changes affected late Proto-Slavic, the continuing contact between Uralic and Baltic and between Uralic and Slavic in the north would make us expect to find more evidence of Uralic influence in the northern languages and dialects than in Slavic as a whole. One reason is that a longer period of intimate contact is likely to result in more overall interference, especially if borrowing occurs as well as shift-induced change; another reason is that at least some of the northern changes will have been more recent and thus easier to detect. This expectation is in fact borne out by what we do find: a few features that suggest Uralic interference in late Proto-Slavic, a number of additional features in Russian and its nearest Baltic and Slavic neighbors, and still other Uralic interference features confined to northern Russian dialects and/or one or both extant Baltic languages, Lithuanian and Latvian.

The following discussion of Uralic interference features in Baltic and Slavic is not meant to be exhaustive. The sources we cite, espe-

cially Veenker (1967) and V. Kiparsky (1969), give further examples
for Slavic; we know of no thorough investigation of Uralic interference in Baltic. Our goal is to show that the presence of numerous
solid examples in the northern languages and dialects makes it imperative to give careful consideration to claims of such interference in the
entire Slavic subfamily. We will not consider other possible sources
of interference features in any detail. Proto-Slavic was apparently in
contact with Iranian, as is shown by a number of early loanwords,
such as the word for 'hundred' in Common Slavic. But we have seen
no discussion of possible nonlexical Iranian influence in early Slavic.
Caucasian languages are sometimes proposed as sources of interference features in Indo-European as a whole, but we know of no
instances of Caucasian interference in Slavic or Baltic alone.

To take the clearest evidence first, we find examples of phonological, syntactic, and morphological interference from Uralic (specifically the Finnic subgroup) in Latvian, Lithuanian, and northern Russian dialects. Two of these are prosodic features. Latvian has acquired
a rule of fixed word-initial stress from Livonian (Comrie 1981*b*:149;
other examples of Livonian influence on Latvian are also found in
this source); Veenker (1967) reports the same innovation in some
Lithuanian and northern Russian dialects. And according to Jakobson
(1962 [1938]:239), several Russian dialects of Olonets, influenced by
the typical Uralic word-initial stress pattern of the Finnic language
Karelian, have moved all original word-final stresses to the first
syllable of the word. Since nonfinal stresses remain on their original
syllables, stress is still phonemic in these dialects. (This change is
reminiscent of, though more complicated than, the change induced
by shifting Hungarian speakers in a Serbocroatian dialect, fixing the
stress on the penultimate syllable. See chapter 3.3 for a discussion of
this change.) Both stress changes are perhaps best considered as
simplificatory, since partially or entirely predictable stress patterns
are surely easier to learn than free stress.

Another simplificatory phonological change is the cokan'je found
in northern Russian dialects. V. Kiparsky (1969), Décsy (1967), and
Veenker (1967) agree on attributing this merger of Russian /c/ and
/č/ into /c/ to Uralic influence. Décsy (1967:153–154) reports that
the feature appears already in 11th-century texts.

In morphology and syntax, most of the clearest examples of
Uralic influence in the northernmost languages do not simplify the

grammar (though it is not certain that they constitute overall complications, either). One change, to be sure, is obviously simplificatory:
one Latvian dialect spoken by assimilated ex-Livonian speakers has
lost all gender distinctions (Comrie 1981*b*:147); Livonian, like most
other Uralic languages, lacks grammatical gender. Another
simplificatory change, but one that sets the dialects sharply apart
from the rest of Slavic, is a replacement of the feminine accusative
singular form of nouns by the nominative singular form, in northern
Russian dialects (Veenker 1967:86). This matches the Uralic pattern
in which the nominative case is regularly used for indefinite direct
objects.

A trickier example is that of the nominative object found in
Latvian, to a lesser extent in Lithuanian, and in northern Russian
dialects. Timberlake (1974:220) argues that the use of the nominative
case for the direct object in certain constructions diffused from one
or more West Finnic languages into the IE languages. This claim is
controversial, however. Certainly the construction exists in the Balto-
Finnic languages (Décsy notes, in explanation, that these languages
originally lacked an accusative case [1967:156]). But V. Kiparsky
(1969) credits Finnic only with a "conserving influence" in Slavic—
that is, he argues that the feature is a retention, not an innovation.
Décsy reports that the earliest example in Russian proper dates from
1215 and the latest example from the eighteenth century, but that the
feature remains in northern dialects. In any case, all the authors agree
in attributing its current existence in Russian to Finnic influence,
whether it is to be viewed as an innovation or a retention. If it is the
former, it may count as a grammatical complication. Since, as Timberlake argues persuasively, its specific syntactic behavior varies from
language to language, this construction also provides a nice example
of nonidentity between a source-language feature and the recipient-
language feature.

In the inflectional morphology, Lithuanian has undergone significant complications that look very much like a result of Finnic influence, though concomitant syntactic simplifications may cancel these
out as far as the calculation of overall grammatical effects is concerned. Most notably, Lithuanian has acquired three new cases, an
illative, and allative, and an adessive (Senn 1966:92; cf. Fairbanks
1977:117).[6] Of these new cases, only the illative is in regular use in
modern Standard Lithuanian; but all three cases were used regularly

in the sixteenth and seventeenth centuries, and several isolated south-eastern dialects still have the allative and the adessive (Senn, 92). Both the allative and the adessive were formed by means of a suffix -p(i), derived from a preposition *pie* 'to' (which still occurs, according to Senn, in the same dialects that retain these two cases); this suffix was added to stems already inflected with case endings. The origin of the illative suffix -*n* is disputed. Fairbanks reports a general agreement that it is derived from a postposition. Since, however, the emergence of new cases that are quite foreign to IE but typical of Finnic is hardly likely to be coincidental, we would suggest that the Finnish illative suffix -*Vn*, or rather its analogue in an older Finnic language now replaced by Lithuanian, is a probable source (though quite possibly not the only source) of the Lithuanian illative suffix.

Two Lithuanian inflectional changes that appear to be interconnected are also due to Finnic influence. Lithuanian is unusual among highly flexional IE languages in having lost the distinction between third person singular and third person plural finite verb endings, and its single third person form has a zero marker. Uralic, according to Collinder (1965:58), originally had personal suffixes only for first and second person verbs; third person singular is still often unmarked in Uralic, and some of the languages also still lack suffixes for the third person plural (Comrie 1981*b*:125). The original Lithuanian 3.pl. indicative verb form has become the regular nominative plural active participle, both masculine and feminine, replacing the original participial form (Cowgill 1970). Cowgill is surely correct in attributing this remarkable change to Finnic influence, following a suggestion made by Calvert Watkins (Cowgill 1970:31); compare Collinder's statement (58) that 'Finnish *laulavat* 'they sing' is historically identical with the nominative plural of the present participle *laulava*' (the verb is *laula*-), and Comrie's similar statement about Estonian (125). It looks as if the first of these two Lithuanian changes was motivated by shifting Uralic speakers' tendency to avoid suffixing third-person verbs, and it looks as if the second change was caused by the shifting speakers' transfer of the 3.pl. verb form, which they did not use in its original function, to replace the original plural participle, in a change that mirrored the Finnish functional extension of the participial form to the finite verb.

Both Lithuanian and Latvian have innovated a so-called relative mood in -*ot*, a special verb form indicating that the speaker doubts, or at least declines to take personal responsibility for, the truth of a statement (Comrie 1981*b*:154); this links the two Baltic IE languages typologically with Estonian (thus Comrie). Within the morphology, at least, this change clearly complicates the system.

Northern Russian dialects, finally, have acquired a derivational causative suffix under Finnic influence, e.g., *sosat'* 'suck' : *sositat'* 'to suckle' (Décsy 1967:155). Veenker (1967:152) emphasizes that this suffix is used with native Russian words.

When we broaden our view to include Russian as a whole, with and without Baltic and other northerly Slavic languages, we find more examples of Uralic interference in several grammatical subsystems. There are no certain phonological innovations in this category, however. One candidate might be the development in Russian of prothetic *v* before back rounded vowels and of prothetic *j* before front unrounded vowels. Collinder (1965:92–93) cites both changes within the Finnic branch of Uralic. But, though the development of these prothetic consonants may be more consistent in Russian, the *j-*, at least, occurs elsewhere in Slavic too, e.g., in *jem* 'I eat', with *j-* in all Slavic languages (but cf. the Lithuanian *ěmi* and other IE cognates in *ēd-*). These changes are likely to be linked to the set of changes known as the Law of Open Syllables, which led to a more consistent realization of C(C)V as the preferred canonical syllable type in the entire subfamily. If it is due to Uralic influence at all, then, it would have to belong to the small group of early Uralic influences on Proto-Slavic rather than with later influence on Russian alone—if the date of the Uralic changes in question was sufficiently early. From a systemic viewpoint, it is neither clearly simplificatory nor clearly complicating, since the addition of two segments (which already existed in Slavic as phonemes) is offset by the greater regularity in canonical syllable type.

Another possible Russian phonological example is actually restricted to southern and central Russian dialects (including Standard Russian). This is the akan'je innovation which changed *o* to *a* or *ə* in unstressed syllables. Its origin has been much disputed, and the precise form of the rule varies considerably from dialect to dialect. Besides Russian, it occurs in Belorussian (and, according to Černyx [1962:139], in two South Slavic languages, Slovenian in the west and eastern Bulgarian dialects in the east); it also occurs in (among other non-Slavic languages, again according to Černyx) the Volga Finnic language Mordvin, but not in Finnic languages to the north of Mordvin territory. Décsy (1967:152) cites Stipa as a source for the proposal that akan'je arose in Slavic through the influence of Mordvin, whose speakers were "russianized" between the tenth and the thirteenth centuries. We have not investigated the matter thoroughly, but from the facts presented by the authors just cited it looks as if two opposite proposals are about equally likely: either Slavic acquired the akan'je rule(s) through Mordvin (and perhaps other Uralic) substratum influence, or Mordvin borrowed the rule from Russian. Clearly, since akan'je was present neither in Proto-Slavic nor (apparently) in Proto-Uralic, the respective periods of innovation in Slavic and relevant Uralic languages are crucial for deciding this question. There is no general agreement on the age of the rule(s) in Russian, and estimates vary widely. We do not know of any estimates about the period of origin in Mordvin. However, Veenker's argument (1967:29–35) that the change was due to early influence from Volga Finnic (the ancestor of Mordvin and Cheremis), rather than to influence from Mordvin itself, looks quite promising.

Some examples of morphosyntactic interference in Russian are clearer. The so-called second genitive, a partitive construction that arose through reinterpretation of a vanishing noun-class distinction, is surely due to Uralic influence; in Finnish, for instance, the partitive case is consistently distinguished from the genitive case. In Russian, this change complicates the case system, but the partitive suffix -u is a relic of a set of forms (the old u-stem inflections) that were lost in a series of simplifying changes. In Finnish the partitive is also used as the direct object of a negative verb; this usage seems too close to the Russian genitive object of negated verbs to be coincidental (though Finnic influence here may be conserving rather than innovative, since other IE languages share this feature). If it is an innovation, this feature might count as a syntactic complication.

The Russian second locative case, though less well developed than the second genitive, is also probably due to Uralic substratum influence. Its suffix, like that of the second genitive, comes from a now vanished noun class, the old u-stems. Functionally, it can be compared with the adessive and inessive cases of Finnish and other Finnic languages.

The common imperative suffix -ka, which is added to the simple imperative to soften the force of an order, is said by Décsy (1967:155–

156) to be derived from a Uralic imperative suffix; compare the
widespread Uralic imperative suffixes *-k, -ka* (Collinder 1965:131).

The lack of a verb 'have' in Russian and Latvian is ascribed by
V. Kiparsky, Décsy, and Veenker to Uralic influence. The possessive
construction used in Russian is common in Uralic, e.g., Finnish
minulla on paketti 'I have a package' (literally 'me-to is package').
This corresponds closely to Russian *u m'en'a pak'et* (literally 'at me
[is] package'), and the construction cannot have been inherited by
Russian, according to Décsy (158–159), because it doesn't appear
until the fifteenth century. Other Slavic languages use an inherited
verb 'have' whose syntactic properties are more or less equivalent to
those of English 'have'.

These two sample sentences show, in addition to the Finnish case
ending as opposed to the Russian preposition, a difference in copula
usage: the Finnish sentence has one, the Russian sentence doesn't.
Proto-Uralic apparently lacked the copula in such sentences (Collinder 1965:62), and some of the Finnic languages are said to have
acquired one under IE influence. It is sometimes claimed that Russian
lost its present-tense copula under other (and/or earlier) Uralic substratum influence. Both Décsy and V. Kiparsky reject this proposal,
but for different reasons. We have already discussed Décsy's objection in 3.3; it is based on the erroneous assumption that an exact
correspondence between source-language structures and target-language structures is to be expected. As we argued in chapter 5, learners
are quite likely to overgeneralize or reinterpret their own native
language features when speaking the target language. Kiparsky's objection to the hypothesis of Uralic interference here cannot be set
aside easily, but we do not find it conclusive. He argues that other
IE languages, and even some other Slavic languages, have the trait
(i.e., copula drop). But most other Slavic languages retain the inherited verb 'to be', so no general drift to lose it can be established within
Slavic; and even if there were a drift in that direction, the other Uralic
influence on Russian makes it likely that Uralic contributed to this
change too. Veenker (1967:109–117) considers other objections to the
hypothesis of Uralic influence on this Russian development; like us,
he concludes that such influence is probable.

We come now to Slavic as a whole. The historical and inferential
evidence indicates a long history of shifts by Uralic speakers to Slavic
(and Baltic) languages; as we have seen, at least some of these shifts

have left linguistic traces in the target languages. The dates of earliest contact, as far as we know, do not set the beginning of this process at a time too late for Proto-Slavic to have been a target of the first shifts. Any evidence for Uralic substratum interference in late Proto-Slavic must be indirect, since there are no records for the period. All the examples we have found are problematic in one way or another (though not all in the same way); nevertheless, we feel that, as a set, they suggest an origin in Uralic substratum interference. They occur both in the phonology and in the morphosyntax, so they meet the linguistic criterion we have set for establishing contact-induced language change. In a case of this sort, where the social prerequisite of sufficiently intimate contact at a relevant time period is hard to pin down, a convincing demonstration will probably require showing that some innovated features were unlikely to have arisen through drift. This requirement is met here, we believe.

There are several promising phonological features. In the consonant system, a contrast between plain and palatalized consonants is particularly pervasive in Russian, but it occurs to some extent in most other Slavic languages as well (and also in Lithuanian). In some of the languages, e.g., Serbocroatian, it is confined to apical consonants, but in Russian almost every nonpalatalized consonant in the phonemic inventory has a palatalized counterpart. Slavic did not inherit this contrast, though it arose in Common Slavic through a series of developments with plausible internal motivations. A look at the areal context, however, makes the development suspicious as a strictly internal phenomenon. Palatalization in the apical series is one of the most striking characteristics of Uralic consonant systems, occurring in Proto-Uralic and in most of the modern languages (though not in Finnish). Jakobson (1962 [1938]), in noting the areal feature, cites numerous other northern Eurasian languages that have it; but most of these either owe the feature to Slavic (e.g., some Yiddish dialects and Romani dialects in Russia and Poland) or were not in contact with Slavic at the relevant period (e.g., some Chinese dialects). If, as Jakobson says, North Caucasian languages have the feature, they might be candidates for sources of influence on Slavic, but there is no other solid evidence of interference or for extensive early shifts from these languages.

One objection that might be raised against the proposal of Uralic influence on Slavic in this feature is that, especially in Russian, the contrast extends far beyond its exclusive Uralic domain in the apical series. Our response to this objection is the same as to the similar problem with the fate of the copula in Russian: imperfect learning during language shift very frequently leads to a broader distribution of features carried over from the native language. The expansion of palatalization in Russian vis-à-vis Uralic strikes us as analogous to the distributional expansion of retroflex consonants in Indic vis-à-vis Dravidian, or of clicks in Zulu vis-à-vis Khoisan (see chap. 5 for discussion).

In the vowel system, the Proto-Slavic restructuring of the inherited IE system has a distinctly Uralic flavor. Steinitz (1964), in fact, argues that the Proto-Slavic and Proto-Finno-Ugric vowel inventories are essentially the same (and that a Uralic substratum underlies the Slavic system). This may be overstating the case—Uralic lacks nasalized vowel phonemes, for instance—but the change from IE length distinctions to Proto-Slavic quality distinctions that match typical Uralic vowel qualities closely is striking. Steinitz compares the Old Russian vowel phonemes /i e ě a o u ï ĭ ŭ/ to a typical Uralic inventory, Cheremis (Mari) /i ü e ä a o u ï ʌ ə/. The Slavic jers, front /ĭ/ and back /ŭ/, were apparently extra-short, but they also differed in quality from the other vowels; specifically, they were probably centralized. It is noteworthy that Old Russian lacks the typically Uralic front rounded vowel /ü/ (though it has lost, or is losing, the non-Uralic nasalized vowel phonemes inherited from Proto-Slavic). But it is likely that late Proto-Slavic actually did have at least one front rounded vowel, /ü/ (namely, what others call /ju/): this is one solution proposed for certain disputed spellings in Old Church Slavic (see Lunt 1966:17); Old Church Slavic, though based on a South Slavic dialect, is generally considered to be virtually identical to late Proto-Slavic phonologically.

The Slavic innovation of a high back unrounded vowel /ï/ (< IE *ū) is particularly unlikely to be due to drift. So, to a lesser extent, is the emergence of a second nonhigh front unrounded vowel /ě/, the jat', which is the reflex of IE *ē and, in part, of the IE diphthongs *ay and *oy. The East Slavic languages Russian, Ukrainian, and Belorussian, and also eastern Slovak dialects, still lack distinctive vowel length.

As a final phonological note, Menges (1945) says that Old Church Slavic has a vowel harmony rule that affects its weakest vowels, the two jers. He believes that this feature is due to Uralic and/or Altaic influence. Linguistically, either group would fit, since front/back vowel harmony occurs in both; for the reasons given above, we think Uralic influence is more likely here.

It should be noted that, of the phonological changes just mentioned—phonemic palatalization, replacement of vowel length distinctions by quality distinctions, including the rather highly marked vowel /i/, and development of a restricted vowel harmony rule—none can reasonably be claimed as a simplificatory change.

Only three general Slavic morphosyntactic features are promising candidates for Uralic interference features. The first and most interesting one is the animacy category, because it is unlikely to have arisen through drift. Although an animate/inanimate gender distinction is perhaps the most widespread (and thus least marked) noun-class distinction in the world's languages, its appearance in Slavic is decidedly adventitious. Slavic inherited a complex set of noun-class distinctions from Proto-Indo-European; one system, comprising six classes whose original semantic base is unknown, was already partly lost by late Proto-Slavic times, but the other system, based on biological gender, was and is quite stable throughout Slavic. So the development of yet another noun-class system was hardly to be expected as a result of internally motivated drift.

In fact, none of the rather tortured attempts at internal (mainly analogic) explanations for the appearance of animacy has met with general acceptance among Slavists. Two authorities recently concluded independently that the category is an "example of spontaneous morphological innovation" (Klenin 1980:253–254; cf. H. Andersen 1980). It apparently entered Proto-Slavic just before the first written records, to judge by its shaky foothold in the language of the oldest texts. Animate nouns were originally marked in Slavic by the use of the genitive case instead of the accusative singular in the major masculine noun declension, the o-stems. In some Uralic languages, direct objects are expressed by a genitive case form. More significantly, in Proto-Uralic the case used for an indefinite direct object was probably the nominative, as it is in some of the modern languages; a definite direct object was in the accusative case, which in Finnic languages and Mordvin has fallen together through sound change with the old genitive case (Collinder 1965:55, 122–123).

Now, Uralic languages have no grammatical gender. But it is possible that shifting Uralic speakers, in their struggles with the unfamiliar Common Slavic gender distinctions, introduced their native definite/indefinite distinction, with its genitive-accusative definite marker, into their version of the Slavic target language. As examples given in chapter 5 show, this sort of reinterpretation is common in interference through shift; moreover, it is somewhat analogous to shifting Uralic speakers' reinterpretation of a noun-class distinction (*o*-stems vs. *u*-stems) in Russian case forms as a case distinction, genitive proper vs. partitive. One piece of evidence that supports our hypothesis about the source of the animacy category is Huntley's argument (1980:196, following Meillet) that the earliest Slavic distinction actually did involve definiteness—specifically, definite mature human ("animate") vs. other singular masculine *o*-stem nouns. So the semantic shift from definite to animate is not a stumbling block for the hypothesis. (Semantically, the category developed from definite/indefinite in the earliest attestations to personal/impersonal and then, in modern Slavic languages, to animate/inanimate.)

The second general Slavic feature that might be due to Uralic influence is the emergence of the predicative instrumental construction. This also occurs in Lithuanian and in most other Slavic languages as well as in Russian; in Slavic, it is best developed in Polish and Russian (Veenker 1967:131). In Russian and Finnish, for instance, the construction is used for temporary states, e.g., Russian *on byl soldatom* 'he was a soldier' (where 'soldier' has the instrumental suffix *-om*) and Finnish *isä on pappina* 'father is a minister' (where 'minister' has the essive suffix *-na*). V. Kiparsky and Veenker both argue against Uralic influence in this Balto-Slavic development precisely because it occurs in other Balto-Slavic languages besides Russian. But if we are correct in believing that the available historical evidence suggests that old Uralic influence in both groups was possible, then this is not a cogent objection.

The third Slavic morphosyntactic feature that might have been influenced by shifting Uralic speakers is a retention, not an innovation. A shared retention is, of course, much harder to establish as an interference feature than an innovation. Nevertheless, the high level of maintenance of the inherited IE case system by all but the most balkanized Slavic languages (as well as Lithuanian) seems unlikely to be coincidental, in view of the intimate contact between these IE languages and the case-rich Uralic languages, and the fact that case systems have been reduced in number of categories in all other IE subfamilies to a maximum of four.

The foregoing analysis of possible Uralic interference features in Baltic and Slavic suggests the following historical picture. In the northernmost languages and dialects—Lithuanian, Latvian, and northern Russian—the process of shift from Uralic left indisputable linguistic traces in the target languages. The influence is so clear here partly, perhaps, because the Uralic presence was numerically stronger in the north. More importantly, the shifts were more recent in this area, so that interference features are still structurally transparent and thus easy to identify—that is, the shift-induced changes have not been obscured by subsequent changes. Russian as a whole, and its neighbors, also show a number of definite Uralic substratum features. All the evidence for Uralic interference in Slavic as a whole is problematic, but it seems likely to us that the difficulty arises primarily from the fact that the structural links are harder to verify at the relatively great time depth—a thousand years or more. In any case, Uralic substratum interference throughout Balto-Slavic territory is moderate rather than heavy: structural interference features can be found in several grammatical subsystems, but most of the inherited Indo-European grammatical patterns remain intact.

9.6. AFRIKAANS

Controversy about the development of Afrikaans has been sharper than for any other putative creole, largely (apparently) for political reasons. The extreme positions are these: (a) Afrikaans developed out of Dutch exclusively through internally-motivated changes of a type found in Dutch dialects of Europe and/or in other Germanic languages; and (b) Afrikaans is a creole, the result of relexification of a Portuguese-based creole with, maybe, some influence from Hottentot (i.e., Khoisan), Malay, and other languages spoken in and around Cape Town during the seventeenth and eighteenth centuries. Between these two extremes are various intermediate positions, such as the view that Afrikaans is a semi-creole which arose partly through internally-motivated changes in Dutch but partly through influence from other South African languages. We have not carried out independent study either of the linguistic features of Afrikaans or of its social history; our comments on the case therefore rest entirely on secondary sources. We offer them here for their possible methodological value. In particular, it seems to us that the published social and linguistic facts about Afrikaans have not been sufficiently studied together, as a package, to see what conclusion best fits them. This case study is based on an unpublished section of the original version of Thomason (1980a).

Certainly Afrikaans seems at first glance to be an unlikely candidate for creole status, because the socially dominant core of its speech community is now, and always has been, the descendants of the original Dutch settlers at Cape Town after its founding in 1652. The Dutch colonists could reasonably have been expected to pass their language on to their descendants in a continuous unbroken process of normal transmission, in sharp contrast to, say, the transmission of Portuguese by Portuguese slavemasters to enslaved Africans. However, Valkhoff's careful study (1966) of the external history of Afrikaans shows that the process of transmission of Dutch in the Cape Colony was not as clear-cut as one might have assumed. Our sketch of this history is based on Valkhoff's account.

Two major factors complicate the picture. First, chronologically speaking, is the fact that few Dutch women accompanied the first Dutch settlers to Cape Town. A natural consequence of this situation was that, in the first twenty years of the Cape Colony, some 75 percent of the children born to female slaves were fathered by Dutch colonists (Valkhoff, 206). (Valkhoff refers to documentary evidence that refutes "the persistent legend"—fostered, by implication, by Afrikaners who hated the idea of miscegenation—"that the Cape Coloured had been begotten only by passing sailors, not by the White colonists themselves" [75].) Now, the slaves were Asian and would have been speaking a Portuguese-based Creole and/or Malay, and the Dutch, according to Valkhoff, would also have known Portuguese and/or Portuguese Creole. Nevertheless, the language passed on to these children—whose descendants later formed the Cape Coloured community—was a form of speech with Dutch vocabulary.

Valkhoff's claim is that the Dutch learned by the children must have been very heavily influenced by Portuguese Creole in particular—that, in effect, the transmission process was not normal, since the children's slave mothers would have spoken at best broken Dutch. Valkhoff estimates that 45 percent of the nearly four million current (as of 1966) speakers of Afrikaans are coloureds, which means that the coloureds' influence on the further development of Dutch in

South Africa could have been considerable if the early proportions of coloureds to whites were similar.

Meanwhile, the second complicating factor entered the picture once white families settled in numbers in the Cape Colony. It was common practice for Dutch mothers in southern Africa and the East Indies to turn over the duties of bringing up their children to servants. From these servants the children learned both Portuguese Creole and Dutch but, according to an eighteenth-century German traveler named Kolbe, the servants' poor command of Dutch meant that the children were learning "from the outset a very pitiful Dutch" (cited by Valkhoff, 176). By 1685, high officials of the Dutch East India Company were expressing fears that the broken Dutch which had become established, especially among White **children**, "would prove to be ineradicable" (209). In this way, Valkhoff believes, Portuguese Creole (and perhaps also Hottentot, whose speakers were prized as interpreters for their linguistic skills) interference features found their way into the Dutch of South Africa.

The transmission process, as Valkhoff describes it, would have been bent rather than broken in the early years of Cape Colony Dutch. Valkhoff points to the "advanced" (i.e., more creole-like) Afrikaans of certain subgroups of the coloureds as evidence of coloured participation in the process; he also remarks on the continued influence of High Dutch on Afrikaans as spoken by whites. Some recent comments by Hans den Besten (personal communication, 1984), however, indicate that the distinction between the Afrikaans of coloureds and the Afrikaans of whites is by no means so simple. White farmhands in the West Cape, he observes, speak the same type of Afrikaans that West Cape Coloureds speak—a dialect which is, moreover, hard for Afrikaners from the East Cape to understand, thanks primarily to several sound changes that have occurred in West Cape Afrikaans. He also points out that the high "bookish" style of spoken Afrikaans is relatively easy for Dutch speakers to understand, while the "deep," or colloquial, register of spoken Afrikaans is very difficult for Dutch speakers to follow.

When we look at the linguistic features of Afrikaans, we find no obviously marked features from any language other than Dutch. One possible exception to this generalization is the double negative marker, which den Besten (1985) suggests as a Khoisan interference feature. Another possible exception is the development of nasalized vowels, e.g., *ons* [ɔ̃:s] 'we, us' (Lockwood 1965:208), which could have arisen under Portuguese influence. We also find more marked features of Dutch grammar in Afrikaans than we find from the vocabulary-base language in any languages that are uncontroversially classed as creoles; even possible semi-creoles such as Réunion Creole, which might have as much French grammar as Afrikaans has Dutch grammar, also have features from substrate languages in addition to their French features. The information we give below about Afrikaans structure comes from Lockwood (1964:208 ff.)

A number of phonological changes from Dutch to Afrikaans simplify the phonological inventory. An example is the loss of voiced fricatives through merger with their voiceless counterparts.

Morphological simplification has occurred to some extent in nominal inflection and to a great extent in verb inflection. Nouns and plural personal pronouns lack case distinctions, though singular personal pronouns retain the Dutch distinction between the subject and object cases. In verbs, Dutch itself has a more analytic system than some other Germanic languages, such as German; but Afrikaans has lost all personal endings and much of the tense system, so it is much more analytic even than Dutch. The Dutch preterite has been lost except in auxiliaries, and the original perfect has become the ordinary Afrikaans past tense (cf., analogous changes in French, southern German, Yiddish, Italian, etc.). The past participle is now derived from the present stem, and Afrikaans has entirely lost the characteristic Germanic distinction between strong and weak verbs. Among Lockwood's examples (210) are these: *ek, ons* (etc.) *skryf* 'I, we (etc.) write'; *ek, ons* (etc.) *het geskryf* 'I, we (etc.) wrote, have written'. Lockwood (210) says that the loss of Dutch structure has not impoverished the expressive possibilities of Afrikaans, because new verbal constructions have developed, e.g., a periphrastic progressive aspect construction: *ek was aan die skryf* 'I was writing' (literally 'I was on the write').

The syntax of Afrikaans, according to Lockwood, is similar to that of Dutch. The main innovations he mentions are the double negative and a few Malay features, e.g., a reduplication process. The lexicon is mainly Dutch, though there are numerous English loanwords; there are also a few Malay loanwords and some African words for "purely African objects and conditions" (210 f.).

Opponents of Hesseling's original suggestion (1897, 1923) (and of Valkhoff's, following Hesseling) that Afrikaans arose by (semi-) creolization with "Malayo-Portuguese" are assiduous in their efforts to identify all features of Afrikaans with dialect developments in European Dutch. But many of these identifications are of dubious historical value, since they do not occur in clusters in one or more dialects that can be shown to have been spoken in the Cape Colony during the formative period of Afrikaans. That is: it is not enough to show that a particular change is a possible development in a Dutch dialect; in order to connect a feature of Afrikaans with a particular dialect feature in Holland or Belgium, one must show that speakers of the relevant European dialects were present at the relevant time in sufficient numbers to have influenced the development. Such a demonstration will be most convincing, moreover, when it involves the development of arguably marked features. In any case, the drastic inflectional simplifications and consequent remodelling of Dutch structures in Afrikaans are not typical, as a set of changes, of any European Dutch dialect or dialect group. To argue that Afrikaans arose by a series of perfectly ordinary internally motivated changes from Dutch flies in the face of everything we know about ordinary rates of internally-motivated change. We do not suggest that we can specify precise rates of change, but rather that the changes from Dutch to Afrikaans, apparently during the early years of the Cape Colony, were much too extensive to have arisen solely by internal means in the elapsed time. However, as we observed above, they show little positive interference from any other languages, as far as we can tell; nor are Afrikaans structures similar in detail to structures of most abrupt creoles with European lexicons.

Neither the social situation nor the linguistic facts, therefore, seem to support a claim that Afrikaans is a creole in origin. Both sets of facts do support the claim that speakers of other languages shifted to Dutch in the years following the founding of Cape Town, and that the children of Dutch fathers and, later, of Dutch mothers and fathers learned a form of Dutch that was significantly different from the Dutch spoken natively by adult Dutch settlers. The essence of the difference appears to lie in the simplification of the inflectional systems, and the (concomitant?) emergence of analytic constructions to take the place of certain inflectional features that were lost. In terms of our framework, this looks like a failure to learn the most difficult features of the target language during a process of language shift, if one is willing to accept the Dutch children's "bad Dutch" as the first stage in the TL population's acceptance of the shifting speakers' errors. The absence of many accompanying interference features from adult learners' original native languages is, we believe, explained in part by the continuing influence of native Dutch speakers on Afrikaans as it developed and in part by the fact that the learners' languages—Malay, Portuguese Creole, and Hottentot and other African languages—were sufficiently diverse typologically that their combined effect would have been to promote the emergence only of unmarked structures, not of marked ones. On this view, Afrikaans is historically a descendant of Dutch, as the Afrikaners claim, because it preserves a significant portion of Dutch structures in all its grammatical subsystems, even (though much reduced) in the morphology. But its development into a separate language was in fact heavily conditioned by nonwhites who learned Dutch imperfectly as a second language.

9.7. CHINOOK JARGON

The linguistic and social information in this case study are for the most part based on Thomason (1983a); see also Kaufman (1968, 1971). We present an outline of relevant facts here as an illustration of our claim, in chapter 7, that pidgin structures result primarily from mutual simplification and accommodation by speakers of all the languages in contact.

Chinook Jargon flourished in the Pacific Northwest of the United States and Canada during the nineteenth and early twentieth centuries. Extensive attestations date from the late 1830s, from the Columbia River; they occur primarily in the writings of missionaries and traders, people who dealt regularly with Indians. Some earlier possible attestations, dating from as early as the late eighteenth century and from the same region, consist of only a word or two each, so that their historical significance is hard to interpret. This means that a decision about the period of origin for Chinook Jargon must rest on indirect evidence.

It is not surprising, then, that the origin of Chinook Jargon is controversial: the major split is between those who believe that pidgins are an extremely rare linguistic phenomenon and those who believe that pidgins are likely to be a rather common development in multilingual contact situations which require regular, but functionally restricted, intergroup communication. The former tend to argue that Chinook Jargon arose in the early decades of the nineteenth century, after whites settled in numbers in the region and as a direct or indirect result of that contact situation; the latter tend to argue that Chinook Jargon is quite likely to have arisen before extensive white settlement, as a result of contacts of various sorts among the Indians themselves. As we said in chapter 7, we belong to the latter group.

There is no doubt that intergroup contacts were frequent and regular before whites settled along the Columbia. It is also certain that many Indians were sophisticated multilinguals. The question, therefore, is whether a pidgin would have been needed by the Indians before European settlements both changed the nature of the contacts among Indians and necessitated communication between Europeans and Indians. Although no definite answer can be given to this question, we believe that the weight of the indirect evidence is on the side of the earlier origin hypothesis, i.e., that Chinook Jargon owes its existence to contacts among Indians before extensive white settlement. Hymes (1980), arguing for the same position, presents a picture of prewhite Indian contacts—for instance, in a trade center near the Dalles on the Columbia—that resemble the classic trade settings in which other pidgins have arisen. Moreover, even in two-language contact situations, the possibility that speakers simplified their own language to promote social distance must be considered. This would be particularly likely, perhaps, in master-slave communication, but the quotations given in 7.2 indicate that a superordinate/subordinate relationship is by no means the only one in which a distorted version of (at least) one group's language is used as a social distancer.

In any case, whether or not Chinook Jargon arose as a result of contact with whites, its structure (with the possible exception of one prominent syntactic feature) does not reflect any participation by whites in its development. This means that postulating a nineteenth-century period of origin would require an additional hypothesis that the effect of white settlement was indirect only—that is, that white settlement merely provided the catalyst by creating an appropriate social context for pidginization. This hypothesis is not wildly implausible, but it is somewhat dubious in view of the fact that the white settlements were established for the express purpose of trading with Indians, and the white missionaries came to proselytize among the Indians as well as to minister to the spiritual needs of the white settlers and their dependents. It seems probable to us that a Chinook Jargon that arose in the context of white-Indian communication as well as Indian-Indian communication would reflect a structural cross-language compromise that included English and French as factors, in addition to the various Indian languages of the region. But the only demonstrable English or French influence on Chinook Jargon is in the lexicon, which acquired increasing numbers of French and English words throughout the nineteenth and twentieth centuries. The fact that the flood of French and English words did not bring with it any structural interference at all—except for a scattering of unproductive formants such as the plural suffix -s, which is added systematically only to one or two nouns—means, we believe, that the pidgin was fully crystallized before large numbers of whites began to use it.

When we look at Chinook Jargon structure, we must distinguish between two very different kinds of data. For the oldest extensive attestations, i.e., those from the mid-nineteenth century, we must rely on missionaries' and other whites' transcriptions. Starting in the late nineteenth century, we have more reliable transcriptions, including a number of texts and word lists recorded by trained linguists directly from Indians' utterances. Use of the older sources is complicated by the fact that not all of them are independent of each other, because most of the later publications by nonlinguists are based at least in part on earlier published material. However, Kaufman (1968) has established "lines of descent" for the most important of the nineteenth-century sources, so it is possible to determine which ones represent truly independent attestations. These sources can then be compared with the later linguists' elicitations from Indians.

The resulting comparison shows that the structure of Chinook Jargon is remarkably consistent from the earliest attestations to the mid-twentieth century. The difficulties inherent in trying to interpret the early white settlers' attempts to render exotic sounds in English and French orthography do not, as it turns out, hamper this comparison as much as one might expect. To be sure, some of the complex sounds transcribed by linguists in the 1930s are not consistently represented by any "odd" spellings in most of the early sources; nevertheless, all but one of the non-English and non-French sound categories are indeed recorded consistently in one or more of the earliest sources, so that we can be confident that they were present in the Chinook Jargon of the period. The most reliable of the early sources, by far, is the little book by Demers et al. (1871), whose first author was praised by a colleague in 1845 as being particularly expert in speaking Chinook Jargon (*Notices* 1956:19; in the same volume another colleague, also in 1845, refers to the complexity of the language's phonology [150]). Other early sources, including Hale (1846) and other Americans' writings, also represent consistently some of the pidgin's characteristic non-European sounds and sound sequences. As for the syntax, comparison here presents no special difficulties, and grammatical consistency between early and late sources is easy to demonstrate.

The basic vocabulary of Chinook Jargon is derived primarily from Chinook, Nootka, and a Coast Salishan language, perhaps Chehalis. The Nootka element no doubt entered the pidgin through white intermediaries: the marked sounds characteristic of the Chinook- and Salish-derived portion of the lexicon do not occur in any of the Nootka-derived words, except for the voiceless lateral fricative /ł/, and it was apparently late eighteenth-century European traders who first introduced a Nootka-based jargon (or incipient pidgin) to the Columbia River. (This was proposed by William Sturtevant, as reported in the June 1981 edition of the *California-Oregon Languages Newsletter;* see Thomason 1983a, n. 46, for discussion.)

Chinook Jargon consonant phonemes, as established by Kaufman (1968), are given below. Each item represents a unit phoneme.

p	t		ts	tš	k	kw	q	qw	ʔ
p'	t'	tł'	ts'		k'	kw'	q'	qw'	
b	d				g				
		l	s	š	x	xw	X	Xw	
m	n								
	r	l							
w				y					

It should be emphasized that every phoneme in this set is attested in at least two independent sources. One other possible (or probable?) phoneme, /tš'/, cannot be shown to exist by this criterion, because we can find it attested in only one source; and a second possible addition to the inventory, /ŋ/, is primarily attested only in European-language sources. The complex symbols in the inventory above are attested at least twice each in environments where analysis as a consonant cluster is not attractive. Chinook Jargon vowel phonemes are quite ordinary: /i e a ə o u/. The consonant phonemes, though exotic from an Indo-European viewpoint, are also quite ordinary when considered in the context of Northwest Amerindian languages. The most highly marked features—namely, the glottalized series, the labialized dorsals, the lateral obstruents, and the parallel sets of velar and uvular obstruents—all occur in most of the Indian languages of the region. So, although they are marked in universal terms, they are not surprising in a language that arose as a typological compromise among the Indian languages that would have been in contact. That is, Indian creators of the pidgin would have had no difficulty reproducing the marked sounds they heard in Chinook and Salish words. The voiced stop phonemes might have caused trouble for the Indians, and in fact many Indians did not distinguish this set. But these phonemes clearly did enter Chinook Jargon with English and French words. The same is true of /r/, which was used consistently only by Indians in Oregon—not by Indians in the later wider range of the pidgin. Almost all Indian languages in the area lack voiced stop phonemes and /r/. We do not claim that all, most, or even many whites who spoke Chinook Jargon pronounced it as the Indians did. Clearly, they did not. But some did, and others at least acknowledged the Indians' pronunciation as "best" (see Thomason 1983a for sample quotes).

Below are a few illustrations of representative Chinook Jargon words. Entries in parentheses are spellings that do **not** show the marked sound(s) in a given word, an indication that, though Chinook Jargon had a definable consistent structure, it also exhibited considerable variation among users and even in different utterances of the same speaker. In the examples, the native languages of identifiable Indian speakers (i.e., in data elicited by linguists) are indicated by hyphenated designations. References to the sources of the data given here can be found in Thomason (1983*a*). European (nonlinguist) nineteenth-century sources are designated by author. Spellings are the same as in the original sources, except that the truncated versions of *k* and *h* that are used by Demers et al. (1871) to represent glottalized dorsal stops and dorsal fricatives, respectively, are given in the examples here as *k'* and *x*. Stress usually occurs on the first syllable of a word; it is marked here only when it occurs on some other syllable.

(1) /tł'unas/ 'doubtful': Chinook-CJ *tł'unas* : Kalapuya-CJ *t'łu'nas* : Saanich-CJ *t'łunɛ·'s* : Upper Coquille Athabaskan-CJ *t'łu·'nas* : Chehalis-CJ *tł'unas* (Twana-CJ *tłu'nas*, Demers et al. *Tlonas*, Hale *Klunas*).

[2] /tšxi/ 'new': Chinook-CJ *tcxi·'* (where *tc* represents /tš/) : Twana-CJ *tcxi* : Kalapuya-CJ *tchi'* : Chehalis-CJ *tšxí·*; (Saanich-CJ *tci·'*).

(3) /dlay/ 'dry' (an English-origin word; note the impossible—for English—consonant cluster): Chinook-CJ *dlai* : Chehalis-CJ *tlʌ́y* : Hale *tlai* : Demers et al. *Tlaï*; all other Anglo and French speakers also have an /l/ in this word, though some insert a vowel between the /d/ (or /t/) and the /l/.

(4) /yaʔyəm/ 'tell a story': Kalapuya-CJ *ya'ʔum* : Twana-CJ *ya'ʔyɪm* : Chehalis-CJ *yʌ́ʔʔʌyʌm*.

(5) /qw'əláṅ/ '(h)ear': Kalapuya-CJ *q̇wəla·'n* : Chehalis-CJ *q'wʌllá·nʔ* : Demers et al. *k'wolan, k'olan*. It should be noted that no French or English source distinguishes uvulars from velars, though Demers et al. does consistently distinguish glottalized from nonglottalized dorsal stops. Twana-CJ *k'wəlá·n'* also shows glottalization, but no uvular; Hale and other Anglo sources do not show glottalization for this word, or for most others. The final glottalized *n'* in both Chehalis-CJ and Twana-CJ represents a recurring feature of the pidgin, since these two sources are independent of each other, but there are few or no other certain examples of glottalized resonant consonants, though such phonemes do occur in Salish and some other languages of the region.

(6) /makwst/ 'two': Chinook-CJ *ma'kwct* (where *c* represents [š]) :
Twana-CJ *ma'kwst* : Chehalis-CJ *má·kwst* : Snoqualmie-CJ *ma'kws-*
: Kalapuya-CJ *ma'kwst*. Two other Indian sources have nonlabialized
velars in this word, as do most European-language sources; but
compare Hale *makust, makst*: the first variant may reflect a labialized
velar in the speech Hale heard.

(7) /tk'up/ 'white': Twana-CJ *tk'o'p* : Chehalis-CJ *t'k'ú·p* : Saanich-
CJ *tk'u'p* : Demers et al. *tk'op* ; other European-language sources
fail to indicate the glottalization, but several do represent the marked
and non-European consonant cluster, as *t'koop* or *t'kope*.

(8) /ts'əm/ 'mark(ed), figured': Twana-CJ *ts'α'm* : Chehalis-CJ
ts'ʌm' : Demers et al. *Tsom*. Boas (1888) records a glottalized /ts'/
affricate in this word, but the Indian(s) from whom he heard the
relevant song is (are) not identified. All other European-language
sources that have this word agree with Demers et al. in spelling it
with the non-English, non-French affricate (or syllable-initial consonant cluster) *ts-*.

Chinook Jargon lacks the complex morphological structures that
are characteristic of Indian languages in the region, and its syntax—as
is typical of pidgins—is limited. The features it does display, however, can be accounted for as cross-language compromises among the
relevant Indian languages. The only possible exception to this
generalization is the dominant SVO word order of Chinook Jargon.
Kalapuya (Oregon) is an SVO language, but most languages of the
region, including Chinook itself and all the Salishan languages, are
dominant VSO languages. Only the few Athabaskan languages in
Oregon (where, we assume, Chinook Jargon arose) have a different
dominant word order—SOV. Nevertheless, the SVO order of
Chinook Jargon may have an Indian origin after all, because all the
VSO languages have patterns in which a subject noun or (more often)
a pronoun precedes the verb. If the origin of the SVO order does not
lie in these patterns, it may be due at least partially to influence from
French and English. In any case, the pidgin also has a less frequent
but still common VS (or at least Predicate S) word order pattern, as
in (from Hale) *Haias olo tsok naika* 'I am very thirsty' (literally 'much
hungry water I').

Negative words in Chinook Jargon are usually sentence-initial (as they are in all Indian languages of the region), as in *wik ałqi msayka atá nayka* 'you won't [have to] wait for me' (literally 'NEG FUTURE 2.pl. wait for 1.sg.'). The pidgin has an optional yes/no question particle *na*, whose use corresponds to the use of corresponding particles or affixes in the Indian languages. The optional nature of this particle is also reflected in the rather common optional occurrence, in the Indian languages, of yes/no questions marked only by intonation. Chinook Jargon sentences with nouns as subjects also have pleonastic subject pronouns preceding the verb, as in *t'alap'as pi lilu łaska małayt ixt-ixt łaska xaws* 'A coyote and a wolf lived [with] their houses side by side' (literally 'coyote and wolf they live one-one their house'). The same is true of possessive constructions consisting of a possessed noun and a possessor noun. Tense/aspect markers, e.g., the future particle *ałqi*, precede the verb and its subject. Imperatives are formed with *łuš (spus)*, literally 'good (if)', as in *łuš (spus) mayka łatwa* 'go!, you should go' (literally 'good [if] 2.sg. go').

All these features occur regularly in most or all of the Indian languages of the region, so they are all explainable as the result of mutual accommodation by speakers of diverse Indian languages. Except for the dominant (though not exclusive) SVO word order, none of these features is typical of pidgins and creoles elsewhere in the world, so they cannot be explained by the operation of universal structural tendencies alone. An explanation in terms of simplification of Chinook itself is a possibility, but the SVO word order does not fit, and the mixture of vocabulary—especially its Salish component—suggests that Chinook was not a true target language for the pidgin's creators.

9.8. ENGLISH AND OTHER COASTAL GERMANIC LANGUAGES, OR WHY ENGLISH IS NOT A MIXED LANGUAGE

9.8.1. INTRODUCTORY REMARKS

In this, our most extensive, case study we intend to characterize the kinds of contact-induced language change that Old, Middle, and early Modern English (A.D. 900–1500) have undergone in terms of the framework developed in chapters 1 through 8. A number of features wherein Middle English (ME) seems to differ from Old English (OE) in the direction of simplification have been cited in some recent studies as suggesting that in the development from OE to ME there has occurred something other than **normal change** in the sense that we would accept the notion. Such changes are typically associated with the contacts that English has had with Norse and French. In spite of the fact that English is one of the best-documented languages in the world, certain recent discussions of the history of English, based, as their authors claim, on new insights gained in sociolinguistic and creole studies, are both **iconoclastic** in that they reject what they characterize as "traditional" formulations, and **speculative** in that on theoretical or axiomatic grounds they try to devise scenarios for linguistic developments in English for which there is essentially no documentation, namely those in the north of England from 950 to 1250 and those in the whole of England from 1050 to 1150. These issues must be addressed, since they are recent and fairly well represented in the literature. We will argue here against the unjustified, if popular, hypothesis that Middle English underwent extensive contact-induced structural change at the hands of French; we will also argue that the extent of Norse influence on English between 900 and 1100, though remarkable, was not extreme given the preexisting typological and genetic closeness of the two languages.[7]

9.8.2. OUR POSITION

The Old English written in the first two-thirds of the eleventh century was a standardized literary language (the first in medieval Europe, after Irish) and probably represents the spoken language of a particular region, namely Berkshire and Hampshire, of about A.D. 900. The abundant Middle English of about A.D. 1250 represents the spoken language of that period in all its dialectal variety. There does not seem to be any reason to believe that the degree of change exhibited in English between A.D. 900 and A.D. 1250 (350 years) is anything other than normal. The Norse invasion and possibly heavy settlement in certain areas of Britain during the ninth and tenth centuries is a fact with linguistic consequences, and the Norman conquest of England (but not Scotland, where, in the Southeast, Northern English was spoken) in the eleventh century and consequent devaluation of English as a cultivated language are also facts. However, with respect to French, the linguistic consequences for

English do not seem to have amounted to anything other than normal borrowing (a borderline type 2/type 3 case) by a lower language in a situation of occasional bilingualism, as we will see in 9.8.8. The case with respect to Norse is difficult to evaluate without looking at all the facts, since much of the structure of the two languages was identical. When all the relevant data are examined, however, it is apparent that a creolization hypothesis is not required to explain the facts of Northern Middle English, nor is it even likely.[8]

9.8.3. SUMMARY OF ENGLISH SOCIOLINGUISTIC HISTORY DOWN TO A.D. 1400

Pre-English (so called because it is logically the earliest stage and is unattested) was planted on the island of Britain during the fifth and sixth centuries A.D. The English abandoned the Continent at this time, or left but a few rapidly-absorbed stragglers (Chadwick 1907:89, 103, 181–185). When English was introduced into Britain it may already have had some dialectical nonuniformities. For example in some dialects West Germanic *a: was reflected as /ae:/ while in others its was /e:/ (this is paralleled in Frisian). The redistribution of WGmc *a as /ae/ and /a/ was also not uniform, and the existence of [ae] is of continental date (Frisian may have been non-uniform with respect to this as well). The palatalization of WGmc *k and *g near from vowels and *j may not have been quite uniform, either, though it is generally considered to have been so. It is probably not the case that there were just three named groups of English-speaking settlers in Britain (Angles, Saxons, and Jutes), and the "Angle" and "Saxon" Kingdom (later county) names of Anglo-Saxon England do not correlate straightforwardly with either ancient or more recent dialect cleavages. Hence the terms "Anglian" and "Saxon" when describing and naming groups of dialects in OE should be avoided. The first written material in English dates from about 675. By 900, as a result of the passage of time as well as of the spread of English from the eastern third of the island westward to the borders of Cornwall, Wales, Cumberland, and Strathclyde, English had the following known dialects: Kentish, West Saxon, West Mercian, North Mercian (attested only in Rushworth gloss to Mt 1.1–Mk 2.15, Jn 18.1–3), and Northumbrian. Given our knowledge of Anglo-Saxon tribes and petty kingdoms, and the fact that the known Old English (OE) dialects (A.D. 700–1100) cannot be ancestral to all of the known ME dialects (1100–1400) we must suppose the existence of at least the following additional but unattested OE dialects: *East Saxon (Essex), *East Anglian (Norfolk), and *East Mercian (Lincoln-shire). A **Middle Anglian** "tribe" occupied parts of Northampton and Leicester; whether it is necessary to postulate a special dialect of OE for this group is unclear but unlikely. There were OE "king-doms" that did not have dialects of their own: for example Sussex (South Saxons). In ME times the dialect of the area of Hastings (East Sussex) descends from Old Kentish, though by 1250 it has split off from Kentish. The speech of Lewes (West Sussex) is descended from West Saxon OE.

These eight dialects each had a few particular traits, and there were some peculiarities shared by batches of two, three, or four dialects against the rest. The OE dialects were not greatly different from each other, though Northumbrian was the most divergent. Before our earliest records of English such phonological develop-ments as **breaking, velar umalut,** and **palatal umlaut** had occurred on British soil, and not uniformly. It must be kept in mind that from 500 to 800 (at least) English clearly was in contact with its mainland sibling Frisian and its mainland cousin Low Frankish. Such innova-tions as palatal umlaut (600–650), voicing of the spirants /f θ s/ in initial position (before 950:TK), voicing of all four of the spirants non-initially in voiced environments (very early), the raising of [ae] to <e> (650–700), and the change of /y/ to /e/ (eighth century) all seem to have originated on the Continent and spread to Britain (DeCamp 1958).

Probably all the distinct OE dialects were used in writing down to about 1000, but as of about A.D. 900 the West Saxon dialect came to be the one most widely used in writing because of the political ascendancy of the kingdom of Wessex, whose homeland included the modern southwestern counties of Hampshire, Berkshire, Wiltshire, Dorset, and Somerset. Wessex was able to rise at the expense of the other regions of England because for several decades these other regions were being overrun by the "Danish" hosts. Although eventu-ally stopped by Alfred and his Wessexmen from taking over the whole country, a respectable number of "Danes" settled in the North and East of England, in areas where Northumbrian, East Mercian and East Anglian dialects of OE were spoken. This area was later known as the Danelaw (in OE, *Denalagu*) (see map 3). By 1000 a standardized written OE based on the West Saxon (WS) dialect was in use all over England. The non-West Saxon dialects continued to be spoken, of course, but materials written in them without a WS overlay are rare if not altogether lacking.

Norse[9] speakers settled in the North and East of England during the period from 865 to 955 (though not in the East after 920), a period that brackets the settlement of Normandy by the same Northmen. In none of the areas of Europe conquered and/or settled by Northmen—whether Norwegians, Swedes, or Danes—did they maintain their Norse language. Though in England the settlement appears to have been more intensive than elsewhere Norse probably lasted no more than two generations after 955. In Normandy, for example, the first France-born generation had almost only French names.

French-speaking Normans, with Breton and Flemish allies, conquered England between 1066 and 1070. They displaced the heretofore English-speaking higher nobility and much of the clergy. During the reign of William the Bastard, England's new overlords gradually modified the country's political and religious superstructure, and eventually some fairly radical transformations took place.[10] The legal and religious activities of both Normans and Englishmen were recorded mainly in Latin, decreasingly in English, and scarcely at all in French. Though Northern (Picard) and Western (Angevin) French soon became the vehicles of a flourishing "Anglo-Norman" literature in England, French was not used in official legal documents in England until 1215. In court proceedings, at least during William's reign, both French and English were used. This was most probably the case throughout the Middle English period (Mellinkoff 1963:67–70). Written materials continued to be produced in English, though they were scanty. Most of what was written was copies of Old English texts composed several generations earlier. A very small amount of original text in contemporary English began to be written as of about 1150, roughly ninety years after the Norman Conquest. French speakers did not settle in **large** numbers anywhere in England, though they did settle in modest numbers in certain commercial centers in the South. French speakers, however (along with some Flemings and Bretons), became the feudal lords of the most productive agricultural lands of England, as well as of the church. Though they were everywhere, French speakers never made up more than a small fraction of the population (Berndt 1965). Even in 1086 (Doomsday survey), well after the completion of the Conquest, there were a sizable number of English fief-holders; and there had been French fief-holders even during the reign of Edward the Confessor (1042–1066). No doubt French was the principal language of the Norman fief-holders, but they could be numbered in the thousands (perhaps 20,000). England at this time had a population of from 1.5 to 2 million.

From the time of William the Bastard to King John, the king of England was also the duke of Normandy, and held Normandy as a fief from the king of France. Until about 1200, most of the higher nobility divided their time roughly equally between England and Normandy. They probably had no particular cultural motivation either to learn English or to require Englishmen in any numbers to learn French. (It should be remembered that the states of Europe down to the last century were typically multiethnic and multilingual, but not necessarily with many multilingual individuals.) But John got into a war with the king of France, and lost it, and in 1204 lost Normandy to boot. Thenceforth, Normans holding fiefs in both countries were obliged to decide whether they would hold them either in England or in France, but not both. The ranks of the aristocracy began to speak mainly English (many must already have been bilingual in English [Mellinkoff 1963:68]) and to forget how to speak French. Already in the late twelfth century, when the Norman rulers of the English established colonies in Wales and Ireland, the colonies were English-speaking, with (presumably) French-speaking bosses. By the middle of the thirteenth century, a great deal of writing in (Middle) English was going on, no doubt in large part due to the demand of the upper classes for literature in a language they knew. (In the twelfth century, when they still spoke French, the English aristocracy were great supporters of literary efforts in French, more so than the mainland French themselves.) This trend had begun already around 1200. Those nobles retaining fiefs in England came to identify themselves as English by nationality, whatever their language might have been. In the 1250s a barons' revolt against Henry III had as one of its grievances a resentment against the mainland French cronies of Henry III and the inevitable associated French influence. Some of these barons, descended from eleventh century French-speaking Normans, demanded that those fief-holders in England who could not speak English should be dispossessed of their holdings, or even killed! In 1258, at the end of the Barons' Revolt, a proclamation was issued in both English and French, describing some of the settlements made as a result of the revolt. This is the first known official document that was written in English since the time of Henry I (ca. 1154).

Around 1250, between one and two generations after those Norman fief-holders who had so chosen had opted for England rather than France, French words began to pour into ME. This suggests that between 1200 and 1250 the Norman nobility to a great extent began learning English and interacting with monolingual English speakers. By the end of the thirteenth century the French being written in England was simply awful. By the early 1300s there is good evidence that very few nobles spoke French very well, if at all. The maintenance of French, to the extent that it was maintained, seems to have served primarily as a class marker. Also from 1100 to at least 1500 the French were culturally 50 to 100 years in advance of other Europeans, and any cultured person felt he should know French, even if he did not. By 1360 English was officially accepted alongside French as a language usable in parliament, law courts, and legal documents (but Mellinkoff 1963:68–69 shows that English must always have been used, even if alongside French, in the lower and rural courts). After that date, French was little used, though it held out among lawyers till the sixteenth century. Medieval French loans into English ceased for all practical purposes by 1400.

When written English began to be used again at an increasing rate, it was no longer standardized and people wrote basically as they spoke. There were about twenty dialects of English at this time, falling into three main divisions: Northern, Midland, and Southern; the Midland division had two main subgroups: East Midland and West Midland; the Southern division also had two main subgroups: Southeastern and Southwestern (see map 5).

9.8.4. THE ETHNOLINGUISTIC REGIONS OF ENGLISH-SPEAKING BRITAIN

From about 1200 to the present day we have a reasonable to good grasp of what the dialects of English have been, what their boundaries have been, and what at least some of the features have been that define them. To be sure, certain areas of England are known in ME times only through place-names, and in modern times (i.e., since 1430) the dialects of the Southeast became extinct before they could be recorded. But even with these gaps, it can be shown that the outlines of the dialect regions of English have changed relatively little over recorded time; even when the isoglosses that define the regions have changed, they have tended to jump from one boundary to the next. (This, of course, is not done without exception; some areas have spread, others have shrunk, and others have split.) Consequently it is convenient to refer to the distribution of linguistic features by the "ethnolinguistic regions" in which they are prevalent. Since these regions typically do not correspond exactly with the medieval or modern counties, the ethnolinguistic regions must be defined by a one time only listing and/or by a map.[11]

Description of the Ethnolinguistic Areas in Terms of Modern Counties (CAPs name the ethnolinguistic regions, ordinary type the current political units)

GALLOWAY: Kirkcudbright, Wigtown, S Ayr.

STRATHCLYDE: Dumbarton, Renfrew, N Ayr, Lanark, Dumfries, Roxburgh, Selkirk, Peebles.

LOTHIAN: Berwick, Haddington (East Lothian), Edinburgh (Mid Lothian), Linlithgow (West Lothian), Stirling.

NORTHUMBERLAND: Northumberland, N Durham.

DEIRA: North & East Ridings of Yorkshire, N fringe of West Riding.

ELMET: most of West Riding of Yorkshire.

CUMBRIA: Cumberland, Westmorland, N Lancashire.

LANCASTER: M & S Lancashire.

CHESTER: Cheshire, NW Derbyshire.

STAFFORD: Staffordshire, NE Shropshire, NW Warwickshire, SW Derbyshire.

LINDSEY: Lindsey (Lincolnshire).

FOURBOROUGHS: Kesteven & Holland (Lincolnshire), Nottinghamshire, E Derbyshire, NE Leicestershire.

LEICESTER: most of Leicestershire, Rutland, NE Warwickshire, maybe SE Warwickshire, maybe M Northamptonshire.

NORTHAMPTON: SW Northamptonshire, NE Oxfordshire, Bedfordshire, NW Hertfordshire, most of Buckinghamshire, maybe M Northamptonshire, maybe SE Warwickshire.

NORFOLK: most of Norfolk, N Cambridgeshire, Huntingdon-shire, E Northamptonshire.

SUFFOLK: Suffolk, NW Essex, NE Hertfordshire, S Cambridge-shire.

ESSEX: most of Essex, SE Hertfordshire, the City of London.

KENT: Kent.

HASTINGS: Hastings (Sussex), E Surrey.

EAST WESSEX: Middlesex, S Buckinghamshire, most of Berkshire, W Surrey, Lewes (Sussex), most of Hampshire (including the Isle of Wight), SE Oxfordshire.

WEST (or MID) WESSEX: W fringe of Berkshire, W fringe of Hampshire, SW Oxfordshire, S & E Gloucestershire, Wiltshire, Dorset, E Somerset.

DEVON: W Somerset, Devon, E fringe of Cornwall.

THE PALE: Dublin, Wexford, and other places to be determined.

SOUTHMARCH: N & W Gloucestershire, Herefordshire, Wor-cestershire, SW Warwickshire, most of Shropshire.

Certain other terms are used to refer to two or more of the ethnolinguistic regions as a unit. Thus,

BERNICIA = LOTHIAN + NORTHUMBERLAND
NORTHUMBRIA = BERNICIA + DEIRA
EAST ANGLIA = NORFOLK + SUFFOLK
WESSEX = EAST WESSEX + WEST (MID) WESSEX
 (?+ DEVON)
THE PALATINE = LANCASTER + CHESTER

Most scholars (Kaufman among them) have been accustomed to use names for dialect regions of English based on geographical terms, but terms created on such principles are not the same for each scholar and the usages by different scholars are frequently at odds; the reader has to learn what a given term means for each scholar. We have used geographically-based terms for the major divisions and subdivisions of Middle and New English dialects since these pose the fewest problems; however, note that our West Midland does not include

SOUTHMARCH, commonly referred to as "SW Midland."
The dialect divisions and subdivisions of ME are as follows:

NORTHERN DIVISION
  SCOTS SUBDIVISION
    ?ABERDEEN: John Barbour's writings (fifteenth century)
    ?PERTH: Andrew Winton's writings (fifteenth century)
    LOTHIAN: Gilbert Haye's writings (fifteenth century)
    (in modern times GALLOWAY, STRATHCLYDE and
    others needed to be added)
  ENGLISH NORTHERN SUBDIVISION
    NORTHUMBERLAND
    DEIRA
    (in modern times the additional CUMBRIA proves to have
    been colonized from Deira)
MIDLAND DIVISION
  EAST MIDLAND SUBDIVISION
    ELMET
    LINDSEY
    FOURBOROUGHS
    NORFOLK
    LEICESTER
    NORTHAMPTON
    ?SUFFOLK
  WEST MIDLAND SUBDIVISION
    LANCASTER
    CHESTER
    STAFFORD
SOUTHERN DIVISION
  SOUTHEASTERN SUBDIVISION
    ESSEX
    KENT
    HASTINGS
  SOUTHWESTERN SUBDIVISION
    EAST WESSEX
    WEST WESSEX
    THE PALE
    DEVON
    SOUTHMARCH
    (in modern times also CORNWALL)

OVERVIEW OF ENGLISH DIALECTS FROM 700 TO 1900

OE dialect	Division in ME	ME dialect	ModE dialect	Explanations
*East Saxon		Essex		
Kentish	SE	Kent	dead	
		Hastings		
West Saxon	SW	East Wessex	shrunk	
		Mid Wessex	living	
		The Pale	dead	
		Devon	living	
		Southmarch	now 2	+ Shropshire
West Mercian	WM	Stafford	living	
		Chester	living	
		Lancaster	now 2	+ M Lancaster
*East Anglian	EM	Suffolk	shrunk	
		Norfolk	shrunk	
		Northampton	shrunk	
*East Mercian		Leicester	living	
		Fourboroughs	now 2	+ S Lincolnshire
		Lindsey	shrunk	
North Mercian		Elmet	living	
Northumbrian	N	Deira	living	spread to Cumbria
		Northumberland	denatured	
		Scots	now several	

9.8.5. Overview of Linguistic Developments in the Middle English Period

As of 1200 Northern English was thoroughly riddled with Norse traits both in lexicon and grammar. Its grammar was a good deal simpler than that of the other ME dialects. Lindsey, Fourboroughs, Elmet, and Lancaster, like Northern English, had hundreds of lexemes of Norse origin, as well as a sizable but lesser amount of grammatical influence. Norfolk and Chester had a lesser degree of lexical and grammatical influence from Norse. The Norse speakers who had settled in the West Midland area, Cumbria, and Galloway were Norwegians, while the Norse speakers who had settled in the Northern and East Midland areas were Danish speakers. Southern dialects had practically no Norse influence, and their grammatical structure was essentially unchanged from that of OE except for the results of sound change. These had not even been subjected to analogical leveling, so that in some ways the Southern ME dialects were more complex than their OE antecedents. The primary grammatical changes from OE to ME were (a) the loss of grammatical gender, (b) the simplification (but in the South not loss) of gender/number/case agreement on adjectives (qualifiers, quantifiers, and demonstratives), and (c) the loss of the genitive plural and dative (both singular and plural) cases.

French lexical influence was at first (1150–1250) moderate, and then became massive, especially in the Southern and East Midland dialects, by the beginning of the fourteenth century. Yet the Southern dialects remained the most conservative of all ME dialects in grammar, phonology, and morphophonemics throughout the ME period.

Until about 1225 innovations starting in the South were spreading northward (e.g., /aː/ > /oə/, 'gamma' > w/y), after 1250 practically all innovations in English were starting in the North and spreading southward (e.g., lengthening of short stressed vowel in open syllable, dropping of final unstressed schwa, degemination, spread of third person singular present tense -es at the expense of -eth). No explanation (except that York, England's second city, is located in Deira) can as yet be offered for why the North should have been so influential on the Midlands and South from 1250 to 1400, since it was much poorer than the rest of England, and was constantly being raided by the Scots, with whom the Northerners (ruefully, one supposes) shared a dialect. Only near the end of the fourteenth century, when a standardized form of English was developing in London, did traits that originated in the South begin to spread north again (e.g., /Vht/ > /Vit/ and /Vut/ as in **riht** > **riit** > **rəit** 'right', **druht** > **druut** > **drəut** 'drought', **dohtər** > **dahtər** > **dautər** 'daughter').

A Central Midland type of dialect superimposed itself on London through the heavy in-migration of entrepreneurs from the region of Leicester and Northampton in the first half of the fourteenth century. By about 1400, a written standard of English was developing in London that showed traits of the local Southern (Essex) dialect basically as a substratum to this imported Leicester (+ Northampton) speech. By 1430 (Samuels 1963:85, 88) the London dialect, though still rather more complex morphologically and less complicated in the use of modals than current English, became the written standard to which all regional dialects of English have been assimilating ever since—at least till the end of the colonial period, about 1800.

With these basic facts in mind, we can proceed to examine some of the assertions that have been made as to the "unusual" degrees of change that may seem to have taken place between the stages conventionally labeled OE and ME. (In the early nineteenth century, OE was called "Anglo-Saxon," the English of the twelfth and early thirteenth centuries was known as "Semi-Saxon" or "Old English," and "Middle English" was applied to material dating after 1250.) We may take the period of Norse influence (but only in the Northeast and East of England) as lasting from 875 to 1045, as will be explained in 9.8.6. We may take the period of **spoken** French influence to have lasted from 1065 to 1265; although French continued in widespread use until about 1350, its use after 1265 was artificial for all concerned, high and low alike.

9.8.6. NORSE INFLUENCE ON ENGLISH[12]

9.8.6.1. THE NORSE IN ENGLAND

For the 45 years between ca. 875 and 920, Danish Vikings and their descendants ruled (the ethnolinguistic regions of) Norfolk, Fourboroughs, Lindsey, and Leicester. Between ca. 875 and ca. 955, 80 years, these folk ruled Deira. Between 900 and 920 Norwegians settled in respectable numbers in the western parts of Cumbria, Lancaster and Chester (Wainwright 1975), and in Galloway; small numbers of them settled in scattered places in Northumberland and

Lothian. In Elmet there were both Danes and Norwegians. Danish was destined to have a permanent effect on the English of these areas, and an analysis of this effect is the aim of the present section. For a brief summary of the period of Danish settlement we quote from P. H. Sawyer's *The Age of the Vikings* (1971:148, 150, 151):

> In the last quarter of the ninth century the Anglo-Saxon Chronicle reports the settlement in Northumbria, Mercia and east Anglia of two bands of Scandinavian invaders. In 865 what the Chronicler called a *micel here* arrived and campaigned for ten years before beginning to find permanent new homes. In 876 one group, under the leadership of Healfdene, "shared out the land of the Northumbrians and they proceeded to plough and support themselves." In the following year another group, apparently from the same *micel here* "went away into Mercia and shared out some of it" and very early in 878 the remainder "came stealthily to Chippenham and occupied the land of the West Saxons and settled there. . . . " In the spring and early summer of that year Alfred rallied the West Saxons . . . and the intruders were defeated in battle. . . . [T]hey reatreated to Cirencester where they stayed for a year, and then in 880 they "went from Cirencester into East Anglia and settled there and shared out the land" [148]. Long after they had found new homes in the north and east of England these settlers continued to trouble the English of western Mercia and Wessex. . . . [T]hey continued to venture on plundering expeditions in the south and west. . . . The best answer to such attacks was the system of strongpoints [called "boroughs"] established by Alfred and his children [150]. In the shelter of such defences counter-attacks could be prepared and these boroughs were soon turned to offensive use. The extension of the authority of the West Saxon kings largely depended on the extension of this system of boroughs year by year deeper into the Danish-held lands . . . [B]y 920 Edward had been acknowledged as overlord throughout the greater part of southern England. North of the Humber the situation was more complicated. The native Northumbrians seem to have been . . . reluctant . . . to acknowledge the overlordship of a southerner . . . until Eric Blood-Axe, the last of the Scandinavian kings of York, was deposed in 954 and Northumbria finally became part of the united kingdom of England. [151][13]

9.8.6.2. NORTHERN ENGLISH

In comparison with other dialects of ME, the dialects of the Northern division seem to be simpler in structure and to be quite heavily influenced by Norse. Before examining the ways that Northern ME English is unlike Southern, let us list how Northumbrian

OE, the apparent ancestor of Northern ME, differed from West Saxon in ways that bear on the ME outcome.

(1) Where most early West Germanic languages dropped the original short vowel /i/ in the second and third person singular of the present indicative of strong verbs, Old Northumbrian (ONhb) retains a vowel /e/, or else reinstated one through pattern pressure. Such forms (in dialects that drop the vowel in question) are known as "contract presents."

(2) ONhb had dropped word-final /n/ in inflectional suffixes, except in the past participles of strong verbs and in the preterit plural. Consequently, when (in late OE/early ME) posttonic short vowels all merged as schwa, weak nouns had no distinctive case or number forms, and neither the infinitive nor the subjunctive plural had a distinctive ending.

(3) For the person/number agreement suffixes on verbs, late ONhb had different phonological shapes from those of WS.

Table 4 continues with a display of how, as of about 1300, the Northern division can be contrasted with the Southern division, without reference to the Midland division. There are two rubrics: (4a) where the North preserves what late Old Northumbrian had; (4b) where the North is not conservative.

The Northern dialects, but not typically those of the rest of the Danelaw, show a good deal of morphological simplification when compared to the OE stage or even to Old Norse. A fairly full selection of these simplificatory changes can be seen in table 4b. This degree of simplification in the North, versus its rarity in the rest of the Danelaw, correlates with the rather high level of social upheaval prevalent in the North betwen 920 and 1100. It does not, however, correlate with anything in the structure of Norse.

There are phonological simplifications (table 4b 6–9), and grammatical simplifications that result from dropping final schwa (table 4b 10–13) (final schwa dropped in the North between 1250 and 1300. Schwa drop reached the south around 1400). These latter changes may not seem particularly noteworthy, but the dropping of this phoneme results in *the wiping out of four grammatical categories*. However, schwa drop occurred in the North long after Norse had died out there, so even though there is "simplification" here, it can't be blamed on a language contact situation. The grammatical changes 14–18 of table 4b are **not** phonologically motivated, and are not found in the rest of the Danelaw.

TABLE 4
NORTH VERSUS SOUTH CA 1300

4a. CONSERVATION (1–5)

Feature		North	South
1) V]nd		short	long
2) OE /a:/		/aə/ (no structural change)	/oə/
3) surviving OE n#		kept [sic]	dropped [sic]
4) contract presents of sv		absent	present
5) person/ number markers in present indicative	1 2 3 pl	-e ~ es -es -es -es ~ e	-e -st -th -eth

Note: (The CONSERVATION table is misleadingly short because the vast list of features wherein all dialects of ME keep what OE had is left out.)

4b. SIMPLIFICATION (6–18)

Feature	North	South
6) French #v	> /w/	kept
7) /ö/,/ü/	absent	present
8) final /š/	> /s/ in Deira	kept
9) final schwa	dropped	kept
as a result of schwa drop:		
10) definite adjectives	unmarked	-e

TABLE 4 *(continued)*

4*b*. SIMPLIFICATION (11–18)

Feature	North	South
11) weak nouns	absent	present
12) infinitive suffix	absent	-e(n)
13) present subjunctive	unmarked	-e:-e(n)
14) class 2 weak verbs	lost	kept [-ie(n)]
15) preterit of strong verbs	one vowel	two vowels
16) gender/case inflection of pronominal modifiers	absent	traces
17) preterit plural	unmarked	-e(n)
18) preterit 2s strong:weak	unmarked	-e:-est

Note: (The SIMPLIFICATION table does not list those ways in which all ME dialects simplified OE structure. These are given elsewhere: 9.8.5, 9.8.6.5, 9.8.8, 9.8.11.)

These features of simplification and Norsification (except for schwa drop and its consequences) do not appear gradually; they appear in the earliest ME documents of the Danelaw, and they do not diminish in frequency until after 1430, that is, until the development of a written standard of English. In fact, many of these Norse-origin features entered into the formation of standard English *only after the development of the standard* (see Chambers and Daunt 1931). From ca. 1250 to ca. 1450 NME is stable in all its traits (except for the increasing French-origin lexical component), until Standard London English begins affecting its written form.

9.8.6.3. DANELAW ENGLISH

By reference to seven traits table 5 shows how dramatically changed the dialects of the Danelaw are when compared to those of the South. Points 1, 5, and 6 have appeared in table 4*b* above, where only North and South were contrasted. Point 7, which has not yet been discussed, is more a correlation with the South:Danelaw split than clear evidence of foreign influence. The dialects of the South voice initial /f θ s/ and the dialects of the Danelaw do not. Dutch has this voicing while Frisian does not; hence, it is probably originally foreign to English. But the voicing of these initial spirants, even though originating on the Continent, must have occurred in the OE period (at least by 950). The ME distribution does not correspond to OE dialect boundaries any more; but we hypothesize that initial voicing affected East Saxon, Kentish, West Saxon, and West Mercian. It may have affected the other OE dialects as well, but this can't be proven. Later, in the Danelaw, the allophonic voicing of initial spirants was abandoned because Norse lacks such a rule. Each of the seven features is given a score of from 1 to 4 to reflect our evaluation of the seriousness of the change.

The Middle English of the Danelaw, in spite of its Norse component, its greater phonological and morphological simplicity, and its other regional peculiarities neither simple nor Norse, is **English**. It is part of the network of ME dialects. Several dialects are involved: the Northern dialects are (in part only) a continuation of Old Northumbrian, the Lincolnshire dialects (Lindsey and Fourboroughs) are a continuation of Old East Mercian, and the Norfolk dialect is a continuation of the OE dialect of that region (see OVERVIEW in 9.8.4).

A majority of the inflexional affixes of the Northern dialect(s), for example, can be traced to Old Northumbrian; some of the grammatical simplification that characterized Northern ME already existed in late Old Northumbrian, even the partial replacement of arbitrary gender by natural gender (a notable exception is that in unstressed syllables there was still a two-way contrast between a rounded (/u/) and an unrounded (/a/) vowel; they had not merged as /ə/ nor dropped off). Most simplifications of Northern ME from the late

TABLE 5
DIFFERENTIAL SIMPLIFICATION AND FOREIGNIZATION OF SELECTED
ME DIALECTS ca 1250–1300

Feature	Southmarch	Wessex & Kent	Leicester	Deira
1) gender/case agreement (= 4.b.16)	no (1)	traces (lost MWx by 1300)	no (1)	no (1)
2) Norse grammar	slight (1)	no	moderate (2)	heavy (3)
3) Norse vocabulary	slight (1)	slight (1)	heavy (3)	massive (4)
4) French vocabulary	moderate (2)	heavy (3)	heavy (3)	moderate (2)
5) final schwa (= 4.b.9–13)	yes	yes	yes	drops (1) (between 1250–1300)
6) 2 different vowels in sv preterite (= 4.b.15)	yes	yes	yes	no (1)
7) #/f/ is [v]	yes	yes	no (1)	no (1)
SCORE	5	4	10	13

Old Northumbrian stage are not unusual when compared with Modern Dutch, Low German, Danish, or Swedish, but in A.D. 1250 these languages were not anywhere nearly as evolved as Northern English was (see EXCURSUS, 9.8.9).

The use by some Danelaw ME dialects of pronouns and auxiliaries of Norse origin suggests an intense contact situation, either category (3) borrowing or considerable influence through shift, or (more likely) both. It should be noted, however, that the pre-existing close typological fit between OE and Norse might have permitted borrowing of such features even with less intensive contact (and we tend to be swayed by Sawyer's evidence and arguments, which point to a modest number of Norse-speaking settlers in England). In any case, we are convinced that Norse was largely or entirely absorbed by English in the Danelaw by A.D. 1100. Up to that time there must have been heavy borrowing between the two languages before the Norse speakers in the end switched to English. If the Norse had survived we would have seen a Norse equally riddled with English traits. We would not, technically speaking, characterize the situation as of a Sprachbund type, since English and Norse were already structurally more similar than any two languages in a typical Sprachbund, being closely related genetically, with a maximum separation of perhaps 1000 years.

It must be borne in mind that it is a historical accident that late Middle English and early Modern English have borrowed heavily from northerly English dialects that happen to be the ones that were strongly influenced by Norse. If the capital of England had remained Winchester, for example (where the Anglo-Saxon and early Norman kings were buried), the chances are good that the portion of Modern Standard English structure that is of ultimate Norse origin would be no more than one-third of what it actually is, given that London was the capital de facto by the middle of the thirteenth century.

Shetland Norse (which was Norwegian and called "Norn" in English) as it was being replaced by English in the eighteenth century is scantily recorded, but it gives a bit of an idea as to how Norse probably was affected by English before it died out in the Danelaw (Jakobsen 1897, 1908–1921). The vernacular English of the Orkneys (Marwick 1929) and the Shetlands is Scots English superimposed on Norwegian, in the first case in the 1600's and in the latter case as late as 1800. These dialects of English deviate in various ways from Scots, and Norwegian is a clear contributor to the deviance. Orkney and Shetland Scots have not been studied carefully by linguists, but we expect that careful study of these dialects would yield some useful insights into the origins of Danelaw English.

9.8.6.4. NORSIFICATION

Northern Middle English (NME) is quite clearly the most Norse-influenced of the ME dialects (see map 9). It is therefore the logical place to begin a study of Norse influence on English. Kaufman assembled data to establish:

(a)   a grammatical profile of NME;

(b)   all of the linguistic peculiarities of NME, including lexicon, as compared with other forms of ME;

(c)   the origin, whether in Old English or Old Norse (ON), of all the above linguistic elements. It should be noted that virtually **every** inflectional affix and function word of NME has been identified and its origin determined.

The results were somewhat of a surprise, because the English component of NME owes more to the Midlands than it does to Northumbrian (Nhb) OE. Among grammatical (closed-class) words, affixes, and inflexional processes, whereas NME has 15 elements of distinctively Nhb origin it has 33 elements of distinctively Midland origin (with doublets in four cases).

To the extent possible, a comparable data assemblage was done for the remaining Norse-influenced dialects of ME, namely Lindsey, Fourboroughs, Norfolk, Elmet, Lancaster, and Chester (see maps 3, 6, and 9). All these dialects, plus the Northern ones, we term **Norsified**, because they have not only heavy lexical influence from Norse, but also have adopted a significant number (between 24 and 57) of Norse derivational and inflectional affixes, inflectional processes, and closed-class grammatical words. Apart from the fact that some of these Norsified dialects have more Norse-origin traits than others, and that NME has some 11 Norse-origin traits unique to itself, the Norse-origin grammatical traits found in the Norsified dialects of ME are a subset of the trait set found in Lindsey and Fourboroughs. This trait set we call the **Norsification package**; the term refers to the part of any dialect that is of Norse origin, but what we mean to imply is that the late OE Norsified dialect of Lincolnshire was spread to the rest of the North Midlands, to Norfolk, and to Deira, and that in the latter case Nhb OE was essentially transformed in the process such that the ME dialects known from Northumbria can only in part be considered as descending from the Nhb dialect of OE. We further claim that Lincolnshire English was carried over into Deira at a time when Norse was still spoke in Deira, whereas Norsification due to spread of Lincolnshire English to the other dialects of the North Midlands took place after Norse was no longer a spoken language in the Midlands. Part of the evidence for these claims will be presented below (see maps 7 and 8).[14]

In a broader sense the Norsification package was made up of:

(1) Midland (specifically *East Mercian, a kind of English not attested in writing in the OE period) phonology, morphology, syntax, and lexicon;

(2) 45 Norse-origin grammatical traits, some morphological and some lexical; and

(3) several hundred Norse-origin lexical items, in basic vocabulary, tending to displace native equivalents.

Although those Midland dialects lying directly to the south of NME do receive some grammatical traits from it *after 1200* (see map 10), Norsified Midland English was already in existence well before 1150 (cf. Peterborough Chronicle, entries for 1132–1154, written in the latter year). There are no Nhb traits involved in the formation of Norsified Midland English.

The simplest way to account for these facts is to hypothesize that Norsified English arose in the Midlands, in the Midland dialect known in ME times to be fullest of Norse elements, namely that of Lindsey, as represented by *Havelok* (written ca. 1250, copied ca. 1300 in Leicester or Northampton). *Ormulum* (ca. 1200) and *Robert Manning's Chronicle* (ca. 1340) represent the neighboring region of Fourboroughs, which lacks only two of the 45 Norse-origin grammatical traits found in *Havelok*.

9.8.6.5. A MODEL FOR NORSIFICATION

Our scenario for the development and spread of Norsified English has the following essential assumptions.

(1) Norsified English arose in the Midlands and not the North, because NME has Midland elements at its very heart.

(2) Norsified English arose in the part of the Midlands that later had the greatest grammatical component of Norse origin.

(3) Norsified English arose at a time when Norse was still spoken but going out of use in its area.

(4) Norse began to go out of use in any area when the area was reintegrated (through conquest) to the English polity, and was effectively defunct within two generations (of thirty years each) of this reintegration (see map 6).

(5) Norsified English spread to other parts of England that were receptive to it due to Norse having been spoken there earlier with a consequent heavy lexical influence having taken place on the local English (see maps 3 and 7).

(6) When Norsified English spread to other areas where Norse was no longer spoken the number of grammatical features of Norse origin found in the model Norsified dialect was subject to attrition proportional to the distance from the point of origin of Norsified English (see map 8).

(7) However, when Norsified English spread to an area where Norse was still spoken, the whole Norsification package was accepted entire, with local additions from the resources of the still-spoken local Norse (The only case where this happened was in Deira; see map 8).

Assumptions 1, 2 and 6 taken together point to the area of origin of Norsified English as being Lindsey and Fourboroughs. Assumptions 3 and 4 taken together point to the period 920–980 as the time of origin of Norsified English. In this time period English is known as "Old English," and it is quite possible that down to 1100 Norsified English everywhere observed the case marking rules of Old English (see the last two paragraphs of this section). Lack of gender-number-case agreement on noun modifiers and loss of dative singular and plural and genitive plural case marking is the primary way that ME differs morphologically from OE in any area.

As to assumption 4: All the objects with Norse inscriptions found in England, insofar as they were not made in Scandinavia or by resident foreign Scandinavians, are dated before the projected demise of Norse in each area of Britain, i.e., two generations or sixty years from the time that the Norsemen of the region came under direct control of the English crown (see map 6). Thus, the Pennington church in Furness, Lancashire, contains an inscription dated (Gordon 1957:186) to about 1150, though some (Geipel 1971:58) date it about 1100. In any case the area, Cumbria, was brought under English control between 1090 and 1100. An inscription from Carlisle, also in Cumbria, is dated "12th century" by Gordon (1957:327), but earlier than the Pennington inscription; three "illegible" inscriptions from Yorkshire (Deira) are dated "11th century" by Gordon. Since the conquest of England by Swein Forkbeard and his son Knuut resulted in Knuut's assuming of the crown in 1016, even though Danes did not settle in England as a result (Knuut sent his armies back to Denmark), Norse may have gotten a cultural boost in the one part of England where it was probably (barely) still spoken, namely Deira (Cumbria did not belong to England at the time). So though we would judge Norse to have been on its last legs at this time, it may have survived for another generation, say till about 1045.

When did Norsified English spread to Deira? The earliest possible date is 1000, since pure Nhb OE was being written there until that date (there are no more than 10 Norse loan words in tenth-century Nhb OE). This was *not* a traditional or standardized written variety of English since there was no known literary tradition to which a speaker of Nhb OE could refer. Whether the Vikings are to blame for it or not, there simply is *no* connected text in Nhb OE that dates before 900, with the exception of "Caedmon's Hymn," "Bede's Death Song," the "Leyden Riddle," and a few inscribed objects. The tenth-century Nhb that we have consists entirely of interlinear glosses to Latin texts, specifically the gospels and the *Durham Ritual*. The total vocabulary is several thousand words, however, and there is complete documentation of the inflectional morphology of Nhb OE.

The latest date for the introduction of Norsified Midland English to Deira is about 1035, since Norsified Northern English had to spread to Northumberland, a region never settled by Norsemen in significant numbers, and do so before the Normans harried Yorkshire in 1069–1070, that is while Yorkshire was rich and prestigious in comparison to Northumberland and Lothian. Norsified Midland English could not have spread to Deira after the time that Lindsey English had acquired the enclitic **hes** "her, them" from Flemish sometime around 1100 (see 9.8.10), since NME never had this pronoun. After about 1150 Yorkshire was more or less recovered economically and after about 1200 linguistic influences began flowing southward from the northern area, where York, the second city of England, was located. The earliest text written in NME that has come down to us may have been composed around 1250 (*Prose Rule of St Benet*, though surviving manuscripts are much later, e.g., B. M. Lansdowne 376, ca. 1400). The earliest surviving manuscript with a NME text is B. M. Cotton Vespasian A3, from about 1330, which contains the *Cursor Mundi* or *Renner of the Werld*.

The following is our scenario for the development and spread of Norsified English:

In the two generations after the Southern Danelaw was reintegrated into the English polity, Norse went out of use. In Lindsey, in the process, a good deal of Norse grammatical material was absorbed into the local "East Mercian" (unattested) dialect of Old English, between 920 and 950.

Between 950 and 980 this Norsified English became the model for linguistic developments in neighboring Fourboroughs.

After 980, when Danish was no longer used in Norfolk, Norsified English (including twenty-eight Norse-origin grammatical features) spread to that area.

Between 1005 and 1035, when Norse was still spoken in Lindsey, though barely, Norsified English spread to Deira from Lindsey. The Deirans took the whole package (with the exception of just one Norsification feature), including weak noun plurals of Southumbrian type, and merely substituted the Nhb person markers on verbs. They also added 11 grammatical traits of Norse origin.

Between 1035 and 1065 Deiran Norsified English spread to neighboring Northumberland, which lies to the north. Here there was no Norse to interact with. In fact, only five of the eleven new Norse-origin grammatical features added to Norsified English were actually passed on to Northumberland. Further, in Deira, a great amount of Norse-origin vocabulary was in use that was never used elsewhere in England, except Cumbria, to which Deiran English spread after 1100.

Since Lothian was Nhb-speaking, though sparsely populated, Norsified Deiran English tended to spread from Northumberland to Lothian during the same period, since, although Lothian had been ceded to/annexed by Scotland in 1018, the Scots had little control over it. In the winter of 1069–1070, William the Bastard laid waste large parts of Yorkshire, killing or making refugees of about half the population. Those refugees who fled north to the North Riding and Durham were carried off as slaves in large numbers by Scottish raiders, and they doubtless reinforced the Norsified English of the English-speaking Lothian folk. From this point on we will refer to Norsified Deiran English and its northward extensions as Northern (Middle) English.

Northern English was introduced into Cumbria after 1192, when that region was definitively annexed to England by William the Red, who began settling English peasants there. Previously the inhabitants had spoken British (in a dialect collateral with those of Wales, Cornwall, and Brittany), Norwegian, Danish, and Irish.

When Normans began receiving fiefs from King David of Scotland in the period 1124 to 1135, more English was introduced into Scotland; in 1138 David invaded Northumberland and carried off many English women as slaves; and after that Northern English spread within Scotland on its own. By the end of the fourteenth century English was spoken (presumably by all) as far north as Aberdeen and probably throughout southern Scotland.

Because Elmet English is hardly attested before 1400, and because time has not been available to search through the texts in that dialect for a complete list of the Norsification traits current there in ME times, it is not feasible to date the Norsification of that dialect any more narrowly then between 980 and 1070. In effect Elmet English may have received its Norsification traits from Lindsey and Fourboroughs relatively early, with later influences from NME, or it may have gotten most of its Norsification traits from NME at a later date. If the former, Norse may still have been spoken at the time, though this was an area of only moderate Norse influence on the lexicon. Elmet ME is apparently descended from the OE dialect of the Rushworth Gloss to Matthew 1.1 through Mark 2.15 plus John 18.1–3. The gloss was produced by a man named Farman, evidently in Harwood (OE *Harawudu*) which is in the West Riding not far from and straight north of Leeds. We call this dialect North Mercian.

The Palatine, whose dialect descends from West Mercian, was Norsified via Elmet no later than the period 1070–1100. Since the Palatine has only five of the Norse-origin grammatical features that are basically peculiar to the North, The Norse-origin features of the Palatine are probably for the most part from the East Midlands. Lancaster has thirty-six Norse-origin grammatical traits and Chester has twenty-four.

Thus, in the number of Norse-origin grammatical traits passed on to them, Lancaster is comparable to (Elmet and) Fourboroughs (roughly thirty-eight) and Chester is comparable to Norfolk (roughly twenty-six). This correlates with assumption 6, at the beginning of this section.

Because the Norsification package spread to Fourboroughs, Norfolk, the Palatine, and probably Elmet after Norse was no longer spoken in those regions, for many of the Norse-origin elements there survives a native English equivalent engaged in competition with it, ranging from weak to strong.

The only historical facts that we can correlate with the transfer of linguistic habits from Lindsey to Deira are mentioned by Sawyer (1971:174–175): there was a great growth of quite profitable sheep-farming at the hands of Norse-origin or even Norse-speaking entrepreneurs in the eleventh century in the Lincolnshire Wolds (which lie in Lindsey, the major town being Louth) and in the Yorkshire Wolds (which lie in the East Riding of Yorkshire part of Deira, the major town being Bridlington), which lie right across the Humber from each other (see map 4).[15]

Evidence for the spread of Norsified Midland English into Deira and the development of Norsified Deiran English (the stage immediately antecedent to NME) within the time frame of the above scenario is provided by an inscription in OE on a sundial at Kirkdale, North Riding, Yorkshire (Deira), dated 1060 by Gordon (1957:327). It is not in Nhb but in a form of Midland English. It has five traits that characterize NME, though the writers of the text were evidently trying to write Standard West Saxon.

(1)   Personal names and kin terms in possessive function do not take the genitive case suffix:
    <in eadward dagum> "in Edward's days"
    <[i]n tosti dagum> "in Tosti's days"

(2) /y/ has been shifted to /i/:
    <minster> "minster"; see also the next example.

(3) "each" is <ilcum> (dative singular); Nhb has <aelc ∼ elc>, whereas NME has **ilk** from Mercian OE <ylc>.

(4) "to make" is <macan>; this form has the Midland infinitive suffix -**an**, and, as in Norsified English, the mark of class 2 weak verbs is missing. Nhb has <maciga> /maki(j)a/.

(5) "wrought" is <wrohte>; Nhb has <worhte>, but NME has **wrohte**.

The text on the sundia is as follows:

ORM GAMALSUNA BOHTE S[AN]C[TU]S GREGORIUS MINSTER ÐONNE HIT WES AEL TOBROCAN & TOFALAN & HE HIT LET MACAN NEWAN FROM GRUNDE CHR[IST]E & S[AN]C[TU]S GREGORIUS IN EADWARD DAGUM C[I]NG AND [I]N TOSTI DAGUM EORL. ÐIS IS DAGES SOLMERCA AET ILCUM TIDE. & HAWARD ME WROHTE & BRAND PR[EO]S[T].

This means: "Orm son of Gamal bought Saint Gregory's minster when it was all broken up and fallen down and he had it made new from the ground up for Christ and Saint Gregory in King Edward's days and in Earl Tosti's days. This is the sunmarker of the day at each hour. And Haward and Brand the Priest wrought me." The personal names (except Eadward) are Norse and **solmerca** is a lexical borrowing from Norse.

9.8.6.6. LINGUISTIC EVENTS AFTER NORSIFICATION

Around 1190 /aː/ shifted to /ɔə/ somewhere in the Southeast of England. This change reached Norfolk by 1200 and Fourboroughs between 1225 and 1275. It reached the Palatine by 1300 but by 1350 had still not affected Lindsey (Kristensson 1967), though it did by 1400. Even though this is a sharing by rejecting an innovation, it shows a close connection between Lindsey and Deira throughout the ME period. Another sound change, which began in the South of England around 1180, affected all ME dialects except possibly that of Kent. This is the change of **gh** (i.e., gamma) to /y/ or /w/ depending on whether a preceding vowel was front or not. It reached NME by 1250–1275.

Apart from these two changes, however, after 1200, linguistic innovations in the northern part of the Midlands tended to come from the North. For instance the basic verb marking of early Midland ME was

-e	1sg pres indic
-est	2sg pres and pret (wk vb only) indic
-eth	3sg pres ind and impv pl
-en	pres and pret pl
-en	inf

This is attested as such in the *Peterborough Chronicle for 1132–1154* (composed in the Norfolk dialect in 1154), the *Ormulum* (Fourboroughs dialect, ca. 1200), and the *Bestiary* (Norfolk dialect ca. 1225) and must have existed as such by 1050–1100 (see map 10).

On the other hand the verb marking system of NME was different, being based on that of Nhb OE. It had:

NME		Nhb OE
-e ~ -es	1sg pres ind	-o
-es	2sg and 3sg pres ind	-es, -as

-es	impv pl	-as
-es ~ -e	pl indic	-as ~ -e
-e	inf and pret indic pl	-a resp. -o(n)
-e	subjunctive	-e

(by 1250 final schwa had dropped in NME).

By 1225–1250, under NME influence, Lindsey had changed both -est and -eth to -es. Between 1225 and 1300 Fourboroughs borrowed the same person markers that Lindsey had done. Elmet and the Palatine are only known from about 1400, so we cannot date the events in question very narrowly, but Elmet has exactly the same person marking on verbs as NME, though it began with the Midland system specified above. Palatine ME changed -est and -eth to -es, and inf -en to -e, and in 1400 had changed pl ind -en to -es in Lancaster. The changes outlined above and their distributions remain unchanged to the present day.

9.8.6.7. DIALECTS THAT WE CONSIDER NOT TO HAVE BEEN NORSIFIED

Leicester was not Norsified, though 18 Norsification features crept into Leicester from the North and East. The English of Leicester became the basis of London Standard English, which is why Standard English shows a number of Norsification traits (*though, they, them/ their, till, fro, again(st), give, run, thrive, get*).

Stafford has nineteen Norsification traits, via Leicester, Fourboroughs, and Chester.

These figures may make it seem rather unlikely that Leicester and Stafford, with eighteen to nineteen features, should be placed in a different category from Chester, with twenty-four features. However, most (not all) of the features found in Leicester and Stafford fall under the heading of "replace an English word with a similar-sounding one of Norse origin."

Southmarch has just eight Norsification features.

Suffolk might have shown a few such traits, but it is undocumented before 1430 (the date of the effective supremacy of Standard London English in Southeastern England), this is too late for a genuine local dialect to be attested in that part of England.

The remaining dialects of ME have no Norse-origin grammatical traits worth mentioning: **taken, boadhe(n), with, nay** are so widespread as to be nondiagnostic.

9.8.6.8. THE DATA

We now proceed to list the grammatical features of Norse origin appearing in ME dialects. Not every trait is equally "intimate," and the inclusion of strong verbs in the list may be seen by some as passing fully into the realm of simple lexical borrowing. However, this list is intended to be as exhaustive as possible (for "grammatical" traits loosely defined), and though the list is rather long, it will be seen that many of these Norsifications are of a rather trivial nature.

The table that follows (table 6) needs a couple of explanations. "Viking Norse" refers to the historical state of Norse during the period 700–1100. The term "Old Norse" covers roughly the period 1100–1500. There is not much written in Viking Norse and what there is is in runes; consequently in the phonological state of VN is extrapolated from Old Norse plus whatever needs to be assumed to account for the shapes of loanwords into English and other languages at the time in question (see Gordon 1957:326–329).

The symbol x occurs before a ME form that is a phonological blend of a VN form with a cognate OE form. sv means strong verb. EVN means East Viking Norse.

The following Norse-origin grammatical traits in ME are so widespread as not to serve in an index of Norsification: **take(n):took: taken** 'to take'; **baadhe/boadhe(n)** 'both'; × **with** 'with'; **nay** 'no!'.

The preceding chart has four instances (22, 38, 46, 52) where a Norse-origin form has a distinctively East Norse (i.e., Danish) shape. There are no forms in this list that have a distinctively West Norse (i.e., Norwegian) shape. Hence Norsification occurred in a Danish-settled area.

The fifty-seven grammatical traits of Norse origin examined here make up no more than 20 percent of the total set of comparable traits in NME (out of at least 260). The percentage is smaller for other dialects of ME. About 5 percent of the grammatical traits of Norse-influenced dialects of ME are pure innovations. This leaves an English-origin grammatical component of 75 percent *and upwards.*

Of the at least 260 grammatical processes, affixes, and function words used in Norsified Middle English, apart from the fifty-seven of Norse origin (many of which are in competition with native English items of the same function and meaning) there are at least 160

TABLE 6

NORSE GRAMMATICAL ELEMENTS IN NORSIFIED DIALECTS OF ME

Middle English	Viking Norse	Old English
I. Processes		
1) no *i-* on perf pcp	no such prefix	*je-*
2) no wk vb class 2	wv2 has vowel *-a-*	wv2 has *-ija-*
3) /a:/ > /oə/ in	/a:/	/e:/
pret pl of sv4,5 (EM)		
II. Affixes		
4) *umbe-* 'around'	*umb*	*ymbe*
5) *-leik* '-ness'	*-leik-r*	*-la:k*
6) *-ande* pres pcp	*-ande*	*-ende*
7) *-scap* '-ship' (Dei)	*-skap-r*	*-sčip*
III. Phonetic trait		
8) #[f] not #[v]	#[f]	?#[v]
IV. Copula		
9) × *ert*	*est* > *ert*	*aearθ* (WM)
'(thou) art'		= *arθ* (Nhb)
		= *aeart* (NM)
& *ere* 'are' (Dei)	& *ero*	& *aron*
10) *es* 'is'	*es*	*is*
11) *waare/woaren*	*wa:ro*	*we:ron*
V. Auxiliaries		
12) *mun* (*man* Sc, WM):	*mun* ~ *man*:	no equivalent
munde	*munda*	
'must, will'		
13) × *sall:sulde* (N) 'shall:should'	*skal:skylda*	*sčal,sčalde* (Nhb)
		sčael,sčulde (M)
VI. Pronouns		
14) *they* 'they'	*θei-r*	*hi:e, he:o*
15) *theim* & *theire* 'them, their'	*θei-m,*	*him,hira* (Nhb)
	θei-ra	*heom,heora* (M)
16) *sliik* 'such' (Dei)	*sli:k-r*	*swelk* (Nhb)
		= *swylč* (WM)
		= *swylk (EM)*
17) × *thir(e)*	cf *θei-r* (#14)	*θis(s)-* + *-e* pl
'these' (N)		
18) *same* 'same'	*same*	*ilka, seolfa*
VII. Noun Plurals		
19) *breedher*	*brö:θr*	*bro:θor(o)*
'brothers'		
20) *dehter(es)*	*döhtr*	*dohter(o)*
'daughters'		
21) *hend* 'hands'	*hend-r*	*hand(a)*

Table 6 (*Continued*)

Middle English	Viking Norse	Old English
VIII. Strong Verbs		
22) *give(n):gaf:geeven (EM goaven):geven* 'to give' sv5	EVN *gifa,gaf, ga:fo,gifen-n*	*jefa(n)/jifan,jaef, je:fon,jefen/jifen*
23) *gete(n):gat:geeten (EM goaten):geten* 'to get' sv5	*geta,gat, ga:to,geten-n*	*jeta(n)/jitan,jaet, je:ton,jeten/jiten*
24) *ligge(n):lay: leeyen:lein* 'to lie (down)' sv5	*leggja,lah, la:go,legen-n*	*liğğa(n),laej, le:gon,lej(e)n*
25) *renne(n):rann: runnen* 'to run' sv3	*renna,rann, runno,runnen-n*	*iorna(n),arn, urnon,urnen*
26) *breste(n):brast: brusten:brosten* 'to burst' sv3	*bresta,brast, brusto,brosten-n*	*bersta,baerst, burston,borsten*
27) *late(n):leet:laten* 'to let' sv7	*la:ta,le:t,la:ten-n*	*le:ta(n),leort* (Nhb) = *le:t* (M),*le:ten*
28) *riive(n):raaf/roaf: riven* 'to tear' sv1	*ri:fa,reif, rifo,rifen-n*	cf *teren* sv4
IX. Quantifiers		
29) *twinne* 'two'	*twinn-r* 'twofold'	*twejen,twa:*
30) *thrinne* 'three'	θ*rinn-r* 'threefold'	θ*re:o*
31) *ahte* 'eighth' (Dei)	*ahte*	*aehto*θ*a* (Nhb) = **ehtunde* (EM)
32) *hundreth* 'hundred'	*hundra*θ	(Nhb *hundra*θ is from Norse)
33) *faa/foa* 'few'	*fa:-r*	*fae:awa*
34) *minne* 'less'	*minne*	*lae:ssa*
35) *seer* 'various'	*se:r* dat sg and pl of refl/recip pron	*syndrij* *sundrij*
X. Comparatives		
36) *werre* 'worse'	*werre*	*wyrsa*
37) × *werse* 'worse'	*werre*	*wyrsa*
XI. Place Words		
38) *whedhen* 'whence'	*hwa*θ*an*	*hwana(n)*
hedhen 'hence'	*he*θ*an*	*heona(n)*
thedhen 'thence'	EVN θ*e*θ*an*	θ*ana(n)*
39) × *whaare* 'where'	*hwar*	*hwe:r*
40) × *thaare* 'there'	θ*ar*	θ*e:r*
41) *til* 'to'	*til*	*to:*
42) *fraa/froa* 'from'	*fra:*	*fram/from*
43) *samen* 'together'	*saman*	*aet-gaedere* (Nhb) = *to:gadere* (Shb)

Table 6 (*Continued*)

Middle English	Viking Norse	Old English
44) *end(e)lang* 'along'	*endelang-r*	*andlang*
45) *a-gein(es)* 'again(st)'	*(i:) gegn*	*on-jaeɲn,*
		to:-jaeɲnes
46) *a-mell* 'between, among' (Dei)	EVN *(a:/i:) mellom*	*be-twih/be-twi:en,*
		on-mang
XII. Time Words		
47) *ay* 'always'	*ei*	*a:*
48) *aar/oar* 'before'	*a:r* early	*ae:r*
49) *efter* 'after'	*efter*	*aefter*
XII. Conjunctions		
50) *ook* 'also' (EM)	*ouk ~ ok*	*e:k*
51) θ*oh* 'though'	θ*oh*	θ*eh* (Nhb & *EM)
		= θ*ah* (WM)
52) *sum* 'as, so'	EVN *sum*	*swa:*
53) *at* [+ Sen 'that' (N)	θ*at ~ at*	θ*aet*
54) *at* relative particle 'that' (N)	*at*	θ*e*
55) *at* [+ Vb '(for) to'	*at*	*to:*
XIV. Interjections		
56) *yaa* 'yes!'	*ja:*	*je:*
57) *way* 'alas!'	*wei*	*wa:, wae:,*
		wejla:(wej)

of undoubted English origin. About forty of these could come from either English or Norse (but these need not be credited to Norse). It may provide some perspective on Norsification simply to cite most of these items without further commentary. The forty or so items that would turn out homophonous whether from English or Norse are in parentheses.

Affixes (16 +): *-es* plural, all verb suffixes but *-and* (7), *-ward*, *-ness*, *-head*, *-lik*, (*-er*, *-est*, *'s*-genitive, *mis-*) plus many other English-origin derivational affixes, e.g., *-dam*, *-th*, which were not exhaustively cataloged for this study.

Auxiliaries (11): *may:maht ~ miht ~ moht, will:wald, dar:durst, cann:cuudh, moot:moost, doht, be-hoov-es/-ed, bee:am:been:(was), (thar:thurt, aw:aht, bir-s/-d).*

Personal Pronouns (9): all but *they/theim/their* (7), *whaa, man.*

Demonstratives (15): *awen, the, this, yon, whenn, thann ~ thenn, yonder, aidher, whider/h-/th-, whilk, (that:thaa, heer, nuw, what, self/ven).*

Noun Plurals (11): *shoon, een, childer, gees, teeth, wi(m)men, (menn, kiy, feet, miis, liis).*

Quantifiers (53 +): *a(n),* all cardinal numerals but *hundreth* (21 +), all ordinal numerals (15 +), *aller-* ∼ *aldher-, few, whoon* ∼ *foon, i-nooh, naa(n), mani* ∼ *moni, ani* ∼ *oni, oodher, oht/noht, oudher/noudher, ilk, maa(r):maast, less:least, (liitel, mikel, sum).*

Irregular Strong Verbs (2): *hatt:hiht:hatten,gaa/gang:yeed/ yood:gaan.*

Irregular Weak Verbs (16): *rekk:roht, teach:taht, strekk/ streak:straht, think:thoht, wirk:wroht, bring:broht, reach:raht, lacch:laht, biy:boht, sell:sa(a)ld, kiidh:kidd, haa(v):ha(v)d, doo:did:doon, (seek:soht, cleadh:cledd, think:thuht).*

Comparatives (4): *ald:eld-er/-est, lang:leng-er/-est, good/ weel:(better:best), (neest).*

Place Words (29 +): *be-for(n), be-hind, buut, a-buve(n), widh-uut(en), a-pon, on, of, over, biy, be-twix* ∼ *be-tween, for, a-mang(es), duun, be-yond, a-buut, foorth, fordher, thurh, to-gedder* ∼ *to-gidder, to-ward, neeh, on bak, (up, at, under, in, uut, be-neadhen).*

Time Words (7 +): *eft-soon(es), ever/never, sidhen, whiilum, yeet* ∼ *yitt, yisterday, (oft).*

Manner Words (10): *thus, too, i-wiss, swiidh, noht, (s(wa)aa, whiy, than* ∼ *then, thaa, ne(e)).*

Conjunctions (7 +): *for-thiy, but, als* ∼ *os, and, or, never-the-less, if,* and many others.

9.8.6.9. DISTRIBUTION OF THE NORSIFICATION DATA

In order to state the distributions of the 57 Norsification features displayed in table 6 as revealingly as possible, the ME dialects of Lindsey, Fourboroughs, and Norfolk together will be called "East."

The Norsification features are distributed as follows. (The figures in parentheses following features indicate the numbering of these items in table 6.)

East only (2): *ook* (#50), *a:(* > *oa)* in pret pl of sv4,5 (#3).

Lindsey + North (2): *hend* (#21), *efter* (#49).

East (w/o Norfolk) + North (5): *at* + Vb (#55), *way* (#57), *umbe-* (#4), *same* (#18), *endelang* (#44).

East + North (w/ Norfolk) (4): *yaa* (#56), *es* (#10), *whaare* (#39), *aar* (#39).

East + North + Palatine (w/o Norfolk) (8): *seer* (#35), *thrinne* (#30), *sum* (#52), *they* (#14), *theim/theire* (#15), *mun* (#12), *given* (#22), *-leik* (#4).

East + North + Palatine (w/ Norfolk) (24): no *i-* (#1), no wv2 (#2), *-ande* (#6), *thaare* (#40), *laten* (#27), *bresten* (#26), *fraa* (#42), *a-gein(es)* (#45), *liggen* (#25), *waar* (#11), *riiven* (#28), *faa* (#33), *twinne* (#29), *samen* (#43), *thoh* (#51), *werse* (#37), *ay* (#47), *rennen* (#25), *geten* (#23), *whedhen/h-/th-* (#38), *werre* (#36), *til* (#41), *breedher* (#19), #[f] (#8).

North only (of these 6 are Deira only) (10): *thir(e)* (#17), *sliik* (#16), *ert/ere* (#9), *sal/sulde* (#13), *a-mell* (#46), *at* (rel) (#54), *ahte* (#31), *-scap* (#7).

North + Palatine (w/o Chester) (3): *dehter(es)* (#20), *at* 'that' (#53), *minne* (#34).

North + Palatine (w/ Chester) (1): *hundreth* (#32).

We will point out some important subsets by grouping some of the above distributions (see map 8).

The largest single set of shared features is that between Lindsey and the North: 43 features. This, we claim, is the initial form of the Norsification package (insofar as grammatical traits are at issue).

The set of features shared by Lindsey and Fourboroughs (and in turn with the North) is forty; given that the documentation of no ME dialect can be considered really exhaustive, the difference between Lindsey and Fourboroughs is probably not meaningful.

Lancaster has thirty-six Norsification features, Norfolk has 28, and Chester has twenty-four.

Two Norsification features are uniquely Eastern; they did not get taken over in Northern English. One is the conjunction **ook** 'also,' for which NME uses English **eek**. The other is more "intimate," and common only in Norfolk; this is the use of the vowel /oə/ (</a:/) in the preterit second person singular, plural, and subjunctive of strong verbs of classes 4 and 5. The attested instances of the use of this vowel instead of the native /iə/ < /e:/ or /eə/ < /ae:/ are the following: **goaven** 'gave', **goaten** 'got', **droapen** 'killed', **boaren** 'bore', **cwoadhen** 'said', and **spoaken** 'spoke'. While the first two are of Norse origin, and the second two are found in both OE and

ON, the last two are English without Norse cognates (Björkman 1900:85–86, Jordan and Crook 1974:78).

9.8.6.10. CHARACTERIZATION OF THE NORSE INFLUENCE ON ENGLISH STRUCTURE

In spite of the relatively large number of grammatical elements of Norse origin in Norsified ME, their effect on English structure was almost trivial. Thirty-eight of the fifty-seven traits, or 67 percent, are mere phonological variants of what English had had in the first place. It is as though Norsification largely reflects a fad whereby an English speaker would parade his knowledge of Norse while speaking English (4, 5, 6, 7, 9 , 10, 11, 13, 16, 19, 20, 21, 22, 23, 24, 25, 26, 27, 29, 30, 31, 32, 33, 36, 38, 39, 40, 42, 44, 45, 47, 48, 49, 50, 51, 53, 56, 57). Such knowledge of Norse by English speakers may nevertheless have been considerable.

Some 11 items (20%) were in competition with a native item of considerably different phonological shape (14, 15, 18, 34, 35, 41, 43, 46, 52, 54, 55).

One item (2%) had no functional equivalent in OE (12).

There were four kinds of structural influence that were perhaps not trivial: Items 1, 2, and 8 involved giving up something that English had but Norse lacked. Item 3 involves using a Norse-origin inflexional feature in place of a native one. It is more abstract than the noun plurals 19, 20, and 21 because it is used with native English words. These four features, of which the fourth has a fairly restricted distribution, make up only 7 percent of the Norse grammatical influence on ME.

9.8.6.11. HOW NORSIFICATION TOOK PLACE

What then was the nature of the Norse influence in the formation of Lindsey English?

Norse was not structurally different from English in significant ways. It had no sounds lacking in English, though Norse lacked the English sounds /č/ and /ǧ/ and replaced them with /k/ and /g/ when it borrowed words from English. Norse did not use a prefix equivalent to OE **je-** on the perfect participles of verbs and did not have a phonologically salient analogue of the OE second class of weak verbs; whereas Norse had a thematic vowel **-a-** (which would later go to schwa in English mouths) in these verbs throughout the paradigm, OE had a characteristic theme ending in **-ija-** in the infinitive, the plural present indicative, the imperative plural, and the present subjunctive; this theme normally develops in ME as /iyə/ or /ii/. In Norse initial spirants have always been voiceless, whereas in the OE of the Danelaw they *may* have been voiced, as they certainly were in the South. Elimination of **je-** and **-ija-** may be taken as instances of structural interference by Norse on English. Since the best evidence suggests a relatively small percentage of Norse speakers in the Danelaw (Sawyer 1971:168 and passim),[16] local English speakers are probably responsible for these innovations. On the other hand, if the numbers of Norse speakers in the Danelaw had been relatively large, such modifications in the structure of Danelaw English may have been partly brought about by interference through the shift of Norse speakers to English.

For the rest, Lindsey English borrowed 26 Norse forms to replace similar-sounding English ones; it formed three blends: **werse, whaare, thaare**; it borrowed nine Norse word-forms that were in competition with native forms that were considerably different in pronunciation: **they, theim/theire, same, samen, endelang, til, sum, at, riven** (In the cases of **they, theim, theire,** and **same** a motivation for borrowing may have been avoidance of uncomfortable near-homophony, since the OE equivalents are potentially homophonous with the words meaning 'he' and/or 'she', 'him', 'her', and 'each' respectively); it borrowed five Norse elements that were frills, in that they did not threaten to displace an English equivalent: **-leik, mun, twinne, thrinne, seer**.

9.8.6.12. THE ORIGIN OF NORTHERN MIDDLE ENGLISH

When Norsified English spread to Deira, the Deirans, in contact with obsolescent Norse, accepted the whole Lindsey Norsification package, with the exception of **ook**, and added the following Norse-origin features: five items replacing similar-sounding English forms: **sliik, dehter, ere, hundreth, ahte**; three blends of Norse and English: **thir(e), ert, sall/sulde**; two items that competed with a native form of a different sound: **minne, a-mell**; one frill: **-scap**, for a total of eleven. Six of these new Norse-origin features remained peculiar to Deira, that is, they never spread to Northumberland and Scotland: **sliik, ere, ahte, ert, a-mell, -scap**.

The influence of Lindsey English on Deira was not just in the

Norsification package, however: among the at least 75 percent of English-origin grammatical traits thirty-three Midland English features entered the English of Deira.

A Midland Form in Northern Middle English:	Replacing a Northumbrian (OE) Form:
1) *uur(es)* 'our(s)'	*u:ser, u:sr-* ~ *u:s-*
2) *a-bu(v)en* 'above'	*bufa*
3) *be-forn* 'before'	*bi-fora*
4) *widh-uuten* 'without'	(*wiθ-)u:ta*
5) *be-neadhen* 'beneath'	*bi-nioθa*
6) *thurh* 'through'	*θerh*
7) *yis* ~ *yus* 'yes'	*je:*
8) *elder, eldest* 'elder, eldest'	*aeldra, aeldesta*
9) *shoon* 'shoes'	*ji-sčoe:*
10) *ee(ghe)n* 'eyes'	*e:gu*
11) *childer* 'children'	*čild(u)*
12) *moht, miht* 'might' (aux)	*maehte*
13) *durst* 'dared'	*darste*
14) *art* '(thou) art'	*arθ*
15) *bee* 'be' - inf, subj, impv	*wosa, si:e, w(a)es*
16) *rekk* 'to heed'	**rečča*
17) *(be-)seek* 'to seek/beseech'	*(bi-)soe:ča*
18) *strekk, streak* 'to stretch'	**strečča*
19) *think* 'to think'	*θenča*
20) *think* 'to seem'	*θynča*
21) *wirk:wroht* 'to work'	*wyrča, worhte*
22) *bring* 'to bring'	*brenǧa*
23) *-ness* abstract noun suffix	*-nisse*
24) *-head* abstract noun suffix	*-ha:d*
25) *whilk* 'which'	*hwelk* or *hwelč*
26) *swilk* 'such'	*swelk* or *swelč*
27) *ilk* 'each'	*(a)e:lč* or *(a)e:lk*
28) *thridd* 'third'	*θirdda*
29) *ahtend* 'eighth'	*aehtoθa*
30) *ni(gh)end* 'ninth'	*ni(g)oθa*

31) *teend* 'tenth'   *teiθa*
32) *(e-)leaven* 'eleven'   *aellef(n-)*
33) *e-leavend* 'eleventh'   *aellefta*

Contrasted with the 33 features of Midland origin in NME, there are only 11 features of undoubted Northumbrian origin among the closed-class words of the dialect; of these 11, four have variants of Midland origin.

Northern Middle English: Is from Northumbrian:

a) *whenn* 'when'   *hwenne*
b) *be-hind* 'behind'   *bi-hionda*
c) *buut* 'without'   *bu:ta*
d) *be-yond* 'beyond'   *bi-jeonda*
e) *a-buut* 'about'   *bu:ta*
f) *wald* 'would' (aux)   *walde*
g) *whuw ~ huw* 'how'   *hwu: ~ hu:*

The *n*-less forms in the following three sets of phonological variants are of Nhb origin, while the forms with -n are of Midland origin: **be-for ~ be-forn, a-bu(v)e ~ a-bu(v)en, widh-uut ~ widh-uuten.** Nhb OE **maehte** 'might' also survives as **maht** in NME (see item 12 in the above list).

Besides the above-mentioned traits, only the person marking on verbs in NME is of undoubted Nhb origin: **-es** (2s and 3s pres indic and impv pl), **-e ~ es** (1s pres indic), **-es ~ -e** (pres indic pl), **-e** (infinitive). The remaining English-origin grammatical traits are indistinctly Nhb or Midland.

Apart from the grammatical traits that have been focused on in this section, we remind the reader that there are hundreds of English-origin lexical items in NME whose pronunciations derive from Midland English and not from Nhb OE. A full study of the origins of NME will be undertaken in a separate work.

9.8.6.13. ON THE QUESTION OF SIMPLIFICATION

There are only two kinds of grammatical regularization that English dialects in Norse-influenced areas carried out that dialects in the

South did not do. These have no obvious relation to structural properties of Norse, except that in the first case Norse lacked the alternations in question, and the phonemes /č/ and /ǧ/ that were involved in the alternations.

(a) In the first type of change verbs that had a final consonant $k \sim č$, $j \sim ǧ$, or $ng \sim nǧ$, normally selected the variant with k, j (= ME y), or g respectively (k, j, and g occurred $\angle$C, $č$ and $ǧ$ occurred before certain suffixes, $č$, V]j, and n]$ǧ$ occurred $\angle$_# and before certain other suffixes). Nhb OE had no verb suffixes beginning with C that /k/ (rather than /č/) could have stood before, hence /k/ in these forms in NME is a borrowing from Midland English (see items 16, 17, 18, 19, 20, 33 in the above list; cf. also 21).

(b) In the second type of change, in NME only, strong verbs that had two different root vowels in the preterit, one vowel for the first and third person singular and the other vowel for all the other forms (2 sg, pl, and subjunctive), have lost the form with the latter vowel. Verbs in the preterit are marked for neither person nor number of subject: except for the verb 'to be', which has **was** 'was' (sg) and **waar** 'were' (pl and subj).

Neither of these two types of simplification occurred in the Southern dialects of ME, but this cannot be taken as evidence that an unusual linguistic situation existed in Norse-influenced parts of England. The case that has been made above for Norsified English arising in Lindsey in the period 920–950 at a time when Norse was going out of use suggests that NME's simplification of the preterit inflexion is not related to the rise of Norsified English, though it could be related to the rise of NME (and absorption of Norse) in Deira in the period 1005–1035. The leveling of the vowels of the strong preterits began to appear in other parts of England near the end of the 14th century. The leveling of $k \sim č$, $j \sim ǧ$, and $ng \sim nǧ$ occurred as well outside the Norse-influenced area and is a perfectly pedestrian form of analogical leveling.

9.8.6.14. EVALUATION[17]

The Norse influence on English was pervasive, in the sense that its results are found in all parts of the language; but it was not deep, except in the lexicon. Norse influence could not have modified the basic typology of English because the two were highly similar in the first place. Norse did not stimulate simplification in English, since the simplifications we see in ME when compared to OE probably were taking place in OE before Norse influence became relevant.

What Norse did was to add a few subtleties of meaning and a large number of new ways of saying old things, often by replacing an English item of similar but not identical sound. The hundreds of semantically basic lexical borrowings from Norse assured that in Norsified English one could hardly speak a sentence of English without using a Norse-origin element. In many ways Norse influence on English was a kind of prestige borrowing that took little effort to implement.

The fact that Norse and English at the time of their contact were structurally and lexically so similar meant that

(a) it was relatively easy to learn the other language; and

(b) it was relatively easy to learn to understand the other language without learning to speak it. Nevertheless, one could never be in doubt which language was being spoken.

Because Southern ME in the thirteenth century has very little of Norse origin in it, and little more French material than any other dialect of ME, the Norse element in Danelaw English may create a deceptive impression that Norsified English is qualitatively different from Southern English. We hope to have provided the evidence for moderating any such extreme view.

Since the Norse in 900 may have been proportionally no more numerous than French speakers in 1100, the willingness of English-speakers to learn Norse (or features of Norse) must have been related to the cultural or economic advantage accruing thereto. That Norse influenced Danelaw English more than French did English generally is due to the closer genetic relationship and (hence) greater typological similarity of Norse and English.

Neither large armies nor large numbers of poor Danish and Norwegian peasants are necessary to explain the structural influence of Norse on Norsified English, and Sawyer (1971:99–212, passim) has given strong arguments that they did not exist. On the other hand, the large proportion of Norse-origin terminology in the rural life of Northern England suggests that the influence of Norse-speakers on rural pursuits was decisive. Whether this was through administration, trade, or a large number of settlers is not clear at this time, though it is clear that Norsemen, even if they were a small elite, were perfectly familiar with all aspects of agriculture and animal husbandry, and could have influenced the vocabulary of English-speaking peasants merely through a prestigious status.

We consider an important accomplishment of this survey the determination that the Norse influence on ME (particularly Northern ME) was not nearly as overwhelming as it is often thought to have been; but the demonstration that *Northern Middle English is essentially Midland English with Northumbrian person markers* is even more revealing of the linguistic history of England, and should inspire controversy as well as further research. Whether or not the notion strikes the reader as likely on the face of it (Kaufman certainly did not anticipate this result), a close examination of the facts of NME renders inescapable the conclusion that most of the distinctive traits of a Midland dialect were borrowed into the rather spare inflectional framework of late Nhb OE. Future research may identify some of the reasons for this and suggest some of the mechanisms. For the present we point to the growth of sheep-farming in Lindsey and the Yorkshire Wolds in the eleventh century, and observe that this correlates with the linguistic sharing between Lindsey and Deira.

The above survey deals with essentially **all** the discoverable grammatical influence of Norse on English (apart from syntactic rules); though some of the features dealt with are hardly instances of intimate influence, there will not be any significant additions to the list of features treated above. We avoided treating lexical influence as such, because such influence can in no way demonstrate serious influence of one language on another's structure. Though the total set of relevant data can rarely be assembled for the languages involved in a contact situation, when it can be done, there is an obligation to do it, that is, if one wants to draw believable generalizations.

9.8.7. THE BEGINNINGS OF LONDON STANDARD ENGLISH

The Standard English that arose in London beginning around 1400 has numerous Norse traits brought in from the East Midlands, traits originally absent from the South of England. Some of the East Midland (EM) traits imported to London in turn originated in Northern ME, but assuredly arrived in the East Midlands after 1250. G. V. Smithers provides a sketch of how an East Midland and dialect became established in London:

It is clear that the later fourteenth-century written English of London must, as an Anglian-derived [we eschew this terminology: TK and SGT] type, be in some sense an intrusion there. The personal names preserved in London documents of the ME period have lately been used to show how this happened. . . . Ekwall has . . . been able to establish that, out of 2,900 odd such names, c[a]. 1,970 attest E[ast] M[idland] origins for the persons concerned, as against c[a]. 350 from the North, and 380 from the W[est] M[idlands]. He has thus solved a major problem in the history of London (and therefore standard) English, since these figures led him to deduce that the displacement of an antecedent type of London ME by an EM one was due to the immigration of merchants, &c., from the E[ast] M[idlands] who became well-to-do and thereby gave their form of English a prestige that caused its adoption as an upper-class one in London. (Bennett and Smithers 1968:lvi)

The London Standard was somewhat simpler in morphophonemics than the neighboring indigenous Southeastern and Southwestern dialects, and perhaps a hair more complex than its East Midland (basically Leicester with a bit of Northamption, thus more specifically Central Midland) template. Written English used in London from about 1380 to about 1430 was not uniform (see the texts in Chambers and Daunt 1931, and also the vocabulary). Some writers used a preponderance of Southeast Midland traits while others had a healthy percentage of generic Southern features and even specifically some that were peculiar to the Essex dialect, London's indigenous dialect.[18]

The following list illustrates the ongoing competition between Southern and Central Midland dialect features in written London English between 1385–1425. Both sets of features were found at the time in written London English. For all but the last item the CM features are of Norse origin.

Southern Feature		Central Midland Feature
aye(i)n	'again'	*agein*
aye(i)ns	'against'	*agein(e)s*
yildhall(e)	'guildhall'	*gildhall(e)*
suster	'sister'	*sister*

theih	'though'	*thouh*
hem	'them'	*theim*
her	'their'	*their*
hiy	'they'	*they*
-eth	pres indic pl	*-en*

In this period the forms **given** and **gift(e)** are not found in London English, only **yiven/yeven** and **yift(e)**.

None of the texts is in a "pure" dialect, though some of the within-text variation may reflect ongoing change as much as dialect mixture. But when things eventually shook down in London English (around 1500), the resultant system was a mixed one, with Central Midland traits predominating (Among the dialects of the Danelaw, the Stafford, Leicester, and Northampton dialects were not as heavily Norsified as the Palatine and remaining Danelaw dialects). Like most standard dialects, Standard English tended to be simpler than the regional vernaculars on which it was based, at least at its inception. Because standard dialects often become codified and are then resistant to change, a standard dialect examined after it has been codified for 200 or 300 years may give the false impression that a standard dialect is conservative. By then it may be: at its inception it probably was not. It is misleading to compare Standard English of the nineteenth or twentieth century with rural dialects of the same period, because they have been receiving harsh treatment at the hands of Standard English for at least 500 years. Even now the dialects of southwestern England are still more conservative phonologically and grammatically than Standard English, but not by much. Not any more. In fact, in southeastern England, rural speech is nothing more than countrified Standard English. Kentish died.

9.8.8. FRENCH INFLUENCE ON MIDDLE ENGLISH AND THE QUESTION OF CREOLIZATION

In recent years certain scholars (especially Domingue 1975, Bailey and Maroldt 1977, and Milroy [in Trudgill, ed. 1984]) have suggested that in the contact situations between English and Norse, and also between English and French, pidginization and creolization took place.

Though it cannot be denied that Norse influence on English was extensive (it is on the borderline of types 2 and 3 of our borrowing scale), the foregoing discussion, along with the essentially exhaustive data examined there, makes such an assumption in the case of Norse-English contact unlikely and unnecessary. The very close similarity between the two languages makes the emergence of a pidgin language as unlikely on linguistic grounds as it is on social grounds: linguistically, communication could be effected without drastic elimination of linguistic complexities, and socially the need (at least in most places) was for an all-purpose language, not merely for a restricted-purpose minimal language. Creolization is also unlikely on social grounds, and again the languages seem too close linguistically for such an extreme response to communication difficulties.

As to whether "creolization" occurred somewhere/sometime in England in the contact between English and French, such an issue, it seems to us, could hardly be raised by scholars familiar with the social and linguistic history of England, unless by "creolization" they understand something greatly different from what we do, something which robs the notion of "creolization" of much meaning. In fact Bailey and Maroldt (1977:27, 33, 35, 38) suggest that the linguistic system we know as Middle English is really the result of the massive importation of English lexicon into the Old French spoken by the upper classes of medieval England. Outrageous? Yes. Likely? No. The only way in which this could have happened—given that the *basic* vocabulary of English is overwhelmingly of OE origin—would have involved extremely unsuccessful learning of English by French speakers during a process of shift to English. (Borrowing by French speakers into a maintained French language would not have replaced so much basic French vocabulary unless French grammar had also been replaced by English grammar—but that is just what B&M reject.) However, imperfect learning of the requisite degree, which corresponds to what we have called abrupt creolization (chap. 6), always involves several languages, and (partly for that reason) always involves a forced shift because of an urgent need for a contact medium in a new multilingual contact situation. The case of the French in England is not a promising place to look for such a dramatic linguistic result, with only two languages and ample opportunity for bilingualism to develop—and, in any case, no question of a socially forced shift that could affect the victorious invaders. The specific circumstances of French in England also militate against any such theory:

1. There were never many speakers of French in England.

2. They began giving up French by 1235 at the latest.

3. There is no reason to suppose that any large proportion of native English learned French between 1066 and 1250; after that point they had no reason to do so.

4. Dialects of English most in contact with French underwent no simplification that can be traced to French; they are among the most conservative ME dialects, and no doubt would have been so with or without contact with French.

5. Simplifying traits in Standard English are imported from the East Midlands; sometimes these traits originated in the North.

6. The massive French influence on English vocabulary, *followed* by the mild influence on English morphology and syntax, and the practically trivial influences on English phonology, took place at a time when there were practically no competent French speakers around for an Englishman to talk to.

The kinds of influence we may suppose that French has had on English are also no more extreme than the kinds found in many other normal cases in history, for example, the influence of Turkish on Greek (*in Greece*). English has borrowed heavily from the French lexicon (mainly from 1200–1400). It has also phonologized certain allophonic pairs such as initial [f]:[v] and [ǰ]:[j] through French influence, though not a single foreign sound (phone) has been introduced from French (or Norse, for that matter). It has borrowed particles. Because of massive lexical borrowing, certain derivational affixes occurring in words of French origin have been abstracted and applied to relevant roots and stems of any origin whatsoever (for example, **-abel**, which first entered English through French-origin lexical borrowings consisting of a French verb and the French suffix **-able**; this suffix does not become at all popular on English verbs until the late 14th century).[19] Influences on word order are almost impossible to prove, except in certain fixed phrases whose influence is trivial on the syntax in general, and there are no influences at all on rules of concord.

In fact, in the history of contact between English and French in England, there is abundant evidence that while *some* English speakers learned French (and naturally their prestige influenced their monolingual compatriots in many ways), virtually *all* Normans and Angevins became bilingual in English within no more than 250 years of the Conquest, and that their French suffered as a result. There is more than one instance in medieval French literature where the speech of French-speaking English nobility is characterized as bad and/or specifically mimicked in ways that demonstrate the influence of English on it (Rickard 1956, Matzke 1905). This is apart from the fact that the Norman conquerors mostly spoke Northern and Western dialects (and later shifted to the by then more prestigious Central dialect when their French became largely a second language for them as of about 1265).

The remarks of G. V. Smithers (Bennett and Smithers 1968:xxi, xxii) on the transition from OE to ME are to the point:

> The question "What marks off Middle English from Old English?" which sounds a reasonable and proper one, proves to be unanswerable in that form. The changes that go really deep in the language up to 1400 (in both the written and the spoken form), and whose effects go really deep in English since 1400, are changes in accidence [i.e., inflexion:TK&SGT]. As a result of the drastic simplification of the system of endings, grammatical gender was eliminated, and case ceased to be expressed by endings. It is these things that one commonly thinks of as the distinctive characteristics of "Middle" English; and what one commonly forgets is that they occur in a well-developed stage in the Northumbrian "Old" English of the Lindisfarne Gospels in the late tenth century [xxi]. (We have already pointed out that there was no more Norse influence on Nhb OE than there was of Powhatan on Virginia English:TK&SGT)
>
> The example of the Lindisfarne Gospels is a warning that the date of the Norman Conquest may have no essential bearing on the emergence of "Middle English." [xxii]

Given these facts, it can in no way be considered reasonable to suppose that any of the conditions for pidginization, creolization, or language mixture existed between English and French in the Middle Ages, and it is our firm conviction that **no** such events occurred between English and French.

Since, however, the 1977 article by C.-J. Bailey and K. Maroldt titled "The French lineage of English" has received considerable attention and even, apparently, is considered by some creolists to be a plausible scenario for England in the Middle Ages, we will discuss it briefly here. Their scenario has two main components:

First, sometime between 900 and 1066 a creole arose in the North as a result of contact between Old English and Viking Norse. It is not clear which is supposed to have been the base language.

Second, sometime between 1066 and 1200 English and French together produced a creole, which we know as Middle English (B&M refer to Old English as "Anglo-Saxon" in order to emphasize that it and ME are, in their view, two different languages. They also suggest that twelfth-century writings in English may be "Anglo-Saxon" and not Middle English). ME is claimed to be an obvious mixed language made up of Old English and Old French components (pp. 22–23). As for which language forms the framework into which the other language's materials were incorporated, B&M think it most likely that ME arose by incorporating English lexicon into Old French (pp. 33, 35).

Concerning the first phase of the scenario, B&M write:

> . . . Old Norse contributed anticipatorily to the creation of Middle English. (26)

> Anglo-Saxon had already a clear tendency to reduce its inflections as the result of the Nordic creolization, and a number of analytic expressions had also come into existence as possible options. (41)

> The Nordic creolization of Anglo-Saxon caused inflections to be phonetologically reduced; their final loss can be attributed to the general creole tendency to simplify morphology. (45)

The detailed examination we have presented above should make it clear that in the contact between Norse and English no case can be made for anything other than rather heavy linguistic borrowing by English from Norse.

Concerning the second phase of their scenario, B&M have this to say:

> French creolization seems to have proceeded in two steps—a major creolization, before 1200, and a minor one (mainly with Central French) that involved massive borrowing during the thirteenth and fourteenth centuries. (27)

> . . . consider the possibility . . . that Middle English began with a heavy admixture of Anglo-Saxon elements into Old French. (38)[20]

A comment regarding morphological simplification is in order. In the Southern dialects, only the following morphological simplifications took place: (a) loss of the dative case (but in early ME, down to 1250, singular nouns ending in consonants optionally suffixed -e after prepositions); loss of the genitive plural (though the original genitive plural ending, -ene, came to function as a derivational suffix forming adjectives from nouns); (c) reduction of gender/case agreement markers on prenominal modifiers; (d) elimination of certain minor subclasses of OE nouns that had no more than 10 members each. There is no simplification of the inflection of verbs. There is general reduction of posttonic short vowels to schwa, but that is of eleventh-century date. The constantly-repeated claim by B&M concerning simplification and creolization is simply not true of the ME dialects of the Southern division from 1200 to at least 1350. They were hardly "Anglo-Saxon," even in B&M's terms! Conversely, if (as we claim) Southern ME is not simplified morphologically from the OE stage, that means that *OE is basically as analytic as Southern ME.* There is a problem here that B&M's ad hoc logic does not encompass. We do not, of course, wish to deny that Northern ME has a good deal of morphological simplification (though much of it occurred before Norse or French speakers ever set foot in Britain), or that Midland ME has a moderate amount. We have already discussed these matters.

B&M do discuss a large number of the grammatical features of ME, and are reasonably well-informed about the facts. They compare parts of the noun and verb inflection patterns between OE and Old French (OF) and discuss the ME situation. They concede that in cases of non-overlap between English and French, English-origin morphological markers win out, but belabor their supposition that since some OE and OF morphs of parallel function have similar shapes, French must have contributed to Middle English in such cases (pp. 48–51). One wonders how by such reasoning they expect to convince the reader that ME is a French-based creole. There is no question about whether the facts are so confusing that B&M are wallowing in uncertainty; they have an axe to grind. They start by claiming that what they want to demonstrate is obvious, and spend most of their time arguing against the obvious interpretation of a large proportion of the facts they bring up. They state: "The linguistic consequences of the Conquest have been subject to varying judgments, . . . mainly by the fact that the historical data are given to diverse interpretations" (27). But B&M continue to press their claim that it is self-evident that ME is a mixed language and must have creolization in its pedigree. The scenario described relies on the times when nothing was being written in contemporary vernacular English. Bailey is well-known to believe that creolization is happening all the time; "creolization," as the term is used by him, means any kind of structural interference from another language, and any kind of "analytic" development in a language is taken as evidence of foreign interference (see chap. 2 n. 8). Few (or no) languages have escaped foreign influence, and our model does not consider that "analytic" developments are either necessarily evidence for foreign interference, nor that, whatever their cause, they should be labeled "creolization" or call for different interpretive techniques. B&M say they fully expect strong opposition from "traditionalists." In this they are quite correct, because the available evidence puts ME squarely in the large group of normally transmitted languages, not in the smaller group of mixed languages which (in our view) have no genetic affiliations.

West Saxon English existed in a standardized form from ca. 950 to 1100. The only way we can see what was going on in spoken English of that period is from the mistakes, i.e., failures to reproduce the standard, that writers made. Such errors show, for example, that the older dative plural -**um** became -**an** in late OE, and that the various posttonic vowels /e a o/ all merged (as schwa) by A.D. 1000.[21] Other information that may be gleaned from such texts awaits the researcher. The fact that straightforward vernacular texts from this period are not available does not permit *either* of the following two assumptions:

(a)   that the spoken language was as unchanging as the written; or

(b)   that the spoken language was undergoing large-scale simplification.

The reasonable assumption is that gradual change was going on, and no matter what C.-J. Bailey says, gradual simplification and regularization of linguistic subsystems are typical, and normal. When vernacular English reappears (around 1150 in the Midlands, around 1200 in the South, and around 1250 in the North), the well-known facts (given A.D. 900 as the last reliable point of reference) are:

(a)   Southern has very little change from OE;

(b)   some Midland is Norse-influenced and shows moderate change;

(c)   Northern is Norse-influenced and shows a great deal of either change or idiosyncrasy, though most of it is attributable to Old Northumbrian itself, or Old *East Mercian; and

(d)   all show superficial French influence, stronger in the South. This is the framework within which hypotheses about the linguistic habits of English speakers from 900 to 1200 must be formulated.

We specifically deny that French has had a disruptive influence on English in the sense of having promoted simplification or denaturing. Simplification and denaturing have occurred in written English, but not at the right times to be explainable through language contact with French at a face-to-face level. The simplification is both earlier than and later than the period of close contact with French (1065–1265) and the denaturing is *much* later than the period in question; it reflects a cultural peculiarity of English speakers probably akin to the one that led Japanese to adopt thousands of Chinese borrowings in our Middle Ages.

Concerning the influence of French on Middle English, to our own statements we add the following healthy-minded quotes from G. V. Smithers (Bennett and Smithers 1968):

> . . . [T]he fundamental changes in the inflexion of nouns, adjectives, and pronouns, since they were under way before the Conquest (p. xxi), were the outcome of internal processes likely to operate in any language with a moderately ample system of accidence. The main changes in the endings of verbs, being due to the need for unambiguous expression of grammatical meaning, are likewise the product of purely internal factors. And though the causes of unconditioned (i.e., 'isolative') phonetic changes are complex and notoriously hard to determine, it is clear that, for example, the reduction of OE diphthongs to what was in effect their first element had set in before the Conquest. . . . "Thus the impact of an alien language spoken by a new ruling class did not substantially affect or modify the structure of English." (xlviii–xlix)

> From what has been said above, it should be clear that the structure and organization of a language and its characteristic trends of change are what matter. It is the vocabulary that lies nearest the surface, and is therefore most easily touched by an alien tongue; it is the vocabulary of ME (and hence of present English) that has been affected by OF. (xlix–l)

A point commonly overlooked in attempts to assess the contribution of French to the vocabulary of English is the crucial difference in this regard between colloquial and other forms of English. It is a curious and impressive fact that one can compose a piece of English conversation without using a single French word; and one can often hear or take part in conversations containing very few. (lii)

It was probably not only an author's audience [in ME times: TK&SGT], but also his own background endowments, and tastes that determined the number of adoptions from OF that he used. This is one of the reasons why the first record of a French word in ME should not necessarily be assumed (as is commonly done) to imply that it was, or even soon became, generally current in the "language." In fact, so long as we are dealing with any one ME work, the influence of French vocabulary on the "language" is an abstraction: such a notion applies only to words which are found, on analysis of many works, to recur in several of them. (lii)[22]

J. Milroy (Trudgill, ed. 1984:11) presents a scenario for the breakdown and reassembly of English structure under Norse and French influence that is very reminiscent of B&M's:

Certain general principles that operate in language contact situations are now well known to sociolinguists and creolists. These include (1) gross morphological simplification (2) some loss of segmental phonological distinctions; relexification (i.e., replacement of much of the lexicon of one language—the subordinate one—with the lexicon of the other); and (4) a preference for a fixed SVO word order. ME shows clear signs that at least three of these (1, 3 and 4) had operated: loss of a number of consonantal distinctions seems also to have taken place if the orthography of some thirteenth-century texts is to be trusted. (Milroy 1983)

Gross morphological simplification only *seems* to have occurred in NME. Loss of segmental phonological distinctions does not need to be abnormal, though nothing of the sort occurred in ME.[23] In the case of French lexical influence on English, in the ME period French lexical influence expanded the total vocabulary of English but did *not* for the most part displace native vocabulary; this happened later. The claim about SVO word order is one of the most touted and least convincing of the begged questions of the creolist zealots. It explains nothing, and is unnecessary for the English case. We deny gross morphological simplification in any kind of ME, and we also deny that the Norse lexical influence on Norsified English can be viewed as relexification. As for Milroy's orthographic evidence for phonemic mergers, medievalists know how difficult it is to interpret medieval scribal practice; they must find a particular pattern repeatedly attested before being able to draw reliable conclusions from orthography. If such phonological simplifications as suggested by Milroy do not appear in later forms of English, it is highly unlikely that they ever occurred.

9.8.9. EXCURSUS: SIMPLIFICATION AND FOREIGNIZATION OF OTHER GERMANIC LANGUAGES

Students of the history of the English language, at whatever depth, are aware of how thoroughly the English vocabulary is riddled with French, Latin, and Greek terms. What concerns us here is the French influence on *Middle English*, which involved much lexicon, some affixes, a few particles, and a handful of syntactic devices. The student of English may not be aware that the medieval influence of Low German on Danish, Norwegian, and Swedish through the activities of the Hanse after about A.D. 1200 was every bit as deep as the influence of French on English. A person who learns continental Scandinavian may well not also learn Low German or Icelandic, and continental Scandinavian looks just as overwhelmingly Germanic as High German; however, there is much that continental Scandinavian has that Icelandic lacks, and it is mostly of Low German origin.

In fact, most other Germanic languages show about as much simplification and foreignization in their histories as English does. Twenty features have been identified wherein a number of Germanic languages have undergone these kinds of changes and the results are displayed in table 7. Icelandic has been surveyed, but the results have been left off the table, because it has undergone such changes in only three cases, points 7, 19, and 20, a truly atypical outcome. Each feature is assigned a weight of one point, and a marginal or less decided feature is given half a point. Plus (+) means present; minus (–) means absent; marginal features are in parentheses; (?) means unknown or unclear.

Scores of 13.5 to 15.5 are associated with English, Standard Dutch (vs. Eastern Netherlandish), North Low German and Mecklenburgish (vs. Westfalian, Eastfalian, and Brandenburgish), Danish and Bokmaal (vs. Landsmaal), and Swedish. These are all *coastal-insular* languages and dialects.

TABLE 7

SIMPLIFICATION AND FOREIGNIZATION IN MODERN GERMANIC LANGUAGES

Feature	Standard English	Danish & Bokmaal	Swedish	North Low German & Mecklenburgish	Standard Dutch	Saterland East Frisian	Standard High German
1. reduce unstressed V to /ə/	+	+	−	+	+	+	+
2. lengthen stressed V in open syll.	+	+	+	+	+	+	+
3. degeminate	+	+	−	+	+	+	+
4. drop final /ə/	+	−	−	+	+	−	(dialects)
5. lose /θ/	−	+	+	+	+	+	+
6. lose /h/ before /w/	(+)	+	+	+	+	+	+
7. change /w/ to [v]	−	+	+	+	−	+	+
8. devoice final obstruents	−	−	−	+	+	+	+
9. massive word-of-mouth lexical borrowing	French	Low German	Low German	French: moderate	French	Low German	French: moderate

10. foreign deriv. affixes from same (#9)	+	+	+	+	+	+	+
11. dative > TO + N	–	+: too	+: aan	+: ?	+: til	+: til	+: to
12. two genitive constructions	–	+: 's & fon	+: 's & van	+: 's & fon	+: 's & av	+: 's & av	+: 's & of
13. lack gender on def. art.	–	–	–	?	–	–	+
14. lack gender on modifying adj.	–	+	+	+	–	–	+
15. lack distinct pers/# markers on verbs (pres.)	–	–	–	–	+	+	–
16. same as #15 (past)	–	–	–	–	+	+	+
17. use WHO/WHICH/ WHAT in restr. rel. cl.	–	–	(literary?)	?	(literary)	(literary)	(literary)
18. use MORE/MOST in comparison	–	–	?	?	+	+	+
19. use polite YE	+ (obsol.)	?	+	?	+	+	+
20. exclusive SVO	–	–	–	–	+	+	+
SCORE	10	12	13.5	13.5	13.5	15.5	15

Scores of 10 to 12 are associated with Saterlandish East Frisian, High German, and the excluded/contrasted dialects mentioned above (except Landsmaal). These are all *inland* languages and dialects.

But Icelandic, the most coastal-insular of all these languages, has undergone practically no simplification or foreignization with respect to the traits dealt with here.

In considering changes in this set of languages, it is clear that

(a)   the sociolinguistic circumstances have not been uniform; furthermore

(b)   Standard Dutch, North Low German and Mecklenburgish, Danish and Bokmaal, and Swedish are *not* "creolized" nor do they show abnormal development; and

(c)   the "simplification" features can plausibly be explained by drift and diffusion from one Germanic language to another. However

(d)   when they are considered together with the "foreignization" features they may/should be viewed in the context of the **gradual convergence of most Western European languages.** Here, clearly,

(1)   most innovations began in the Mediterranean (Roman Empire);

(2)   French is the next most important source of foreign linguistic influence; and

(3)   coastal languages and dialects have converged more than those further inland.

Some scholars make much of the degree to which English has become analytic in its syntax. Except for gender (neuter vs. common) agreement on noun modifiers and the definite forms of adjectives *Danish and Swedish are every bit as analytical as English.* (Though their Germanic-origin derivational system is more in evidence, much of this is borrowed from Low German.) Apart from a more complex person/number marking system on verbs and the survival of neuter vs. common gender marking on the definite article, *Dutch and North Low German are just as analytical as English.* Though these dialects do have a small number of French-origin derivational affixes, their number does not come near what is found in English. But in English *the foreign derivational patterns are of Latin, not French, origin* and are the result of massive borrowing of the written, not spoken, word.

We now proceed to a discussion of most of the points of table 7.

All dialects of English, Frisian, Dutch, Low German, High German, and Danish have undergone the following sequence of sound changes:

(1) Reduce unstressed final (and some nonfinal) short vowels to schwa;[24]

(2) Lengthen (or add a centering glide to) a short stressed vowel in an open syllable;

(3) Degeminate consonants.

In addition, English, Dutch, some Frisian, some Low German, and some High German

(4) Drop final schwa.

These four changes occurred between 1200 and 1600. They may be connected via diffusion, though they are not remarkable and could have occurred independently. For example, changes (1–3) also occurred in French before A.D. 900, and (4) occurred in spoken French by A.D. 1600. Degemination has occurred before A.D. 1000 in all Romance languages except Central and Southern Italian, and Sardinian, and has been eliminated from Celtic.

(5) *Loss of /θ/.* Except for English, Icelandic, Wangeroogish East Frisian, Welsh, Albanian, and Greek, no European language currently has /θ/, and every European language that had it has changed it to something else. Thus,

in High German, Low German, and Dutch /θ/ > /d/;

in continental Scandinavian and Frisian /θ/ > #[t and V[d; and in French /θ/ > ∅.

(6) *Loss of /h/ before /w/.* Most Germanic languages lost /h/ before /w/, but many English dialects retain it, and Icelandic and Landsmaal Norwegian shift it to /k/.

(7) *Substitution of [v] for [w].* Most European languages lack [w] and have [v] instead. Except for English and some dialects of Danish, Polish, and Ukrainian, all European languages (including Turkish) that had [w] earlier have changed it to [v] or [β]. Greek changed earlier [b] to [v]. In Welsh earlier [w] became [gw]. It should be kept in mind that [v] is not an especially common sound in the world's languages outside Europe, Iran, India, and parts of Africa.

(8) *Devoicing of final obstruents.* This change affects many European languages, e.g., French, Provençal, Catalan, Maltese, all Slavic languages except Ukrainian and SerboCroatian, Turkish, High German, Low German, Dutch, and Frisian. It also affects the English

spoken by Greek immigrants, so that although most Greek dialects offer little for such a rule to act on, it is plausibly part of Greek's phonology (see 9.1 for discussion of such a rule in Northern Greek dialects after the drop of word-final high vowel). It affected Proto-Norse at a time when certain final vowels had not yet been dropped (before A.D. 700). Maltese must have gotten the rule from Sicilian, which had even less scope for the rule in native material than Greek has. As is well known, many phonologists believe final devoicing of obstruents is natural, and needs no explanation.

(11) *Loss of dative case.* As in Western Romance, most Germanic languages, as well as Bulgarian, Macedonian, and Greek, have lost the dative case. (In many SerboCroatian dialects the dative and locative cases differ only in their accent patterns.)

(12) *Two genitive constructions.* Except for High German and Icelandic, all Germanic languages have two ways of expressing the genitive, the *'s*-genitive used mostly with personal names, and the *of*-genitive used with inanimate nouns and parallel to the devices used in Western Romance.[25]

(13–14) *Loss of gender agreement on definite article and modifying adjectives.* English is the only Germanic language to completely lose grammatical marking of gender agreement.[26]

(15–16) *Loss of person/number marking on verbs.* While English has simplified person/number marking on verbs, continental Scandinavian has eliminated it altogether.

(17) *Use of interrogative words in restrictive relative clauses.* The use of the words **who/which/what** (originally only interrogative/indefinite in Germanic) in restrictive relative clauses is found in several Germanic languages, but it is limited to formal usage, and seems clearly to be modeled on French or Latin usage.

(18) *Use of* **more/most** *in comparative and superlative forms.* In the comparison of some adjectives **more** and **most** are used in continental Scandinavian as well as in English and this is parallel to Romance and Greek usage.

(19) *Use of polite* **ye.** The use of **ye** for polite second person goes back to the Roman Empire and is extremely widespread in Europe. In several languages, for example, Standard English, Standard Dutch, and Brazilian Portuguese, **thou** has become obsolete.

(20) *Exclusive SVO order.* Exclusive (or predominant) SVO constituent order is characteristic of Greek and most Western European

and Slavic languages.[27] Frisian, Dutch, Low German, and High German have SOV in some kinds of dependent clauses, as did Old English. Runic Germanic had both SVO and SOV in main clauses. Hungarian and Turkish have SOV in main clauses. Latin had SOV, but medieval Romance languages had SVO (or verb second). We suggest that SVO order may have originated in Greek and spread to Latin; though Germanic and Slavic may have had SVO as one of their available constituent orders, their preference for SVO in main clauses could well owe something to Popular Latin and Greek respectively.

We would like to stress that ten of the traits listed on table 7 (i.e., 5–8, 11–12, 17–20) are widespread in the languages of Europe. They may all be diffused, but

(a) their immediate source is not necessarily known for each language that has them; also

(b) many of them are not at all unnatural and so particular changes might have occurred more than once;

(c) these changes are in no way evidence for "creolization" or any other kind of disruptive linguistic change.

We rather suspect that some of the writers whose interpretation of the history of English[28] we are objecting to might interpret the evidence from Dutch, Low German, Danish, and Swedish as being evidence for "creolized" stages in these languages' developments; however, such a use would rob the term "creolization" of its distinctive content, and certainly we do not use the term in the way these authors do. The languages in question were not colonized in quite the same way that English was by Norse and French (though Flanders was dominated by France, and parts of Scandinavia by Low German speakers). Our point is this: English is not significantly more simplified or foreignized than Danish, Swedish, Dutch, or Northern Low German. Most of the simplification that has occurred in Standard English and in Southern English dialects has occurred while English speakers were overwhelmingly monolingual.

9.8.10. LOW DUTCH GRAMMATICAL INFLUENCE ON MIDDLE ENGLISH

A third language to influence English in our time period (900–1500) was Low Dutch. Low Dutch means both Low Frankish (or Netherlandish) and Low Saxon (or "Low German"). Three kinds of Low Dutch speakers found homes in Britain:

1. Flemings: those who invaded with William the Bastard; later refugees from Flanders who would be accepted in England when the King of France put down Flemish moves toward independence; wool merchants; and marauding mercenaries in the twelfth century;

2. Hollanders who came to build dikes and brew beer; and

3. Low Saxons who represented the mercantile interests of the Hanse.

Down to 1150 probably the only Low Dutch speakers in England were Flemings. Low Dutch speakers may or may not have been as numerous as the Norman and Angevin French, but they were not evenly spread over the country; rather they were concentrated where their interest lay. For example, the merchants and brewers settled in cities and towns, while the dike-builders settled near the fenlands of the Wash, which they drained. The Flemish mercenaries were brought under control and allowed to settle in large numbers in South Wales (Gower, Tenby, Haverford West, and Milford Haven) as early as 1100, where they eventually switched to English. They also formed a large colony at Berwick-upon-Tweed, in Northumberland. Flemings settled in smaller numbers in towns throughout England, with the following exceptions: in the twelfth century the East Northern and Southeast Midland areas had few or no Flemings, and the same was true of the counties of Sussex, Gloucester, Somerset, Dorset, Hertford, and Nottingham. There were Flemish mercenaries and town-dwellers in Scotland at least as early as 1138. The English colonies in twelfth-century Ireland (especially Wexford) contained Flemings. J. Bense (1925:22) informs us: "There were more than fifty small Flemish settlements in Great Britain and Ireland in the 12th century." In his opus *A Dictionary of the Low-Dutch Element in English Vocabulary* (1938:xxiv), Bense provides a summary of the contacts between English and Low Dutch speakers in the Middle Ages, from which we quote excerpts:

> . . . (1) one wave of Flemish and Dutch immigration after another flowed over Great Britain and Ireland from the time of William the Conqueror to that of William the Third; (2) thousands came to stay, lived with English hosts, taught their trade to English apprentices, and married English wives . . . (5) from the Middle Ages to the middle of the 16th century . . . the Hanse merchants . . . had their Guildhall in more than one town; (6) the carrying trade between

Great Britain and the Continent was chiefly in the hands of the
Dutch until Cromwell's Navigation Act.

Low Dutch, with perhaps 600 years of separation from it, was much
more closely related to English than Norse was; consequently, less
scope existed for possible effects of Dutch influence on English. The
number of words of Low Dutch origin recorded in ME down to 1400
does not exceed 100. Yet there was a striking grammatical influence
of Low Dutch on ME that is little known, because though introduced
sometime before 1150, it is found in certain dialects only and disappeared by the end of the fourteenth century (see map 11).

In the Lindsey (Grimsby?), Norfolk, Essex, Kent (Canterbury
and Shoreham), East Wessex (Southhampton?), and West Wessex
(Bristol?) dialects of ME, attested from just before 1200 down to at
least 1375, there occurs a pronoun form that serves as the enclitic/un-
stressed object form of SHE and THEY. Its normal written shape is
<(h)is> or <(h)es>, presumably /əs/; one text occasionally spells
it <hise>. This pronoun has no origin in OE. It does have one in
Low Dutch, where the unstressed object form for SHE and THEY
is /sə/, spelled <se> (this is cognate with High German **sie**). If the
ME <h> was ever pronounced it was no doubt on the analogy of
all the other third person pronoun forms of English. We do not know
whether Low Dutch speakers settled in sizable numbers in all of the
dialect areas where this pronoun occurs, but there is one striking
correlation: all these dialect areas abut on the sea (see map 11), and
after 1070 the seas near Britain, along with their ports, were the
stomping grounds of the Flemings, Hollanders, and Low German
traders. These facts should remove all doubt as to whether this pronoun is foreign or indigenous (and just happened not to show up in
any OE texts!).

This phenomenon raises the question as to just how telling the
borrowing of pronouns between closely related languages is. Maybe
it is not noteworthy. It is possible that Northern ME acquired Norse
pronouns to avoid homophony problems. Let us look at the third
person pronouns of Old Northumbrian, Northern ME, late West
Saxon, and Southern ME. Note that OE has four case forms, and
ME has three (actually until about 1225 ME has four case forms also,
but the dative and accusative are rapidly merging). Note also that
Southern ME has enclitic object forms.

TABLE 8

OLD ENGLISH AND MIDDLE ENGLISH THIRD PERSON PRONOUNS

ONhb	IT	HE	SHE	THEY	NME	IT	HE	SHE	THEY
nom	hit	he:	hi:o	hi:e	subj	it	hee	yhoo >shoo	they
acc	hit	hine	hi:e	hi:e					
					obj	it	him	hir	theim
dat	him	him	hir	him					
gen	his	his	hire	hiora	poss	his	his	hir	theire

OWS	IT	HE	SHE	THEY	SME	IT	HE	SHE	THEY
nom	hit	he:	he:o	hi:e	subj	hit	hee	höö	hüi, hii
acc	hit	hine	hi:e	hi:e	encl	hit	hine	hese	hese
dat	him	him	hire	him/heom	obj	hit	him	hire	höm/ham
gen	his	his	hire	hira/heora	poss	his	his	hire	höre/hare

NOTE: The OE forms are given in their normal spellings with length marks added to vowels where appropriate.

In late OE /i:o/ > /e:o/ > /ö:/, and then in the North sometime before the ME attestation /ö/ > /e/ and /ü/ > /i/. This would have made HE and SHE homophonous. There must have existed a variant /hjo:/ < /hi:o/ for SHE and that is what survived, to avoid homophony. ONhb /hi:e/ 'they (,them,her)' had a diphthong that otherwise occurred in **si:e   se:** the present subjunctive of "to be," and in **bi-twi:en** which became ME **be-tween.** Thus it is to be expected that ONhb **hi:e** would have given ME ***hee.** This did happen in other dialects of ME, for instance that of East Anglia (Norfolk). A change of /i:e/ to ME /e:/ would have created homophony between HE and THEY. In ONhb the datives HIM and THEM were already homophonous. Borrowing **they** and **theim** from Old Norse eliminated two real homophonies. Though the Norfolk dialect was able to live with HE/THEY homophony, in the light of this inconvenience, the borrowing by Northern English of the Old Norse form seems less likely to be a sign of the break-down of English in the North than might otherwise be thought.

Sound change operating on the late West Saxon system, on the other hand, produced no homophonous developments, so there was no need to upgrade rare variants. Nevertheless, the dialects named above, which are both East Midland and Southern, but all coastal, have added a foreign pronoun form to their system with no apparent need. Only fashion and a fairly good knowledge of Low Dutch would seem to be able to account for this. Yet this clear instance of structural borrowing from Low Dutch into Middle English seems to be an isolated phenomenon. It disappeared, to be sure, but not because it was foreign—rather, because the ME enclitic forms were eliminated, English and foreign alike (though an enclitic /ən/ 'him' does survive in Wessex).

There is a lesson here: an overarching theory that uses isolated traits to reconstruct detailed sociolinguistic scenarios should be viewed with some suspicion. It follows that other possible grammatical (as well as phonological) influences of Low Dutch on ME should be sought. Actually, there is one other instance of grammatical influence (indirect, however) of Low Dutch on Middle English, which is well known. The use in English of the suffix -kin to form diminutives from names and other nouns dates from 1250: examples are **Watekin, Wilekin, Malekin** from the ME equivalents of "Walter," "William," and "Mary." Also, M. L. Samuels (in Aitken et al. 1971:3–19) presents evidence that in the Kentish dialect (spoken in Kent, East Sussex, and East Surrey) the voiced allophone [ð] of /θ/ shifted to /d/ around 1400, under the influence of Flemish. Since Standard English was coming into existence about that time, this development leaves only traces in the twentieth century, since, as mentioned earlier, in rural Kent what is spoken these days is countrified Standard English.

9.8.11. ON ORDERLINESS OR THE LACK OF IT IN THE RATES OF LINGUISTIC CHANGE IN ENGLISH

Four hundred years have passed from Shakespeare's time to our own (1580–1980). With some difficulty we can read and understand Shakespeare.

From King Alfred (ca. 900) to *Robert of Gloucester's Chronicle* or the *South English Legendary* (ca. 1300) 400 years also had passed. Was the linguistic difference any greater here than between Shakespeare's times and our own?

We must not be misled by the fact that Alfred and Robert use different orthographies while we and Shakespeare use the same one, because it is quite certain that Shakespeare's pronunciation was different from ours, both phonetically and phonemically.

We doubt that from Alfred to Robert more change occurred than between Shakespeare and us. While we do not undertake here a full demonstration of our viewpoint, we will give an outline of the most meaningful changes.

Changes from 900 to 1300:

1. Changes in case system: loss of dative, loss of genitive plural; acquisition of *of*-genitive;

2. Vowel reductions: certain posttonic and all final short vowels become schwa;

3. Restructuring of OE vowel system: /V:/, /Vj/, and /Vw/ are reinterpreted as /Və/, /Vi/, and /Vu/ (not necessarily respectively); shift of /a:/ to /oə/; allophonic lengthening of short stressed vowel in open syllable (or adding phonemic schwa to them);

4. Loss of arbitrary gender and most of the agreement marking associated with it;

5. Acquisition of a sizable amount of French vocabulary, *without* the displacement of any meaningful amount of English vocabulary; use of a few derivational suffixes of French origin with words of all origins.

Changes from 1600 to 2000:

1. Modern English vowel changes (1600–1700). The third column shows to what extent the contemporary SW dialects have shared the post-Shakespeare vowel changes.

phonologically	orthographically	is it SW now?
a) /e:/ > /i:/	\<ea>	no
b) /ai/ > /eə/	\<ai>	no
/ou/ > /oə/	\<ou>	yes/no
c) /eə/ > /e:/	\<a. .e>	no
/oə/ > /o:/	\<ou>	no
d) /aə/ > /oə/ and /aə/	\<au>	yes
/eu/ > /iu/ > /yu:/	\<eu>	yes/no
/ui/ > /oi/	\<oi>	no
/u/ > /ə/ and /u/	\<u>	yes

2. Lexical attrition and amplification;

3. Changes in the auxiliary system, e.g., progressive aspect, use of passive in all tenses, moods, and aspects;

4. Loss of syllable-final /r/ (in the East of England).

From Robert of Gloucester to Shakespeare, 300 years, there *does* appear to have occurred proportionally more linguistic change than in the two other 400-year periods. But beyond the passage of time there are two other factors:

Robert and Shakespeare use *different dialects*; and second,

Shakespeare's English is standardized, while Robert's is not. After 1500 essentially no one wrote dialectal or non-standard English and few did after 1450 (notable exceptions are *Promptorium Parvulorum* (Norfolk) and *Catholicon Anglicum* (Deira), two English-Latin word-lists of several thousand words each (PP 12,000 words; CA 8,000 words). These word-lists will provide the careful reader with a sense of what the ordinary English vocabulary of the late fifteenth century was. Inflated claims about French lexical influence on English are not supported by the contents of these vocabularies).

Changes from 1300 to 1600:

1. Complete displacement of much native vocabulary by French loans (15th century);

2. Latinization of the lexicon (16th century);

3. Loss of final schwa; degemination (ca. 1400);

4. Shift of /h/ to /i/ and /u/ before /t/ (ca. 1410);

5. The Great Vowel Shift:

    a) /ii/ > /əi/; /uu/ > /əu/ except before

                               labials and velars (ca. 1420)

    b) /iə/ > /i:/ and /uə/ > /u:/ (ca. 1430)

    c) /eə/ > /e:/ and /oə/ > /o:/ (ca. 1475)

    d) /aə/ > /eə/ (ca. 1500)

    e) /au/ > /aə/ (ca. 1525);

5. Loss of infinitive suffix;

6. Ability to use any major lexeme as a noun, adjective, or verb;

7. Ability to use any particle as a noun, adjective, or verb: e.g., "if me no ifs, but me no buts";

8. Changes in the auxiliary system (Lightfoot 1979);

9. Acquisition of the so-called Romance Phonological Rules, which make up most of what SPE (Chomsky and Halle 1968) deals with; PLUS

10. Beyond all this, Standard English has a Central Midland basis while Robert wrote in the dialect of Mid Wessex; this should be discounted in order to make the comparison fair.

We would like to stress that the period from 1300 to 1600 was one in which

(a)   massive lexical borrowing was going on from French;

(b)   knowledge of French by Englishmen was quite poor and never native;

(c)   the English had a love/hate attitude toward the French people and culture.

It seems to us that efforts to relate the massive French influence on English to a face-to-face language contact situation between French and English are misguided. We would also like to point out that while the theories that we object to claim to explain observed facts, we say they fail; furthermore we cheerfully admit it when we can't explain something. We also acknowledge, albeit not cheerfully, that overarching models that use a small number of axioms and try to explain practically everything annoy us. We dislike reductionism (ad absurdum). We are splitters, not lumpers. The purpose of this book is to introduce some *subtlety* into the thoughts and words of historical linguists.

To return to the issue of the change in English from 1300 to 1600: is the amount of change roughly expectable, given the amount of change from 900 to 1300 and from 1600 to 2000? Either way we win. If it is more than expectable, there is no way that a creolization hypothesis can explain the degree of change, given our knowledge of the sociolinguistic situation. If it is about as much as expected, there is no issue. If the amount of change from 1600 to 2000 is less than expected, this must have something to do with prior standardization. That would mean that the changes from 900 to 1300 and from 1300 to 1600 would be roughly comparable and characteristic of pre-industrial society. "Creolist" hypotheses are unnecessary for the period 900–1000 and inapplicable to the period 1300–1600. Even if we were to concede that the murkiness of the period from 1000 to 1200 at least offers a chance that "creolization" might have occurred, in the exercises carried out by Domingue as well as by Bailey and Maroldt we see no useful results, and especially, we see no demonstration of the creolist hypothesis.

To summarize our views on the "creolization of English" issue:

(1) In the context of Europe, the kinds of simplification and foreignization undergone by Southern English down to 1400 were typical.

(2) The degree of morphological simplification seen in Northern, East Midland, and Standard English may owe something to the tumultuous history of the North of England in the 9th, 10th, and 11th centuries. The degree of borrowing from Norse is heavy but not abnormal between closely-related languages (It straddles types 2 and 3 of our borrowing scale). The degree of phonological (i.e., morphophonemic) and morphological simplification reached by Northern English by 1300, apart from gender loss, was eventually reached by Dutch by 1600, so it can hardly be seen as abnormal in the long run.

(3) Standard languages tend to be simpler (at least at the time of codification) than many of the vernacular dialects on which they are based, partly because they must accommodate the production habits of speakers on the low end of the range of structural complexity within a network of dialects.

(4) Massive foreign lexical influence on English (particularly on the derivational phenomena observable in the English lexicon, which is productive for uncultivated speakers to a limited extent only) occurred only in the Modern English period, say from 1450 to 1550 and later, and reflects the rather odd cultural values of the literate class in England at that time. This lexical stock, while in many cases mediated by *written* French, is almost entirely of Latin origin. Even the material of Greek origin is latinized. While the importation of extensive lexical resources via the written word is of some interest, it can in no way be construed as a kind of creolization or abnormal linguistic change.

(5) The linguistic influence of French on Middle English folk speech was normal for coastal Northwestern Europe (Katara 1966, a dictionary of French loans in MLG, has some 5000 words of French origin attested in the period 1300–1600). The fact that French was the medium of instruction in the universities down to about 1460 (Oxford was founded in 1168), as well as the language of the courts, a situation unlike that of other Germanic-speaking countries (except possibly Flanders), probably promoted in England a somewhat greater familiarity with French vocabulary and idiom than was true on the Continent. While the proportion of French-origin items in English basic vocabulary is 7 percent, the amount of useful and frequently-used French-origin vocabulary is rather large. It should be noted that non-literary dialects of Dutch and all dialects of Low

German have a much higher proportion of French-origin vocabulary than Standard Dutch or Standard High German. This means primarily that written Dutch and High German tolerate a lower percentage of French-origin items than the spoken language, though Dutch is more tolerant than German.

9.8.12. CONCLUSIONS

Our survey (in 9.8) of Norse, French, and Low Dutch influence on English (and other coastal Germanic languages) has yielded a variety of both specific and generally applicable results.

1. Speakers of the languages of Western Europe were in regular (though not always intense) contact with each other throughout the Middle Ages (ca. 800–1500). English, Low Dutch, and German, as well as Spanish, Portuguese, and Italian, were all strongly influenced lexically by French, beginning around 1100. Norse in mainland Europe (but not the islands of the North Atlantic) was strongly influenced by Low Dutch after about 1100 (9.8.3, 9.8.8–9.8.9). Yet all these influences are moderate (ranging up to type 3 on our borrowing scale) compared to what has been exemplified elsewhere in this book.

2. From Norse, French, and Low Dutch, English accepted linguistic traits according to the degree of typological overlap and the intensity of contact with these languages (9.8).

3. We did not survey in detail the ways that French influenced English in the period 1065–1265, while French was a living language in England. The details are numerous and not hard to come by. In rejecting the exaggerated claims of Bailey and Maroldt, Domingue, and J. Milroy we do not mean to deny that the degree of French influence on English was meaningful: it was meaningful, but moderate and fairly commonplace (9.8.8).

4. We have conducted a thorough examination of Norse structural influence on English that shows the hypotheses of the above-mentioned scholars to be unnecessary and misguided (9.8.6–9.8.7).

5. We have also shown that Northern Middle English proves to owe virtually 90 percent of its distinctive structural traits to the spread of the Norsified English dialect of Lindsey (= North Lincolnshire) into the North of England probably during the eleventh cen-

tury. This result is a spin-off of the investigation into Norse influence on northerly dialects of ME (9.8.6–9.8.7).

6. From 900 to 1600 English overall shows no evidence of having undergone either unevenly distributed degrees of linguistic change, or simplification due to language contact (9.8.11).

7. Only thorough/complete surveys of well-documented cases should be taken as a basis of serious generalizations and claims about the nature of linguistic change in contact situations. That is precisely what we have tried to do in this book. Models that are built by picking out from the mass of data only those data that support the model are to be avoided.

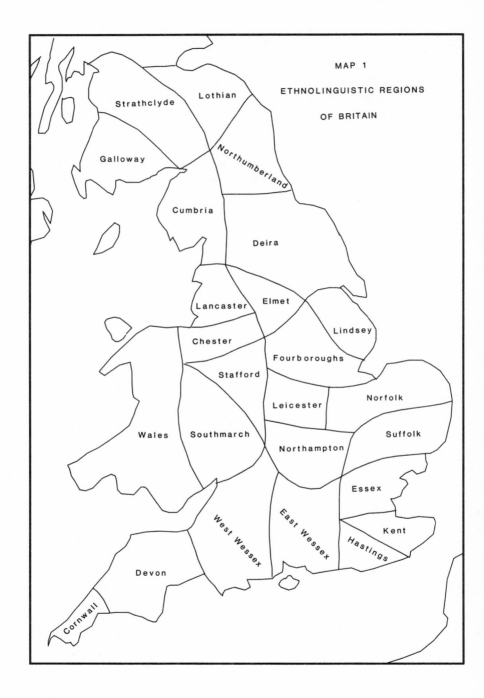

MAP 1

ETHNOLINGUISTIC REGIONS

OF BRITAIN

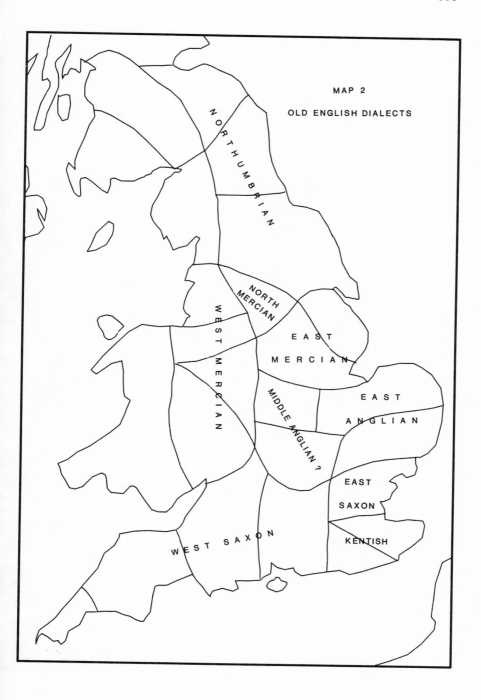

MAP 2

OLD ENGLISH DIALECTS

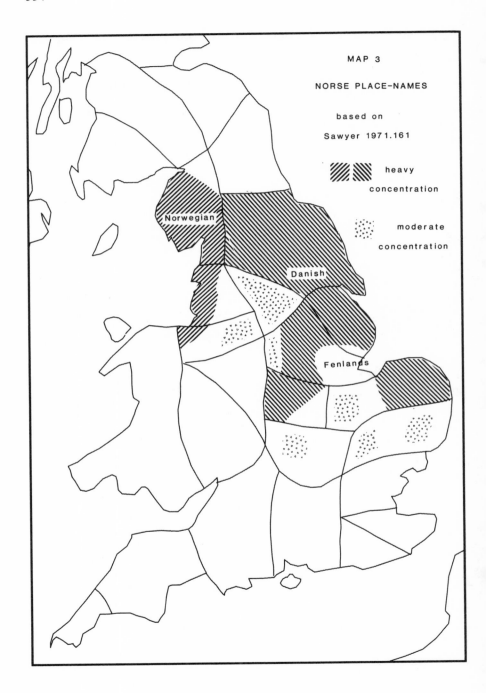

MAP 3

NORSE PLACE-NAMES

based on
Sawyer 1971.161

heavy
concentration

moderate
concentration

Norwegian

Danish

Fenlands

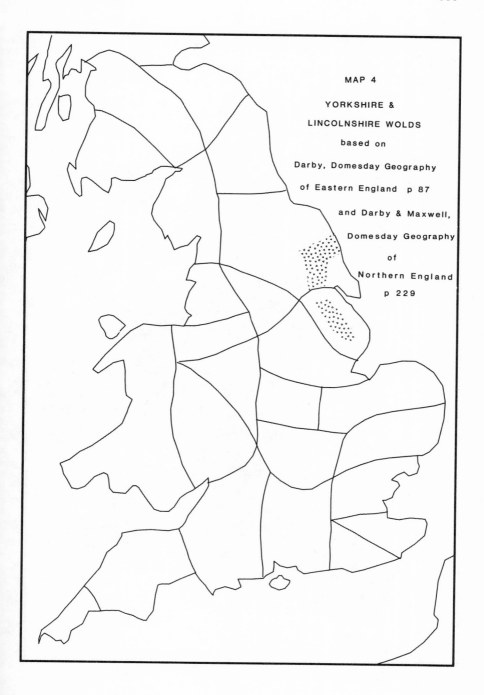

MAP 4

YORKSHIRE &
LINCOLNSHIRE WOLDS
based on
Darby, Domesday Geography
of Eastern England p 87
and Darby & Maxwell,
Domesday Geography
of
Northern England
p 229

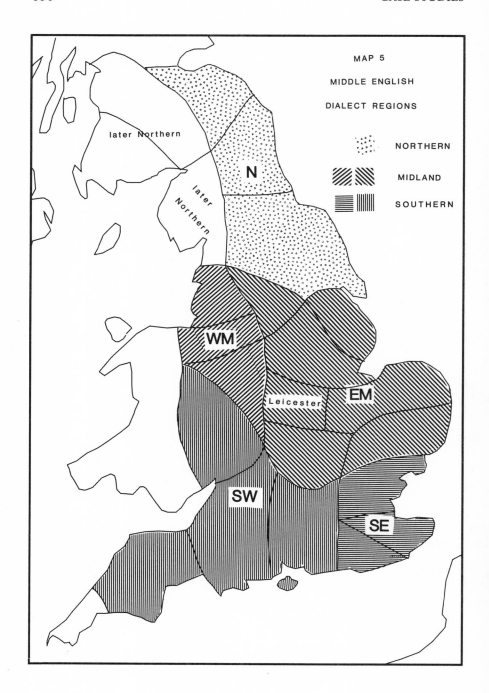

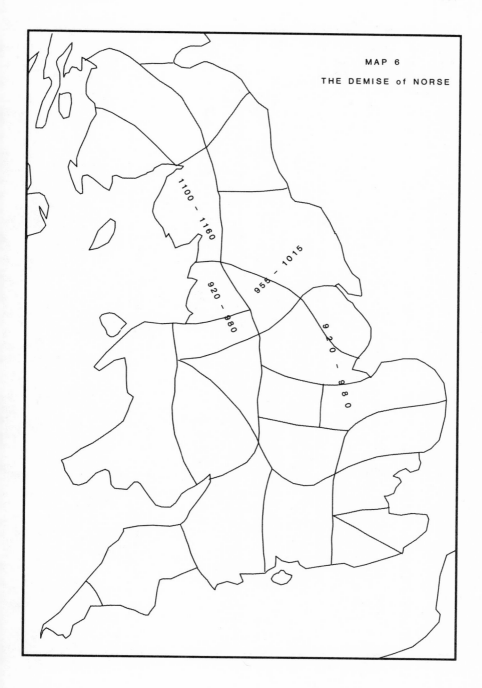

MAP 6

THE DEMISE of NORSE

1100 – 1160

955 – 1015

920 – 980

920 – 980

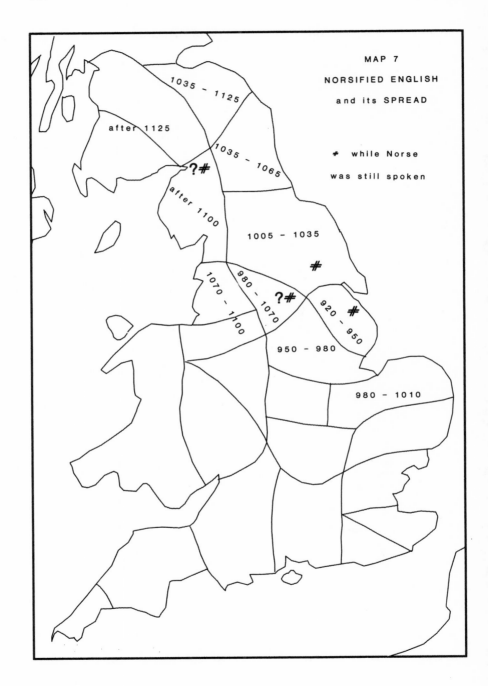

MAP 7

NORSIFIED ENGLISH

and its SPREAD

⚹ while Norse

was still spoken

1035 – 1125

after 1125

1035 – 1065

?#

after 1100

1005 – 1035

#

1070 – 1100

980 – 1070

?#

920 – 950

#

950 – 980

980 – 1010

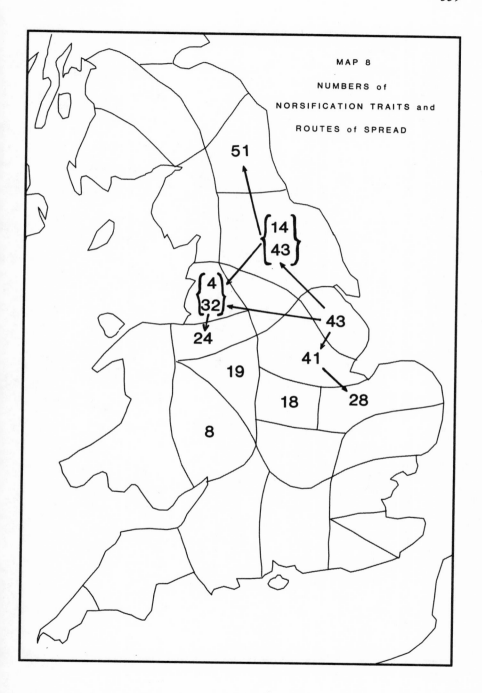

MAP 8

NUMBERS of

NORSIFICATION TRAITS and

ROUTES of SPREAD

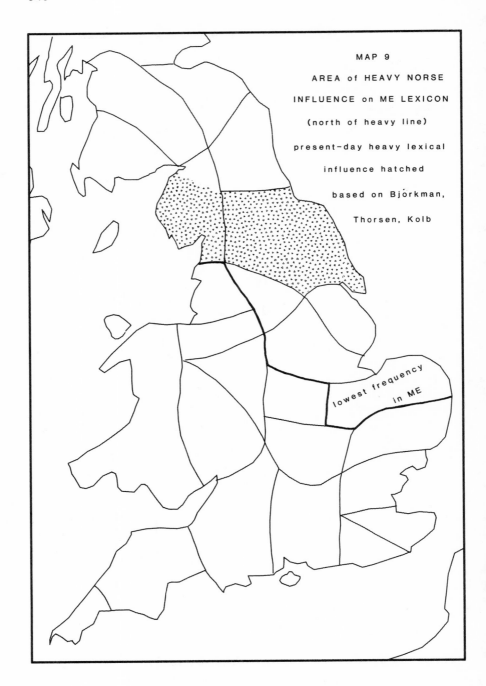

MAP 9

AREA of HEAVY NORSE

INFLUENCE on ME LEXICON

(north of heavy line)

present–day heavy lexical

influence hatched

based on Bjórkman,

Thorsen, Kolb

lowest frequency in ME

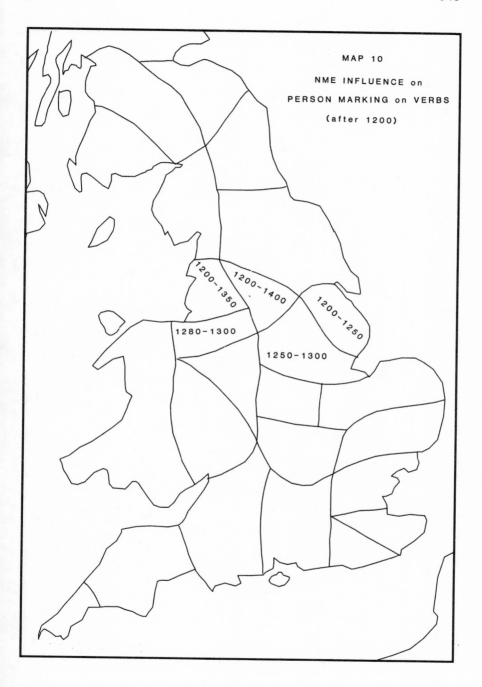

MAP 10

NME INFLUENCE on

PERSON MARKING on VERBS

(after 1200)

1200-1350

1200-1400

1200-1250

1280-1300

1250-1300

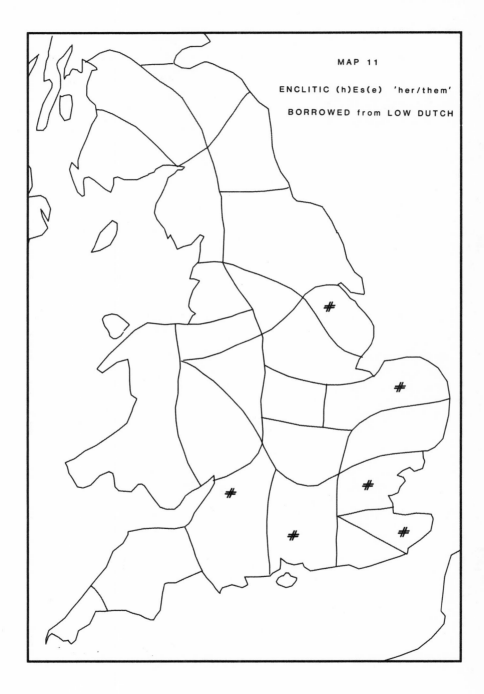

Notes

1: INTRODUCTION

1. We should emphasize that we are not the only linguists to adopt Boas' position on this issue. We first noticed the quote from Boas 1917 in Haas (1966:102), where it is also given as an indication of how things should be done; and see Goddard (1975) and Campbell & Mithun (1979). In fact, as we argue below, proper application of the Comparative Method has always demanded the establishment of such correspondences.

2. This generalization is, of course, a considerable oversimplification of the facts, as the evidence presented over the years by dialectologists, and more recently by scholars such as Labov (on ongoing sound change) and Wang (on lexical diffusion), attests. Labov (1981) provides a useful review of the Neogrammarian controversy—the hundred-year argument about the Neogrammarian hypothesis that sound change is regular. Our main reason for giving only the traditional generalization here is that our focus is on retrospective interpretation of the results of language change, and we believe that both kinds of sound change—phonetically gradual + lexically abrupt, and phonetically abrupt + lexically gradual—usually result, in the end, in regular change. (But cf., e.g., Wang 1977 on lexical diffusion.)

Several types of exceptions have been identified by the scholars just mentioned. A lesser-known class of exceptions occurs in what might be called, from a retrospective viewpoint, "minor sound changes," which have an analogic motivation of exactly the same sort as analogic changes in morphology and syntax. Romance languages seem to be particularly notorious for having irregular sound changes; Malkiel (1976) gives a thorough and insightful analysis of two such changes in Spanish, monophthongizations originating in diminutive suffixes and other morpheme classes. We suspect that markedness plays an important role in determining the fate of sound changes triggered by analogic associations: it may well be that many regular changes are initiated in this way and sweep through the entire language because they increase the naturalness of the system in some way. Certainly markedness plays just such a role, under appropriate social circumstances, in determining the fate of contact-induced sound and other changes, as we will argue in chapter 3.2.

3. Whinnom (1971) also argues that pidgins and creoles should not be classified genetically. Our reasoning differs from his, however, and we disagree with some of his conclusions. He does not emphasize normal transmission, and, in fact, his elaborate biological analogy is fundamentally asocial and therefore cannot (in our opinion) be taken as a realistic model of what goes on in language change or in pidgin/creole genesis.

2. THE FAILURE OF LINGUISTIC CONSTRAINTS

1. This section and the next are a revised and expanded version of the first part of a paper entitled "Are there linguistic prerequisites for contact-induced language change?", written by Thomason for the Tenth Annual University of Wisconsin-Milwaukee Linguistics Symposium: Language Contact, Milwaukee, 1981.

2. A constraint recently proposed by Bickerton (1980) also seems to fall into this general category, although Bickerton's formulation and supporting examples are not clear enough to make the classification certain. Bickerton distinguishes between "spontaneous" and "nonspontaneous" change, a distinction that is, as Hymes (1980: 400–401) suggests, fuzzy: "in spontaneous change, an already existing form or structure acquires a new meaning, function or distribution. In decreolization [a special case of non-spontaneous change], an already existing function or meaning acquires a new form or structure" (Bickerton 1980:113). Bickerton says that further research will be necessary to show whether or not the decreolization case is applicable to all nonspontaneous (i.e., contact-induced) change. But his distinction is surely invalid both for "spontaneous" and for decreolization changes. First, new structures and forms arise through various mechanisms, for example sound change and analogy, in internally motivated language change. Second, as the examples below show, contact-induced change does frequently lead directly to the emergence of new functions and meanings, so even if his characterization were true of decreolization, it could not be generalized to all externally motivated change. But it cannot be true that all decreolization involves new structures for old functions, because that would mean, as Thomason (1982:482) has observed, either that complete decreolization is an impossibility, or that a creole in continuum has always shared all its functions and meanings with its vocabulary-base language. Neither alternative is attractive, given the large numbers of non-European grammatical features in, for instance, the Caribbean creoles (some of them identified by Bickerton himself) and the current state of Black English, with its at least partially creole origin. For further discussion of Bickerton's generalizations about decreolization, see chapter 4.3.

3. Smith (1977) emphasizes that this feature of Sri Lanka Portuguese Creole, like its new phonemic vowel length distinctions, is a result of convergence **after** the original period of creolization, and not a product of the creolization process itself.

4. A typical objection to this interpretation is Heath's argument (1978:60 et passim), with respect to his Australian data, that "what is diffused is a surface pronunciation pattern, not a rule as such." On this point we agree emphatically with Campbell (1976:185). Campbell comments that he has heard the objection, to claims of rule borrowing, that "what is borrowed is not really a rule, but merely a phonetic

constraint or habit akin to . . . borrowed segments . . . , borrowed only in phonetically determined positions. This, however, begs the question, how is a rule to be defined?". Campbell adds that the argument on this point is "more terminological than substantive" and that, in any case, the demonstrable transfer of morphophonemic alternations should settle the question.

5. Like many other pidgin/creole specialists, Mühlhäusler confines his predictions about contact-induced changes to pidgins, as if pidgins (and perhaps also creoles) will be different from other languages in their behavior in this domain. We will argue that fully crystallized pidgin and creole languages are **not** unique in their ways of changing, but that they fit in general into ordinary patterns of development, both internally and externally motivated. (We do not, however, agree with the rather common view that the crystallization of a pidgin or creole is just like ordinary language change, only faster. This point is discussed further in chaps. 6 and 7.)

6. The exception is the devoicing of final obstruents, which is common in the Asia Minor dialects and which Dawkins attributes to Turkish influence. Word-final stops are devoiced also in the dialect of Saranda Ekklisies in eastern Thrace (Newton 1972:103, citing Psaltis 1905). Many Greek dialects lack final obstruents entirely, but the northern dialects, like the Asia Minor Greek dialects, have them as a result of such processes as the loss of unstressed word-final high vowels.

7. Dawkins's Asia Minor Greek data and the Dravidian-to-Indic inflectional changes discussed earlier in this section also refute Winter's assertion that "there are no data of an incontrovertible nature within the group of Indo-European languages that would prove the transfer of morphological features that form part of grammatical paradigms" (1973:144).

8. Bailey does, in fact, include numerous hedges with his $\overset{>}{m} > \overset{<}{m}$ prediction (see especially 1977:11–19). But he offers so many ways of accounting for changes that appear to be exceptions to his basic prediction that it is not clear to us what, if anything, would count as a genuine counterexample for him. Our doubts on this point are heightened by several vague and (in our opinion) methodologically unsound aspects of his approach. Here are some examples. Bailey appeals to unidentified substrata to explain away exceptions that don't fit into any of his fourteen "higher-level unmarking" processes (e.g., 1977:46–7; in 5.1 we discuss methodological problems in the identification of substrata). He does not define "higher-level unmarking process" precisely; for instance, he does not justify his apparent assumption (1977:16, in a discussion of polarization) that perceptual ease produces a "higher-level unmarking" than articulatory ease. He asserts that "it is now believed that languages do not have enough inner resources to adapt to every new circumstance: their resources must be supplemented by borrowing" (1980:7)—but he does not say who (besides him) believes this, or, more importantly, **why** anyone believes it. He says that "it is only drift towards synthetic formations which is the natural one, and drift towards analytic constructions that results from contact" (1977:20). But he offers no evidence at all to support this claim. This aspect of many of his recent writings—that is, much theory accompanied by little empirical evidence (Bailey 1973 is a notable exception)— is troubling in view of the fact that counterexamples are rather easy to find. To give just one example, he believes that the presence of /θ/ implies the presence of /f/, because [θ] "changes to [f] in various languages" (1977:35). But several Amerindian

languages of the Pacific Northwest (among them the Athabaskan languages Chasta Costa and Chipewyan, and the Coast Salishan languages Halkomelem and Comox) have /θ/ although, like many other languages in the area, they are notoriously labial-poor and, in particular, lack /f/. (These languages cannot all have acquired /θ/ from neighboring languages that do have /f/ as well as /θ/, because /f/ was apparently virtually nonexistent in the region until English and French speakers arrived.) See chapter 9.8 for a detailed criticism of aspects of Bailey's theory as represented in Bailey & Maroldt (1977).

9. Bickerton observes in this connection that "SVO languages cannot borrow a set of postpositions, to take an extreme and obvious case" (1981:50). Actually, "extreme cases" of this general type are common enough, and we have at least one example that fits his hypothetical situation almost exactly: according to Sapir, Upper Chinook has acquired postpositions from neighboring Sahaptin languages (1921:206); and Chinook is VSO, so we would expect it to have prepositions, but not postpositions.

10. The difficulty with Lovins's arguments arises also with Hyman's, which we have discussed elsewhere (Thomason & Kaufman 1976). Hyman's argument does not, however, emphasize naturalness per se.

11. The data in Table 1 are from Menovščikov (1969:122), and the sociolinguistic distinction just described is based on his account.

Parallel situations can be found elsewhere. Compare, for instance, Bonvillain's observation (1978:32) about borrowings in Akwesasne Mohawk from French and English: " . . . the early loan words replace the European labials /p, b, m, f, and v/ with indigenous Mohawk nonlabials. Later loan words incorporate the foreign labials without phonemic modification." (In this case the early loanwords are from French, while later loanwords are from English; but the two European languages have the same inventory of labial phonemes.)

3: A FRAMEWORK FOR CONTACT-INDUCED CHANGE

1. "The ability of the so-called 'homogeneous' languages to receive borrowings (common words of Europe) depends **not** on the linguistic structure of the language, but on the politico-social position of the speakers."

2. "In our opinion, this question does not depend on the character of the grammatical structure of the languages in contact, but on a series of factors of a social nature. . . . "

3. Sometimes, as in the case of Ma'a, the entire borrowing-language population will be bilingual in the source language. But sometimes not. In the case of Asia Minor Greek, all the men in some Greek villages spoke Turkish, but not the women (9.1). In Arnhem Land, Australia, a wife from a different clan would join her husband's clan, but her son would have to learn her clan's language, for ritual purposes, as well as the language of his own clan (Heath 1978:19). We disagree, therefore, with Nadkarni's claim that universal bilingualism among borrowing-language speakers is necessary before structural borrowing can occur (1975:681); there are counterexamples.

4. This case represents an intermediate stage in a process of language shift. The interference from any group's L_1 in their L_2 will be of the same type regardless of whether or not the group gives up their original L_1. So the label "interference through shift" is in a sense misleading; it is the imperfect learning that is criterial, not the social fact of shift from L_1 to L_2. From the historical linguist's perspective, however, a group's SECOND language normally poses no problems for historical interpretation; hence our use of the phrase "interference through shift."

5. It should be noted that Deshpande (1979) has argued that the time period relevant for consideration of Dravidian substratum influence on Indic is later than previous authors have thought—namely, **after** the time at which the Rigveda was originally composed. On his theory, features like retroflexion were not present in the original oral version of the Rigveda, but were introduced later, through oral transmission of the text.

6. "Contrary to current opinion, the pressure that a language exerts on the phonological structure of another language does not necessarily presuppose political, social, or cultural dominance of the nation speaking the first language."

7. This is true more for flexional than for agglutinative morphology, however. In this context, note Heath's observation (personal communication, 1985) that "several of the [Arnhem Land] language pairs have very similar typological structure, yet the morphological borrowings appear to be limited to particular types of affix." Heath's comment suggests that close matching of categories will not always be a crucial factor in the diffusion of linguistic features.

8. There are also some aspects of Heath's proposal that we disagree with. First, he lists a number of morphosyntactic features that he claims as "nondiffusable": independent pronouns, bound pronominals, verbal inflectional affixes, demonstrative stems, and demonstrative adverbs (1978:105). It is not entirely clear from the context, but he seems to be hypothesizing that these features are nondiffusable in general—rather than merely nondiffused among the Arnhem Land languages he has studied. We have counterexamples to the general hypothesis for every feature he lists. For instance, Flathead has borrowed a first person plural pronoun from Kutenai; Mednyj Aleut has borrowed verbal inflectional suffixes from Russian; and English borrowed a third person pronoun from Norse. Other examples can be found throughout this book.

Our second disagreement with Heath has to do with his view that his study "suggests what kinds of diffusion are possible when linguistic structural (and functional) factors are primary" (1978:143), as opposed to cases like Kupwar (Gumperz & Wilson 1971), in which social factors are primary. It is true that in Heath's Arnhem Land case the situation looks like a classic Sprachbund, with bi- and multilingualism among most speakers and mutual (rather than clear one-way) interference. Nevertheless, we would argue that the fact that specific social pressures are complex or even undiscoverable does not make them irrelevant.

9. This proposal partly resembles Heath's suggestion (1978:124) that a claim of indirect diffusion is strengthened when a whole series of changes can be attributed to foreign interference; he makes a similar point in 1981:335.

One reason for insisting on the presence of changes in different grammatical subsystems is that we need to be wary of chain reactions. Twenty-five years ago, for instance, changes from VSO, NA, and NG word order with prepositions to SOV, AN, and GN word order with postpositions would have been considered a series of independent changes; nowadays, many linguists would consider these changes as interconnected in such a way that whichever one occurred first, the others would be likely to follow. So the whole set would only count as one change as far as the initial cause is concerned.

10. Another criterion that is sometimes invoked is expressed by Lightfoot (1979:382): in order to prove that external influence produced a given syntactic change, he argues, one must prove that "the innovating forms were first used by bilingual speakers." Insistence on this criterion would of course make it impossible to consider external causation for the vast majority of all completed syntactic (and other) changes. But such a narrow restriction is unnecessary if our criterion is adopted, because our approach offers a unified explanation for a variety of changes in each case.

4: LANGUAGE MAINTENANCE

1. The reader should keep in mind that few or none of the authors quoted in this chapter distinguish borrowing in our narrow sense from interference through shift. As we argued above, tendencies in borrowing proper do not always hold for interference through shift. Aside from the linguistic differences, there are important social differences between the two processes—including differences in the level of bilingualism within the group that introduces the interference features. Specifically, shifting speakers who introduce interference features typically do not speak the target language fully, but in pure borrowing situations the speakers who introduce the interference features are native speakers of the borrowing language—and are at least reasonably bilingual in the language the features come from. Although the authors we cite are generally using the term "borrowing" to include all kinds of interference, we discuss their comments here only with reference to borrowing in our narrower sense.

2. The presence of numerous transferred grammatical morphemes makes borrowing somewhat more likely than shift, but not enough so to be very useful for prediction. See chapter 5 for more discussion on this point.

3. It is often said that many languages can't or won't borrow verbs. Meillet believed this for French, for instance, on the ground that French verbs have such an elaborate inflectional structure that it is difficult to incorporate foreign verbs into the system (1921b:84, cited by Vildomec, 1971:100). But Weinreich (1953:36–37), pointing out that most languages with much verb inflection have means of converting words into verbs, remarks—cogently, in our opinion—that the reason for the predominance of nouns over verbs in loanword lists is "probably of a lexical-semantic, rather than a grammatical and structural nature." (He also gives examples of verb borrowing in this passage.) We find Moravcsik's proposed constraint against borrowing single-morpheme verbs as verbs (1975:4) labored (and also, surely, false for borrowing between languages **without** any verb morphology).

Here are some examples, to add to Weinreich's, of verb-borrowing and mechanisms. Mayan languages are indeed inhospitable to the borrowing of verbs as verbs, for the reason Meillet gave. But they have two devices for borrowing Spanish verbs. The more common one is to borrow a Spanish infinitive (which is a noun) as such and use a Mayan verb meaning 'do' as an auxiliary, thus creating a syntactic verb phrase functioning as a lexeme. The other is to borrow the infinitive and add a verb-forming suffix (N $\rightarrow$ tv). Both of these devices are very common in borrowing languages. The former is also used, for instance, in Persian borrowings from Arabic (Heath 1978:119–120, citing Telegdi 1973) and American Greek (Moravcsik 1975); the latter is used in, for example, German borrowings from French and Russian borrowings from various languages.

4. This borrowing scale is a revised version of a scale originally presented in Thomason & Kaufman 1975. Though there is some overlap with the borrowing constraints proposed by Moravcsik (1978)—such as in our claim that derivational affixes are more easily borrowed than inflectional affixes—we have not found her approach generally useful for our purposes. We have counterexamples to most of her constraints. The typological basis of our hierarchy also differentiates our approach from hers; moreover, while we try to develop a hierarchical scale, her constraints are atomistic.

5. It should be noted that American and British English speakers differ in the extent to which they nativize Modern French loanwords: the British anglicize the stress placement on words like *ballet* and *pâté*, shifting the stress to the word-initial syllable, while Americans—as in category (2) borrowing—tend to retain the final stress.

6. Sometimes grammarians can even successfully impose invented features. Oksaar (1972:491) gives the following example: "The innovations of the Estonian language reformer Aavik are proof that arbitrarily coined new derivational and inflectional morphemes and new grammemes—such as the synthetic superlative—can be wholly accepted by the language users and . . . incorporated into the language."

7. Both these German examples, and others in this chapter, are clearly related to the kinds of synchronic language mixing that Pfaff (1979) found in Spanish/English bilinguals' speech. Her argument that "surface structures common to both languages are favored" (315) is intimately connected with our diachronic predictions based on typological distance. See chapter 6 for discussion of the importance of her findings for a theory of creole genesis.

8. Kupwar Kannaḍa apparently has an inclusive/exclusive 'we' distinction, while other dialects of Kannaḍa do not. However, since Standard Kannaḍa has lost this typically Dravidian category, we do not know whether its presence in the Kupwar dialect is due to retention or to borrowing from Marathi.

9. This hybrid construction with double comparative marking is reminiscent of the occasional hybrid plural form in Ma'a, with double plural marking—both a borrowed Bantu plural/noun-class prefix and a native Cushitic plural (or collective) suffix. As noted in Thomason (1983b:209), double marking of this sort may suggest one mechanism for the replacement of native patterns by borrowed ones. Another example is the optional double marking of coordinate noun phrases in Asiatic

Eskimo, a combination of the native comitative suffix and a conjunction borrowed from Chukchi (see 3.2 for sample sentences). Unfortunately, we have few other examples of this type; but a search for further examples might be fruitful.

10. In fact, Bickerton's examples must reflect imperfect learning of the vocabulary-base language, because they are typical of the sorts of changes that arise through language shift. Compare, for instance, the very close analogues in the examples from lexical semantics given in chapter 6. This suggests that decreolization (not surprisingly) is a complex combination of shift and borrowing. That is, some changes involve acquisition of acrolectal vocabulary, including function words, as basilectal speakers (attempt to) shift to the acrolect; these include Bickerton's "new forms first" examples. But if decreolization is going on, there must be structural convergence as well, and it must be initiated by bilingual speakers—speakers who actually know the source-language structures and borrow some of them, with or without the forms that express them. (In using the terms "acrolectal" and 'basilectal', we are of course oversimplifying the actual social and linguistic situation, which is in many cases a continuum. But the shift and borrowing aspects of the changing situation should be essentially the same for a continuum.)

We should note, incidentally, that Bickerton's 1981 formulation of this proposal differs significantly, in its implications, from his 1980 proposal about "spontaneous" vs. "non-spontaneous"—specifically decreolizing—linguistic change (see chap. 2, n. 2 for a discussion of the earlier proposal). If his 1980 and 1981 versions are in fact supposed to be compatible (this is not clear from the 1981 exposition), then Bickerton seems to be suggesting that the later acquisition of new functions by a diffused morpheme, in a decreolizing creole, is a case of **spontaneous**, i.e., internally-motivated, change. But this would not account for the fact that such changes demonstrably represent convergence toward the superstrate language, in the decreolization case.

5: LANGUAGE SHIFT WITH NORMAL TRANSMISSION

1. Compare a comment made by Emeneau (1980 [1962]:60–61): " . . . the only really valid evidence [of structural interference] is that derived from bilingual situations in which the languages on both sides are well known. It will not do to deal in substrata that have long vanished entirely from our control. That way lie uncontrolled hypotheses, alias guesses, and the mysticism of so many substratum theories." We agree with Emeneau, but we would stress that the two languages may be well known indirectly rather than directly. That is, it is possible to find out about the structure of a long-vanished undocumented substratum language by studying its surviving relatives and/or its reconstructed parent language, and by similar means to get information about the pre-shift structure of the target language.

2. This tendency in cases of shift is occasionally noted in the literature. Moreno (1948, quoted in Hetzron 1975:109), for instance, observes of Cushitic-influenced Ethiopic Semitic that "Semitici i materiali, ma cuscita l'artefice."

The distinction between diffused structure with diffused morphemes and diffused structure expressed by native morphemes in the recipient language corresponds to Heath's (1978) distinction between direct and indirect diffusion. We do not adopt Heath's terminology here because the two mechanisms strike us as equally direct.

3. Our evidence does not support Mühlhäusler's (1980:36) more extensive differentiation between substratum and superstratum interference (although, since he does not distinguish between borrowing and shift situations, his classification may not refer exclusively to shift situations). In particular, though his emphasis on "lexical form" in superstratum interference matches our distinction here, we do not agree that superstrata contribute more segmental phonemes than substrata do, or that substrata are more likely to contribute prosodic features, semantics, and lexical semantics.

4. But since Old French had a verb-second rule, which was later replaced by an SVO pattern in Modern Standard French, there may be chronological problems in attributing the SVO word order of English even partly to Old French influence. An added complication is that the old Germanic verb-second trait persists in some modern Germanic languages, including Scandinavian ones, and even Modern English preserves a few of the construction types, for example *here comes John, there goes Bill,* and *then came spring.*

5. We could of course say more about the probability of structural borrowing by (original) native speakers of Semitic directly from Cushitic if we had information about the extent to which Semitic invaders were bilingual in Cushitic languages: if they were not bilingual, then they cannot have borrowed structure from Cushitic. It is much too late to get such information about the earliest period of contact, but since Semitic and Cushitic speakers are still in contact in parts of Ethiopia, it would be helpful to know who speaks which language(s) now in the area. We could then perhaps draw tentative conclusions abut earlier periods.

6. It has also been suggested that Burushaski is the remnant of a very ancient widespread linguistic substratum that could have influenced Proto-Indic, at least. Such a substratum could conceivably have contributed the retroflex series to both Proto-Dravidian and Proto-Indic. But, though there is historical evidence of a Burushaski presence outside the Karakoram (Grierson 1927, I:192), there is no linguistic evidence about the age of these features in Burushaski. So the present chances for establishing any nonlexical Burushaski interference outside the Karakoram are nil.

7. Most scholars consider the Dardic languages to be a subgroup of Indic, but some claim Dardic as a third branch of Indo-Iranian, coordinate with Indic and Iranian.

8. This is especially true given Hock's idiosyncratic definition of the phrase "beyond a reasonable doubt." A circumstantial case (i.e., an external explanation), he says (1984), "should be established in the same manner as circumstantial cases in a court of justice . . . [i.e.] *beyond a reasonable doubt.* That is, in each case it ought to be established that the nature of the evidence is such that it precludes any interpretation other than the one advocated." In U.S. law, at least, this is too high a standard of proof for "beyond a reasonable doubt."

6: SHIFT WITHOUT NORMAL TRANSMISSION: ABRUPT CREOLIZATION

1. The Arabic-based creole Ki-Nubi may also belong in this category. However, though Ki-Nubi differs structurally from the Arabic-based pidgin spoken near the region from which the original Ki-Nubi speakers came, the creole is likely to have historical links to the pidgin.

We do not include Hawaiian Creole here, because in this case (*pace* Bickerton 1981) there is considerable evidence for a pre-existing pidgin; see Goodman (1985:110ff.) for discussion.

2. The traditional view is still held by some, possibly most, scholars. It seems popular, for instance, among specialists in second language acquisition who take their departure from Schumann's pidginization hypothesis (e.g., 1978)—apparently on the assumption that you have to pidginize (i.e., simplify, in their view) the TL completely before you can creolize (expand) it. Note, for instance, R. Andersen's assertion (1980:292–293), presented without argument or evidence: "Only a fully pidginized (individually and probably group-pidginized) second language will do for true creolization to take place."

3. This is true, of course, even if the slaves shifted to an already existing pidgin with a European vocabulary base. But in that case the historical picture would look quite different; there would be no question of language genesis in the new slave communities, only (at most) of relexification and nativization.

4. It is doubtful, in fact, that we can reasonably speak of a true target language under these circumstances. Still, the European language in a given community would be the closest thing to a TL that was available.

5. This is another oversimplification: sometimes shifting speakers may, for all we know, be quite aware that the TL has certain features, but they may decide not to follow the lead of original TL speakers.

6. But this is neither a case of creolization nor a case involving shift, to judge by the sociohistorical and linguistic evidence presented by Gumperz & Wilson. It looks, rather, like a case of moderate to heavy borrowing interference, for each language. See chapter 4.3.1 for discussion.

7. Kwa and Bantu languages are probably no more similar typologically than the Niger-Congo mixtures in other creole contexts. But, as Ferraz's examples show, the Bantu segment of the substrate population was strong enough in the Gulf of Guinea settings to contribute some marked Bantu features to the developing creoles.

8. The term "substratomaniac" actually comes from Hall (1966:108), as John Holm (personal communication, 1984) reminded us. Hall says that "'substrato-maniacs' see the influence of linguistic substrata everywhere, and ascribe virtually every linguistic change to one substratum or another, whether anything is known about the presumed substratum or not; 'substratophobes' deny such influence in almost all instances. . . . " It is worth noting that Bickerton never refers to the "substratophobe" segment of the sentence. It is also worth noting that Hall's immediate reference is not to pidgin/creole genesis, but to discussions of language change, and his "substratomaniacs" are the people who—as we pointed out in

chapter 5—gave substratum explanations a bad name in historical linguistics. No one in pidgin/creole studies (*pace* Bickerton) belongs in that group, however.

9. Actually, Bickerton states his position in two fundamentally different forms. In his 1981 book and in most of his other writings, he presents the bioprogram (or simply, in the earlier writings, universal structural tendencies) as **the** basis for the early-creolizing creole grammar. This is the strong version of his position, and the one criticized here. But in at least one place (Bickerton 1977:64–65) he says that "the central argument of natural semantax" is the proposition that "there can be rules of language that are not derived from any linguistic input." This, of course, is a much weaker claim, and we do not dispute it—though trying to account for such phenomena by reference to universal structural tendencies based on markedness considerations strikes us as a much more promising enterprise than Bickerton's later appeal to genetic programming for which direct evidence is unavailable.

10. Corne attributes the other feature he discusses, reduplicated distributive numerals, to Indic substratum influence. But since Indic speakers did not arrive on Mauritius until after 1835, i.e., after the creole was fully crystallized, this influence would be ordinary interference through shift, and not due to creolization *per se*. That is: the Indic contribution to the dialect of Isle de France Creole spoken on Mauritius constituted contact-induced change in an already existing language and did not belong to the process of creolization itself.

7: PIDGINS

1. We should note here that there are difficulties with using lack of mutual intelligibility as a criterion for deciding when one is dealing with dialects of one language and when with separate languages; and these difficulties will carry over to the problem of deciding when a speech form is to be considered an independent pidgin language. One major problem is that mutual intelligibility may be asymmetrical: speakers of A may have trouble understanding speakers of B, but not vice versa. This is said to be the case, for instance, with Swedish (A) and Danish (B). Another problem is that attitudes affect the extent to which speakers of a dialect or language A understand a language or dialect B. A third difficulty (but one that is often not relevant to the pidgin situation) is that there is no sharp historical dividing line between "intelligible" and "nonintelligible"—indeed, there can't possibly be, since the process of normal language split is gradual.

2. However, Bickerton's picture of Hawaiian Pidgin English is almost certainly wrong; see Goodman (1985:110–114). In particular, as Goodman notes, Hawaiian Pidgin English has a longer history than Bickerton assumes for it, and "it is very doubtful that the speech of B's informants is a reliable guide either to the form of the pidgin out of which Hawaiian Creole English evolved or **even to the degree of homogeneity which it exhibited**" (112–114; emphasis ours).

3. Even though pidgin genesis often involves no social distinction between "substrate" and "superstrate" speaker groups, we will use the term "substrate" throughout this chapter to refer to (potential) source languages other than the pidgin's

vocabulary-base language. This usage is a convenience only; we intend no social implications. Similarly, we use the terms "lexical source language" and "vocabulary-base language" throughout this chapter, even for pidgins whose vocabularies are drawn from several languages—notably Chinook Jargon.

4. This view is in apparent conflict with his earlier position (in Bickerton & Givón 1976), cited above, though as far as we know Bickerton has not repudiated the earlier proposal. It may be that he has in mind a distinction between the group's norm (nouns and verbs only) and the individual's behavior (relexification of native-language structures), but even so we cannot reconcile the two claims; if individual relexifications are claimed to be confined to nouns and verbs strung together, the data presented by Bickerton himself and by Nagara on Hawaiian Pidgin English does not fit the hypothesis. In any case, as we will argue below, the evidence of **attested** pidgin structures in various parts of the world does not support the nouns-and-verbs-only claim, and the evidence of individuals' behavior in contact situations does not support any general version of the relexification claim.

5. We are skeptical, however, of Naro's claim (1978) that Portuguese teachers taught captive Africans a pidginized form of Portuguese in the early mid fifteenth century, in Portugal. According to Naro, this happened when Prince Henry ordered captured Africans to be trained as interpreters in order to facilitate Portuguese trade in Africa, and the practice is documented as early as 1435—that is, thirty to forty years before there is any evidence of "Portuguese" spoken in Africa. Naro says that the captive Africans had little or no contact with other Africans in Portugal, but that as more and more captives arrived knowledge of the incipient pidgin spread **among the Portuguese** in Portugal. Eventually, he says, it was transplanted into Africa (ca. 1476) by the Portuguese lançados, who settled in African towns and set up households with African women there.

We do not doubt Naro's documentary evidence, but the scenario he proposes seems to us to be very implausible sociolinguistically. If Prince Henry ordered that the captive prospective interpreters be taught Portuguese, and if (as Naro suggests) the teachers were educated people and the Africans isolated from one another, then it seems likely that the Africans would in fact have learned Portuguese, not (only) foreigner-talk Portuguese. Passages in literary texts that show pidgin-like features might simply represent the Africans' (temporary?) imperfect learning of Portuguese rather than the result of a deliberate teaching strategy. And it is hard to imagine that uneducated people learned an incipient Portuguese pidgin *en masse* and took it to Africa with them. It is, in fact, easier to imagine that what the lançados took with them to Africa was Portuguese, and that the Portuguese/African households were the birthplace of the pidgin—together with the Portuguese traders' ships, with their polyglot crews. Similarities between earlier literary renditions of Africans' imperfect speech and later attestations of "Portuguese" in Africa could be accounted for by the fact that, as we argue here, imperfect learning of a TL and pidgin genesis are in many ways similar in their linguistic results.

6. This claim rests on his theory of developmental linguistics, in which he follows Bailey. In note 8 to chapter 2 we give some reasons for our skepticism about the general theory.

7. Mühlhäusler (1980:34) suggests that Hiri Motu is "a partial relexification of Papuan Pidgin English rather than a genuine indigenous lingua franca." But, though its spread was encouraged during the colonial period by the first governor, Sir Hubert Murray (because he hated Tok Pisin), the origin of Hiri Motu seems more likely to lie in the ancient Motu tradition of the *hiri* trading expeditions, as described by Dutton (1983). Dutton describes two other trading pidgins used by the Motu and NAN trading partners; these pidgins lack some of the more striking features of Hiri Motu itself. This might indicate that several different pidgins arose in the course of Motu trade and/or that Hiri Motu has changed since it first crystallized. Or, perhaps most likely, it might indicate that the other two speech forms never became fully crystallized pidgin languages. In any case, Hiri Motu can hardly be viewed as a relexification of Papuan Pidgin English unless it is grammatically identical to the English-based pidgin.

8. It is not clear, however, how unlikely a combination of SOV with NA order actually is. Sumerian and Akkadian were both SOV and NA (the latter perhaps because of influence from the former); so is Persian. Classical Latin was an SOV language with NA and AN orders in about equal frequency.

9. The Papua New Guinea government's *Dictionary and grammar of Hiri Motu* (1976:18) gives the following example: *inai mero boroma badana ia alaia* (literally 'this boy pig big + adj.sg. 3.sg.subj. kill + tr.sg.') can mean either 'This boy killed a big pig' or 'A big pig killed this boy'. The grammar goes on to explain that one can disambiguate the sentence by adding the optional agent/subject marker *ese* after *mero* for the first reading or after *badana* for the second reading.

10. This situation lasted until the late nineteenth century when, according to Lehiste, "a period of intense Russification set in; Russian became the language of the schools. The social conditions changed so that the servants and the lower middle class in the towns did not feel the same need to acquire German at any cost. Education became more widespread among all classes; more importantly, there was a tremendous increase in the number of Estonians who acquired a university education, and a corresponding rise of an Estonian-speaking upper middle (professional) class. The conditions for the use of Halbdeutsch simply weren't there any more" (personal communication, 1975). Accordingly, Halbdeutsch vanished.

8: RETROSPECTION

1. The results of (5) and (6) in turn permit the construction of a family tree diagram. But of course no two-dimensional diagram of the diversification of a family of languages can be adequate as an account of the ways in which the languages are mutually related. A family tree diagram can only be an abbreviation, with certain necessary oversimplifications, of a fully elaborated theory of diversification. Among other complications, any family tree diagram ignores the results of waves of changes in a long-settled dialect complex; see, for instance, Krauss's discussion (1976 [1973]) of difficulties in establishing a conventional family tree for Athabaskan languages.

2. See Mithun & Campbell (1982) for a good discussion of some of the problems involved in carrying out syntactic reconstruction.

3. We are assuming, of course, that the third main possible source of shared features—chance—can be ruled out. This is not a trivial problem; the methodology involves considerations of universal markedness. Chance is the only source of shared features that does **not** signal a historical link between the languages. (We have not mentioned drift; like direct inheritance from a common ancestor language, it occurs in the course of normal transmission.)

9: CASE STUDIES

1. These three villages illustrate three different sociolinguistic settings of Asia Minor Greek. Dawkins records 2000 Christians and 800 Moslems for Malakopí. Many of the village's male inhabitants commuted to work in Istanbul, which increases the tendency toward efficient bilingualism and, as a result, Turkish interference in the locak Greek. However, Malakopí possessed a flourishing Greek school, a circumstance that put the local dialect under pressure from Common Greek and at the same time retarded its incorporation of Turkish elements (24).

By contrast, the dialect of Phloïta, a village with 1500 Christians and 650 Moslems, was in no danger from Common Greek, because its school was not so efficient as that of Malakopí (25). The school would therefore also offer no effective hindrance to the borrowing of Turkish features into the local dialect.

The smallest of the three villages, Ulaghátsh, had 1000 Christians and 250 Moslems in 1905. This is the official count, but Dawkins comments that there must be more Turkish speakers than the religious figures would suggest, given the extreme turkicization of the local Greek. Greek, he believed, would soon vanish as a vernacular from the local scene; he even heard Greek women speaking Turkish to their children. The dialect's lexicon is filled with Turkish, and its syntax is more turkicized than that of any other dialect he studied (18). Significantly, there is no mention of a local Greek school here.

2. In 1899, 1800 Christians and 400 Moslems lived in Semenderé; in 1905, there were 1300 Christians and 700 Moslems. Like the Ulaghátsh dialect, the Greek dialect of Semenderé was rapidly dying out when Dawkins studied it (18).

3. Ferték, in 1895, had 2700 Christian and 300 Moslem inhabitants; in 1910 it had 1100 Christians and 2000 Moslems. The men of Ferték commuted to work in Istanbul and generally spoke Turkish among themselves. They also knew Common Greek and understood, but (according to Dawkins) did not speak fluently, the local dialect. The use of the dialect was therefore almost entirely confined to women and children. But since Turkish women frequently entered Greek households to do housework, the Greek women generally spoke Turkish too, among themselves as well as to their husbands (14).

4. References to our data sources are given in the article. This study (like the article it is based on) owes a considerable debt to Christopher Ehret, who generously provided substantive and bibliographical help, as well as useful critical comments on an early draft of Thomason 1983b. We should also mention another source which

(though we have not used it) provides valuable further Ma'a data and further comparisons with Bantu: this is an unpublished 1977 paper by Derek Nurse, entitled "Ma'a/Mbughu." Nurse's analysis partly overlaps with Thomason's, but the two are independent of each other: Thomason 1983*b* is an elaboration of a case study written for Thomason & Kaufman 1975, and we received a copy of Nurse's paper only in 1983, when Thomason 1983*b* was already in press. Nurse's paper is particularly interesting for its more extensive syntactic data and details on Ma'a morphophonemics.

5. We have, however, found one case reported in the literature that is not covered in this analysis. This is the Media Lengua described by Muysken (1981). He identifies it as an Amerindian contact language spoken in the Ecuadorian Highlands, with almost 90 percent Spanish vocabulary and Quechua grammar. His analysis is based on a recording of four hours of conversation with five speakers, three of them (according to Muysken) native speakers of the Media Lengua. Muysken argues that the process by which this language arose was relexification—that is, borrowing of almost the entire Spanish lexicon, including (to judge from his examples) numerous grammatical morphemes. We don't know what to make of this case; it resembles nothing we have encountered elsewhere. Our efforts to find more data and more analyses have so far proved fruitless. Muysken's own analysis raises some questions that he does not answer, particularly about the social circumstances in which the language is used and about the degree of difference between the Quechua grammatical features of the Media Lengua and the grammatical structures of ordinary Quechua dialects. We would need to know more about the Media Lengua before we could tell how (and whether) it fits into the framework we have developed in this book.

6. We are grateful to Brian Joseph (personal communication, 1981) for bringing this example to our attention.

7. A recent collection of articles surveying the linguistic and sociolinguistic situation in the British Isles (Trudgill, ed. 1984) contains an article by J. Milroy 'The history of English in the British Isles' (pp. 5–31), that has in it a number of poorly-supported claims and outright mistakes. We discuss (in the appropriate places) those mistakes that are related to our concerns because the book as a whole is likely to be widely read and perhaps quoted. We have perhaps given this article more attention than it deserves, but it illustrates the creolist faddism that we are attempting to combat in this work.

8. On the spelling of Middle English. In order to represent ME phonology accurately we use a systematic spelling for ME that is based on the medieval practice to the extent possible and reasonable. The following symbols have values other than current linguistic ones:

c (not before i,e)	/k/
ch	/č/
dg	/ǰǰ/
gh	/h/ [γ]
j	/ǰ/
sh	/š/
th, dh	/θ/

wh	/hw/
yh > sh	/hy/ > /š/
aa	/aə/
ee	/iə/ < /e:/
oo	/uə/ or N [ü:] < /o:/
öö	/üə/ < /ö:/
ea	/eə/
oa	/oə/
Vy	/Vi/
Vw	/Vu/

The phonemes and graphemes we use for writing ME are the following:

consonants   vowels

p	t		ch	c/k
b	d		j/dg	g
f	th	s(s)	sh	h
v	dh	s/z		gh
m	n			
	l			
	r			
w			y	

i	ü	u
e	ö	o
	a	

diphthongs

ii	iu	ee
ei	eu	ea
ai	au	aa
oi	ou	oa
ui	uu	oo
üi or üü	üu	öö

The Old English orthography has been followed largely, with the following deviations: θ **k j** (yod) (**ǧ**)**ǧ č ae oe aea** are written instead of the customary ortho-graphic <*thorn* or *edh* c ġ cg ċ ae-digraph oe-digraph *ea*>; vowel length is marked by a postposed colon. The same transcription practices have been followed for writing Old/Viking Norse; however for Norse **ö** (not **oe**) and **ä** (not **ae**) are written.

9. The term **Norse** is used here to mean any of the languages and dialects of the North Germanic branch of Germanic languages. It is synonymous with "Scandina-vian," which we avoid as being latinate and polysyllabic. **Norse** here does not mean Norwegian, as it often did in writings near the turn of the 20th century. **Norseman** refers to any Norse speaker. In Viking times there were three well-defined dialects of Norse: Norwegian (=West Norse), DanoSwedish (=East Norse), and Gautish. From 700 to 1400 both the English and the Norse referred to the Norse language as "Danish," a usage we do not follow.

10. Milroy (1984:10) has the following observations on the effects of the Norman Conquest:

. . . whereas *Saxon* bishops and other leading men were rapidly replaced by Normans in many areas, the West Midlands remained less directly influ-enced . . . [emphasis ours. We have no quarrel with the content of this statement, but "Saxon" is a term that was never used of the English, except by their Welsh, Irish, and Gaelic neighbors and often enemies. "Saxon" appears only in the fiction of Walter Scott and others of his romantic ilk. The English language and people have always been called by themselves only *English*. Such terms as *Wessex* (or West Saxon), *Essex* (or East Saxon), *East Anglia*, and the like, are names of tribal subgroups of the English people and do not and never did correlate with linguistic differences in any straightforward way (Chadwick 1907:86–87) TK&SGT].

11. The ethnolinguistic regions have been established (by Kaufman, over a period of 27 years) using as data the works of Duncan (1972); Ek (1972); Ellis (1889); Glauser (1974); Jordan & Crook (1974); Kolb (1965, 1975); Kolb, Glauser, Elmer, and Stamm (1979); Kristensson (1967); Kurath (1954); Moore, Meech, and Whitehall (1935); Mosse (1952); Murray (1873); Oakden (1935); Orton, et al.: Survey of English Dialects Basic Material (1962–1968); Orton and Wright (1974); Orton, Sanderson, and Widdowson (1978); Pogatscher (1900); Ritter (1914); Rubin (1951); Samuels (1963, 1972); Serjeantson (1922, 1927a, 1927b); Sievers & Brunner (1951); Stratmann & Bradley (1891); Wright (1905); Wyld (1920, 1921); and others. Since the relevant material from the Linguistic Survey of Scotland is not yet available, no attempt has been made to define the ethnolinguistic regions of Scotland, apart from "Lothian." Though our ME sources allow us to know that by 1400 English was spoken from Berwick to Aberdeen, we do not know its total extent in Scotland at the time, nor whether Aberdeen, Perth, and Lothian had as yet distinct dialects.

The names for the ethnolinguistic regions have been chosen from any time in history when an ethnic or political entity had a distribution roughly equivalent to that established on linguistic grounds for the period 1200–1900. Thus, LOTHIAN, GALLOWAY, ELMET, STRATHCLYDE, and CUMBRIA have roughly the same shapes as the corresponding political entities of the Anglo-Saxon period, when the last two were British-(i.e., P-Keltic)speaking, and during which Elmet was annexed by Northumbria (ELMET was christened by Kolb [1975]). When a particular region contains the major part of a medieval or modern county, or all of a county plus parts of adjoining counties, that county has the honor of naming the whole region, except that if the county's name is formed by adding -*shire* to the name of the county town, only the county town's name is used as the region's name. Thus, NORTHUMBERLAND, NORFOLK, SUFFOLK, ESSEX, KENT, CORNWALL, DEVON; but LANCASTER, CHESTER, STAFFORD, LEICESTER, NORTHAMPTON. Some dialect regions correspond to parts only of medieval or modern counties, and are so named: LINDSEY (Lincolnshire), HASTINGS (Sussex). Some regions do not correspond well with any past or present political or ethnic area and have been assigned names that are suggestive but might be improved upon on discovery of an apter regional name: SOUTHMARCH, FOURBOROUGHS. The part of eastern Ireland colonized by English in the middle ages is called THE PALE. Finally, the names EAST WESSEX and WEST WESSEX have been assigned to two regions both of which formed part of the Anglo-Saxon Kingdom of Wessex, though if DEVON is considered part of Wessex, WEST WESSEX should perhaps be called MID WESSEX.

It should be noted that the precise boundaries of certain ethnolinguistic regions may be fuzzy owing to lack of documentation, but such fuzziness does not extend more than a few (3–8) miles from the line assigned on the map. Nevertheless some lines on the accompanying map (map 1) are rather approximate, especially those defining STAFFORD, LEICESTER, NORTHAMPTON, and SUFFOLK, and further research might change the courses of some of them by more than just a few miles.

12. In this part of the English case study we will quote at some length from P. H. Sawyer, *The Age of the Vikings,* 2d edition, Edward Arnold 1971. Sawyer's is the most up-to-date analysis of the archeological and historical data on the Viking raids on and settlement of parts of Britain, and will be taken as essentially the latest word for the purposes of this study. The quotes from Sawyer amount to a framework/outline of the argument we will develop with respect to Norse influence on English.

13. The following quotes from Sawyer (1971) indicate how and where the Norsemen settled in England:

The first evidence of the extent of the Danish conquests is the treaty agreed between Alfred and Guthrum, a Danish leader, possibly in 886. The boundary between their kingdoms is said to be 'Up the Thames as far as the River Lea, then up the Lea to its source, and then straight to Bedford, and then up the Ouse to Watling Street.' It seems probable that Watling Street marked the boundary for some 50 miles . . . The area to the north and east of this line was later called the Danelaw. [151] The area under Danish law, that is the area in which the law was administered by a predominantly Danish aristocracy, would tend to be much larger than the area of dense Danish settlement . . . There is, however, no evidence . . . to suggest that the customary law observed in the shire courts of Middlesex, Buckinghamshire, Hertfordshire and Bedfordshire had ever been Danish, or that these counties had ever had a Scandinavian aristocracy . . . [152] The heart of the Danelaw lay where Scandinavian settlement was densest, in Leicestershire, Lincolnshire, Nottinghamshire and Yorkshire. It is probable that in this region, between the Welland and the Tees, Scandinavians or men of Scandinavian descent ruled locally for a long time after they had accepted the West Saxon overlordship . . . [153] Attempts have been made to determine the extent and character of the Scandinavian settlements . . . with the help of place-names and archaeological evidence . . . [T]here is a large number of stone carvings which show Scandinavian influence and . . . they help our interpretation of the settlement . . . [T]he Scandinavians brought with them, and used, a distinctive stock of words and personal names which they used to describe farms and villages and features of the landscape such as hills, streams, woods and fields . . . [154] Not all the names and words are recognizably Danish or Norwegian; . . . but the differences are clear enough to show that most of the settlers in the eastern parts of England were from Denmark and that the settlers in the northwest were predominantly of Norwegian descent. The names in the north-western group have other characteristics showing that the settlers came from Celtic areas . . . [158].

[An] early group of names are the hybrids in which Scandinavian personal names are compounded with English elements . . . [T]his type of name is generally described as a 'Grimston hybrid' . . . The fact that these hybrid names are generally found on good settlement sites that were unlikely to have been left vacant by the English together with the use of English elements, strongly suggests that, as a class, these names represent an early stage of the Scandinavian colonization when the invaders were seizing the best estates they could find . . . [163–164] There are in the north of England a large number of stone carvings by English craftsmen in the English tradition in which attempts have been made to satisfy Scandinavian tastes . . . [A] few may even have been carved before the end of the ninth century . . . [163, 166] The evidence of these [stone carvings] and of the Grimston hybrids suggests that the Scandinavian conquerors first seized the best land, the already existing villages . . . [166] The survival of English place-names in the areas that were first colonized by the Scandinavians, together with the English element in the hybrid names, show that a substantial native population survived in those areas, a population that was in time to be deeply influenced by their Scandinavian masters . . . [166].

14. The major part of the data used in this section was found in the ME texts listed below (other data is found in Björkman [1900, 1902], Rynell [1948], and Thorsen [1936]):

Northern

> *Prose Rule of St Benet.* orig ca. 1250; ms ca. 1400.
> *Cursor Mundi,* orig ca. 1300; ms ca. 1330.
> Writings of School of Richard Rolle. 1350–1400.
> *Northern Passion.* orig ca. 1300; ms ca. 1350.
> Poems of Lawrence Minot. orig ca. 1350; ms ca. 1400.
> John Barbour's *Bruce.* orig ca. 1375; ms 1467.
> John Barbour's Saints' Legends. orig ca. 1375; ms 15th c.
> Andrew Winton's *Original Chronicle.* orig ca. 1375; ms ca. 1440.
> *Catholicon Anglicum.* ca. 1440.

Lindsey

> *Havelok.* orig ca. 1250; ms ca. 1300.

Fourboroughs

> *Ormulum.* ca. 1200.
> Robert Manning's Chronicle. ca. 1340.

Norfolk

> Peterborough Chronicle 1132–1154. 1154.
> *Bestiary.* ca. 1225.
> *Genesis & Exodus.* ca. 1275.
> *Promptorium Parvulorum.* ca. 1460.

Lancaster

> Works of the Gawain Poet. orig ca. 1375; ms ca. 1400.

Chester

> *Stanzaic Life of Christ.* orig ca. 1400; ms ca. 1450.

See special bibliography to 9.8.6–9.8.7 following main bibliography.

15. The following are the relevant comments by Sawyer (1971:174–175):

In the Danelaw the destruction of the established church and the replacement of the power of the English kings and lay lords by the Scandinavian invaders meant that new land could be more freely occupied . . . [A]nother powerful motive for expansion [was] the natural desire of the leaders of the Scandinavian colonists to reward and provide for the sons of the first generation warriors. All this combined with the economic stimulus afforded by invaders who brought with them the accumulated loot of years spent plundering Christendom encouraged the extension of the settlement and with it of Scandinavian influence in England. [174] The main driving force behind that internal colonization was economic . . . In the eleventh century the demand seems to have been above all for an extension of sheep farming to satisfy the looms of Flanders and those parts of the Danelaw that were well suited to sheep farming [namely the Yorkshire and Lincolnshire Wolds] prospered greatly. [174–175] It is likely that the initial Danish conquest and colonization affected the southern parts of the Danelaw, including Northamptonshire and East Anglia, as much as it did Lincolnshire and Yorkshire. The differences in the apparent degree of Scandinavian influence may be explained in part . . . by the earlier and more effective submission of the southern Danelaw to the English kings, but it probably owes more to the fact that Lincolnshire and Yorkshire offered opportunities for an expansion which soon proved prosperous . . . [175]

16. The following are some relevant quotes from Sawyer on the numbers of Norse settlers in England:

When allowance is made for . . . the fact that this fleet brought women and children as well, the probability is that [the] *micel here* [of 892], the largest force ever described in detail in ninth-century English sources, was well under 1,000 men. There is nothing in the ninth-century sources to suggest that the Viking armies were ever larger than this and the probability is that most, if not all, the raiding bands were about three or four hundred men. [127–128] The prolonged existence and occasional rapid movement of the Viking bands in the ninth and early tenth centuries would not have been possible had they contained more than a few hundred men at the most . . . [129] The Danish and Norwegian conquerors of Britain had little contact with Scandinavia . . . in the tenth century. The Vikings who . . . [took] for themselves the Scandinavian kingdom of York did not come fresh from Scandinavia, but were recruited from families already established in Britain . . . [210]

It is commonly accepted that the scale of Scandinavian influence was so great that there must have been a very numerous Scandinavian population . . . It is, however, also accepted that the Viking armies were not very large and it has therefore become necessary for those who believe the Scandinavian colonization to have been on a massive scale, to assume that there was a secondary migration from Denmark under the shelter of the Viking armies that had established themselves in England . . . [167] The fact that no such secondary migration is reported in contemporary sources does not necessarily rule out the possibility . . . It would, however, not be unreasonable to expect a migration on such a massive scale to have left some trace in later traditions, but apparently there is none . . . [T]he absence of any . . . indications that the areas of supposed 'secondary migration' were in any . . . sense . . . subordinate to the centers of Danish power [in England] . . . strongly suggests that no such . . . peasant migration ever took place . . . [T]he apparent difficulty experienced by the [later Danish] 'army' of 892 in finding somewhere to settle [in England] suggests that newcomers were not welcome . . . *The Danish colonisation of England was not achieved . . . by a silent stream of peasants sheltered by the Danish 'armies' . . . It was, in fact, the work of the 'armies' themselves* <emphasis ours> [168].

It has been suggested, on the basis of place-name evidence, that Denmark, like Norway, experienced a remarkable growth of population in the early Viking period, but doubt has recently been cast on this interpretation of the evidence. It can, however, be said that if such an expansion had occurred, the Danes would not have needed to journey to England in search of new homes, there was ample space for expansion in Denmark itself and in Ska<o>ne . . . The Danish Vikings were, therefore, not colonists, in the same sense as the Norwegians, but pirates who extended the range of their activities into western Europe . . . [208] The Danish Vikings appear to have been exiles from their homeland . . . In the middle of the [ninth] century the Danes began to operate from bases in England. At first they were temporary but by 880 they had settled permanently in the north and east of the country. The Danish colonization of England was, therefore, not the result of a mass migration of land hungry peasants but was, in contrast, achieved by a relatively small group of warriors who had made themselves rich by plunder and hoped to continue in that way of life. [209]

The first Danish settlers, or conquerors, of England were joined by a second group of Danes in 898 that had, for more than a decade, campaigned in Frankia [sic] and England, but there is no evidence of any later invasions by Vikings from Scandinavia until the end of the tenth century . . . [209] One of the most interesting and remarkable characteristics of the Scandinavian [archaeological] material is the scarcity of ninth-century western European coins. This was a century of raids on western Europe, large areas of which had long been familiar with coin . . . [T]here is no reason to doubt that large sums were paid to Scandinavian raiders at this time . . . [99] There is . . . good reason to believe that, by the end of the ninth century, the raiders did not take their winnings home, but rather used them as a sort of capital with which to settle. The Anglo-Saxon Chronicle describes, in 898, how Haesten's army broke up, 'the Danish army divided, one force going into East Anglia and one into Northumbria; and those that were moneyless got themselves ships and went south across the sea to the Seine.' The implication is clearly that those who settled in East Anglia and Northumbria had money; it was to win such wealth that they had joined the raiding band, and having won it they did not return home to Denmark, they settled . . . [100–101]

17. Sawyer, while not claiming to be a linguist, is able to reconcile small numbers of Norse speakers with a notable degree of linguistic power, as the following quotes show:

The Scandinavian colonists of western Europe were soon assimilated. Only those who found homes in the virtually uninhabited islands of the north Atlantic preserved their native speech, the others soon adopted the language of their neighbors. They also adopted the religion of their neighbors . . . [211–212] The belief in very large numbers [of Norse settlers] rests not only on the numbers of place-names, but on the scale of general Scandinavian linguistic influence . . . (Recent studies of linguistic change and, in particular, of bilingualism have shown how very complex . . . the effect of one language on another can be . . .) [169–170] Although English and Danish are closely related languages it would have hardly been possible for the Scandinavian colonists to communicate with the native English, unless each group had learnt at least something of each other's language . . . The bilingualism needed for the communication would doubtless have been facilitated by the similarity of the languages . . . [170] <quoting Weinreich, *Languages in*

Contact> . . . 'whereas the unilingual depends, in replenishing his vocabulary, on indigenous lexical material and whatever loan-words may happen to be transmitted to him, the bilingual has the other language as a constantly available source of lexical innovations.' . . . [and] 'even for extensive word transferring, large numbers of bilingual speakers need not be involved and the relative size of the groups is not necessarily a factor' . . . Linguistic arguments, on their own, are insufficient to prove the scale of the Scandinavian settlements. [170–171]

18. Milroy (1984:10) shows he is either out of his depth or unwilling to be precise when he states:

. . . the Modern English standard language that began to form after the Norman Conquest was based not on West Saxon but chiefly on the South-east Midland (Mercian) dialect of London [Standard English began to form in the 1380s, not at 1066. The dialect of London was not originally Southeast (our Central) Midland but Southeastern (Essex Dialect), but during the 14th century massive in-migration to London took place, from the Central Midland area of Leicester and Northampton where Central Midland dialects were at home (and still are) TK&SGT].

19. The following remarks by Milroy (1984:28) are inappropriate:

French influence was not confined to the borrowing of single [lexical] items, but extended to the general rules of word-formation in English. Many of the prefixes and suffixes that we still use to form complex words are taken from French . . . Thus, derivational systems exemplified by: *nation, national, nationality, nationalize, nationalization* were imported into English from French, and we can still attach French suffixes to native words, as in *like/able, word/age* . . . [The words based on *nation* were assembled in **Latin**, then borrowed by English from French, or directly from Latin: only *nation* and *national* probably come directly from French. The suffixes *-able* and *-age* are in fact more common now in English than they were in ME. They are also used in Dutch and Low German. TK&SGT].

20. The following comment by Milroy (1984:11–12) is in a similar vein:

Contact with Norman French was of a somewhat different kind [than that between English and Danish in Northern England, where Milroy thinks an Anglo-Norse pidgin arose, was then creolized, and then entered into a post-creole situation]. The Norman settlers were quite few in number, . . . But it is clear that in daily life between 1066 and the early thirteenth century, pidgin-type contact forms or interlanguages *must often have been used,* continuing and spreading the tendencies to structural simplification that were already present in the Anglo-Norse areas [emphasis ours: We find the idea that there "must have been" pidgins used between French and English speakers between 1066 and 1250 to be a totally specious bit of question-begging. There is no evidence for it and creolists and sociolinguists are simply not in a position to make such predictions given the empirical base available TK&SGT].

21. Note how Milroy (1984:22] is off the mark in this remark:

Some fossilized [morphological] forms . . . survive to the present day: *whilom, seldom, random* are OE dative plurals, but that fact has been irrelevant to English synchronic morphology since before 1300. [ModE **whilom** (<ME **whiilen**) and **seldom** (<ME **selden**) have final /m/ for the same reason as **ransom** (<OF **rançoun**) and **random** (<OF **randoun,** *not* from OE!), namely a late ME dissimilation of

final /n/ to /m/ after an apical consonant in a preceding syllable. See also **venom** (<OF **venin, vellum** (<OF **velin, pilgrim** (<OF **pelerin**). All these words ended in /n/ in Early ME. There is no question of the preservation of the OE dative plural in -**um** (with /m/), though the final syllables of ME **whiilen, selden** are phonologically descended from the OE dative plural TK&SGT].

22. Domingue (1975:3) says that:

Pyles (1964, 1971) computed that 85 percent of the ME lexicon is made up of words of French origin.

Baugh (1957:215) says that there were 10,000 words of French origin in ME. ME surely had more than 12,000 words. Domingue concedes that only eight French-origin words made their way into the 200-word lexicostatistics list. A calculation by Kaufman of French influence on Modern English lexicon shows 7 percent on the Swadesh 200-word list (i.e., 14 items), and 7 percent out of a 700-word non-cultural, non-regional diagnostic list constructed by Kaufman. Norse influence is also about 7 percent on both the 200-word and 700-word lists. This means that between them French and Norse account for about 14 percent of the basic vocabulary of Modern English, though in the ME period some of these words had not yet displaced the native English synonyms. This degree of influence is, we think, normal. We would not be surprised at such a rate of lexical influence by Middle Low German on modern High German, Danish, or Swedish, or of French on Dutch (see 9.8.9). Jespersen, who counts French loanwords in ME (1938:87), points out that in many cases the Oxford English Dictionary (OED) identifies as from French words he would claim come from Latin, though he adopts the OED's attribution in making his calculations. It is true that early Modern English was heavily latinized, but this is not relevant to the question of Medieval French influence. We think that it is a fairly improbable notion that 85 percent of the words forming the active vocabulary of any English speaker at any time between 1250 and 1400 could have been of French origin. It must be borne in mind, as Smithers warns, that many French words occur in just one ME text and there is no assurance that such words were known generally to English speakers. It should also be noted here that the French lexical influence on the everyday vocabulary of the dialects of the South was greater than what shows up in Standard English.

23. The appearance of OE <y> [ü] as /i/ in ME has been referred to by some scholars as evidence for imperfect transmission due to sociolinguistic upheaval in England. However, this change had already taken place by 900 in some kinds of West Saxon (A. Campbell 1959:132), that is, outside the Norse settlement area and long before the Norman Conquest. In ME the change was universal in areas of Danish (not Norwegian) settlement (see Table 4.A.7); unrounding of /ü/ to /i/ did not occur in the rest of England till between 1350 (or even later) and 1400. Furthermore, both Norse and French had the phoneme /ü/. The same change occurred in Central and Southern Germany several hundred years ago. It is quite natural.

Words having medial /d/ in Old English have /θ/ [ð] in Old Norse. Thus OE <faeder> = ON <faðir> "father." Domingue suggests that Modern English /faaðǝr/ has /ð/ under Norse influence. Actually English has /fadǝr, vadǝr/ throughout ME until after 1400. In early Modern English -d- > -ð- next to /r/, thus:

/fadǝr/ > /faaðǝr/ "father" : German /Vater> (Gmn *d)

/wedər/ > /weðər/ "weather" : German <Wetter> (Gmc *d)
Conversely, -ð- > -d- next o /l/:
/fiðələ/ > /fidəl/ "fiddle" : German <Fiedel> (Gmc *θ)
These are ModE changes with no connection whatsoever with the English-Norse contact situation.

24. Some scholars have seen this as a sign of simplification that could only be the result of foreign influence, since the reduction of unstressed vowels to /ə/ renders homophonous many grammatical suffixes originally distinct. The fact is that OE had distinct vowels /a o e/ in unstressed syllables. During the period 875–950 unstressed /a/ and /o/ merged as /a/ *throughout* England, long before French influence, and including areas never in contact with Norse (A. Campbell 1959:161). *All* unstressed vowels had gone to /ə/ by the middle of the 11th century (Moore 1928:238–266; A. Campbell 1959:161; Moore 1951:72). This "simplification" cannot have been motivated except by factors internal to the language. It can reasonably be argued that the phonological merger would not likely have taken place unless there *already* existed alternative devices, largely syntactic, to express the grammatical categories masked by the phonological simplification (unless the category was semantically redundant, in which case it could be allowed to vanish, as has happened in uncounted languages) (see table 7.1,4).

25. This trivializes Domingue's (1975:5) idea that the expression of possession in these precise two ways in English is abnormal except as the result of serious foreign interference.

26. There are two subparts to this issue: (a) third person pronoun reference assigned naturally, and not agreeing with the grammatical/arbitrary gender of the noun antecedent; (b) reassignment of gender to nouns on the basis of natural or figurative associations, with agreement marked on modifying adjectives and demonstratives, including the article. Situation (a) had already developed by 950 throughout England. Situation (b) was already in effect by 1150, even in areas outside Norse settlement (Jones 1967). Also by 1150, there was no gender agreement of any kind in the Danelaw, but it persisted on noun modifiers until after 1350 in the South. Therefore, whereas it is basically an imponderable whether contact with Norse may have had anything to do with the loss of gender agreement in the North, French clearly did not interfer with gender agreement (albeit based on natural gender) in the South.

27. English's exclusive SVO constituent order, with Auxiliary preceding Main Verb when relevant, is viewed by some as a kind of contact-induced simplification. OE has an *optional* order with finite verb last in dependent clauses (in Modern German and Dutch this is obligatory; Yiddish has abandoned it, apparently under Slavic influence). ME lacks verb-last dependent clauses in ordinary prose, though they do occur in poetry. Even in prose, an unstressed object pronoun may precede a finite verb in ME. This simplication or regularization to SVO in prose is already universal in the earliest ME by 1150, in all dialects. It is not likely to be the result of French influence, at such an early date. It is also true that Norse never has finite verb last in dependent clauses, but Norse influence never extended to the South of England. Whatever the origin of preferred SVO word order in English, it can hardly be seen as a kind of simplification associated with sociolinguistic breakdown.

28. Here is our last batch of quotes from Milroy (1984:5):

During the past nine centuries, English has undergone more dramatic changes than any other major European language in the same period. There have also been many phonological changes . . . the lexicon has been altered from mainly Germanic to a mixed Germanic-Romance type . . . OE . . . , unlike, for example, medieval Icelandic, is not immediately accessible to the modern native reader. [Old English dates from A.D. 700–1000. (Standard OE was codified during the tenth century and then got a fixed form.) Old Norse dates from 1200–1400 and is temporally parallel to Middle English, not Old English. Modern Standard Icelandic is deliberately archaizing. The Viking Norse that influenced ME was not even a written language. The Icelanders learned to write in Roman letters from the English TK&SGT].

References

Adams, G. B. 1975. Hamito-Semitic and the pre-Celtic substratum in Ireland and Britain. In James Bynon and Theodora Bynon, eds., *Hamito-Semitica*. The Hague: Mouton, 233–247.

Aitken, A. J., Angus McIntosh, and Hermann Pálsson. 1971. *Edinburgh Studies in English and Scots*. London: Longman.

Alleyne, Mervyn C. 1971. Acculturation and the cultural matrix of creolization. In Hymes, ed., 169–186.

———. 1979. On the genesis of languages. In Kenneth C. Hill, ed., *The genesis of language*. Ann Arbor: Karoma, 89–107.

———. 1980a. *Comparative Afro-American: an historical-comparative study of English-based Afro-American dialects of the New World*. Ann Arbor: Karoma.

———. 1980b. Introduction. In Valdman and Highfield, eds., 1–17.

Andersen, Henning. 1980. Morphological change: towards a typology. In Jacek Fisiak, ed., *Historical morphology*. The Hague: Mouton, 1–50.

Andersen, Roger W. 1980. Creolization as the acquisition of a second language as a first language. In Valdman and Highfield, eds., 273–295.

———. 1983. Introduction. In Roger W. Andersen, ed., *Pidginization and creolization as language acquisition*. Rowley, Mass.: Newbury House, 1–56.

Andronov, M. 1964. On the typological similarity of New Indo-Aryan and Dravidian. *Indian Linguistics* 25.119–126 (Baburam Saksena Felicitation Volume).

Apte, Mahadev L. 1974. Pidginization of a lingua franca: a linguistic analysis of Hindi-Urdu spoken in Bombay. *International Journal of Dravidian Linguistics* (Special issue on Contact and Convergence in South Asian Languages, ed. by Franklin C. Southworth and Mahadev L. Apte) 3/1:21–41.

Aquilina, Joseph. 1975. The Berber element in Maltese. In James Bynon and Theodora Bynon, eds., *Hamito-Semitica*. The Hague: Mouton, 297–313.

Bailey, Charles-James N. 1973. *Variation and linguistic theory*. Arlington, Va.: Center for Applied Linguistics.

———. 1977. Linguistic change, naturalness, mixture, and structural principles. *Papiere zur Linguistik* 16:6–73.

———. 1980 MS. Note: developmental linguistics.

Bailey, Charles-James N., and K. Maroldt. 1977. The French lineage of English. In J. M. Meisel, ed., 21–53.

Baker, Philip, and Chris Corne. 1982. *Isle de France Creole: affinities and origins.* Ann Arbor: Karoma.

Baron, Naomi. 1975. Trade jargons and pidgins: a functionalist approach. Paper presented at the International Conference on Pidgins and Creoles, Honolulu.

Baudet, Martha M. 1976 MS. The case for an African substratum in French-based Caribbean creoles. M.A. thesis, University of Pittsburgh.

———. 1981. Identifying the African grammatical base of the Caribbean creoles: a typological approach. In Arnold Highfield and Albert Valdman, eds., *Historicity and variation in creole studies.* Ann Arbor: Karoma, 104–117.

Baugh, Albert C. 1957. *A history of the English language.* 2d ed. N.Y.: Appleton-Century- Crofts.

Bender, Jan E. 1980. The impact of English on a Low German dialect in Nebraska. In Paul Schach, ed., *Languages in conflict: linguistic acculturation on the Great Plains.* Lincoln: University of Nebraska Press, 77–85.

Bennett, J. A. W., and G. V. Smithers. 1968. *Early Middle English verse and prose.* 2d ed. London: Oxford University Press.

Bennett, William H. 1955. The southern English development of Germanic initial [f s þ]. *Language* 31:367–371.

Bense, J. F. 1925. *Anglo-Dutch relations from the earliest times to the death of William the Third.* The Hague: Nijhoff.

———. 1938. *A dictionary of the Low-Dutch element in the English vocabulary.* Oxford: Oxford University Press.

Berndt, Rolf. 1965. The linguistic situation in England from the Norman Conquest to the loss of Normandy (1066–1204). *Philologica Pragensia* 8:145–163.

Besten, Hans den. 1985. Die doppelte Negation im Afrikaans und ihre Herkunft. In N. Boretzky, W. Enninger, and T. Stolz, eds., *Akten des 1. Essener Kolloquiums über "Kreolsprachen und Sprachkontakte."* Bochum: Studienverlag Dr. N. Brockmeyer, 9–42.

Bever, Thomas, and D. Terence Langendoen. 1972. The interaction of speech perception and grammatical structure in the evolution of language. In R. Stockwell and R. Macaulay, eds., *Linguistic change and generative theory.* Bloomington: Indiana University Press, 32–95.

Bickerton, Derek. 1977. Pidginization and creolization: language acquisition and language universals. In Valdman, ed., 49–69.

———. 1979. Beginnings: the genesis of language. In Kenneth C. Hill, ed., *The genesis of language.* Ann Arbor: Karoma, 1–22.

———. 1980. Decreolisation and the creole continuum. In Valdman and Highfield, eds., 109–127.

———. 1981. *Roots of language.* Ann Arbor: Karoma.

Bickerton, Derek, and Talmy Givón. 1976. Pidginization and syntactic change: from SXV to SVX. In Sanford B. Steever et al., eds., *Papers from the parasession on diachronic syntax.* Chicago: Chicago Linguistic Society, 9–39.

Björkman, Erik. 1900, 1902. *Scandinavian loan-words in Middle English*. Part I, Part II. Halle: Niemeyer.

Bloomfield, Leonard. 1933. *Language*. New York: Holt, Rinehart & Winston.

———. 1970 (1927). Literate and illiterate speech. In Charles F. Hockett, ed., *A Leonard Bloomfield anthology*. Bloomington: Indiana University Press, 147–156. Reprinted from *American Speech* 2:10.432–439.

Boas, Franz. 1888. Chinook songs. *Journal of American Folklore* 1:220–226.

———. 1911. Introduction. *Handbook of American Indian languages* (Bureau of American Ethnology, Series B 40:1), 1–83. Washington, D.C.: Government Printing Office.

———. 1917. Introductory. *International Journal of American Linguistics* 1:1–8.

———. 1929. Classification of American Indian languages. *Language* 5:1–7.

Bokamba, Eyamba G. 1977. The impact of multilingualism on language structure: the case of central Africa. *Anthropological Linguistics* 19/5:181–202.

———. 1982. The africanization of English. In Braj B. Kachru, ed., *The other tongue: English across cultures*. Urbana: University of Illinois Press, 77–98.

Bonvillain, Nancy. 1978. Linguistic change in Akwesasne Mohawk: French and English influences. *International Journal of American Linguistics* 44:31–39.

Boretzky, Norbert. 1983. *Kreolsprachen, Substrate und Sprachwandel*. Wiesbaden: Otto Harrassowitz.

Bradshaw, J. 1979 MS. Causative serial constructions and word order change in Papua New Guinea. Paper presented at the Annual Meeting of the Linguistic Society of America, Los Angeles.

Bray, Denys deS. 1909. *The Brahui language*. Part I: *Introduction and grammar*. Calcutta: Superintendent Government Printing, India.

———. 1913. *Census of India, 1911*. Vol. IV: *Baluchistan*. Calcutta: Superintendent Government Printing, India.

Bright, William. 1976 (1960). Animals of acculturation in the California Indian languages. In *Variation and change in language*, ed. Anwar S. Dil. Stanford: Stanford University Press, 121–162. Reprinted from *University of California Publications in Linguistics* 4:4.215–246 (1960).

———. 1976 (1973). North American Indian language contact. In Thomas A. Sebeok, ed., *Native languages of the Americas*, vol. 1: *North America*. New York: Plenum Press), 210–227. Reprinted from T. A. Sebeok, ed., *Current Trends in Linguistics*, vol. 10: *North America*.

Broch, Olaf. 1927. Russenorsk. *Archiv für slavische Philologie* 41:209–262.

Bruce, R. 1970. *Cantonese*. (Teach Yourself Books). New York: David McKay Co.

Burling, Robbins. 1973. Language development of a Garo and English-speaking child. In Charles A. Ferguson and Dan I. Slobin, eds., *Studies of child language development*. Holt, Rinehart & Winston, 69–90.

Burrow, Thomas, and S. Bhattacharya. 1970. *The Pengo language*. London: Oxford University Press.

Burrow, Thomas, and Murray B. Emeneau. 1961. *A Dravidian etymological dictionary*. London: Oxford University Press.

Bybee Hooper, Joan. 1973. *Aspects of natural generative phonology.* UCLA Ph.D. dissertation.

Camden, W. G. 1975 MS. Parallels in structure of lexicon and syntax between New Hebrides Bislama and the South Santo language spoken at Tangoa. Paper presented at the 1975 International Conference on Pidgins and Creoles, Honolulu.

Campbell, A. 1959. *Old English grammar.* London: Oxford University Press.

Campbell, Lyle. 1976. Language contact and sound change. In W. Christie, ed., *Current progress in historical linguistics.* Amsterdam: North-Holland, 181–194.

———. 1980. Explaining universals and their exceptions. In E. C. Traugott et al., eds., *Papers from the Fourth International Conference on Historical Linguistics.* Amsterdam: Benjamins, 17–26.

Campbell, Lyle, and Marianne Mithun. 1979. Introduction: North American Indian historical linguistics in current perspective. In L. Campbell and M. Mithun, eds., *The languages of native America: historical and comparative assessment.* Austin: University of Texas Press, 3–69.

Cassano, P. 1972. The influence of native languages on the phonology of American Spanish. In A. Rigault and R. Charbonneau, eds., *Proceedings of the 7th International Congress of Phonetic Sciences.* The Hague: Mouton, 674–678.

Černyx, P. Ja. 1962. *Istoričeskaja grammatika russkogo jazyka.* Moscow.

Chadwick, H. Munro. 1907. *The origin of the English nation.* Cambridge: Cambridge University Press.

Chambers, R. W., and Marjorie Daunt. 1931. *A book of London English 1384–1425.* London: Oxford University Press.

Chatterton, Percy. 1970. The origin and development of Police Motu. *Kivung* 3:95–98.

Chaudenson, Robert. 1977. Toward the reconstruction of the social matrix of creole language. In Valdman, ed., 259–276.

Chomsky, Noam, and Morris Halle. 1968. *The sound pattern of English.* New York: Harper & Row.

Clyne, Michael G. 1981. *Deutsch als Muttersprache in Australien: zur Ökologie einer Einwanderersprache.* (Deutsche Sprache in Europa und Übersee, 8.) Wiesbaden: Steiner.

Cole, D. T. 1964 (1953). Fanagalo and the Bantu languages in South Africa. In Dell Hymes, ed., *Language in culture and society.* New York: Harper & Row, 547–554. Reprinted from *African Studies* 12:1–9 (1953).

Collinder, Björn. 1965. *An introduction to the Uralic languages.* Berkeley and Los Angeles: University of California Press.

Comrie, Bernard. 1981a. *Language universals and linguistic typology.* Chicago: University of Chicago Press.

———. 1981b. *The languages of the Soviet Union.* Cambridge: Cambridge University Press.

Cook, Albert S. 1894. *A glossary of the Old Northumbrian gospels.* (Lindisfarne Gospels or Durham Book.) Halle: Max Niemeyer.

Corne, Chris. 1983. Substratal reflections: the completive aspect and the distributive numerals in Isle de France Creole. *Te Reo* 26:65–80.

Coteanu, I. 1957. A propos des langues mixtes (sur l'istro-roumain). Bucharest: Mélanges linguistiques.

Cowgill, Warren. 1970. The nominative plural and preterit singular of the active participles in Baltic. In Thomas F. Magner and William R. Schmalstieg, eds., *Baltic linguistics*. University Park, PA.: The Pennsylvania State University Press, 23–37.

Craton, Michael. 1982. *Testing the chains: resistance to slavery in the British West Indies*. Ithaca: Cornell University Press.

Crawford, John C. 1981. What sort of thing is Michif? Working paper for Workshop on The Metis in North America, Newberry Library Center for the History of the American Indian.

Crowley, Terry. 1983. *Introduction to historical linguistics*. (Studying Pacific Languages Series, no. 3). Port Moresby: Department of Language, University of Papua New Guinea.

Darby, H. C. 1952. *The Domesday geography of eastern England*. Cambridge: Cambridge University Press.

Darby, H. C., and I. S. Maxwell, eds. 1962. *The Domesday geography of northern England*. Cambridge: Cambridge University Press.

Darnell, Regna, and Joel Sherzer. 1971. Areal linguistic studies in North America: a historical perspective. *International Journal of American Linguistics* 37:20–28.

Davis, John H. 1971. Notes on Mainland Comox phonology. In James Hoard and Thom Hess, eds., *Studies in Northwest Indian languages* (Sacramento Anthropological Society, Publ. 11), 12–31. Sacramento.

Dawkins, R. M. 1916. *Modern Greek in Asia Minor: a study of the dialects of Sílli, Cappadocia and Phárasa with grammars, texts, translations, and glossary*. Cambridge: Cambridge University Press.

DeCamp, David. 1958. The genesis of Old English dialects: a new hypothesis. *Language* 34:232–244.

Décsy, Gyula. 1967. Is there a Finnic substratum in Russian? *Orbis* 16:150–160.

Deeters, Gerhard. 1939. Réponse au questionnaire. *Ve Congrès Internationale de Linguistes, 1939: Ire publication: Réponses au questionnaire*. Bruges: Imprimerie Sainte Catherine, 52–53.

Demers, Modeste, F. N. Blanchet, and L. N. St. Onge. 1871. *Chinook dictionary, catechism, prayers, and hymns*. Montreal: Quebec Mission.

Deshpande, Madhav M. 1979. Genesis of Ṛgvedic retroflexion: a historical and sociolinguistic investigation. In Madhav M. Deshpande and Peter Edwin Hook, eds., *Aryan and non-Aryan in India*. Ann Arbor: Karoma, 235–315.

The dictionary and grammar of Hiri Motu. 1976. The Papua New Guinea Government Office of Information.

Dolgopol'skij, A. B. 1973. *Sravnitel'no-istoričeskaja fonetika Kušitskix jazykov*. Moscow: Nauka.

Domingue, Nicole Z. 1975. Another creole: Middle English. Paper presented at the 1975 International Conference on Pidgins and Creoles, Honolulu.

Dorian, Nancy C. 1973. Grammatical change in a dying dialect. *Language* 49:414–438.

————. 1981. *Language death*. Philadelphia: University of Pennsylvania Press.

Douaud, Patrick C. 1980. Métis: a case of triadic linguistic economy. *Anthropological Linguistics* 22:392–414.

Douglas, David C., and George W. Greenway, eds. 1953. *English historical documents 1042–1189*. London: Eyre & Spottiswoode.

Drachman, Gaberell. 1969. *Twana phonology*. (The Ohio State University Working Papers in Linguistics, 5) Columbus: The Ohio State University Department of Linguistics.

Drechsel, Emanuel J. 1984. Structure and function in Mobilian Jargon: indications for the pre-European existence of an American Indian pidgin. *Journal of Historical Linguistics and Philology* 1:141–185.

Dressler, Wolfgang. 1972. On the phonology of language death. In *Papers of the Chicago Linguistic Society* 8:448–457. Chicago: Chicago Linguistic Society.

Duncan, Pauline. 1972. Forms of the feminine pronoun in modern English dialects. In Martyn Wakelyn, ed., *Patterns of folk speech in the British Isles*. London: Athlone Press, 182–200.

Dutton, Tom. 1983. Birds of a feather: a pair of rare pidgins from the Gulf of Papua. In Ellen Woolford and William Washabaugh, eds., *The social context of creolization*. Ann Arbor: Karoma, 77–105.

Dutton, Tom, and H. A. Brown. 1977. Hiri Motu: the language itself. In Stephan A. Wurm, ed., *New Guinea area languages and language study*, vol. 3 (Pacific Linguistics C-40). Canberra: Australian National University, 759–793.

Ek, Karl-Gustav. 1972. *The development of OE y and eo in south-eastern Middle English*. Lund: Gleerup.

Ekwall, E. 1956. *Studies of the population of medieval London*. Stockholm: Almqvist and Wiksell.

Elderkin, E. D. 1976. Southern Cushitic. In M. Lionel Bender, ed., *The non-Semitic languages of Ethiopia*. East Lansing, MI: African Studies Center, 278–297.

Ellis, Alexander J. 1889. *On early English pronunciation with especial reference to Shakespear and Chaucer, Part V: Existing dialectal as compared with West Saxon pronunciation*. London: Trübner.

Emeneau, Murray B. 1962. *Brahui and Dravidian comparative grammar*. (University of California Publications in Linguistics 27.) Berkeley and Los Angeles: University of California Press.

————. 1964 (1956). India as a linguistic area. In Dell Hymes, ed., *Language in culture and society*. New York: Harper & Row, 642–653. Reprinted from *Language* 32:3–16.

————. 1980 (1954). Linguistic prehistory of India. In *Language and linguistic area*, ed. Anwar Dil. Stanford: Stanford University Press, 85–104. Reprinted from *Proceedings of the American Philosophical Society* 98:282–292 (1954).

————. 1980 (1962). Bilingualism and structural borrowing. In *Language and linguistic area*, ed. Anwar Dil. Stanford: Stanford University Press, 38–65. Reprinted from *Proceedings of the American Philosophical Society* 106:430–442 (1962).

————. 1980 (1965). India and linguistic areas. In *Language and linguistic area*, ed.

Anwar Dil. Stanford: Stanford University Press, 126–165. Reprinted from *India and historical grammar* (Annamalai University Department of Linguistics Publication No. 5), 25–75.

———. 1980 (1971). Dravidian and Indo-Aryan: the Indian linguistic area. In *Language and linguistic area*, 167–196. Reprinted from Andrée F. Sjoberg, ed., *Symposium on Dravidian Civilization*. Austin and New York: Jenkins Publishing Co. and Pemberton Press, 1971, 33–68.

Evans, Donna. 1982. On coexistence of two phonological systems in Michif. In Desmond C. Derbyshire, ed., *Work papers of the Summer Institute of Linguistics, University of North Dakota Session*, vol. 26. Huntington Beach, CA.: Summer Institute of Linguistics, 158–173.

Fairbanks, Gordon. 1977. Case inflections in Indo-European. *Journal of Indo-European Studies* 5:101–131.

Ferguson, Charles A. 1971. Absence of copula and the notion of simplicity: a study of normal speech, baby talk, foreigner talk and pidgins. In Hymes, ed., 141–150.

———. 1976. The Ethiopian language area. In M. Lionel Bender, J. Donald Bowen, R. L. Cooper, and C. A. Ferguson, eds., *Language in Ethiopia*. London: Oxford University Press, 63–76.

Ferraz, Luiz. 1974. A linguistic appraisal of Angolar. *In memoriam António Jorge Dias*, vol. II: 177–186. Lisbõa: Instituto de Alta Cultura Junta de Investigações Científicas do Ultramar.

———. 1975 MS. The origin and development of the creoles of São Tomé, Príncipe, and Annobón. Paper presented at the International Conference on Pidgins and Creoles, Honolulu.

———. 1976. The substratum of Annobonese Creole. In J. L. Dillard, ed., *Sociohistorical factors in the formation of the creoles* (special issue of the *International Journal of the Sociology of Language*, 7), 37–47.

———. 1983. The origin and development of four creoles in the Gulf of Guinea. In Ellen Woolford and William Washabaugh, eds., *The social context of creolization*. Ann Arbor: Karoma, 120–125.

Fink, Deborah. 1983 MS. Notes from field methods class on Michif, Summer Institute of Linguistics, University of North Dakota Session.

Fowkes, Robert A. 1973. Review of Ternes (1970). *Language* 49:195–198.

Frachtenberg, Leo J. 1918. Comparative studies in Takelman, Kalapuyan and Chinookan lexicography: a preliminary paper. *International Journal of American Linguistics* 1:175–182.

Garvin, Paul L. 1948. Kutenai I, Phonemics; Kutenai II, Morpheme variations; Kutenai III, Morpheme distributions. *International Journal of American Linguistics* 14:37–42; 87–90; 171–187.

———. 1951. Kutenai IV: Word classes. *International Journal of American Linguistics* 17:84–97.

Geipel, John. 1971. *The Viking legacy: The Scandinavian influence on the English and Gaelic languages*. Newton Abbot: David & Charles.

Geoghegan, Richard Henry. 1944. *The Aleut language*, ed. Fredericka I. Martin. United States Department of the Interior.

Gevenich, Olga. 1918. *Die englische Palatalisierung von k > č im Licht der englischen Ortsnamen.* Halle: Niemeyer.

Givón, Talmy. 1979. Prolegomena to any sane creology. In Ian F. Hancock, ed., 3–35.

Glauser, Beat. 1974. *The Socttish-English linguistic border: lexical aspects.* Bern: Francke Verlag.

Goddard, Ives. 1975. Algonquian, Wiyot, and Yurok: proving a distant genetic relationship. In M. Dale Kinkade, Kenneth L. Hale, and Oswald Werner, eds., *Linguistics and Anthropology: in honor of C.F. Voegelin.* Lisse: The Peter de Ridder Press, 249–262.

Goodman, Morris. 1964. *A comparative study of Creole French dialects.* The Hague: Mouton.

———. 1971. The strtange case of Mbugu. In Hymes, ed., 243–254.

———. 1985. Review of Bickerton 1981. *International Journal of American Linguistics* 51:109–137.

Gordon, E. V. 1957. *An introduction to Old Norse,* 2d ed.; revised by A. R. Taylor. Oxford: Oxford University Press.

Greenberg, Joseph H. 1953. Historical linguistics and unwritten languages. In A. L. Kroeber, ed., *Anthropology today.* Chicago: University of Chicago Press, 265–286.

———. 1963. Some universals of grammar with particular reference to the order of meaningful elements. In J. Greenberg, ed., *Universals of language* (2d ed.). Cambridge, MA.: MIT Press, 73–133.

Grierson, George A. 1927. *Linguistic survey of India.* vol. I, Part I: *Introductory.* Calcutta: Superintendent of Government Printing.

Grønbech, Kaare, and John R. Krueger. 1955. *An introduction to Classical (Literary) Mongolian.* Wiesbaden: Otto Harrassowitz.

Gumperz, John J., and Robert Wilson. 1971. Convergence and creolization: a case from the Indo-Aryan/Dravidian border in India. In Hymes, ed., 151–167.

Haas, Mary R. 1966. Wiyot-Yurok-Algonkian and problems of comparative Algonkian. *International Journal of American Linguistics* 32:101–107.

———. 1969. Internal reconstruction of the Nootka-Nitinat pronominal suffixes. *International Journal of American Linguistics* 35:108–129.

Hale, Horatio. 1846. *United States exploring expedition during the years 1838–1842: Ethnography and philology.* Philadelphia: Sherman. Reprinted: Ridgewood, N.J.: Gregg (1968).

Hall, Robert A., Jr. 1958. Creolized languages and 'genetic relationship'. *Word* 14:367–373.

———. 1966. *Pidgin and creole languages.* Ithaca, N.Y.: Cornell University Press.

Hancock, Ian F., ed. 1979. *Readings in creole studies.* Ghent: Story-Scientia.

———. 1980. Lexical expansion in creole languages. In Valdman & Highfield, eds., 63–88.

———. 1985 MS. The domestic hypothesis, diffusion and componentiality: an account of Atlantic Anglophone creole origins. Paper presented at the Workshop on Universals vs. Substrata in Creole Genesis, University of Amsterdam.

Haugen, Einar. 1950. The analysis of linguistic borrowing. *Language* 26:210–231.
———. 1954. Review of Weinreich (1953). *Language* 30:380–388.
Havránek, Bohuslav. 1931. Remarques sur l'interférence linguistique. *Travaux du Cercle Linguistique de Prague* 4:304.
Heath, Jeffrey. 1978. *Linguistic diffusion in Arnhem Land.* (Australian Aboriginal Studies: Research and Regional Studies #13.) Canberra: Australian Institute of Aboriginal Studies.
———. 1981. A case of intensive lexical diffusion. *Language* 57:335–367.
———. 1984. Book Notice on Clyne (1981). *Language* 60:192–193.
Heine, Bernd. 1975. Some generalizations on African-based pidgins. Paper presented at the International Conference on Pidgins and Creoles, Honolulu.
Hesseling, Dirk Christiaan. 1897. Het Hollandsch in Zuid Afrika. *De Gids* 61:138–162.
———. 1923. *Het Afrikaansch: Bijdrage tot de Geschiedenis der Nederlandsche Taal in Zuid-Afrika.* 2d ed. Leiden.
Hetzron, Robert. 1975. Genetic classification and Ethiopian Semitic. In James Bynon and Theodora Bynon, eds., *Hamito-Semitica.* The Hague: Mouton, 103–127.
Hock, Hans H. 1975. Substratum influence on (Rig-Vedic) Sanskrit? *Studies in the Linguistic Sciences* 5/2:76–125.
———. 1984. (Pre-)Rig-Vedic convergence of Indo-Aryan with Dravidian? Another look at the evidence. *Studies in the Linguistic Sciences* 14/1.
Hoenigswald, Henry M. 1971. Language history and creole studies. In Hymes, ed., 473–480.
Hoijer, Harry. 1948. Linguistic and cultural change. *Language* 24:335–345.
Holm, John. 1976 MS. Copula variability on the Afro-American continuum. Paper presented at the Society for Caribbean Linguistics Conference, University of Guyana.
———. 1978. *The Creole English of Nicaragua's Miskito Coast: its sociolinguistic history and a comparative study of its lexicon and syntax.* University of London Ph.D. dissertation.
———. 1980. African features in white Bahamian English. *English World-Wide* 1:45–65.
———. 1982. Review of Bickerton (1981). *English World-Wide* 3:112–115.
———. 1984. Variability of the copula in Black English and its creole kin. *American Speech* 59:291–309.
———. Forthcoming. Creole influence on Popular Brazilian Portuguese. To appear in G. Gilbert, ed., *Pidgin and creole languages: essays in memory of John E. Reinecke.* Honolulu: University Press of Hawaii.
Holm, John, and A. Goke Oyedeji. 1984. The Yoruba language in the New World. *Oso* 3/1:83–89 (University of Leiden, Netherlands).
Hombert, Jean-Marie, and John J. Ohala. 1982. Historical development of tone patterns. In J. Peter Maher et al., eds., *Papers from the Third International Conference on Historical Linguistics.* Amsterdam: Benjamins, 75–84.
Hraste, Mate. 1935. Čakavski dijalekat ostrva Hvara. *Južnoslovenski Filolog* 14:1–59.

Huntley, David. 1980. The evolution of genitive-accusative animate and personal nouns in Slavic dialects. In Jacek Fisiak, ed., *Historical morphology*. The Hague: Mouton, 189–212.

Huttar, George L. 1975a. Sources of creole semantic structures. *Language* 51:684–695.

———. 1975b MS. Some Kwa-like features of Djuka syntax. Paper presented at the International Conference on Pidgins and Creoles, Honolulu.

Hyman, Larry M. 1970. The role of borrowing in the justification of phonological grammars. *Studies in African Linguistics* 1:1–48.

Hymes, Dell H. 1955. Positional analysis of categories: a frame for reconstruction. *Word* 11:10–23.

———. 1956. Na-Dene and positional analysis of categories. *American Anthropologist* 58.624–638.

———. 1971. Introduction to Section III. In Hymes, ed., 65–90.

———. 1980. Commentary. In Valdman and Highfield, eds., 389–423.

Hymes, Dell H., ed. 1971. *Pidginization and creolization of languages*. Cambridge: Cambridge University Press.

Ivić, Pavle. 1964. Balkan linguistics. Lecture course taught at the Linguistic Institute of the Linguistic Society of America, Indiana University, June–August, 1964.

Jacobs, Melville. 1954. The areal spread of sound features in the languages north of California. In *Papers from the Symposium on American Indian Languages* (University of California Publications in Linguistics 10), 46–56. Berkeley and Los Angeles: University of California Press.

Jacobsen, William H., Jr. 1966. Washo linguistic studies. In Warren L. d'Azevedo et al., eds., *The current state of anthropological research in the Great Basin: 1964*. Reno: Desert Research Institute, 113–136.

———. 1979. Hokan inter-branch comparisons. In Lyle Campbell and Marianne Mithun, eds., *The languages of native America: historical and comparative assessment*. Austin: University of Texas Press, 545–591.

Jakobsen, Jakob. 1897. *Det Norrøne Sprog på Shetland*.

———. 1928–1932. *An etymological dictionary of the Norn language in Shetland*. 2 vols. London: David Nutt.

Jakobson, Roman. 1955. *Slavic languages: a condensed survey*. New York: King's Crown Press, Columbia University.

———. 1962 (1938). Sur la théorie des affinités phonologiques entre des langues. In *Selected writings*, vol. 1:234–246. The Hague: Mouton. Reprinted from *Actes du Quatrième Congrès Internationale de Linguistes*, 48–59. Copenhagen: Einar Munksgaard.

Jameson, J. F., ed. 1909. *Narratives of New Netherland: 1609–1664*. New York: Scribner.

Jeffers, Robert J., and Ilse Lehiste. 1979. *Principles and methods for historical linguistics*. Cambridge: MIT Press.

Jespersen, Otto. 1938. *Growth and structure of the English language*. 9th ed. Garden City, N.Y.: Doubleday.

Jones, Charles. 1967. The grammatical category of gender in Early Middle English. *English Studies* 48:289–305.

Jordan, Richard. 1974. *Handbook of Middle English grammar: Phonology*, translated and revised by Eugene J. Crook. The Hague: Mouton.

Joseph, Brian. 1983. *The Balkan infinitive.* Cambridge: Cambridge University Press.

Kapelle, William E. 1979. *The Norman Conquest of the North: the region and its transformation, 1000–1135.* Chapel Hill: University of North Carolina Press.

Katara, Pekka. 1966. Das französische Lehngut in Mittelniederdeutschen Denkmälern von 1300 bis 1600 (Mémoires de la Société Néophilologique de Helsinki: Tome 30). Helsinki: Société Néophilologique.

Kaufman, Stephen A. 1974. *The Akkadian influences on Aramaic.* Chicago: University of Chicago Press. Assyriological Studies No. 19.

Kaufman, Terrence. 1968 MS. Chinook Jargon vocabulary with grammatical notes.

——. 1971. A report on Chinook Jargon. In Hymes, ed., 175–178.

——. 1973 MS. Gypsy wanderings and Romani linguistic borrowing.

Kelkar, Ashok R. 1957. "Marathi English": a study in foreign accent. *Word* 13:268–282.

Kiparsky, Paul. 1973. Phonological representations. In Osamu Fujimura, ed., *Three dimensions of linguistic theory.* Tokyo: TEC Co., Ltd., 1–136.

Kiparsky, Valentin. 1938. Comment on Vočadlo, 'Some observations on mixed languages'. *Actes du Quatrième Congrès Internationale de Linguistes.* Copenhagen: Einar Munksgaard, 176.

——. 1969. *Gibt es ein finnougrisches Substrat im Slavischen?* Helsinki: Suomalainen Tiedeakatemia.

Klaiman, M. H. 1977. Bengali syntax: possible Dravidian influences. *International Journal of Dravidian Linguistics* 6.303–317.

Klenin, Emily. 1980. Conditions on object marking: stages in the history of the East Slavic genitive-accusative. In Elizabeth Traugott et al., eds., *Papers from the Fourth International Conference on Historical Linguistics.* Amsterdam: Benjamins, 253–257.

Knab, Tim. 1980. When is a language really dead? The case of Pochutec. *International Journal of American Linguistics* 46:230–233.

Kolb, Eduard. 1965. Skandinavisches in den nordenglischen Dialekten. *Anglia* 83:127–153.

——. 1975. "Elmet": a dialect region in northern England. *Anglia* 91:285–313.

Kolb, Eduard, Beat Glauser, Willy Elmer, and Renate Stamm. 1979. *Atlas of English sounds.* Bern: Francke Verlag.

Kozinskij, I. Š. 1974. K. voprosu o proisxoždenii kjaxtinskogo (russko-kitajskogo) jazyka. As reported by A. N. Golovastikov, Ju.X. Sirk, *Izvestija AN SSSR, Serija literatury i jazyka* 34/1:94–96. (1975).

Krauss, Michael E. 1976 (1973). Na-Dene. In Thomas A. Sebeok, ed., *Native languages of the Americas,* vol. 1: *North America.* New York: Plenum Press, 283–358. Reprinted from T. A. Sebeok, ed., *Current Trends in Linguistics,* vol. 10: *North America.*

Kristensson, Gillis. 1967. *A survey of Middle English dialects 1290–1350: the six northern counties and Lincolnshire.* (Lund Studies in English 35.) Lund: Gleerup.

Kuiper, F. B. J. 1967. The genesis of a linguistic area. *Indo-Iranian Journal* 10: 81–102.

Kurath, Hans. 1954. *Middle English Dictionary: plan and bibliography.* Ann Arbor: University of Michigan Press.

Labov, William. 1981. Resolving the Neogrammarian controversy. *Language* 57: 267–308.

Laverdure, Patline, and Ida Rose Allard. 1983. *The Michif dictionary: Turtle Mountain Chippewa Cree,* ed. John C. Crawford. Winnipeg, Manitoba: Pemmican Publications.

Lehiste, Ilse. 1965. A poem in *Halbdeutsch* and some questions concerning substratum. *Word* 21:55–69.

Leopold, Werner F. 1939–1949. *Speech development of a bilingual child: a linguist's record.* Evanston: Northwestern University Press.

——. 1948. The study of child language and infant bilingualism. *Word* 4:1–17.

Le Page, Robert B. 1977. Processes of pidginization and creolization. In Albert Valdman, ed., 222–255.

——. 1982. Preface to Baker and Corne 1982, vii–viii.

Leslau, Wolf. 1945. The influence of Cushitic on the Semitic languages of Ethiopia: a problem of substratum. *Word* 1:59–82.

——. 1952. The influence of Sidamo on the Ethiopic languages of Gurage. *Language* 28:63–81.

Lewis, G. L. 1967. *Turkish grammar.* London: Oxford University Press.

Li, Charles N. 1983. Languages in contact in western China. *Papers in East Asian Languages* 1:31–51.

——. 1984. From verb-medial analytic language to verb-final synthetic language: a case of typological change. In Claudia Brugman et al., eds., *Proceedings of the Tenth Annual Meeting of the Berkeley Linguistics Society.* Berkeley: Berkeley Linguistics Society, 307–323.

Lickey, Sara. 1985. Khoisan influence in southern Bantu: an investigation. University of Pittsburgh M.A. thesis.

Lightfoot, David. 1979. *Principles of diachronic syntax.* Cambridge: Cambridge University Press.

Lindelöf, Uno. 1897. *Glossar zur Altnorthumbrischen Evangelienübersetzung in der Rushworth-Handschrift* (die sogenannte Glosse Rushworth/2). Helsingfors: Finnische Literatur-Gesellschaft.

——. 1901. Wörterbuch zur Interlinearglosse des Rituale Ecclesiae Dunelmensis. *Bonner Beiträge zur Anglistik* 9:105–220.

Lindenfeld, J. 1975 MS. Spanish influence in Yaqui syntax.

Little, Greta D. 1974. Syntactic evidence of language contact: Cushitic influence in Amharic. In R. W. Shuy and C.-J. N. Bailey, eds., *Towards tomorrow's linguistics.* Washington, D.C.: Georgetown University Press, 267–275.

Lockwood, W. B. 1964. *An informal history of the German language, with chapters on Dutch and Afrikaans, Frisian and Yiddish.* Cambridge: Heffer.

Lorimer, D. L. R. 1937. Burushaski and its alien neighbors: problems in linguistic contagion. *Transactions of the Philological Society*, 1937: 63–98.

Louw, J. 1962. The segmental phonemes of Zulu. *Afrika und Übersee* 46:43–93.

Lovins, Julie. 1973. *Loanwords and the phonological structure of Japanese.* University of Chicago Ph.D. dissertation.

———. 1974. Why loan phonology is natural phonology. In A. Bruck et al., eds., *Papers from the Parasession on Natural Phonology.* Chicago: Chicago Linguistic Society, 240–250.

Loyn, H. R. 1977. *The Vikings in Britain.* New York: St. Martin's Press.

Lunt, Horace G. 1966. *Old Church Slavonic grammar.* 4th ed. The Hague: Mouton.

Lydall, Jean. 1976. Hamer. In M. Lionel Bender, ed., *The non-Semitic languages of Ethiopia.* East Lansing, MI: African Studies Center, 393–438.

Malkiel, Yakov. 1976. Multi-conditioned sound change and the impact of morphology on phonology. *Language* 52:757–778.

Marouzeau, J. 1960. *Slovar' lingvističeskix terminov.* Translated from French by N. D. Andreev; ed. A. A. Reformatskij. Moscow: Izdatel'stvo inostrannoj literatury.

Martinet, André. 1955. *Economie des changements phonétiques.* Berne: Francke.

Marwick, Hugh. 1929. *The Orkney Norn.* London: Oxford University Press.

Masica, Colin P. 1976. *Defining a linguistic area: South Asia.* Chicago: University of Chicago Press.

Matzke, John E. 1905. Some examples of French as spoken by Englishmen in Old French literature. *Modern Philology* 3:47–60.

Mayhew, A. L. 1908. *The Promptorium Parvulorum, the first English-Latin dictionary.* Early English Text Society, Publication no. 102. London: Kegan Paul, Trench, Trübner.

Meillet, Antoine. 1921a. *Linguistique historique et linguistique générale.* Paris: Champion.

———. 1921b. Le problème de la parenté des langues. Reprinted in Meillet 1921a, 76–101.

Meisel, Jürgen M., ed. 1977. *Langues en contact—pidgins—créoles—languages in contact.* Tübingen: TBL Verlag, G. Narr.

Mellinkoff, David. 1963. *The language of the law.* Boston: Little, Brown.

Menges, Karl H. 1945. Indo-European influences on Ural-Altaic languages. *Word* 1:188–193.

Menovščikov, G. A. 1968. Aleutskij jazyk. *Jazyki narodov SSSR,* vol. 5: *Mongol'skie, Tunguso-Man'čžurskie i Paleoaziatskie jazyki.* Leningrad: Nauka, 386–406.

———. 1969. O nekotoryx social'nyx aspektax èvoljucii jazyka. In *Voprosy social'noj lingvistiki.* Leningrad: Nauka, 110–134.

Miller, Roy Andrew. 1967. *The Japanese language.* Chicago: University of Chicago Press.

———. 1971. *Japanese and the other Altaic languages.* Chicago: University of Chicago Press.

Milroy, J. 1984. The history of English in the British Isles. In Trudgill, ed., 5–31.

Mithun, Marianne, and Lyle Campbell. 1982. On comparative syntax. In J. Peter

Maher et al., eds., *Papers from the Third International Conference on Historical Linguistics*. Amsterdam: Benjamins, 273–291.

Mitzka, Walther. 1943. *Deutsche Mundarten*. Heidelberg: Carl Winter.

Moore, Samuel. 1928. Earliest morphological changes in Middle English. *Language* 4:238–266.

———. 1951. *Historical outlines of English sounds and inflections*. Revised by Albert H. Marckwardt. Ann arbor, MI: George Wahr.

Moore, Samuel, Sanford Brown Meech, and Harold Whitehall. 1935. Middle English dialect characteristics and dialect boundaries: preliminary report of an investigation based exclusively on localized tests and documents. *Essays and studies in English and comparative literature*. Ann Arbor: University of Michigan Press, 1–60.

Moravcsik, Edith A. 1975. Verb borrowing. *Wiener Linguistische Gazette* 8:3–31.

———. 1978. Language contact. In J. H. Greenberg, ed., *Universals of human language*, vol. 1. Stanford, CA: Stanford University Press, 93–122.

Moreno, Martino Mario. 1948. L'azione del cuscito sul sistema morfologico delle lingue semitiche dell'Ethiopia. *Rassegna di Studi Etiopici* 7:121–130.

Mossé, Fernand. 1952. *A handbook of Middle English*, translated by James A. Walker. Baltimore: Johns Hopkins University Press.

Mühlhäusler, Peter. 1980. Structural expansion and the process of creolization. In Valdman and Highfield, eds., 19–55.

———. 1981. The development of the category of number in Tok Pisin. In Pieter Muysken, ed., *Generative studies on creole languages*. Dordrecht: Foris, 35–84.

Müller, Max. 1871–1872 (second revised edition: 1890). *Lectures on the science of language*, vol. I. New York: Scribner.

Murray, J. A. H. 1873. *The dialect of the southern counties of Scotland*. London: Philological Society (Transactions of the Philological Society).

Muysken, Pieter. 1981. Halfway between Quechua and Spanish: the case for relexification. In Arnold Highfield and Albert Valdman, eds., *Historicity and variation in creole studies*. Ann Arbor: Karoma, 52–78.

Nadkarni, Mangesh V. 1970. *NP-embedded structures in Kannada and Konkani*. UCLA Ph. D. dissertation.

———. 1975. Bilingualism and syntactic change in Konkani. *Language* 51:672–683.

Nagara, S. 1972. *Japanese Pidgin English in Hawaii*. Honolulu: University of Hawaii Press.

Naro, Anthony J. 1978. A study on the origins of pidginization. *Language* 54:314–347.

———. 1981. The social and structural dimensions of a syntactic change. *Language* 57:63–98.

Neumann, Gunter. 1966. Zur chinesisch-russischen Behelfssprache von Kjachta. *Die Sprache* 12:237–251.

Newton, Brian. 1964. An Arabic-Greek dialect. In Robert Austerlitz, ed., *Papers in memory of George C. Pappageotes* (supplement to *Word* 20), 43–52.

———. 1972. *The generative interpretation of dialect: a study of Modern Greek phonology*. Cambridge: Cambridge University Press.

Nichols, Johanna. 1980. Pidginization and foreigner talk: Chinese Pidgin Russian. In Elizabeth C. Traugott et al., eds., *Papers from the Fourth International Con-*

ference on Historical Linguistics. Amsterdam: Benjamins, 397–407.

Nida, Eugene, and Harold W. Fehderau. 1970. Indigenous pidgins and koines. *International Journal of American Linguistics* 36:146–155.

Noreen, Adolf. 1923. *Altnordische Grammatik I.* Tübingen: Max Niemeyer.

Notices. 1956. *Notices and voyages of the famed Quebec Mission to the Pacific Northwest. Being the correspondence, notices, etc., of Fathers Blanchet and Demers, together with those of Fathers Bolduc and Langlois . . . mission to the engagés of the Hudson's Bay Company and the pagan natives. 1838 to 1847.* Portland, OR: Oregon Historical Society.

Nurse, Derek. 1977 MS. Maʔa—Mbughu.

Oakden, J. P. 1935. *Alliterative poetry in Middle English: a survey of the traditions.* 2 vols. Manchester: Manchester University Press.

Ohala, John J. 1974. Phonetic explanations in phonology. In A. Bruck et al., eds., *Papers from the parasession on natural phonology.* Chicago: Chicago Linguistic Society, 251–274.

————. 1975. Phonetic explanations for nasal sound patterns. In Charles A. Ferguson et al., eds., *Nasalfest.* Stanford, CA: Language Universals Project, 289–316.

Oksaar, Els. 1972. Bilingualism. In Thomas A. Sebeok, ed., *Current trends in linguistics,* vol. 9, *Linguistics in western Europe.* The Hague: Mouton, 476–511.

Orton, Harold, et al. 1962–1968. *Survey of English dialects (B): the basic materials.* Four 3-part volumes. Leeds: E. J. Arnold & Sons.

Orton, Harold, and Nathalia Wright. 1974. *A word geography of England.* London: Seminar Press.

Orton, Harold, S. Sanderson, and J. Widdowson. 1978. *The linguistic atlas of England.* London: Croome Helm.

Pandharipande, Rajeshwari. MS. Two faces of language change: Marathi and Hindi in central India.

Pandit, P. B. 1964. Indian readjustments in the English consonant system. *Indian Linguistics* 25:202–205 (Baburam Saksena Felicitation Volume).

Paul, Hermann. 1909. *Prinzipien der Sprachgeschichte.* 4th ed. Halle: Niemeyer.

Pfaff, Carol W. 1979. Constraints on language mixing: intrasentential code-switching and borrowing in Spanish/English. *Language* 55:291–318.

Pinnow, Heinz-Jürgen. 1969. Entlehnungen von Tiernamen in Tsimshian und Na-Déné sowie Grundsätzliches zur Entlehnungsfrage bei Indianersprachen. *Zeitschrift für Ethnologie* 94:82–102.

Pogatscher, Alois. 1900. Die englische ae/e-Grenze. *Anglia* 11:302–309.

Polomé, Edgar. 1968. Lubumbashi Swahili. *Journal of African Languages* 7/1:15–25.

————. 1980. Creolization processes and diachronic linguistics. In Valdman and Highfield, eds., 185–202.

Poole, Austin Lane. 1955. *From Domesday Book to Magna Carta 1087–1216.* 2d ed. Oxford: Oxford University Press.

Powell, J. V. 1975. Proto-Chimakuan: materials for a reconstruction. *University of Hawaii working papers in linguistics* 7(2):i–xv, 1–202. Honolulu: University of Hawaii Linguistics Department.

Psaltis, S. 1905. *Thrakikà ē melétē perì toū glōssikoū idiómatos tēs póleōs Saránta Ekklēsiōn.* Athens.

Rayfield, J. R. 1970. *The languages of a bilingual community.* The Hague: Mouton.

Reinecke, John E. 1969. *Language and dialect in Hawaii.* Honolulu: The University of Hawaii Press.

———. 1971. Tây Bôi: notes on the Pidgin French spoken in Vietnam. In Hymes, ed., 47–56.

Rhodes, Richard. 1977. French Cree—a case of borrowing. In William Cowan, ed., *Actes du Huitième Congrès des Algonquinistes.* Ottawa: Carleton University, 6–25.

Rickard, P. 1956. *Britain in medieval French literature 1100–1500.* Cambridge: Cambridge University Press.

Rickford, John R. 1977. The question of prior creolization in Black English. In Valdman, ed., 190–221.

Ritter, Otto. 1914. Zur englischen ae/e-Grenze. *Anglia* 25:269–275.

Rollins, Oneta. 1978 MS. A comparative study of Gullah and Tok Pisin. University of Pittsburgh M.A. thesis.

Ross, Alan S. C., and A. W. Moverley. 1964. *The Pitcairnese language.* New York: Oxford University Press.

Rubin, Sven. 1951. *The phonology of the Middle English dialect of Sussex.* Lund: Carl Blom.

Rynell, Alarik. 1948. *The rivalry of Scandinavian and native synonyms in Middle English, especially TAKEN and NIMEN.* Lund Studies in English 13. Lund: Gleerup.

Samuels, M. L. 1963. Some applications of Middle English dialectology. *English Studies* 44:81–94.

———. 1971. Kent and the Low Countries: some linguistic evidence. In A. J. Aitken et al., eds., 3–19.

———. 1972. *Linguistic evolution (with special reference to English).* Cambridge: Cambridge University Press.

Sandfeld, Kristian. 1938. Problèmes d'interférences linguistiques. *Actes du Quatrième Congrès Internationale de Linguistes.* Copenhagen: Einar Munksgaard, 59–61.

———. 1968 (1930). *Linguistique balkanique: problèmes et résultats.* Paris: Klincksieck.

Sankoff, Gillian. 1979. The genesis of a language. In Kenneth C. Hill, ed., *The genesis of language.* Ann Arbor: Karoma, 23–47.

———. 1980. Variation, pidgins and creoles. In Valdman and Highfield, eds., 139–164.

Sanzheyev, G. D. 1973. *The modern Mongolian language.* Translated from Russian by D. M. Segal. Moscow: Nauka.

Sapir, Edward. 1921. *Language.* New York: Harcourt, Brace and World, Inc.

Sawyer, P. H. 1971. *The age of the Vikings.* 2d ed. London: Edward Arnold.

Schuchardt, Hugo. 1884. *Slawo-deutsches und Slawo-italienisches.* Graz: Leuschner & Lubensky.

Schumann, John H. 1978. *The pidginization process: a model for second language acquisition.* Rowley, MA: Newbury House.

———. 1979. The genesis of a second language. In Kenneth C. Hill, ed., *The genesis of language.* Ann Arbor: Karoma, 48–61.

Sekhar, A. C. 1959. *Evolution of Malayalam*. Poona: Deccan College Post-Graduate and Research Institute.

Senn, Alfred. 1966. *Handbuch der litauischen Sprache*. Heidelberg: Carl Winter Universitätsverlag.

Serjeantson, Mary S. 1922. The dialectal distribution of certain phonological features in Middle English. *English studies* 4:93–109, 191–198, 223–233.

———. 1927*a*. The dialects of the West Midlands in Middle English. *Review of English studies* 3:54–67, 186–203, 319–331.

———. 1927*b*. The development of Old English *eag, eah* in Middle English. *Journal of English and Germanic philology* 26:198–225, 350–400.

Sherzer, Joel. 1976. *An areal-typological study of American Indian languages north of Mexico*. Amsterdam: North-Holland.

———. 1977. Universals of linguistic structure: a North American perspective. *Lingua* 42.177–189.

Shi, Dingxu. 1986. Chinese Pidgin English: its origin and linguistic features. M.A. thesis, University of Pittsburgh.

Sievers, Eduard, and Karl Brunner. 1951. *Altenglische Grammatik* nach der *Angelsächsischen Grammatik* von Eduard Sievers; neubearbeitet von Karl Brunner. 2d ed. Halle: Max Niemeyer.

da Silveiro Bueno, Fr. 1963. Les langues indigènes du Brésil et leur influence sur le Portugais. *Orbis* 12:226–240.

Silverstein, Michael. 1972. Chinook Jargon: language contact and the problem of multilevel generative systems. *Language* 48:378–406, 596–625.

———. 1974. Dialectal developments in Chinookan tense-aspect systems: an areal-historical analysis. *International Journal of American Linguistics* 40/4/2.S45–S99 (Memoir 29).

———. 1977. Person, number, gender in Chinook: syntactic rule and morphological analogy. In K. Whistler et al., eds., *Proceedings of the Third Annual Meeting of the Berkeley Linguistics Society* (Berkeley: Berkeley Linguistics Society, 143–156.

Singler, John Victor. 1984 MS. Remarks in response to Derek Bickerton's "Creoles and universal grammar: the unmarked case?" Linguistic Society of America Colloquium, Annual Meeting. Baltimore.

Sjoberg, Andrée F. 1962. Coexistent phonemic systems in Telugu: a socio-cultural perspective. *Word* 18:269–279.

Smith, Ian R. 1977 MS. Stress and vowel length in Sri Lanka Portuguese Creole.

Smithers, G. V. 1968. Early Middle English. In Bennett and Smithers, eds., xxi–lxi.

Smyth, Alfred P. 1977. *Scandinavian kings in the British Isles 850–880*. Oxford: Oxford University Press.

Snyder, Eileen. 1984 MS. Has there been convergence between Munda and other languages of India? University of Pittsburgh M.A. thesis.

Sommerfelt, Alf. 1960. External versus internal factors in the development of language. *Norsk Tidsskrift for Sprogvidenskap* 19:296–315.

Southworth, Franklin. 1971. Detecting prior creolization: an analysis of the historical origins of Marathi. In Hymes, ed., 255–273.

———. n.d. Linguistic archaeology in India.

Sridhar, S. N. 1978. Linguistic convergence: Indo-Aryanization of Dravidian languages. *Studies in the Linguistic Sciences* 8/1:197–215.

Steinitz, Wolfgang. 1964. *Geschichte der Finnisch-Ugrischen Vokalismus*. 2d ed. (Finnisch-Ugrische Studien, Nr. 4.) Berlin: Akademie Verlag.

Stenton, F. M. 1927. *The Danes in England*. Oxford: Oxford University Press.

———. 1947. *Anglo-Saxon England*. 2d ed. Oxford: Oxford University Press.

Stratmann, Francis Henry. 1891. *A Middle English dictionary* (containing words used by English writers from the twelfth to the fifteenth century); new revised and enlarged edition by Henry Bradley. Oxford: Oxford University Press.

Sturtevant, William. 1981. Report on the Nootka jargon. *California-Oregon Languages Newsletter*, June 1981.

Suarez, V. 1945. *El Español que se habla en Yucatán*. Merida, Diaz Massa.

Suttles, Wayne. 1965. Multiple phonologic correspondences in two adjacent Salish languages and their implications. Paper presented at the 18th Northwest Anthropological Conference, Bellingham, Washington.

Sweet, Henry. 1885. *The oldest English texts*. London: Trübner.

Sylvain, Suzanne. 1936. *Le créole haïtien: morphologie et syntaxe*. Port-au-Prince: Wetteren.

Takaki, Ronald. 1983. *Pau hana: plantation life and labor in Hawaii, 1835–1920*. Honolulu: University of Hawaii Press.

Takano, Sono. 1985. A study of the effect of English loanwords on Japanese phonology. University of Pittsburgh M.A. thesis.

Taylor, Douglas. 1956. Language contacts in the West Indies. *Word* 12:391–414.

———. 1960. Language shift or changing relationship? *International Journal of American Linguistics* 26:155–161.

Teeter, Karl V. 1976 (1973). Algonquian. In Thomas A. Sebeok, ed., *Native languages of the Americas*, vol. 1: *North America*. New York: Plenum Press, 505–525. Reprinted from T. A. Sebeok, ed., *Current Trends in Linguistics*, vol. 10: *North America*.

Telegdi, Z. 1973. Remarques sur les emprunts arabes en persan. *Acta Linguistica (Hungarica)* 23.

Ternes, Elmar. 1970. *Grammaire structurale du Breton de l'Ile de Groix*. Heidelberg: Winter.

Tesnière, Lucien. 1939. Phonologie et mélange de langues. *Travaux du Cercle Linguistique de Prague* 8:83–93.

Tewksbury, M. Gardner. 1948. *Speak Chinese*. New Haven, CT: Yale University Press.

Thomas, Alan R. 1982. Change and decay in language. In David Crystal, ed., *Linguistic controversies: essays in linguistic theory and practice in honour of F.R. Palmer*. London: Edward Arnold Publishers, Ltd.; distributed in North America by University Park Press, Baltimore, 209–219.

Thomason, Sarah Grey. 1976. Analogic change as grammar complication. In William Christie, ed., *Current progress in historical linguistics*. Amsterdam: North-Holland, 401–409.

———. 1980*a*. Continuity of transmission and genetic relationship. In Elizabeth Traugott et al., eds., *Papers from the Fourth International Conference on Historical Linguistics*. Amsterdam: Benjamins, 27–35.

———. 1980*b*. Morphological instability, with and without language contact. In Jacek Fisiak, ed., *Historical Morphology*. The Hague: Mouton, 359–372.

———. 1980*c*. On interpreting "The Indian Interpreter." *Language in Society* 9: 167–193.

———. 1981 MS. Are there linguistic prerequisites for contact-induced language change? Paper presented at the Tenth Annual University of Wisconsin-Milwaukee Linguistics Symposium: Language Contact.

———. 1982. Review of Albert Valdman and Arnold Highfield, eds., *Theoretical orientations in creole studies*. New York: Academic Press, 1980. *Language in Society* 11:478–483.

———. 1983*a*. Chinook Jargon in areal and historical context. *Language* 59:820–870.

———. 1983*b*. Genetic relationship and the case of Ma'a (Mbugu). *Studies in African Linguistics* 14:195–231.

———. 1986*a*. On changes from palatalized labials to apical affricates. *International Journal of American Linguistics* 52:182–186.

———. 1986*b*. On establishing external causes of language change. In Soonja Choi et al., eds., *Proceedings of the Second Eastern States Conference on Linguistics*. Columbus, OH: The Ohio State University, 243–251.

Thomason, Sarah Grey, and Alaa Elgibali. 1986. Before the Lingua Franca: pidginized Arabic in the eleventh century A.D. *Lingua* 68:317–349.

Thomason, Sarah Grey, and Terrence Kaufman. 1975. Toward an adequate definition of creolization. Paper presented at the 1975 International Conference on Pidgins and Creoles, Honolulu.

———. 1976. Contact-induced language change: loanwords and the borrowing language's pre-borrowing phonology. In William Christie, ed., *Current progress in historical linguistics*. Amsterdam: North-Holland, 167–179.

Thompson, Laurence C. 1965. More on comparative Salish. Paper presented at the Fourth Conference on American Indian Languages, Denver.

———. 1979. Salishan and the Northwest. In Lyle Campbell and Marianne Mithun, eds., *The languages of native America: historical and comparative assessment*. Austin: University of Texas Press, 692–765.

Thorsen, Per. 1936. *Anglo-Norse studies: an inquiry into the Scandinavian elements in the Modern English dialects*. Amsterdam: Swets & Zeitlinger.

Thumb, Albert. 1912. *Handbook of the Modern Greek vernacular: grammar, texts, glossary*. 2d ed. Translated from German by S. Angus. Edinburgh: T. & T. Clark.

Timberlake, Alan. 1974. *The nominative object in Slavic, Baltic, and West Finnic*. Munich: Verlag Otto Sagner.

Todd, Loreto. 1975 MS. Pidgins and creoles: the case for the creoloid. Paper presented at the 1975 International Conference on Pidgins and Creoles, Honolulu.

Traugott, Elizabeth Closs. 1973. Some thoughts on natural syntactic processes. In C.-J. N. Bailey and R. Shuy, eds., *New ways of analyzing variation in English.* Washington, D.C.: Georgetown University Press, 313–322.

———. 1977. Pidginization, creolization, and language change. In Valdman, ed., 70–98.

Trudgill, Peter, ed. 1984. *Language in the British Isles.* Cambridge: Cambridge University Press.

Vachek, Josef. 1962. On the interplay of external and internal factors in the development of language. *Lingua* 11:433–448.

Valdman, Albert, ed. 1977. *Pidgin and creole linguistics.* Bloomington: Indiana University Press.

Valdman, Albert, and Arnold Highfield, eds. 1980. *Theoretical orientations in creole studies.* New York: Academic Press.

Valkhoff, Marius F. 1966. *Studies in Portuguese and Creole.* Johannesburg: Witwatersrand University Press.

Veenker, Wolfgang. 1967. *Die Frage des finnougrischen Substrats in der russischen Sprache.* (Uralic and Altaic Series, vol. 82.) Bloomington: Indiana University Press.

Vildomec, Věroboj. 1971. *Multilingualism.* Leiden: A. W. Sijthoff.

Vočadlo, Otakar. 1938. Some observations on mixed languages. *Actes du Quatrième Congrès Internationale de Linguistes.* Copenhagen: Einar Munksgaard, 169–176.

Vogt, Hans. 1948. Reply to the question, "Dans quelles conditions et dans quelles limites peut s'exercer sur le système morphologique d'une langue l'action du système morphologique d'une autre langue?" In Michel Lejeune, ed., *Actes du VIe Congrès Internationale de Linguistes.* Paris: Klincksieck.

———. 1954. Language contacts. *Word* 10:365–374.

Voorhoeve, Jan. 1961. Le ton et la grammaire dans le Saramaccan. *Word* 17:146–163.

Wagle, Mohini. 1981 MS. Homework essay for Historical Linguistics, on the emerging dialect of Hindi spoken in Bombay. University of Pittsburgh.

Wagner, Heinreich. 1959. *Das Verbum in den Sprachen der Britischen Inseln.* Tübingen.

Wainwright, F. T. 1975. *Scandinavian England* (collected papers edited by H. P. R. Finberg). Chichester: Phillimore.

Wallace, Stephen. 1977 MS. Syntactic imperialism. Paper read at the Annual Meeting of the Linguistic Society of America, Chicago.

Wang, William S-Y., ed. 1977. *The lexicon in phonological change.* The Hague: Mouton.

Wartburg, W. von. 1969. *Evolution et structure de la langue française.* 9th ed. Berne: Francke.

Weaver, Deborah. 1982. Obviation in Michif. In Desmond C. Derbyshire, ed., *Work papers of the Summer Institute of Linguistics, University of North Dakota session,* vol. 26. Huntington Beach, CA: Summer Institute of Linguistics, 174–262.

Weinreich, Uriel. 1953 (reprinted in 1968). *Languages in contact.* The Hague: Mouton.

———. 1958. On the compatibility of genetic relationship and convergent development. *Word* 14:374–379.

Welmers, William E. 1970. Language change and language relationships in Africa. *Language Sciences* 12:1–8.

Whinnom, Keith. 1971. Linguistic hybridization and the 'special case' of pidgins and creoles. In Hymes, ed., 91–115.

———. 1980. Creolization in linguistic change. In Valdman and Highfield, eds., 203–210.

Whitelock, Dorothy, ed. 1955. *English historical documents c. 500–1042.* London: Eyre and Spottiswoode.

Winter, Werner. 1973. Areal linguistics: some general considerations. In T. A. Sebeok, ed., *Current Trends in Linguistics,* vol. 11, *Diachronic, areal, and typological linguistics.* The Hague: Mouton, 135–147.

Wright, Joseph. 1905. *The English dialect grammar.* Oxford: Oxford University Press.

Wurm, Stefan A. 1956. Comment on question: "Are there areas of *affinité grammaticale* as well as of *affinité phonologique* cutting across genetic boundaries?" In F. Norman, ed., *Proceedings of the 7th International Congress of Linguists.* (London: Permanent International Committee of Linguists.) Section B4, 450–452.

———. 1964. Motu and Police Motu: a study in typological contrasts. *Pacific Linguistics* A-4 (Canberra: Australian National University), 19–41.

Wurm, Stephen A., and J. B. Harris. 1963. Police Motu- an introduction to the trade language of Papua (New Guinea) for anthropologists and other fieldworkers. *Pacific Linguistics* B-1 (Canberra: Australia National University).

Wyld, Henry Cecil. 1913–1914. The treatment of OE *y* in the dialects of the Midland, and SE counties, in ME. *Englische Studien* 47:1–58.

———. 1920. South-Eastern and South-East Midland dialects in Middle English. *Essays and studies by members of the English association* 6:112–145.

———. 1921. The Surrey dialect in the XIIIth century. *English studies* 3:42–45.

Zaborski, Andrzej. 1976. Cushitic overview. In M. L. Bender, ed., *The non-Semitic languages of Ethiopia.* East Lansing, MI: African Studies Centre, 67–84.

Zenk, Henry. 1984. *Chinook Jargon and native cultural persistence in the Grand Ronde Indian community, 1856–1907: a study of creolization in process.* University of Oregon Ph.D. dissertation.

Middle English texts surveyed in the research lying behind chapter 9.8.6–9.8.7. EETS = Early English Text Society Publication # . . . ; STS = Scottish Text Society Publication (# . . .).

Allen, Hope Emily, ed. 1931. *English Writings of Richard Rolle, Hermit of Hampole.* Oxford: Oxford University Press.

Amours, F. J., ed. 1903–1914. *The Original Chronicle of Andrew of Wyntoun.* 5 vols. STS. Edinburgh and London: Blackwood.

Bestiary = Morris 1872.

Foster, Frances A., ed. 1913–1916. *The Northern Passion.* EETS 145, 147. London: Kegan Paul, Trench, Trübner.

———. 1926. *A Stanzaic Life of Christ.* EETS 166. London: Oxford University Press.

Furnivall, Frederick J., ed. 1887. *The Story of England by Robert Manning of Brunne.* Rolls Series 87. London: Eyre and Spottiswoode.

Gawain poet = Morris 1864.

Hall, Joseph, ed. 1887. *The Poems of Laurence Minot.* Oxford: Oxford University Press.

Herrtage, Sidney J. H., ed. 1882. *Catholicon Anglicum, an English-Latin Wordbook, dated 1483.* Westminster: Camden Society.

Holt, Robert, ed. 1878. *The Ormulum.* 2 vols. Oxford: Oxford University Press.

Kock, Ernst A., ed. 1902. *Three Middle-English Versions of the Rule of St. Benet.* EETS 120. London: Kegan Paul, Trench, Trübner.

Mayhew, A. L., ed. 1908. *The Promptorium Parvulorum, the First English-Latin Dictionary.* EETS 102. London: Kegan Paul, Trench, Trübner.

Metcalfe, W. M., ed. 1887–1896. *Legends of the Saints.* STS 13, 18, 23, 25, 35, 37. Edinburgh and London: Blackwood. [Scottish Saints' Legends]

Morris, Richard, ed. 1864. *Early English Alliterative Poems.* EETS 1. London: Trübner. [the Gawain Poet]

———. 1865. *The Story of Genesis and Exodus.* EETS 7. London: Trübner.

———. 1872. *An Old Englsh Miscellany.* EETS 49. London: Trübner. [the Bestiary]

———. 1874–1893. *Cursor Mundi.* EETS 57, 59, 62, 66, 68, 99, 101. London: Kegan Paul, Trench, Trübner.

Peterborough Chronicle 1132–1154: in Thorpe 1861.

Scottish Saints' Legends = Metcalfe.

Skeat, Walter W., ed. 1870–1889. *The Bruce.* EETS extra series 11, 21, 29, 55. London: Kegan Paul, Trench, Trübner.

———. 1915. *The Lay of Havelok the Dane.* Oxford: Oxford University Press.

Thorpe, Benjamin, ed. 1861. *The Anglo-Saxon Chronicle, according to the Several Original Authorities,* vol. I. London: Longman.

Index

LANGUAGES AND LANGUAGE GROUPS

NAMES OF SCHOLARS

SUBJECTS

Designer: U.C. Press Staff
Compositor: Janet Sheila Brown
Text: Garamond 11/13
Display: Garamond
Printer: Thomson-Shore, Inc.
Binder: John H. Dekker & Sons